Greening the City

GREENING THE CITY. NATURE IN FRENCH TOWNS FROM THE 17TH CENTURY

Charles-François Mathis
Émilie-Anne Pépy

published by The White Horse Press, The Old Vicarage, Main Street, Winwick, Cambridgeshire, UK.
Based on *La ville végétale* © 2017, Editions Champ Vallon, 01350 Ceyzérieu, France.

Translation by Moya Jones

Set in 11 point Adobe Caslon Pro and Lucida Sans

British Library Cataloguing in Publication Data
A catalogue record for this book is available from the British Library

ISBN 978-1-912186-13-6

Cover image: *The Boulevard Viewed from Above* (1880) by Gustave Caillebotte. *Source*: Wikiart.

TABLE OF CONTENTS

INTRODUCTION. GREENERY SCENERY: PLANT LIFE IN THE CITY, SEVENTEENTH TO TWENTY-FIRST CENTURIES

Sleep is full of miracles!
Obeying a curious whim,
I had banned from that spectacle
Irregular vegetation,

And, painter proud of his genius,
I savored in my picture
The delightful monotony
Of water, marble and metal.

Such is the 'Parisian Dream'[1] conjured up by Baudelaire in *Les Fleurs du Mal*, which was dedicated to Constantin Guys whom he had hailed as the painter of modern life: a town without plants, where the trees are replaced by columns, gigantic and eternally silent, sparkling with precious stones. For his contemporaries at the time and for us today this radical modernity of the denatured town would turn towards something of a nightmare. The demands of urban natures are becoming ever more pressing, as is demonstrated by the new defence of biodiversity within cities, garden festivals which are ever more numerous every spring, or even the exhibition held in 2011 at the Cité de l'architecture et du patrimoine (Centre for Architecture and Heritage) in Paris called 'The Fertile town. Towards urban nature'. A poll carried out in 2013 revealed that seven out of ten French people make it a priority to live near some kind of green space and that ninety per cent of them affirm that they need daily contact with the plant world. The fashion today is moving towards the 'vegetalisation of towns' and not towards the elimination of plant life.[2]

From public actions to urban marketing, this principle is determining the way urban planners think in the twenty-first century, and the background to this is an increase in the questioning of our societies' demand for nature

1 Charles Baudelaire, trans. by William Aggeler, *The Flowers of Evil* (Fresno (CA): Academy Library Guild, 1954).

2 Survey UNEP-IPSOS 2013: www.hopscotch-presse.fr/unep/ipsos_2013/dp_unep_ipsos_2013.pdf

and of the construction of a 'landscaped humanism'.[3] The humanities and social sciences have not been immune to these environmental concerns, which have become more widespread and come to the fore in the media over the last few decades.

These days there are more and more scientific publications and organised events examining the relations between ancient societies and their environment.[4] Urban forms of nature are of prime interest to the historian,[5] who is unable to forget that the mineralisation of the town, under concrete and asphalt, is a fairly recent phenomenon. In his way, Baudelaire understood this, for if he had 'banned' the vegetal it was because greenery had furtively insinuated its way into the city. Gardens, trees, weeds … if we look closely, nature has not deserted the town, far from it. Until quite late in the twentieth century the urban space remained relatively permeable to rurality: there were animals in yards or even in the streets, crops grown within the city walls and market gardens that marked a halfway space between the town and the country. And, of course, we also think of how the city is embellished by the creation of vegetalised spaces and in particular the space taken up in the city by gardens. Hundreds of books and articles have been written about these. Today the fifty largest cities in France spend on average five million euros each year on the creation and upkeep of green spaces, where the average area per inhabitant is 31 square metres (although there are wide disparities: Besançon holds the record with 200 square metres of green space per inhabitant while Paris only manages fourteen!).[6]

The topic of the place of nature in town is therefore not new, but over the centuries its shapes have changed as have its importance and its acceptance. Strictly speaking, the medieval town, the city designed by Haussmann and the city of today are not of the same nature. That is why the period that we

3 See Bernadette Lizet, 'Introduction', in Marie Mianowski, Sylvie Nail and Pierre Carboni (eds), *La nature citadine. En France et au Royaume-Uni. Concevoir, Vivre, Représenter* (Rennes: PUR, 2015).

4 Geneviève Massard-Guilbaud, 'Pour une histoire environnementale de l'urbain', *Histoire urbaine* **1** (18) (2007): 5–21.

5 Of course, they also arouse the interest of sociologists, geographers and urban planners, as shown by the international symposium organised in 2013 at the Maison de l'architecture in Paris on the theme 'Urban Nature in Projects. Towards a new alliance between nature and the city', which in 2015 gave rise to six publications in a series under the responsibility of Catherine Chomarat-Ruiz, entitled *Nature Citadine* and available in digital version only on the Editopics website.

6 See the ranking of the 50 largest cities in France given by the association UNEP – Les entreprises du paysage en 2014. http://www.entreprisesdupaysage.org/document/telechargerDocument.php?id=26829_56862

have chosen to study stretches from the seventeenth century to the present day, in order to take into account all that is permanent but also to reflect how cities change.[7]

When related to the urban fabric, the history of the vegetal is primarily a history of transmission and of heritage, one of transformation rather than upheaval. Comparing maps and plans over the long term shows that a garden generally succeeds a garden, unless buildings became predominant during a period of population growth. The brutalisation of towns is a new phenomenon that arose during industrialisation and that radically changed the town as it was under the *Ancien Régime*.[8] The relations that urban societies had with nature then developed and their environmental sensitivity became keener as the factory chimneys rose. Moreover, as early as the eighteenth century, a Western conception of nature began to evolve and we have partially inherited this. In the great nature / culture divide (which today is widely qualified by anthropologists)[9] the vegetal played a major role insofar as it is doubtlessly the easiest natural element to raise, to arrange according to fashions and to integrate into the planning of the city.

This book traces these developments in France from the seventeenth to the twenty-first centuries.

What is a town?

Defining a town,[10] particularly over a period of several centuries is a challenge to which geographers and historians struggle to provide a unanimous answer. The town evolved between the seventeenth and twentieth centuries and at the very least its definition became more precise with the introduction of statistical thresholds. Under the *Ancien Régime* the town was first defined by its fortifications, its institutions for governance and its privileges. Even though royal power laid hands on the towns in the seventeenth century, the

7 We will only deal with cities once they are fully integrated into French territory. The city of Nice, for example, will not be mentioned before 1860.

8 Jean-Luc Pinol (ed.), *Histoire de l'Europe urbaine*, vol. 1, *De l'antiquité au XVIII*[e] *siècle*, vol. 2, *De l'ancien Régime à nos jours. Expansion et limites d'un modèle* (Paris: Éditions du Seuil, 2003).

9 Philippe Descola, *Par-delà nature et culture* (Paris: Gallimard, 2005).

10 We will limit this study to the cities of the French metropolis, without taking into account colonial cities: the history and diversity of the French colonies give rise to very different problems that would deserve a work in their own right. See Odile Goerg and Xavier Huetz de Lemps, *La ville coloniale XV*[e] *– XX*[e] *siècles* (Paris: Seuil, 2012).

extent of municipal powers still remained considerable to the point of being able to compare towns to 'little patrician republics' which the intendants only partly controlled,[11] despite the monarchy's legislative efforts in the second half of the eighteenth century. (An intendant was the King's agent, sent to a region to administer it in his name.) So, we see demographic criteria giving way to the legal and morphological definition of the town. In any case, how many inhabitants are required to constitute a town? The issue was widely discussed in the historiography of the 1970s when questions were being asked about the drift to urbanisation and the move from the *Ancien Régime* to the industrial age. Statistical scales and thresholds only have meaning when placed in a given context. Since 1846 in France, the definition of 'urban' for public statistics is any *commune* (town or village) that has at least 2,000 inhabitants gathered together in a *chef lieu* (chief town). This demographic criterion has the advantage of apparently quantifiable objectivity but remains inadequate. This is partly due to its arbitrariness, as much geographical – in Denmark, a town begins with 200 residents, while in China the threshold is 50,000 – as historical: a conurbation of 10,000 people does not have the same significance today as it did during the Enlightenment! In the eighteenth century, depending on the region studied, some sparsely populated clusters were recognised as towns (1,000 inhabitants in Dauphiné, 1,800 inhabitants in Bourgogne (Burgundy)). If an agglomeration, even with only 1,000 inhabitants, can count as a town it is because it is defined by its functions: a town is not just a structure or a built-up area, it is also a place which gathers within itself some particular functions: political, of course, when it concentrates national decision-making bodies (Paris), regional ones (parliamentary towns like Bordeaux), or local ones (chief towns after the reorganisations of the Revolution and the Empire); judicial, with the presence of different kinds of courts; economic, naturally, with the head offices of large industrial or commercial firms, etc. But while this functional specialisation of towns marks them out, it does not determine their limits: where does a town start and where does it finish? Of course, there are administrative boundaries which might be the beginning of an answer; but it is well known that urban reality and the density of building that often goes on well beyond abstract borders very often ignore these constraints. So? What is a town?

It is definitely an interweaving of these different criteria but, for a period

11 Jean-Claude Perrot, 'Rapports sociaux et villes au XVIIIe siècle', in Marcel Roncayolo and Thierry Pacquot (eds), *Villes et civilisation urbaine, XVIIIe – XXe siècles* (Paris: Larousse, 1992).

as long as that which we propose to examine, the definition of a town also depends on different contemporaneous perceptions. What is meant by a town and how it is viewed alters according to the era. In any case, before 1789, different words were used which referred to certain qualitative differences linked to the privileges that these conurbations possessed: a *bourg* (little town), a *commune* ('commune'), a *ville* (town), a *village* (village). The night of 4 August 1789 not only abolished social privileges, but also put an end to these distinctions. A municipal law of 1789 brought uniformity to these namings. From then on, after some hesitations, one would refer to a *commune*, rural or urban.

While the gaze that inhabitants have cast on their towns over the years should be taken into account, it must be remembered that the appearance of towns has changed considerably over the centuries and has become less clear. This can basically be explained by demographic changes. From the sixteenth to eighteenth centuries, the general framework of urbanisation in France remained stable. With a few exceptions, there were very few new urban creations and the hierarchy of these was generally only marginally modified. The population of *communes* of over 2,000 inhabitants however never stopped expanding, going from about 2.7 million around the year 1600 (which represented about fourteen per cent of the population), to 3.9 million in 1700 (17.4 per cent) and over five million around 1800 (twenty per cent).[12]

This demographic growth obviously changed the appearance of towns but, apart from a few exceptions such as Paris, this was in no way alarming and integration was progressive, with few upheavals within existing structures. Right up to the end of this modern period, the town thus retained its fairly clear boundaries which were those of mediaeval fortifications, as the *Encyclopédie* testifies: 'an enclosure surrounded by walls, enclosing several neighbourhoods, streets, public squares and other buildings'.

But these walls fell into disrepair and on the whole lost their defensive role. They were covered with plants and people went there for strolls. If, as Marcel Roncayolo says, 'the classic town in western Europe, enclosed within its walls, well defined in contrast to the flat land around it, offers the certainty of landscape',[13] the town at the end of the eighteenth century changed orientation: no longer turned in on itself for protection but outwards to its surroundings. From that point onwards, in order to define the town, should

12 Jean-Luc Pinol, *Le Monde des Villes au XIX*[e] siècle (Paris : Hachette, 1991).

13 Marcel Roncayolo, in Pinol, *Le Monde des Villes*, p. 3.

one take into account the *banlieue* (the suburbs), the territory under the town's *ban* or jurisdiction, which extended for about *une lieue* (a league) and particularly included all the foodstuffs grown for citizens? This is doubtless the case, for the town cannot be understood in isolation. Defining in terms of fortifications then makes less sense than thinking of the functions, the privileges and the specialisations of the town.

This trend towards the dissolving of urban boundaries became more marked at the turn of the eighteenth and nineteenth centuries. The rise in population and the beginning of the industrial revolution in fact helped to blur the definition of the town and especially its outline and its limits. Industrialisation played its part in this, of course, in those towns that were concerned: factories were set up in the hearts of some towns or, increasingly, on their outskirts, thereby drawing in large, often wretched, populations. But it was all of urban France that found itself overwhelmed by an unprecedented influx of people. If we only take into account towns with over 2,000 inhabitants, the 1846 census counted nine million urban dwellers, which suggests an average annual increase of 1.3 per cent since the beginning of the century! The nineteenth century town was also changing its appearance: its morphology was being transformed at different speeds, with the destruction of ramparts and the spread of the suburbs which gnawed at the peri-urban space, absorbing older village centres so that no-one was quite sure where the town ended and the countryside began. Industrial cities and suburbs were that century's great novelty, one that profoundly changed the towns, whose ways of life were totally subverted as was their social make-up. Prevailing views about urban centres were modified everywhere in Europe.[14] From the second half of the eighteenth century onwards, there were two opposing discourses. For some, the town remained the incarnation of the Enlightenment, of Civilisation and of Progress. For others, there were only vice and temptation and towns corrupted the virtuous country folk who were drawn towards these sites of damnation! Moreover, the fetid nature of the soil and the air in an urban environment represented everything for which the town was criticised, and did it not contrast with the ideal of nature, pure and healing? This change in how the town was viewed accompanied the accelerating urban transformations of the nineteenth century, to which Baudelaire testified perfectly lucidly: 'the shape of a city, as we all know, changes more quickly, than the

14 Carl Schorske, *De Vienne et d'ailleurs* (Paris: Fayard, 2000).

mortal heart'.[15] These changes varied considerably from one town to another. There was nothing in common between the rise of Second Empire seaside resorts like Biarritz and Deauville and industrial centres like Le Creusot or Roubaix, and the decline of those towns like Montauban which refused modernity or let it pass by. But overall, despite a few notable exceptions, the deep-lying structures of the *Ancien Régime* stood firm: the Seine area, the Mediterranean south, the Rhône valley and the North had a strong urban structure which endured. The hierarchy of great cities, which in the long run changed relatively little between 1800 and 1945, bears witness to the weight of this inheritance. Up until the Second World War, French urbanisation carried on at very different paces depending on the place (on average 1.1 per cent per year from 1806 to 1931) with a generalised slowdown from the end of the nineteenth century, in particular because of demographic stagnation. While the population of the United Kingdom was largely urban by about 1851, it was not until 1931 that France reached this stage.[16]

It was therefore not until the post-war period that the urban landscape we know today began to emerge and this was the result of several factors. Firstly, there were the soaring demographic figures of the 'baby boom' years and of high immigration: urban populations rose from 21 million inhabitants in 1931 (a little over fifty per cent of the population) to 48 million in 2010 (over 75 per cent of the population). This massive influx was accompanied by urban sprawl and a lessening of urban population density (600 inhabitants per square kilometre on average in 1962, as opposed to 400 today), facilitated by increased car ownership which itself radically changed the physiognomy of towns. Little by little, large urban centres, shopping malls on the outskirts and individual houses in housing estates absorbed surrounding rural areas: the town became tentacular, occupying up to twenty per cent of the national land mass.[17] It is estimated that between 1970 and 2000 the average area of towns increased by fifty per cent.[18] The term 'rurbanisation' precisely evokes this growing interpenetration of the rural and the urban. It is estimated that

15 Charles Baudelaire, trans. Julien Gracq and Ingeborg M. Kohn, *The Shape of a City* (New York: New Turtle Press, 2005).

16 For more details, see Georges Duby, *Histoire de la France urbaine*, vol. IV : *La Ville de l'âge industriel*, ed. by Maurice Agulhon (Paris : Seuil, 1998), from which the information in this paragraph is taken.

17 See Dominique Borne, *Histoire de la société française depuis 1945* (Paris: Armand Colin, 1992), pp. 5–8, 47–49 ; INSEE statistics (insee.fr).

18 Emmanuel Boutefeu, *Composer avec la nature en ville* (Paris: CERTU, 2001), p. 339.

today 95 per cent of the French population lives in the sphere of influence of a town.[19] The very hearts of towns are changing too and this was particularly the case in the 1960s when densification was at its height. The singer-songwriter Jacques Dutronc may well regret, in his song, 'the little garden which smells of the Metro' and criticise real estate promoters and their 'concrete flowers'.[20]

Major real estate developments were modernising town centres ,sometimes by razing old buildings: Montparnasse in Paris, Part-Dieu in Lyon and Mériadeck in Bordeaux are a few examples of this. The consequences of this were as much social as aesthetic, and over the last twenty years at least there has been a backlash with a movement to restore old buildings and with less brutal interventions within the urban fabric.

What nature?

It is paradoxical that, while the definition of the town raises so many difficulties, defining nature is easier for us. In effect, this book will only be looking at what is vegetal or vegetable in nature, excluding the elements – earth, air and water – and animals, on which topics there would nevertheless be plenty to say. Historically, reflections on nature and the town are based above all on an opposition – or a complementarity – between the mineral and the vegetal: the fixity of stone as contrasted with the vitality of plants, the orderliness of stone as opposed to the profusion of flowers, leaves and branches (the 'irregular' vegetal of Baudelaire).

However, in Europe, and even more so in towns, nature is not the opposite of culture, it is not 'virgin' but anthropomorphised and always passes between man's hands or under his feet, being or having been modified in some way by him. These interventions may be involuntary (eutrophication of urban water courses affected by effluents of all sorts, for example); but when they are deliberate, they often bear a social or a political message. To build a garden is to give an image of oneself, of one's town, of one's country. It is also, as it was in the Second Empire, to affirm the victory of a bourgeois social order that one wants to impose.

Besides, if the vegetal is, as we have seen, largely present in the towns of the past, it took on various forms according to the scale of observation

19 Chantal Brutel and David Levy, 'Le nouveau zonage en aires urbaines de 2010', *Insee Première*, 1374 (October 2011), http ://www.insee.fr/fr/ffc/ipweb/ip1374/ip1374.pdf

20 Jacques Dutronc/Jacques Lanzmann, 'Le Petit Jardin', 1972.

adopted. Thus, there will be coexistence of plants which have grown spontaneously and those used to play a structuring role in the spatial and social organisation of the town. In order to see more clearly through this profusion, a distinction must be made at the level of the vegetal itself and the way in which it is present in the town.

In work carried out by historians, priority has been given to vegetal forms rooted in the urban space, to those which have left documentary traces and whose history has been reconstituted from the usages which were attributed to them. This has been the case with cultivated species, grown in gardens or raised for consumption by city dwellers. It has also been the case for natural urban places (parks, gardens, planted esplanades and other 'green spaces' designed to enhance, refresh and amuse the town). As for abandoned spaces, very often grassy waste ground, while their use is less formalised, they are nevertheless integrated into city practices (for recreation purposes, for example). The picture would not be complete without those plants that are deemed undesirable or worthless, such as seaweeds, mosses or lichens. They are the dark side of the vegetal kingdom, only glimpsed in times of town dwellers' grievance in the same way as mud or trash.

Alongside these vegetal forms, which are a long-term presence in the urban space, plants that are 'not rooted in the earth' have a more cursory existence. Yet, although these items of mobile nature occupy an important place in the daily life of town residents, they have only left fleeting and even imperceptible traces in the archives, a situation that is inversely proportional to their visibility in the urban landscape (balconies, gardens, cemeteries, urban decoration). A certain number of historians, mainly Anglo-Saxon, have examined this question of ephemeral nature, varying the scales of observation. For example, in a celebrated book on Chicago, the historian William Cronon showed that a town could not be observed as a monad, a self-contained unit closed in on itself: Chicago has profoundly shaped the American Great West and has built itself up thanks to its natural resources, whence the name that Cronon gives it – 'Nature's Metropolis'.[21] On a lesser scale, every town obviously depends on its hinterland and organises the space around itself. It draws in nature in all its forms and then redistributes it, once it is within. Although light has not been totally cast on the economy of the vegetal in a town, this vast topic cannot be ignored for it risks leaving aside a whole facet of urban life. Therefore, we must attempt to grasp as fully as possible this nature on the move which sometimes

21 William Cronon, *Nature's Metropolis. Chicago and the Great West* (New York: Norton, 1991).

belongs to a more spontaneous order than that of parks and their flowerbeds.

To this spatial dimension must be added reflections relating to time: how do nature time and town time match? The often collisional developments of the latter contrast with the regular, seasonal cycles of vegetation and their mortality. Depending on the month and the year, the urban vegetal aspect is not the same: leaves may be lost in a great wind or flowerings may be variable – which landscape designers and town people very often do not take into consideration. Similarly, episodes in urban life modify the natural landscape in the town: market days and civil or religious holidays are often marked by flowers, thus introducing other cycles into the presence of plants.

Nature in town, nature of the town?

So, we understand better the point of reflecting on nature in its vegetal forms in the town between the seventeenth and the early twenty-first centuries, for, over these four centuries, a number of trends have asserted themselves. While nature never left the town during this period, its presence seems to have been reinforced, if only symbolically. Firstly, in fact, the expansion of towns and their growth in population increased their influence over the surrounding area or space; as towns acquired more residents and opened out, they pushed back the countryside and became more rapacious, as plants of all kinds and in increasing quantities were brought into towns and spread throughout them. At the same time, the greening of towns changed in aspect and tended to become more extended, particularly in the second half of the nineteenth century. The reinforcement of absolutism begun by Louis XIV, just like the influx of social elites into towns during his reign, encouraged the multiplication of formal gardens. As demonstrated by the urban transformations during the Second Empire, nature continued to play a role in the extravagant policies of the ruling powers. This greening would, in the end, be encouraged twofold by science: firstly by the development of botanical science, particularly in the eighteenth century, which aroused astonishing enthusiasm and contributed considerably to the diversification of urban plant species; then, by the rise of hygienics and sanitary movements in general, which saw in natural urban forms a remedy for sicknesses – both physical and social or even moral – which afflicted towns. These developments were accompanied by very many theoretical writings which aptly reflected on nature's place in the town. Thus, when in 1931 the census revealed that the French were mainly urban dwellers, in Great Britain garden cities already existed, since Ebenezer Howard had begun the project in 1898. Nature was no longer opposed to the town or exploited to fill in gaps; in theory, and increasingly in practice, it began to structure the city – which ecological concerns, increasingly significant over the past few decades, have only underlined.

This fact underpins our approach here, an approach which cannot just be chronological because of the coherence over these few centuries as regards the progressive recognition of the urban vegetal. In what follows we will proceed by shedding light on a few major themes raised by this movement. The first point is understanding why nature came into the town: what were the motivations, changing as they did over time, behind its growing hold over urban space – or the feeling that nature is missing … (Chapter 1)? But it is not enough just to want grass or flowers – one has to be able to establish them: whose were the green fingers which set in train this often ambitious greening of cities (Chapter 2)? Moreover, more concretely, how was it possible to vegetalise the mineral and what constraints needed to be overcome (Chapter 3)? Thereafter it will be easier to understand the diverse functions of urban nature, which will be introduced in the rest of the book. Quite paradoxically, urban nature is firstly conceived as being one of the key elements in urbanity, the place where good manners are learnt, where those social classes who do not understand the codes of civility learn to be more refined, the site where a social position or an individual identity are affirmed (Chapter 4). It is also a means towards wellbeing and good-living, a factor in all celebrations where the body, the soul and the mind are improved (Chapter 5). By offering a space for freedom in the heart of the urban structure, nature also offers up the chance to go wild: urban nature is not just a vector of urbanity but also a factor in disorder (Chapter 6). But the town is not just about ostentation; it is also quite simply a place for plant production and consumption: flowers, fruits, vegetables and wood come and go in the urban space, and there they are cultivated, handled, ingested and used on a daily basis (Chapter 7). Finally, parks and gardens are spaces where science has found the ultimate field for special experimentation, whether these places are the subject or simply the setting (Chapter 8).

Finally then, it is nature in many forms and with different usages which has imposed itself on urban spaces over these past few centuries to the point where it has become a constituting element: to ask questions about nature *in* the town is basically asking questions about the nature *of* the town.[22] The

22 See also Sabine Barles and Nathalie Blanc (eds), *Écologies urbaines : sur le terrain* (Paris: Economica, 2016).

modern town wants to be regulated, ordered and strong in its monumental identity; a town shaped by man, who uses vegetal forms worked into the controlled staging of an urban mechanism where gardens, esplanades and other ornamentations serve the common good. From the great classical squares to the parks of the Second Empire, the obsession was definitely with a town that was restrained and of a submissive environment. This urban model has only given way to the 'irregular vegetal', wild weeds, insidious mosses or humble everyday herbs fairly recently and with quite some reluctance! Overshadowed by prestige plants and yet fully vigorous, this nature is confined to urban interstices, from wasteland to the back yard, not forgetting the tradesmen's entrances, and yet it has never been so necessary to urban ecology.[23] Despite the dominance of modern science, the desire for order has been accompanied by an unwavering faith in man's creative power: urban space can and must be adapted for the happiness of ever more numerous citizens. Until very recently nothing opposed this land-based ability, which could move stones and also trees in order to improve the town. The 'terrible' dream of Baudelaire's that was mentioned earlier echoes this inventive optimism wherein man can satisfy his 'whim'. If nature can define the town, it is because the people of France have chosen, over the centuries, to set it at the very heart of the city that they want to arrange and modify to their liking. Even though, since the 1980s, they have seen the limits of their power over nature more clearly they have become 'the architect(s) of (their) fairyland'.

23 Stéphane Van Damme, in *Métropoles de papiers* (Paris: Les Belles Lettres, 2012) has shown how urban archaeology emerged in the seventeenth century to examine the future of large cities: it is necessary to know their past, including their ecological past, in order to ensure their future.

1.

WHY BRING NATURE INTO TOWN?

In the little town of Verrieres in the Doubs where Stendhal's *Le Rouge et le Noir* (1830) begins, M. de Rênal, to give his administration a heritage, had an avenue of plane trees planted under the apt name of 'Cours de la Fidélité' (Avenue of Fidelity) to declare his Legitimist loyalties. Though ridiculously compared with the Promenade in Saint-Germain-en-Laye it constituted glory for *M. le Maire*, and happiness for townsfolk strolling about in its shade, and it excited the acrimony of his opponents who could say nothing against this happy venture except to complain that the trees were badly lopped. At the outset of his novel Stendhal indicates what is at stake regarding the place of nature in the city. Why should it be needed? To what ends? In what way? Such questions only really arose after the eighteenth century. In the seventeenth and eighteenth centuries, urban design was still mainly derived from the medieval period. The town was still shut up within its walls and marked by a network of narrow alleyways in a densely-built centre, whose upper storeys seemed to dominate the sky, absorbing all the light. The eighteenth-century townscape, so out of tune with the dominant neo-classical aesthetic, cannot be called 'Gothic', but rather dirty and decrepit. Greening the cities did not yet have a place in aesthetic considerations: it would go hand-in-hand with a deep urban transformation. The seventeenth and eighteenth centuries were just the first step in a disorderly and non-linear process that improved urban life, uniting the vegetal with aesthetics and hygiene issues. The nineteenth century continued and reinforced this process, as nature would then be a response to the anxieties generated by 'the urban question'. And then, after World War I, considerations focused on what kind of nature one wanted to bring into towns, balancing issues of quality with the demands of scale.

A new requirement in the seventeenth and eighteenth centuries

The end of the sixteenth century saw the beginning of the slow transformation of the city, which was growing, overspilling its walls and giving birth to new spatial forms bringing the mineral and the vegetal closer together. The city became the indisputable site of a would-be-absolute royal power, and the residence of elites who favoured this political drive. Henceforth the urban space formed part of the dominant discourse. To build, to straighten, to aerate and to green: these were the golden rules contributing to reshaping the city, or *beautifying* it, as was then said, in line with a grandeur-smitten monarchical ideal.

Beautification was indeed the priority of classical urbanism, not as an add-on quality but as a principle fundamental to urban improvement, with architectural and natural beauty contributing to citizens' physical and spiritual welfare.[1] Since the sixteenth century, theoretical treatises and urban utopias born of the thinking of architects and engineers approached the town as a global theatre whose staging needed attention, but not at the expense of what was behind the scenes. This endeavour to conceptualise the functioning of the city was associated with the process of investing in urban space by rulers and elites, putting this intersection at the heart of their deliberations. The issue of the urban aesthetic had nonetheless to answer to very practical matters: the circulation and flow of people and goods, hygiene and public health, bringing in water and managing rivers. Beautification of the city was robed in economic, moral and civic values. It was felt that a workable, clean, well-regulated urban space would contribute to prosperity and the common good. Renaissance scholars, painters and architects mastered perspective, a basic tool for classical urbanism. Streets were focused on central points, and their firm geometrical forms would free up traffic while controlling space: symmetry, unity, order and harmony were the keywords of an urban aesthetic that did not preclude practical considerations.[2] Within this theoretical framework the first experiments in vegetal urbanism gradually transformed the constricted traditional city-scape.

The glories of the classical town, or the triumph of vegetal decor

Since the sixteenth century, the city had embarked on a slow process of beautification that involved a new relationship with the vegetal. The links which the great majority of the urban population maintained with nature in accordance with their everyday needs lingered on from the medieval period,

1 Daniel Rabreau, 'Introduction', in Daniel Rabreau and Sandra Pascalis (eds), *La Nature citadine au siècle des Lumières* (Bordeaux: Arts & Arts, 2005), p. 18.

2 Pierre Lavedan, Jeanne Hugueney and Philippe Henrat, *L'Urbanisme à l'époque moderne, XVIe–XVIIIe siècles* (Geneva: Droz, 1982).

without being adorned in aesthetic or hygienic virtues. The town was still lodged within a predominantly agricultural economic system, and empty spaces near the belt of city walls welcomed orchards, kitchen gardens and other forms of market gardening, as we shall see in Chapter 7. If the dense building in the centre of medieval cities displayed an architecture in wood and stone, then the vegetal was by no means absent. It was simply a familiar resource rather than an ornament. Some monumental trees, standing alone in the centre of an urban space, were closely connected with the everyday doings of the townspeople and even embodied the community's identity. The Tree of Beauvais at Limoges was planted by the authorities in 1507 in front of the Notre Dame Convent near the Barres fountain. It was in the centre of a space where there was a market, and it was the subject of modifications to fit it better into the urban economy: a low wall topped with stone slabs made a stall for the merchants, and the lantern at the end of an iron bar fixed into the tree trunk served as public lighting.[3] From the second half of the sixteenth century, this everyday vegetal with which people had a principally utilitarian relationship had been in some measure eclipsed by new contrivances designed to beautify the town, which had now become a show-case for royal power and the residence of elites who wished to establish their superiority within a worthy decor.

The origins of the classical town are inseparable from large developments in *Ancien Régime* society. The town saw a strengthening of the leading functions that ensured its domination of the countryside at the same time as a model of civilisation was being erected on the foundation of urban values. It was shaped by the expectations of social elites, for whom it had become the preferred place to live by the turn of the seventeenth century. This was a major transformation, symbolised by the triumph of the French style garden, an urban vegetal creation stripped of all rural reference from the outset. The elite builders and patrons of the *Grand Siècle*, the seventeenth century, were city dwellers and proud of it: the town was the instrument of their social domination, and their home port and horizon. The traditional urban elites (nobility, businessmen, town worthies) strengthened their position by making themselves indispensable to the monarchical state. At the same time the rural nobility started to become city people, whereas up till then they had deemed the town a place of exchange and transaction,

3 Bfm Limoges, Ms21, Annales manuscrites de Limoges, fol°24. http://omeka.bm-limoges.fr/archive/files/be9016eebc0088c539910164d0d19d9c.jpg (accessed 5 Oct. 2014).

a place for business but unworthy of a residence suiting the aristocratic ethos. In a movement running from the end of the sixteenth century to the middle of the eighteenth, several thousands of the nobility abandoned their country chateaux for a town address, for reasons of family or marriage strategy or for service owed to the king. From the period of the Wars of Religion, towns were endowed with the sovereign's representatives (governors, intendants). Administrative functions were added to military ones. While state apparatus expanded and became more complex, and bureaucratic centralisation increased, the major public administrative bodies (tax, justice, Water and Forests, etc.) came together in towns and an elite of functionaries was required to live there. The town 'made' the elites, and the elites 'made' the town. They shaped spaces conforming to their habits and lifestyle, and so contributed to promoting the symbolic superiority of the town over the rural world. Art and literature reflected the urban civilisation's monopoly. At the end of the seventeenth century, choosing an exclusively country life would have been deemed social suicide: the choice of rural retreat was considered a symptom of social failure, or at best a sign of eccentric devotion. The cultural gaps that opened up between town and country, big towns and small towns, and between Paris and the provinces became a trigger for comedy in the theatre. In Molière, a M. de Pourceaugnac, an arrogant minor country aristocrat from Limoges who has become the butt of a joke orchestrated by some Parisian sophisticates, demonstrates irresistibly the civilising function of the city. Those who cannot, or will not, master the codes of urbanity are relegated into the limbo of the faraway countryside. Urban sociability rested on the exercise of civility and the staging of the self in both public and private spaces, as we shall see in Chapter 4. Noble urban habitat cannot do without the vegetal, for the pleasure of the table, and above all for the pleasure of the eyes. But make no mistake: the garden of the private house knew how to distinguish itself from the country vegetable garden. The artful decoration of French parterre flowerbeds was a marker of social success and not necessarily linked with grand aristocratic names. Among many other examples, we can take the instance of Chamlay, historian and general to Louis XIV:[4] he exploited tastes acquired in the king's service to beautify his Parisian townhouse in the rue du Colombier, and commissioned the great artist Pérelle to design lavish parterres to ornament it.

4 Jean-Philippe Cénat, 'Chamlay (1650–1719), le stratège oublié de Louis XIV', *Revue historique des armées* 263 (2011): 53–62.

Why bring Nature into town?

At the beginning of the seventeenth century, the model of the private townhouse made its mark in the centre of towns: normally adjacent to other buildings, constructed round a principal courtyard with a carriage gate, it was perhaps able to accommodate a small garden, if the land constraints allowed it. The progressive expansion of the town beyond its own ramparts allowed new residential zones to move into free unencumbered spaces suitable for the more systematic organisation of pleasure gardens. The most remarkable noble residences played with really scenographic vegetal effects, exciting public admiration. At the end of the eighteenth century, the Parisian nobility experienced the new art of living in the western neighbourhoods, where urban existence blended harmoniously with country pleasures far from the sicknesses of the city.[5] Valorised socially, this taste for the vegetal was nonetheless the extrapolation of a civilisation of urban pleasures, and of a very artificial relation to nature viewed through the prism of artistic emotions.

If the *Ancien Régime* met with the approval of social elites it was because it declared itself as a site of power, both royal and municipal, of undeniable importance. Symbolically, carving the town in its own image allowed political power to confirm its power there and to appropriate it: thus urban historians pay very close attention to urban workings and what they signify. The art of rhetoric is vital to reinforcing royal power, and the language of absolutism etches itself into the very stone. Large open spaces and uncluttered perspectives staged glorious scenes uniting sites of power with sites of sanctity. Such monumental presentations read like a true symbolic grammar of majestic power. In the city-theatre the vegetal was far from a mere supporting player. The architects were often also garden designers. Living material, plastic and infinitely modulable, the vegetal was better suited to sketches and trial-and-error than stone and marble. The Renaissance garden maze and then the seventeenth century French-style garden were real laboratories for classical urbanism. It is impossible here not to refer to the optical illusion of the Tuileries Garden, forerunner of the large perspective that has fashioned the Parisian cityscape. Two dynasties of master gardeners, the Mollets and the Le Nôtres, shaped the land, sand and vegetal decoration of the Tuileries in the seventeenth century. André Le Nôtre, the ultimate garden scenographer, and as much a creator as he was an heir, was raised on a tradition blending know-how in agronomy with the theoretical mastery of geometry. His fellows, Jean and André Mollet, father and son, left to posterity technical treatises

5 Mathieu Marraud, *La Noblesse de Paris au XVIIIe siècle* (Paris: Seuil, 2000).

comprising the state of the art of the French garden in the middle of the seventeenth century. In his *Jardin de plaisir* (*Pleasure Garden*) which appeared in 1651, André Mollet stages the supreme site of power, the royal residence:

> [It] must be located in an advantageous site, for it to be decorated with all that is required for its embellishment; the first requirement is to be able to plant there a great avenue with a double or triple row of female elms or lime trees ... which should be in a perpendicular line before the façade of the House, and at the beginning of which there should be a half-circle or a square ... Then facing the rear of the said House must be built close-by parterres in Broderie, so that from the windows they may be viewed ... After these parterres in Broderie shall the parterres be placed, or patches of lawn, and little groves as well, alleys and fences high and low, suitable to their position, in such a manner that the said alleys arrive and finish at a statue or a fountain.[6]

The virtuosity of the vegetal composition and the rarity and delicacy of the species revealed to the public show a desire to infuse the space with a luxurious and generous monarchical ideal.

However, with the king lacking the resources to order rearrangements on a grand scale, realising a royal urbanism remained essentially a matter for the capital, with activity being intermittent and in sudden bursts, a 'fluttering'[7] urbanism, as it was pleasingly put. In provincial towns, realising new designs was a matter for the local authorities. At the end of the seventeenth century, the chaotic relations between provincial towns and the monarchy seemed more settled. League towns, Fronde towns and Protestant towns all seemed to have ended up yielding to monarchical order and having to consent to the dismantling of the ramparts that were a symbol of their resistance. Although stripped of part of their political autonomy, towns retained a model of self-administration up until the Revolution. To ensure the continuance of their privileges, municipal elites overinvested in prestige undertakings that concretised their privileged relations with the king, as in the royal squares where statues of kings on horseback prance around. As it was not possible to interfere with existing buildings and make major alterations in a complex of properties fiercely defended by their owners, modifications to the urban structure were going to remain essentially very specific. The town hall, a strong identity symbol, is an architectural object particularly apt for staging municipal power. Lyon's town hall rose out of the earth rather late, in 1647,

6 André Mollet, *Le Jardin de plaisir, contenant plusieurs dessins de jardinage, tant parterres en broderie, compartiments de gazon, que bosquets et autres* (Stockholm: H. Kayser, 1651), chapter IX (n.p.).

7 Emmanuel Le Roy Ladurie and Bernard Quillet, 'Un urbanisme frôleur', in Georges Duby (ed.), *Histoire de la France urbaine*, 5 vols, vol. 3 (Paris: Seuil, 1981) pp. 439–481.

as an initiative by the city consuls who up to then had no settled place to meet. A French-style garden is linked to the town hall to make the view of it more sublime and to impress citizens and visitors with the variety and rarity of the species of trees in the parterres. Another great thing for towns in the seventeenth and eighteenth centuries was the matter of ramparts, when there was royal consent that the ancient walls could be knocked down, which was not always automatic. It was very often through breaches in city walls that the vegetal came right into the town.

For town-dwellers, gardens and promenades represent first of all spaces for relaxation suitable for leisure pursuits, a topic addressed in Chapter 5. But for their councillors there were constraints to be overcome and challenges to be met to make establishing them a success. From the sixteenth century on, the palette of vegetalised spaces within towns was enriched with new shades. Public improvements were now added to old and essentially private vegetal forms inherited from the Middle Ages in the shape of gardens (town gardens, botanical gardens) and of planted promenades organised into a *cours* or *mail* (avenue or mall), or a boulevard, which then prevailed in the eighteenth century.

The first public promenades were introduced in towns under the name of *cours* or *mail.* Use of them was, however, restricted to the most respectable social categories: following the Italian model, the *cours* or *mail* is designed for the pleasure of high society, as a refuge from disturbances, foul air and other disagreeable features of the street. This kind of improvement had several components: a planted alley might have intersecting alleys bordering it, and perhaps parterres and gardens as breathing spaces, and a system of enclosure (ditches, fences, grills) separating this privileged space from the rest of the city structure and preserving the august users from the indiscreet gaze of the vulgar. The first *cours* were established in the capital at the instigation of Marie de Medici: the Mail de l'Arsenal (1604) and above all the Allée du Cours-la-Reine (1616), 1,300 metres long and lined with elms, running along the Seine, from the Tuileries Garden to the high ground of Chaillot. It had intersecting alleys and a roundabout enabling coaches to turn easily. This new form of improvement combining walking and vehicular traffic was rapidly adopted throughout the kingdom: from 1649 it was the same in Rouen as in Aix-en-Provence. The relationship with nature was very tenuous because the vegetal (trees, plants in the ditches, etc.) merged with the staged decor of the grand people of the world, who did not take any particular pleasure in it. A few decades later the boulevard took over from the *cours* as the privileged form of urban beautification. The popularisation of boulevards in French towns from the end of the seventeenth century was the product of several phenomena: a favourable economy driven by a demographic dynamism that literally pushed the town outside its walls; the demilitarisation of urban spaces; thinking about addressing the question of traffic within the town; the spread of leisure and consumption activities; and of course emergent sanitary concerns about public health, which would develop further.[8] A straight path bordered with trees and perhaps doubled by a parallel path, the boulevard often occupied the space formerly devoted to ramparts fallen into obsolescence: sometimes it figured as the city limit, and sometimes as the link between the urban centre and the suburbs. Not being cut off from the rest of the town by physical barriers, the boulevard acted as a kind of junction between the public garden and the street. It represented both a place for promenading and leisure and a traffic route absorbing part of the street traffic and a market space. It accommodated some provision for recreation, chairs and benches for rest, fountains, lighting, restaurants, cafés and shops. In Paris in the spring of 1784, the Englishwoman Mrs Cradock liked both the rural and urban character of this mixed space, forming part of a residential quarter but also open to the market garden area around the town:

> We admired a delightful garden on the boulevards; it was approached by a long alley lined with apricot trees and festoons of vines, all in flower. We went into a café for refreshment and listened to an excellent orchestra … Having rested we strolled along several new streets nearby.[9]

City planners tried harder than ever to think of the city as a comprehensive whole. *Cours*, boulevards and gardens were tools articulating different parts of the urban complex. As agents transforming the cityscape, they introduced perspectives and breathing spaces, and painted green lines into a more unified urban fabric.

It is no chance that the first experiments in vegetal urbanism belong to the eighteenth century, a time of urban expansion sustained by a favourable economic dynamic. Creating green public spaces and great monumental vegetalised perspectives were prestige investments reflecting the good economic health of the urban world. Public works were usually embarked on in times of prosperity and reflected the prosperity and ambition of metropolises. The towns distinguished by expansion and population growth

8 Laurent Turcot, 'L'émergence d'un espace plurifonctionnel: les boulevards parisiens au XVIIIe siècle', *Histoire urbaine* **12** (1) (2005): 115–189.

9 *Journal de Mme Cradock, Voyage en France (1783–1786)*, handwritten document trans. by O. Delphin-Baleyguier (Paris: Perrin, 1896), Thursday 17 June 1784, p. 49.

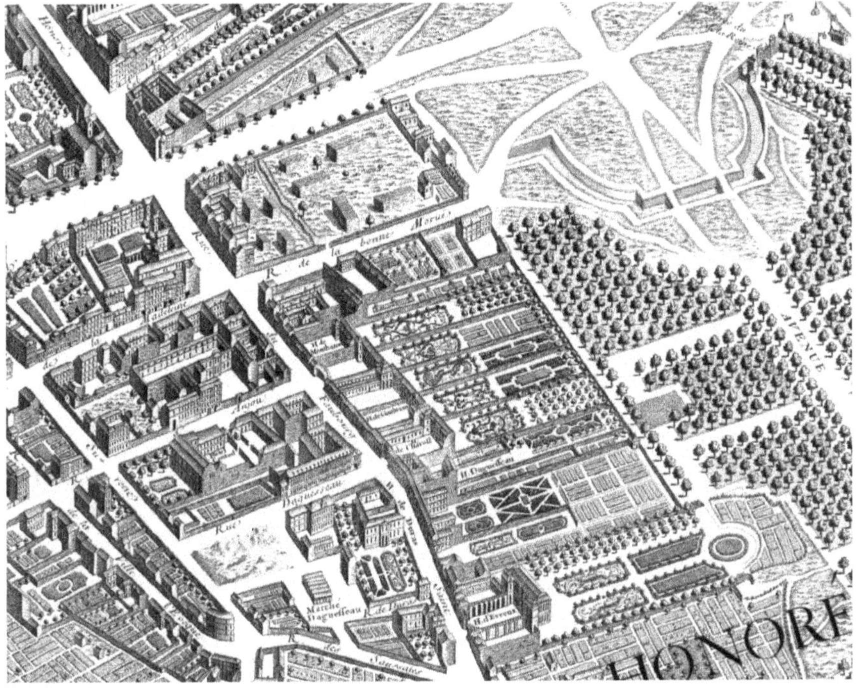

Figure 1.

Turgot's map of Paris, 1739.
Source: Wikimedia Commons, https://commons.wikimedia.org/wiki/Category:Plan_de_Turgot?uselang=fr

had either become outposts of royal power or were economically specialised, such as the great Atlantic ports. There were also particular cases, such as Nancy, whose political destiny gave birth to an urban experimentation in which the vegetal took its place. The city did not become French until 1766 with the death of Stanislas Leszczynski. Louis XV's father-in-law was wholly oriented towards France and, inspired by Louis XIV's urbanism, had built the famous Place Royale, inaugurated in 1755. This was an important moment in Nancy's urbanism as it formed a link between two parts of the city, the medieval hub and the new Renaissance town. Above all, it was an integral part of a plan to reorganise the fabric of the city around this new centre in the most splendid way possible. The vegetal had a central role: the newly established Carrière and the Place d'Alliance were planted with trees, either in the ground or in pots; a huge sixteen hectare nursery garden was established, to link the two towns, to supply trees for the roads of Lorraine and to act as a promenade, in part at least, for the citizens of Nancy.[10] While the mineral fabric predominates, the vegetal is an essential element in this urban project. As with the Atlantic port of Bordeaux, this successful project was cited as an example throughout the kingdom of France. The fall of the monarchy in 1792 did not bring this fundamental movement to an end. What was called the Plan of 'the Artists', devised between 1793 and 1797 by the committee of the same name, made up of some dozen of the period's architects and engineers, sought to address an urban challenge presented by the nationalisation of property in the Revolution: a large part of Paris was under the authorities' control, and this made all imaginable embellishments a possibility. The Artists aspired to present a plan which would include the entire capital, even if in the end they often had to settle for juxtaposing new projects and older ones. It is important to note, however, that natural elements, particularly trees, were incorporated into the thinking, with principally aesthetic ends in view. L'avenue de l'Observatoire leading to the Luxembourg palace and the improvement of the old Chartreux garden and reorganisation of the Tuileries neighbourhood were all envisaged. A shortage of public finance forced the sale of these newly acquired national properties and prevented implementation of the plan: but an idea had been set out, to be taken up in part by later authorities.

Beautification was not the only motive behind the extensive introduction of the vegetal into towns. From the end of the seventeenth century, medical discourse echoed the preoccupations of the public authorities. In order to maintain the health of subjects who were also taxpayers and soldiers of the king, it was necessary to supply the means of limiting the deadly effects of an urban environment whose working was now becoming the subject of theoretical reflection.

Air and space

The eighteenth century is a key period in the emergence of a discourse on health which addressed its arguments to public decision-making and began to influence it. The widespread enthusiasm for public gardens and promenades was explained by both the pleasure they gave to an urban population wanting recreation and the regenerative properties attributed to them.

10 Vincent Bradel, 'Du jardin à la ville : Lunéville-Nancy', in Daniel Rabreau and Sandra Pascalis (eds), *La Nature citadine au siècle des Lumières* (Bordeaux: Arts & Arts, 2005).

Why bring Nature into town?

The introduction of natural spaces into towns was for doctors an indubitable issue of public health. Convinced that bad vapours were carried on the ambient air and corrupted its quality, the medical profession raised more general awareness about the need to improve public health by transforming urban space and by appealing to a wide range of actors – architects, engineers, municipal authorities, etc.[11]

In addition to theoretical studies and pre-statistical enquiries, the dominant discourse deplored excessive urban mortality in comparison with vigorous country life. Called to the bedside of a dying city, doctors blamed the numbers on the wretched quality of the urban environment. Among the 'pre-Pasteurian superstitions' (Alain Corbin) is the notion that air was responsible for spreading illness. In a context of urban growth and increased density, people worried about the vile air expelled by numberless human and animal organisms, whose respiratory mechanism was now well understood, and about the pollution caused by economic activities in the centres of towns (tanneries, butcheries, rendering plants). From the beginning of the eighteenth century the medical profession had harboured a virtual obsession with the free circulation of the elements (air and water). Hippocrates' *On Airs, Waters and Places* was still an essential work of reference in thought about the relation of health to environment, the pathologies observed in a given place being related to its climatic, meteorological and topographical features. From the 1760s on, 'medical topographies' proliferated, aimed at producing detailed observations of individual urban quarters. The diagnoses were in place, but results at the level of action were relatively limited before the Revolution. The monarchy adopted regulations for moving pollution sources away from town centres: the decision to displace cemeteries and graves in 1786 was the most symbolic of these actions, but also the most disputed.[12] On the scale of the town, priority was given to opening up great thoroughfares and to vegetalised spaces, so as to ventilate the urban fabric. Even so, all these measures were dependent on both the goodwill of the local authority and the healthiness of municipal finances. The cartography that has come down to us from the eighteenth century makes it possible to gauge the extent of urban transformations, which often took place within individual *faubourgs* (suburbs). The plan called Du Carla de Puilauron was a projection of the desire for greenery that enthused the

11 Sabine Barles, *La Ville délétère : médecins et ingénieurs dans l'espace urbain (xviiie-xxe siècles)* (Seyssel: Champ Vallon, 1999).

12 Sabine Barles, 'Les villes transformées par la santé, XVIIIe-XXe siècles', *Les Tribunes de la santé 33 (4)* (2011): 31–37.

citizens of Enlightenment Toulouse. Since the end of the seventeenth century, the capital of the Languedoc region had been smothering within its walls. Its population had doubled in the space of a century, and in the eighteenth century population growth showed no sign of faltering: there were 53,000 inhabitants in 1790. During the second half of the eighteenth century there began a phase of major improvement works to contain floods on the Garonne while at the same time developing a network of waterways essential for the vital trade in cereals. The enlightened elites, enthusiastic academicians, hoped to profit from this dynamism by contributing to an improvement in the quality of the life of the majority. Among such good spirits, the marquis Louis de Mondran stands out. He was an enthusiast of architecture and urbanism, and a founder of the Royal Academy of painting, sculpture and architecture of Toulouse. His *Projet pour le commerce et les embellissements de Toulouse* (*Plan for the Commerce and the Beautifying of Toulouse*) published in 1754, presents itself as a design for overall urban planning which should improve the manner of living in the city, of moving around it, of doing business or amusing oneself there. He imagined a network of gardens, boulevards and promenades, of esplanades, quays and canals which would redraw the urban space, at the price of overthrowing the existing street and property plans – which the municipal authorities neither could nor would allow. Only a small part of Mondran's global project was realised, needing only a handful of expropriations outside the city walls. This was a matter of the public promenade of the Grand Rond, executed between 1750 and 1752, and completed by the creation of the Royal Garden in 1754. These reorganisations were made possible through the space gained by the transformation of the old fortification system. From the site of a former earth dyke five large radiating avenues lined with elms and limes stretch out from a great oval space, called Le Boulingrin as a gesture to the Anglomania of the time (on the other side of the Channel a bowling green being a grassed area for playing bowls). The Royal Garden dedicated to botany reinforced the linkage between the town and its new avenues. The example of Toulouse represents a trend which can be seen in most of the kingdom's major cities in the eighteenth century. The introduction of vegetalised spaces answers a strong desire on the part of citizens, and from enlightened elites especially, for a more habitable, less dense town, made airy by roads and pathways for circulation and strolling.

The diagnoses of eighteenth-century doctors helped to initiate the call for air in urban spaces. Investigations into improving public health also led them to look at the earth and to issue warnings about the poor quality of

Figure 2.

The Grand Rond public promenade in the Toulouse city map, by Joseph Marie de Saget (1777). Public domain image from Archives municipales de Toulouse, ii 686.

urban soil, called 'mephitic' in late eighteenth century parlance comparing the urban space to a putrid swamp. The streets were rarely paved and they were not designed for foul water to be evacuated and to flow away; they served as a spillway for organic rubbish and rotten waste matter, producing gases that were deleterious and dangerous for the inhabitants. In the mid-eighteenth century, members of the *Société royale de médecine* (Royal Medical Society) also emphasised the need to carry the battle into humid zones and marshland. The fate of cesspools and ditches at the foot of old ramparts was also sealed: they had to be filled in to give way to public promenades planted with trees which would absorb the dangerous exhalations.[13] The city of Bordeaux, often noted for prestigious improvements in the eighteenth century, rehabilitated an insalubrious quarter running along the walls of the Chateau Trompette between the Médoc and Saint-Germain gates and long abandoned to prostitutes, robbers and crooks. In 1743 the city took back this strip of land, which it owned. The ramparts remained (by royal command) but they were reworked to allow for the establishment of the Allées de Tourny, named after the enlightened official behind the project; this henceforth respectable promenade was planted with 200 Dutch elms and limes arranged in four rows. The vegetal thus figures as the natural ally of doctors in the battle for the beautification and cleansing of the city.

In the eighteenth century, physical activity also became the subject of renewed interest among the social elites, under the influence of neo-Hippocratic medical discourse. There had been no 'medical revolution' in Enlightenment Europe; there was no major medical discovery apart from inoculation for smallpox; knowledge of traditional illnesses had not been renovated, nor was medication enriched with new substances. There was, however, a significant change at the level of social attitudes towards the body, deeply and lastingly transformed with the advent of hygienic practices. From the 1680s onwards, practitioners were updating the lessons of Hippocrates, who emphasised the natural capacity of the human body to keep itself healthy thanks to a vital force capable of launching an illness, but also of putting a term to it. To acquire and keep good health it was best to avoid excess and change, to cultivate tranquillity of mind, to live in pure air, to keep food in proportion to bodily needs and to avoid unnecessary medication. The role of the doctor is to foster the natural curative process. Rather than overprescribing, he should recommend an appropriate dietary regime, cold baths and open-air activities suited to the patient's constitution. The public, both men and women, were quickly convinced of the health-giving value of physical exercise. For those who did not feel themselves capable of sustained effort, doctors recommended activity accessible to everyone within the framework of ordinary exercise associated with a healthy regime. Thus, walking became a mode of preventative medicine. From the end of the seventeenth century, medical literature stresses its beneficial effects on both the respiratory system and the muscular structure. Among its most zealous

13 Patrick Fournier, 'La ville au milieu des marais aux XVIIe et XVIIIe siècle', *Histoire urbaine* **18** (1) (2007): 23–40.

promotors we must cite Doctor Théodore Tronchin (1709–81). Private physician to the Duke of Orleans and a favourite of Parisian high society, for his clientele of both sexes he prescribed moderate exercise (walking, sailing and horse-riding), along with frugal eating and washing in cold water. In the second half of the eighteenth century, society ladies '*tronchined*', walking in flat shoes and holding a stick to help sustain a vigorous rhythm. This practice was so popular that it entailed an adaptation of costume – lower heels, and shorter dresses without side-hoops, the '*tronchines*' or '*polonaises*' which caused a sensation. Another famous eighteenth century doctor, Samuel-Auguste Tissot of Geneva, extended his preventative health practices to the whole body of society, beginning with children (*Avis au peuple sur sa santé* (*Health Advice for the People*), 1761). The eighteenth century hailed the advent of the promenade as a form of urban leisure suitable for everyone, irrespective of status or age, to the point that towns had to make appropriate provision or find themselves suffering unfavourable comments in travel guides. And the very feeling of walking had implications of sensibility: it is written about as a gratifying individual experience.[14] One did not just walk in conformity with the polite codes of the promenade: one walked also for oneself, a healthy walk enabling one to strengthen one's body while enjoying the spectacles of the city and of nature.

Beautification and health were the motives in the seventeenth century, and still more in the next century, for bringing nature into the town. From the end of the eighteenth century, however, while these motives were still there, urban vegetalisation was built on an appreciably different base, associated with a perception of the city as a problem and with new modes of activity.

The vegetal: A therapy for the sick city of the industrial age

The city world

One knows that the city is the very place where authorities stage their power – because it is the place where power is concentrated. And what better manifestation of power is there than power exercised over nature? Technical achievements and the miraculous transformation of wasteland into paradisal parks demonstrate the ability of national and local authorities to master natural space. This mastery over nature increased markedly from the end of

14 Laurent Turcot, *Le Promeneur à Paris au XVIIIe siècle* (Paris: Gallimard, 2007).

the eighteenth century, and throughout the next century, and was extended by virtue of colonial adventure. Explorers were urged to pursue and intensify botanical studies of the regions they traversed. They collected seeds and plants on a large scale and, through the mediation of various botanical gardens, these came to spread through the home-country and even become commonplace. In this way the imperial powers, led by France and Great Britain, made their dominion over the world visible, since even the flora (and the fauna besides) bowed to their will. Transplantation of this kind was on a big scale. For instance, on his return from his voyage to South America with Alexander von Humboldt, Aimé Bompland sent to the *Jardin des Plantes* (Botanic Garden) in Paris a hundred species of orchids, fuchsias, fifty species of passionflowers, etc.[15] While this power over nature was initially celebrated and staged in some great parks belonging to the elite, the phenomenon soon extended to public city gardens. All the great landscapers of the mid-nineteenth century relied on this extraordinary vegetal wealth offering itself to them and they put on display the rare tree or the variegated plant reigning alone in the middle of a lawn and offering itself to the admiring gaze of visitors, happy to find confirmation of European order imposed on the world. Paris, as ever, set the tone: in 1856 in the Square Saint-Jacques, Alphand, the director of the Paris parks and gardens service under Haussmann, tried out the principles that would guide all his subsequent landscape work, and particularly the use of rare and exotic species. The first wigandias were planted here, as well as banana, palm and fig trees, on an area of just sixty ares (6,000 square metres). Extended to all the great parks in the capital, this model was also to be found in the provinces. At Coutances, for instance, the public garden opened in 1855 abounded in foreign species: Virginia tulip trees, araucarias (monkey puzzles), cedar of Lebanon, gingko, sequoia, etc. In Tours, the François Sicard garden created in 1864 by Eugène Bühler also exploited the spectacular or original look of some exotic species: a cedar and a wigandia appear in isolation on the central lawn; bamboos, yuccas and a Japanese sophora add an exotic touch to the surroundings and form a contrast with the usual planes, chestnut trees and limes.

Having all the riches of nature available to them, landscapers could give free play to their creative imaginations and make, as they all declared, a work of art by considering the play of colours and shadows and the relationships of forms and sizes, and so on. They were thus participants in

15 Isabelle Ebert-Cau, 'Aimé Bonpland', *Les Carnets de l'exotisme*, special edition *Les jardins du retour* **13** (1st semester 1994), ed. Nadine Beauthéac.

a sumptuous vegetal politics which celebrated within the town the power industrial societies had acquired over the natural world. Contemporaries were fascinated by this exotic abundance appearing in their streets and parks. In 1861, Édouard Gourdon described the arrival of rare species sent two years earlier by a Belgian nurseryman to ornament the Champs-Élysées:

> It was a true museum of living plants … The whole consignment … consisted of twelve hundred and fifty rhododendrons from one metre to seven metres in height, a thousand kalmias, between one and four metres, three hundred azaleas of two to three metres … four metre *pinus banskiana,* deodar cedars six to eight metres tall … several *araucaria imbricata*, some *pinus cembra*, some *pinus monticola,* a superb collection of magnolias and nearly three hundred other species.[16]

If the botanical gardens, which we will be discussing in the final chapter, were the supreme site for staging colonialism, universal and colonial exhibitions like that at Marseille in 1922 were the occasion for peaceful competition between nations. This is evident, for example, in the 1867 exhibition staged in Paris on the Champ de Mars.

> In the past, from the wooded heights of the Trocadéro … one's gaze would traverse the river to fall firstly on an arid and bare plain of sand. This Parisian desert was called the Champ de Mars … The desert has become the most frequented place in the world; better than that, it is the world itself. Europe, Asia, Africa, America, Oceania with their types of humans, their animals, their plants, their minerals, their natural products, their industry, their sciences and their fine arts are all held in these forty hectares.[17]

One could not better express how this convergence of richness seemed miraculous, and all orchestrated by Napoleonic power, easily combining commercial interests with national glorification, especially in the 'reserved garden' which housed the horticultural exhibition and occupied a quarter of the park surrounding the palace, and whose every flower and shrub was listed in the catalogue. Barillet-Deschamps, chief landscape coordinator, showed both inventiveness and prodigality: nothing was to be omitted that might amaze visitors and excite their wonder. Rare trees and shrubs were literally on display at different points in the park – sometimes at the cost of coherence: 'We hoped to see [in the Chinese pavilion], instead of scrawny Fuchsias from Peru, Alpine Dogwoods and Canadian Elderflowers, the natural vegetation of far-flung regions'.[18]

16 Édouard Gourdon, *Le Bois de Boulogne* (Paris: Bourdilliat, 1861), pp. 288–289.

17 Kaempfen, 'Promenade à l'exposition universelle', *Paris Guide*, 1867, vol. II, p. 2006.

18 'L'exposition universelle d'horticulture', *Mouvement horticole*, 1867, pp. 154–155, quoted in Luisa Limido, *L'Art des jardins sous le Second Empire* (Seyssel: Champ Vallon, 2002), p. 162.

This staging of power benefitted all levels of the hierarchy, and contributed particularly to the acclaim that greeted nineteenth century technical achievement and those responsible for it, the engineers and landscapers. Jules Vacherot, head gardener to the city of Paris and therefore in charge of the vegetal arrangements for the universal exhibition of 1900 concealed neither his satisfaction at the event's success nor the part his department played in it. His work *Les Parcs et Jardins au commencement du XXe siècle* (*Parks and Gardens at the Beginning of the Twentieth Century*) recalled with evident contentment the many challenges he had to face in record time and in ever-changing circumstances to create the magnificent parterres and planted avenues accompanying the exhibition. The many figures given and the quantification of all things were intended to constitute a solid basis for the gardeners' achievements and for their patron, reinforcing their social and professional position.

If the vegetal made such a political affirmation possible, then it is also because its place in the city went on growing, at least in theory. Faced with the city, which was considered infected by all kinds of afflictions, the vegetal became the perfect remedy, raising many expectations.

'Impatience for greenery'[19]

The town was now subjected by municipal and national authorities alike to regulation and scrutiny. Hygienists, who developed as a body during the eighteenth and nineteenth centuries, sought answers to what was called 'the urban question' or even 'the urban crisis'. This comprised a social dimension, which it had not done previously: cities were worried not just that they were harbouring unseen miasmas that carried disruptions to health, but also because they had within them a population that was poor and unsettled, capable of transmitting sickness but also of laying low the social and political edifice. Order had to be reintroduced into chaos, and vegetation was going to both police and cleanse the urban fabric.

In both its social and sanitary aspects this crisis could manifest itself as endemic through the higher mortality levels in towns than in the countryside, and the major variations between neighbourhoods, for instance. Or more brutally, when an epidemic struck and decimated the population: one cannot overstress the trauma of the cholera epidemic that afflicted France in 1832 and took 100,000 victims, including the President of the Council Casimir

19 Alphonse de Calonne, 'Les transformations de Paris', *La Revue contemporaine*, May–June 1866: 739.

Périer and General Lamarque. With two following waves in 1848–49 and 1853–54, this disease became one of the sanitary obsessions of the century, and it concerned towns with their accumulated populations above all. In spite of some doubts, theories about miasmas prevailed: diseases were borne by unhealthy air. Thus, the watchword was ventilation: a strong fresh wind could race through towns and carry far away their toxic emanations. To make this possible, the urban habitat had to be improved by reshaping the slums, driving broad streets through, creating great spaces and bringing some nature into the centre of cities.

Such hopes were expressed in urbanist utopias that proliferated after the French Revolution. Everyone allotted a growing role to nature, thought of as an element of order, beauty and hygiene. For example when Claude-Nicolas Ledoux (1736–1806) constructed a group of buildings for rent for the rich Creole Hosten in the Rue Saint-Georges in Paris in 1792, he took pains to associate them with a large garden; and again, with the model town of Salines de Chaux (Royal Salt Works) at Arc-et-Senans that he realised in part between 1774 and 1779, he introduced nature among the buildings and surrounded the whole site with a circular boulevard planted with trees.

Similarly, Jean-Baptiste Godin, with the Familistère de Guise (built between 1859 and 1884), which was inspired by the theories of Charles Fourier and aimed at improving the living conditions of the proletariat, gave a major role to nature. For instance, the pleasure garden separated the palace from the factory, and so protected the inhabitants from fumes; it was also a productive garden, comprising a greenhouse, a kitchen garden and fruit trees.

One must not exaggerate: finding a place for the natural world in the city was just one element among others in restoring order to the urban space – but in the course of the nineteenth century it was to grow in significance to the point where it ranked among priorities. In Paris, the Prefect Rambuteau, appointed to the post by Louis-Philippe in 1833 just after the shock of the cholera epidemic, reports in his *Mémoires* that he made this promise to the king: 'In the mission which your majesty has entrusted to me, I shall not forget that my first duty is to give Parisians water, air and shade'. He was not content with opening up the heart of Paris with what is now the Rue Rambuteau and improving the Champs-Élysées; he also planted trees along the avenues and improved gardens and squares (the Square de l'Archevêché, now Square Jean XXIII, was the first square in Paris, opened in 1844) with both aesthetics and sanitation in mind: 'Trees, these good friends of mankind, that restore the eyes and purify the air'.[20] He claimed that his obsession with planting had earned him the reputation of preferring to have one of his teeth pulled out than a tree torn down.

After these first steps the next decisive stage in the vegetal organisation of towns came with the Second Empire. Paris was making itself a model for all France: Napoleon III wished to make a modern capital, beautiful and clean, to be admired by all Europe. Nature was recruited to play a big role in this: the vegetal policy implemented by the Prefect Haussmann and especially his director of promenade and garden services, Adolphe Alphand, had no equivalent in the past, uniting as it did an evident ideological structure, apparently limitless means, an almost authoritarian determination and indisputable talents of conception and implementation. Most of the authority's objectives were not basically original: the novelty lay in bringing them together and systematically putting them into effect.

In the words of Baron Ernouf in a piece of propaganda for the imperial work, 'Elegance, health, opulence – these three words sum up the work of the Promenades department.'[21] The beauty lay both in avenues of trees – 100,000 of them in Paris by the end of the 1860s – and in human-made landscapes, exciting the wonder of residents and visitors alike, such as the Buttes Chaumont park, created from scratch on the site of old quarries and a rubbish dump; or the Bois de Boulogne which sparked the liveliest excitement: 'The forest has become a park, a park with sandy pathways, full of flowers and elegant as a garden. This corner of the earthly Eden open to the wide skies could only have been shaped by an excellent landscaper... It is the Tivoli gardens revived for the Parisian's greater happiness, and the immediate gratification of all his tastes.'[22] But over and above aesthetic delights, what commentators ranked first was the effect of the vegetalisation of the capital on Parisians' health. At the time France cherished the idea of the 'green lung', epitomised in the two woods (Boulogne and Vincennes) framing Paris. It was an image that spread throughout Europe. In an article in his journal *Household Words*, Charles Dickens described Hyde Park as though seen from an air balloon: he compares it to a bullfrog's throat, and

20 Comte de Rambuteau, *Mémoires du comte de Rambuteau, publiés par son petit-fils* (Paris: Calmann-Lévy, 1905), p. 377.

21 Baron Ernouf, *De l'art des jardins. Traité pratique et didactique* (Paris: Rothschild, undated [1st edition: 1868]), p. 352.

22 *L'Illustration*, 5 July 1856, quoted in Jean-Louis Cirès, *La Construction des jardins publics à Paris sous le Second Empire*, Master's dissertation supervised by Alain Corbin, University of Tours, 1985.

describes the townspeople as little dots who enter the park pale and fatigued and then leave it radiant and ruddy-cheeked.[23] On a different scale, squares also played their part in cleansing the air. Here is Baron Ernouf again:

> Formerly, to breathe air and enjoy the sunshine, it was necessary either to venture to distant promenades or even to leave Paris; today Parisians have gardens at their disposal spread more or less evenly through all quarters of the town. Mothers ... go there to pass a few hours in the cool shade, to nurse their babies or let them play ... How many charming little ones owe their health and even their lives to them! ... Surely many violent plans and troubled dreams have vanished there, and more than one desperate creature has regained courage in this restful atmosphere.[24]

Pleasure for the eyes, relaxation for the soul, rest for the body: it is hardly surprising that nature makes for 'enrichment', particularly through the valorisation of adjacent neighbourhoods and housing prices.

This programme was implemented rationally and on different scales, with spectacular effects on Paris's urban landscape. At the level of the quarter first of all, the town was dotted with squares designed for everyday relaxation: between 1853 and 1869, 24 were created, seventeen in the old city and seven in the suburbs annexed in 1860 and forming present-day Paris.[25] These green places were augmented by the great Parisian parks, an attempt being made to share them a bit more fairly through the capital: preservation of the Tuileries and Luxembourg in the centre; Montsouris for the south; Buttes Chaumont for the north-east; Monceau for the north-west. Then the last element in the vegetalisation of the city's space, the two woods of Vincennes and Boulogne, the first for the more popular part of the people in eastern Paris, and the other for the finer elites in the west.

The developments were particularly important as French centralisation, like the strong, resolute power of the Second Empire made Paris a model for the rest of the country:

> Civil authorities, governors, prefects, *maires*, aldermen, assistants, may you read these lines! ... Plant a lot in the centre of your towns and around them, but particularly in the middle, and have them properly watered. And create squares and parks, as in Paris, a fine recreation for the eyes, and an abundant source of public health.[26]

France, in fact, was all in tune, and in the provinces, especially in the large regional metropolises (Lyon, Rennes, Bordeaux, Lille, etc.), landscape

23 Charles Dickens, *Household Words*, 12 June 1852.

24 Ernouf, *De l'art des* jardins, p. 347.

25 Cirès, *La Construction des jardins publics à Paris.*

26 *L'Illustration horticole* 11 (1864): 58, quoted in Cirès, *La Construction des jardins publics*, pp. 65–66.

creations copied from the example of Paris and based on the same ideological assumptions flourished.[27] In 1870, when the Empire was collapsing, a professor of hygiene at Montpellier congratulated himself on the transformation brought about by promenades, squares and parks in the centre of provincial towns, creating an illusion of countryside. He emphasised the principle advancement of such changes: their democratic character, because 'the great thing about good hygiene is that it gives the gratifications of wellbeing to the poor as well as to the rich … Everybody has a right to air, light, water and greenery.'[28] Everybody certainly, but social distinctions remained, as we shall see in Chapter 4. The booming tourist resorts set the tone, especially spa towns and the seaside towns of the Riviera and the Atlantic coast: opulent vegetal decor helped to give visitors a change of scene and played a part in staging a style of living still reserved for the regeneration of social elites by way of good air and all kinds of cures. In Pau, the Boulevard des Pyrénées was improved after1893 to offer British aristocrats staying in winter a panoramic view over the mountains. This work was entrusted to Alphand himself, who took his inspiration from the Promenade des Anglais in Nice. To complete the illusion, at the start of the twentieth century the Boulevard des Pyrénées was ornamented with palm trees worthy of the Côte d'Azur.

These fine effects could not, however, conceal another reality: Haussmannian works turned the urban fabric upside-down, and resulted in the disappearance of many private gardens. Essentially, it was the vegetalisation of *public* space that increased, resulting from deliberate choice and considerations not wholly focussed on the physical welfare of townspeople: it was a matter of getting society into order, an enterprise celebrating the then dominant bourgeois civilisation.[29]

One of the consequences of the movement towards the greening of town at any cost was, of course, the *town* of Le Vésinet. In 1856, in a swap with Napoleon III, the industrialist Alphonse Pallu recovered 500 hectares of the wood of Le Vésinet in the forest of Saint-Germain-en-Laye. With the aid of the talented landscaper the Count of Choulot, Pallu created a model residential estate combining town and country. It proved a success and the 'colony' became a *town* in 1875 based on a list of specifications drawn up

27 Louis-Michel Nourry, *Les Jardins publics en province* (Rennes: PUR, 1997).

28 Jean-Baptiste Fonssagrives, *L'Éducation physique des jeunes filles* (Paris: 1870), quoted in Michel Vernes, 'Les jardins contre la ville', *Temps libre* **9** (Spring 1984).

29 On this issue, see Chapter 6.

Figure 3.

The Boulevard des Pyrénées in Pau during the *Belle Époque*.
Postcard from authors' collection.

in 1858 and substantially extended in 1863, protecting its rural character and its boundaries. No industry was tolerated, and business only on certain conditions – except plant nurseries of course. Construction that was allowed had to augment the vegetal presence and maintain the general appearance of the place (for instance, private individuals were forbidden to build on their property within ten metres of a fence giving on to a pathway, a lawn or a river.) Thus Choulot's romantic landscape research, which he theorised in his *L'Art des jardins* (*The Art of Gardens*) in 1863, ensured the aesthetic and financial success of this first park-town, but not its social diversity, as it was generally the well-off who went to live there. Le Vésinet, then, did not really answer the anxieties of the period about the sanitary condition of towns, and ended up as an isolated enterprise with limited ambitions.

Open spaces for sport

It is true that from the last third of the nineteenth century onwards the concern was not just over seeing the labouring classes becoming dangerous but seeing the race become degenerate. In the imperialist context which pitted France against Great Britain and especially against Germany, which had imposed a humiliating defeat in 1871, a eugenicist anxiety permeated all of society. Social Darwinism echoed this, in the writings of Clémence Royer, Darwin's perfidious translator. More than ever, towns were singled out and blamed for the living conditions endured by overcrowded populations which were doomed to decay if nothing was done. This is how tuberculosis came to be seen as the scourge of the century: the ultimate social disease, it undermined the vigour of the French race in urban slums where the sun and the air never entered and whence, haggard and sickly, came the conquered of the future. Despite the discovery of Koch's bacillus in 1882, tuberculosis was still perceived as being the consequence of both living space and the behaviour of the sufferers. The poor were not only the victims of the absence of urban policies, thus being condemned to obscurity, but also victims of their own weaknesses, the first of which was alcoholism. Green spaces could be an answer to this. A public garden would be a healthy distraction for a worker who would no longer have to get drunk in a bar. It would also be the pure air and the ray of sunshine that were so vital in avoiding the disease. However, that would no longer suffice: over and above their role in sanitising the atmosphere, natural spaces would henceforth help to ensure the development of strong and healthy bodies through the recreations and the physical exercise that they had to offer. Here once again there is both a continuity and a break in relation to the neo-Hippocratic discourse of the eighteenth century. The process of rationalising leisure that was at work in European civilisation, as demonstrated by Max Weber in particular, can be partly explained by urban development. The city imposes rational pastimes in limited space and time. It was no longer just a question of recreation but increasingly about proper physical exercise. Sport took over from games. Gardens and parks had until then been designed as places for rest and relaxation; they now became more and more places for exercise.[30]

Aside from workers, children and adolescents were of course the first targets of this desire 'to improve the race', according to the expression in use at the time. They needed to have spaces for the recreation and sport needed for them to develop their physical attributes and this became a real concern from the end of the nineteenth century. Before that, no systematic policy had been discernible. The failure of the transformation of the Feuillants terrace in the

30 Robert de Souza, 'Les espaces libres. Résumé historique', *Le Musée social*, Dec. 1908: 181.

Tuileries Gardens, Paris, by the Public Health Committee, speaks volumes on this point. In a decree dated 15 May 1794 the Committee in fact proposed to install a palestra at the foot of the terrace which would be a place of exercise for young men. All the length of the site a portico was to be erected, inside of which there would be paintings which should be capable of 'developing and channelling the generous passions of adolescence'.[31] This project never came to be: time was limited and, doubtless, it was too soon for this kind of development.

In fact, sports needed to be codified in order for them to benefit from dedicated spaces. And this only happened gradually over the nineteenth century. Ball games in particular, and especially rugby and football, were codified in Britain before being adopted around the world and by France from the 1880s onwards. Men and boys played them, very often on school pitches or on the edges of towns. As for the rest, young people were left to enjoy themselves in the countryside when they had access to it or go walking, calmly it was hoped, in parks. So it was not until the very end of the nineteenth century that thinking came to fruition and there was determined action to create areas for sport in towns. Thus it was that in 1907 a Paris city councillor, Ambroise-Rendu, a member of the French society for open spaces and sports grounds, founded by Jules Siegfried and d'Estournelles de Constant, fought for the creation of spaces for children that were adapted to their age (playgrounds for the littlest and sports grounds for adolescents).

The transition from recreation ground to place for exercise is marked semantically: as opposed to the planned and landscaped parks and gardens, 'open spaces' simply designates unbuilt areas left for public use, without aesthetic dimension. The term was popularised at the very beginning of the century firstly by the Committee for the preservation and creation of open spaces, set up in 1902 by Gabriel Bonvalot, an explorer keen on nationalist theories. The Committee's aim was simple: it was about imposing, for reasons of hygiene, open spaces in all the towns in France. The list of societies that joined forces with the Committee is revealing: the Federation of Anti-Tuberculosis Leagues, the Anti-Alcohol league, the medical press, the newspaper *L'Auto* (!) the Society of Friends of Paris Monuments, the Society for the Protection of the Landscapes of France. Aesthetic and hygienist interests thus merged in this struggle which was not new but which varied slightly from earlier combats. This time nature should explicitly keep a watch over the flourishing of the bodies of the nation.

31 Comité de Salut Public, Arrêté du 15 mai 1794, article 9, quoted in Motoki Toriumi, *Promenades de Paris, de la Renaissance à l'époque haussmannienne. Esthétique de la nature dans l'urbanisme parisien*, Ph.D. dissertation supervised by Augustin Berque, EHESS, 2001, p. 659.

This idea was still apparent if we consider Eugène Hénard, architect for the city of Paris, who in his famous *Études sur les transformations de Paris* (*Studies on the Transformations of Paris*) published between 1903 and 1909, popularised and imposed the expression 'open spaces' (the title of volume III) during the very lively controversy over the future of the Paris fortifications. From 1884, Alphand who was aware of the uselessness of these constructions, had suggested they be torn down. The topic came up regularly since it brought together several interested parties: the army, reluctant to abandon a plot of land, the State, of course, which could have made a large financial profit from the scheme, the city of Paris as a potential purchaser, property speculators and the Parisian people as a whole. Apart from the Bonvalot Committee other associations were involved in the debate including the Social Hygiene Alliance, whose president was Casimir-Périer, the Society of Public Medicine, the Association of Garden cities of France and the Touring Club itself. The issue of the Paris fortifications played a symbolic role in this new health combat which was linked to the upkeep and expansion of green spaces as places for relaxation and leisure for the working classes.

Figure 4.

Vegetable gardens and walks: the new uses of Parisian fortifications. *L'Illustration*, 14 January 1933. Source: Authors' collection.

Why bring Nature into town?

In the run-up to the municipal elections of 1908, the topic was on everybody's lips: the socialist candidate, Albert Thomas, stated very often in *L'Humanité* newspaper the need for the working population to have the open spaces which real estate developers sought to appropriate.[32] The debate focussed on a proposition made by Hénard: the city of Paris should purchase the fortifications and build new, regularly spaced, parks there as well as gardens in such a way that no inhabitant lived more than 500 metres from a square. Hénard also clearly stipulated that in all the parks there should be space set aside for sporting activities while the squares and gardens should enclose vast lawns and sandy paths for games and sports of all kinds. He compared these green spaces to sanatoria. Hénard's plans were strongly backed by the urban and rural hygiene section of the *Musée Social* (social museum),[33] who did not hesitate to apply pressure to future elected representatives, for example by publishing 12,000 copies of a poster entitled 'Air, parks, sports', endorsed by all the candidates and depicting Hénard's project.

In that same year, 1908, Jean-Claude-Nicolas Forestier, one of the greatest landscape architects of the period, working in the Paris promenades department, contributed to this vital discussion by publishing a now classic book entitled *Grandes villes et systèmes de parcs* (*Major Cities and Park Systems*). Forestier had been strongly influenced by the example of Central Park in New York, and in his book he insisted on the need to increase the number of open spaces in large towns and in Paris in particular. He suggested an interesting ranking: great reserves and protected landscapes, suburban parks, great urban parks, small parks, neighbourhood gardens, recreation grounds (sometimes with children's playgrounds) and avenue-promenades. Each level of this *system* (and of course this word is fundamental) is associated with different functions – in particular ventilation, relaxation and sport. Thus, criss-crossed by greenery, the town would make the harmonious development and the wellbeing of its inhabitants possible. And this explains Forestier's famous quip, as related by Giraudoux: 'I am a man of the city. I love fresh air and gardens.'[34]

Because of their symbolic value, these concerns, which were so prominently

32 *L'Humanité*, 28 Apr. 1908.

33 This foundation, created in 1894 thanks to the Count of Chambrun's fortune and the support of eminent people like Jules Siegfried or Émile Cheysson, was central in the elaboration of French social policies at the turn of the 20th century through its surveys and studies, particularly those made by the section of Urban and Rural Hygiene, set up in 1908.

34 Jean Giraudoux, *Pleins Pouvoirs*, quoted in Jean-Pierre Le Dantec, *Jardins et Paysages* (Paris: Larousse, 1996), p. 361.

Parisian, interested all French social reformers and had their equivalents almost everywhere around the country. The most characteristic example at the beginning of the twentieth century was undoubtedly the Parc Pommery in Reims, created under the guidance of the marquis Melchior de Polignac, grandson of Veuve Pommery (the widowed Madame Pommery). There was a dual aim: firstly, to provide a park for the workers in the Pommery champagne house while modifying the landscape of the town, and this was carried out in 1910; and then to respond more directly to sporting concerns. In effect, Polignac was a member of the International Olympic Committee and he worked with Pierre de Coubertin. Like him, he was concerned with improving the fitness levels of the French delegation to the Olympic Games and in particular those destined for the 1916 games due to be held in Berlin. In the context of the heated Franco-German rivalry at the beginning of the century they had to put on a good show! In 1912 the 'College of Athletes' was set up in the park and this was to be run according to the guidelines drawn up by George Hébert and his theories of Natural Movement. This former French navy lieutenant had made himself the defender of open-air sports practised to develop the body to the best of its capacities, by encouraging specific muscle training as well as athleticism and gymnastics. The park was created by the landscape gardener Édouard Redont and took on a specific look since it was a mix of park and sports complex. Even today, it still has a stadium and running tracks alongside extensive lawns and clumps of trees. 'To found a hall for physical training is good, to develop a stadium almost anywhere, almost anyhow, is even better! But to set the stadium in such a way that the child and the athlete both receive training from instructors and the teachings of the landscape, is to create a work of perfection.'[35] This achievement received the enthusiastic support of the authorities: in October 1913 President Poincaré solemnly attended the 'Celebration of muscles' and the 'Celebration of the race and of physical energy regained' organised by the College of Athletes. Apart from these festivities, there were also fifteen children present from the town's hospices, who had been cured of rickets and tuberculosis by physical activities in the open air.

This development at the cusp of the nineteenth and twentieth centuries aiming at the setting up of open spaces besides parks and gardens in fact bore within it the risk of a growing lack of specification regarding vegetalised spaces, now characterised more by quantity than quality. The issue, then,

35 *Le Petit Parisien*, 23 June 1939.

during the twentieth century, was to determine, ultimately, the type of nature that was desired in the town.

Green urbanism: What nature for the twentieth century town?

The garden city

The garden city was an essential stage in thinking about urban vegetalisation in the twentieth century and is testimony to this transition from the qualitative towards the quantitative. It began in England, from the pen of a parliamentary stenographer named Ebenezer Howard who in 1898 published *Tomorrow*, re-titled *Garden Cities of Tomorrow* for its second edition in 1902. In order to restore the benefits of nature to man despite the rural exodus, Howard proposed the creation of a new kind of urban planning which would bring town and country together with all the advantages of both these places of residence. The garden city would be an autonomous community, restricted to a population of 36,000. It would be circular and at its centre would be a park and public buildings while on its outskirts would be the industries necessary for it to prosper. Everywhere, gardens and plants would bring the benefits of the open air and natural beauty. For Howard this was nothing less than the prospect of a new kind of civilisation brought about by the gradual introduction of new towns.

It was through the *Musée Social*[36] that this idea arrived in France, following a trip to England made by one of its members, Georges Benoit-Lévy, who published *La Cité-jardin* (*The Garden City*) in 1904. Here Howard's ideal is well watered-down and the author was inspired more by the industrial communities created by Lever and Cadbury. It was no longer about building a completely new town where everyone could both live and work but rather a question of new neighbourhoods attached to existing *towns*. Moreover, whereas Howard was only aiming at creating a new political and social form of order, Benoit-Lévy was suggesting a model that was rather more paternalistic, where the town was gathered around a factory as an initiative by an industrial magnate caring for the wellbeing of his workers. In 1903 Benoit-Lévy founded the Association of Garden Cities of France whose aim was quite explicit: 'to apply the most recent principles of hygiene to dwellings, to help industrial leaders to build their factories in advantageous

36 The French Society of Urbanists was created in 1913 under its patronage.

conditions for them and healthy conditions for their workers, to encourage the creation of garden cities'.[37]

Philanthropic movements such as the *Musée Social*, which pioneered the defence of social housing, therefore supported garden cities and a more general demand for greenery in order to get their ideas over to politicians who were becoming increasingly aware of this and particularly in the context of rebuilding after the First World War. Several examples of this are most revealing.

In Reims, it was the *Foyer Rémois*, an HBM group (*Habitation à Bon Marché* – office of affordable housing) set up in 1912 that was behind the first plans for garden cities on the eve of the Great War. But it was only after 1920 that the most iconic of Reims' garden cities, called Chemin Vert, was established. This was an English style garden where 371 buildings (houses with two to four homes) were built on a thirty-hectare site along curved pathways, and it became a model of its kind for the whole of France. The social dimension was central: rents would remain moderate and the main tenants were construction workers and labourers. Each home had a garden of 300 square metres where flowers and vegetables could be grown. Social provisions such as a social centre (with a library, public baths, etc.) were there to improve living conditions and emphasise the community spirit. The same ambitions were to be found in the 32 garden cities (for about 31,000 inhabitants in 1923) created after the war by the railway company, Compagnie du Chemin de Fer du Nord, on the initiative of the head engineer, Raoul Dautry. However, the social aspect was twinned with a clear desire to depoliticise the turbulent railway workers by moving them out of town and putting them in touch with nature. This can be seen in the Cité de Tergnier which is spread over 110 hectares with each house having 700 square metres of land, with 450 square metres of garden.[38] On the plan below, kitchen gardens can be clearly seen to the north and probably a little English style garden as well (Dautry liked including 'bachelors' corners' in his housing estates); to the south-east near the railway lines is a cemetery and to the south-west is a stadium which was to help distract the workers and keep them out of the taverns.

Similar to this example of success in the Reims area, between 1920–1930 in the Seine department, the HBM office, set up in 1915 by Henri Sellier,

37 Membership card of the Association of Garden Cities of France, Statutes, art. 2, 1905.

38 Odette Hardy-Hémery, 'Les cités-jardins de la Compagnie du chemin de fer du Nord: un habitat ouvrier aux marges de la ville', *Revue du Nord* **374** (1) (2008): 131–151.

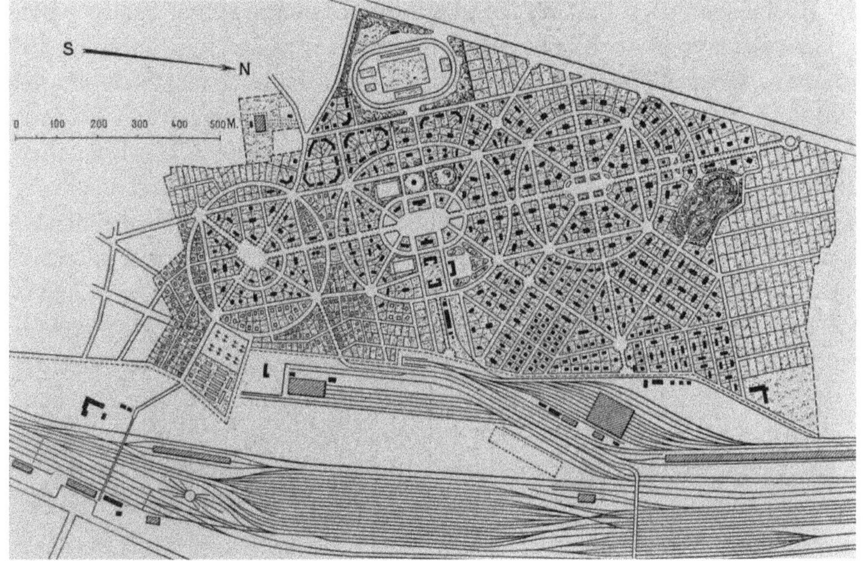

Figure 5.

The Cité de Tergnier in *L'Illustration*, January 1933.
Source: Authors' collection.

mayor of Suresnes and a leading member of the *Musée Social*, began to establish several garden cities around Paris. Financial difficulties as well as demographic pressure and questions about the availability of land meant that the principle of individual dwellings was swiftly abandoned in favour of collective housing, and the garden city of Suresnes bears witness to this. It is composed of buildings four storeys in height which contained 2,500 homes, along with social and cultural installations and of course there was a lot of greenery. In Stains, Gennevilliers and Plessis-Robinson, garden cities on these lines flourished between the two wars, leaving behind the picturesque style of the estate at Épinay-sur-Seine in 1912 for more economic rationality as the buildings grew even higher, culminating in housing developments such as the Cité de la Muette in Drancy in 1933–1935.

Towards progressive urbanism

So, until the middle of the twentieth century, the choice to include greenery in towns was a fundamental part of social policy that aimed at improving the living conditions of city populations and particularly the poorest. As admirable as this scheme was, the policy led to a choice of quantity over quality when it came to greenery. This can be seen in the theories and the realisations of what Françoise Choay has called progressive urbanism, which developed during the inter-war period, particularly within the Congresses of Modern Architecture (*Congrès internationaux d'architecture moderne* – CIAM) founded in 1928.[39] This movement promoted the notion of 'green space' and, as already noted, one of the leaders in this was Eugène Hénard.[40] Tony Garnier can be considered as a precursor of this form of urbanism: appointed as architect of the city of Lyon by Édouard Herriot in 1905, he had already drawn up plans for a modern city by 1901 but these would only be divulged to the general public in 1917, when *La Cité industrielle* (*The Industrial City*), the founding work of modern urban planning, was published. This did not concern the garden city – Garnier stepped away from that by his choice of new materials such as concrete, by more innovative thinking about architecture and by more consolidated reflection on urban planning, particularly in making more systematic zones for different functions (administration, work, residential, leisure activities, etc.). He is nevertheless close to Howard in terms of urban scale – 35,000 inhabitants – and on the primacy of green spaces as structuring elements of the whole. The construction of the États-Unis neighbourhood in Lyon at the beginning of the 1930s is partly an illustration of this, as it is of a mixture of social requirements: inexpensive dwellings (HBM) in five storey buildings, with no closed-in courtyard, well exposed to sunlight and dotted about in a green setting.[41]

While Garnier was a pioneer, the leading figure of this new urbanism was, above all, Le Corbusier. In *The Athens Charter* (1933), as in *La Ville Radieuse* (1934), Le Corbusier wanted to put an end to what he considered to be the chaos and lack of hygiene in contemporary towns by relying on a few principles such as functionalism (each activity had a dedicated space), minimal land use and upwards construction. These last two principles meant

39 To write this paragraph, we have relied on Françoise Choay, 'Pensées sur la ville, arts de la ville', in Maurice Agulhon (ed.), *Histoire de la France urbaine. La ville de l'âge industriel* (Paris: Seuil, 1998), pp. 251–265.

40 For Michel Corajoud, however, it was Alphand, who, in building gardens and parks without taking the original terrain into consideration, viewing it as a 'blank sheet', 'is the true promoter of the "green space". Faced with this almost total disappearance of the idea of territorial character and consequently of the art of gardens, we should not be surprised by the difficulty that today's landscapers have in basing their work on a real cultivation of the landscape'. Michel Corajoud, 'Territorialité du paysage', *Temps Libre* **9** (Spring 1984): 67.

41 Françoise Choay, *L'Urbanisme, utopies et réalités* (Paris: Seuil, 1965), pp. 209–219.

that a considerable area of land could be freed for greenery and for better aeration and sunshine for the home:

> No more courtyards but apartments open on all sides to the air and the light and not giving onto the sickly trees of today's boulevards but onto lawns, games areas and plentiful plants.
> Nature has been brought back into favour. Instead of being pitiless rubble the town becomes a great park … The urban agglomeration (is) treated as a green city …
> Sun, space, greenery.
> The buildings are set in the city behind a lace curtain of trees. The pact with nature has been signed.[42]

It is striking to notice here the relative indeterminacy of these open spaces: it is much more a question of greenery than of landscaped gardens. And, because of this, in the social housing that would be created up until the 1970s, little interest was taken in the shape of the vegetation proposed in these new constructions just so long as it was there and there was plenty of it. Nature was undifferentiated, with no aesthetic idea, the final aim being above all both sanitary and recreational and approved by public authorities who were making green spaces one of the pillars of the norms of urban planning based on essentially quantitative criteria.[43] Landscape gardeners had to battle in order to propose slightly ambitious vegetal designs and they were not always heeded, particularly between 1955 and 1965. This explains the huge housing projects developed in their hundreds between 1953 and 1973 (when they were finally abandoned by public authorities). They incorporated six million homes and forty per cent of their land area was made up of green spaces, which were often just scuffed grass and graceless trees, which were not cared for and resulted from unfinished landscape planning.[44] The vocabulary itself reveals this relative impoverishment: 'open space' and 'green space' were used indistinguishably in the 1950s and it was only then that, gradually, the latter began to take precedence over the former to designate all the green places, private or public, present in the urban fabric. The Cité du Grand Parc, in Bordeaux, is the very example of this transition. This housing development was built in the 1950s and conceived as a park within the city that was

42 Le Corbusier, quoted in Françoise Choay, *L'urbanisme, utopies et réalités*, pp. 242–243.

43 Such a universal statement should not hide local exceptions, more numerous than it might seem. See Bernadette Blanchon-Caillot, 'Pratiques et compétences paysagistes dans les grands ensembles d'habitation, 1945–1975', *Strates* **13** 2007, online 22 Oct. 2008: http://strates.revues.org.janus.biu.sorbonne.fr/5723 (accessed 2 Sept. 2014)

44 Bernard Reygrobellet, *La Nature dans la ville, biodiversité et urbanisme*, Report of the Conseil économique et social, 2007, p. 62.

autonomous. It was made up of a group of high-rise buildings around a vast green space where over half the area was used for parking or for traffic flow.[45] In the same way, Firminy-Vert, a neighbourhood on the outskirts of the small working-class town of Firminy (Loire department) demonstrates very well the mixed outcome of the urban utopia championed by Eugène Claudius-Petit, who was mayor from 1953 to 1971.[46] In the middle of the post-war reconstruction period he wanted to totally transform what was then called 'the road with no joy', a line of hovels, barely alleviated by a few allotment gardens. He convinced the population to abandon their dilapidated individual dwellings and come and live in 'workers' palaces' that were modern and salubrious. The design for the new neighbourhood was granted to a small group of architects close to Le Corbusier and they proposed to build upwards in order to avoid any overlooking and to settle collective housing in the heart of landscaped green spaces. At first, as the showcase for the Modern Movement, Firminy-Vert was criticised just like all the other huge housing estates in France, since they suffered both from a poor image (all the more so as they did not bear the prestigious name of a recognised architectural firm) and from a sometimes random maintenance programme in the common areas. Some neighbourhoods however succeeded in their enterprise and the buildings have aged better than others: in Pau the Aspin towers were built in the 1960s among the gardens of nineteenth century English villas, close to the town centre and to a leisure complex area built for the residents' recreation. Today this is an area that is much appreciated and some of the green spaces at the bottom of the high-rises have been turned into family gardens which strengthens social ties.

But basically, during the three decades of the *Trente Glorieuses*, the Thirty Glorious Years from 1945–75, in the big housing estates useful green spaces were created (playgrounds for children, places for adults to stroll or do sport) that were homogenous and maintained with intensive use of machines and chemicals.[47]

This transformation of the garden into a green space is also the fruit of having adapted to the demands of the population and of the primacy of hygiene and sanitary functions. The landscape arrangements of the second

45 Chantal Callais and Thierry Jeanmonod, *Bordeaux, Patrimoine Mondial* (La Crèche: Geste éditions, 2012), p. 550–551.

46 Clarisse Lauras, *Firminy-Vert, de l'utopie municipale à l'icône patrimoniale* (Rennes: PUR, 2014).

47 Gaëlle Aggeri, *Inventer les villes-natures de demain* (Dijon: Educagri, 2010), pp. 15–20.

half of the nineteenth century were designed for the promenade, the stage setting for respectability. Soon, this green context proved to be inadequate for all the new activities people wished to practise in green spaces. As early as 1914, a group in Paris called *Œuvre des Squares* demanded the installation of sandpits in squares to let babies play safely and in clean conditions.[48] More seriously, as we saw with the debate over the Paris fortifications, it was above all the pressure for sports fields which moved things forward. Integrating these into areas for strolling, as in the Parc Pommery in Reims, was not always possible and this discrepancy continued to grow until there was a crying need after the Second World War, as revealed in a 1952 copy of the magazine *Urbanisme*.[49] Simple, airy stretches of grass for ball games, picnics, races etc. proved to be more pertinent than a landscaped park.

The urban phenomenon of gigantic housing estates gave way to both new towns and the massive spread of individual houses. The former were launched by Paul Delouvrier from 1965 onwards, an initiative decreed by General de Gaulle to bring order to the Paris suburbs: Marne-la-Vallée, Saint-Quentin-en-Yvelines, Sénart, Cergy-Pontoise and Évry were also designed to offer pleasant living conditions, in contact with nature and far from the urban anarchy spreading around just outside Paris. The same ambitions led to the *towns* of Val-de-Reuil near Rouen, of l'Isle-d'Abeau near Lyon and Villeneuve d'Ascq near Lille. Once again, the conception of green spaces was too often too abstract for them to be anything other than simply a sanitary device.

Parallel to this, the aspiration to own a house and to live even closer to nature drove the tidal wave of individual house building. Critics raged against this middle-class ideal by means of which the town invaded the countryside. As early as 1860, in *Le Père La Ruine* (*Old Man Ruin*), Alexandre Dumas was fiercely critical of the 'invasion of barbarians' at La Varenne on the Paris outskirts:

> The urge was instinctive, Panurge's flocks set off, little by little, and in less time than you would have thought, the solitude became peopled, the fields were changed into gardens, the bushes became walls ... The layout of the gardens was even more varied than the aspect of the new village; on the whole it was picturesque: it is difficult to make flowers vulgar and trees ridiculous. Here, one was content with a plot of spinach and a plot of lettuces, modestly mixing the useful with the agreeable; another battled bravely in his twenty square metres in the cultivation of cereals, and having sown seventy-six seeds of rye, was contemplating a report for the Academy of Science.[50]

48 *Les Amis de Paris*, Jan. 1914–June 1923, p. 137.

49 *Urbanisme* 3–4 (1952).

50 Alexandre Dumas, *Le Père La Ruine* (Paris: Le Joyeux Roger, 2013 [1860]), pp. 83–84.

Blaise Cendrars, in *La Banlieue de Paris* (*The Suburbs of Paris*) in 1949 and Jacques Réda at the beginning of the 1980s continued this litany of criticism of the bungalow.[51]

The consequences of this proliferation of little houses are paradoxical. Firstly, they contributed to nature being present in towns. Today, except in very densely populated cities, private green urban spaces in fact often occupy a greater area than public parks and gardens. So, at a national level (including the whole national territory and not just the towns) three out of four French people declare that they have access to a private space for gardening, whether this is a balcony terrace or a garden,[52] and it is estimated that the gardens of individual houses account for two per cent of French land surface.[53] The town of Saint-Cyr-sur-Loire, a suburb of Tours, is a typical example of this proliferation of individual houses. It is a town with 17,000 inhabitants today and it began to grow in the 1920s. However, it was after the Second World War that it really began to expand, particularly between 1950–1960, the model being one of detached houses with a private garden of about 250 square metres on average. This peri-urbanisation began to slow between 1980 and 1990.[54] But while the spread of such housing might favour the presence of nature in the town, one consequence was the devastation of the landscape, with soils becoming seriously altered to the point that biodiversity has been affected.[55] Interest in biodiversity is therefore not just a fad: while the space occupied by each inhabitant in European towns has more than doubled over the last fifty years, urban sprawl has fragmented natural spaces and has meant that biological diversity has to be taken into account in the very heart of the city.

51 Jacques Van Waerbeke, 'Le motif végétal dans les regards portés par les artistes sur les périphéries parisiennes', in Augustin Berque, Philippe Bonnin and Cynthia Ghorra-Gobin (eds), *La Ville insoutenable* (Paris: Belin, 2006), pp. 72–73.

52 UNEP-IPSOS 2009 Survey ('Terrasses et jardins, nouvelles valeurs'), quoted in Pascal Oillic, Jean Louis Yengué and Alain Génin, 'Le jardin individuel au cœur des enjeux fonciers et écologiques dans une métropole régionale : le cas de Tours en France', *VertigO* **12** (2) (2012): 4. http://vertigo.revues.org/13023 ; DOI : 10.4000/vertigo.13023

53 Oillic, Yengué and Génin, 'Le jardin individuel'.

54 Ibid., p. 13.

55 For a good summary on the features of the last forty years' urbanism and its environmental consequences, see Antoine Bailly and Lise Bourdeau-Lepage, 'Concilier désir de nature et préservation de l'environnement : vers une urbanisation durable en France', *Géographie, économie, société* **13** (1) (2011): 27–43.

Towards an ecological town since the 1980s?

The awareness of this ecological impact only dates back thirty years or so and is linked to the emergence of environmental concerns. While the town has become one of the issues in sustainable development, the role of nature in the city has changed very little. Nature was always advocated for health reasons but in the 1980s it regained an aesthetic dimension with the revival of new landscape thinking and it finally acquired an ecological component. Defending the vegetal presence in the town was no longer just about improving man's lot but also about preserving a biological diversity that was under threat. This had a considerable influence on the type of nature that one wanted to see in the city. Gardens and 'old style' parks made up of tamed and constrained vegetation whose beauty was admired by the public would of course be retained. But to these were added wilder spaces (wastelands, *jardins en movement* - Gardens in Movement) where nature was left to her own devices; some public spaces are managed differently to encourage biodiversity and in them green grids like ecological corridors were included, to help wild animals in their movements and the spread of flora. This valorisation of the vegetal in all its forms, and in particular the most *natural* and indigenous species, is based on a well-worn argument that emphasises the ecosystemic services rendered by nature to urban dwellers. A study carried out in 2014 by the *Plante & Cité* association, based on scientific publications, highlights the dozen or so services that nature provides in town.[56] Unsurprisingly, we first find that urban vegetation is good for physical health as well as for the mental wellbeing of urbanites. It is therefore particularly well adapted for sick people; the garden becomes therapeutic.[57] The idea is not new, for one only has to think, for example, about the importance of gardens in religious establishments. At the end of the eighteenth century in particular, according to the medical research done by Philippe Pinel on the mentally ill, the emphasis was laid on the healing role of gardens and horticultural activities in hospital establishments. The psychiatric hospital at Rouffach, opened in 1909, has devoted an important area to green spaces where the structure is one of individual houses with a park, a farm and a market garden business where the men worked.

56 Pauline Laille, Damien Provendier, François Colson and Julien Salanié, *Les Bienfaits du végétal en ville : étude des travaux scientifiques et méthode d'analyse* (Angers: Plante & Cité, 2014).

57 See, for instance, the scientific and philanthropic activities of the association *Jardins et Santé*: http://www.jardins-sante.org/ See also Éric Lambin, *L'Écologie du bonheur* (Paris: Éditions Le Pommier, 2009).

Figure 6.

Le jardin thérapeutique. Pau: Hôpital auxiliaire 137 de l'U.F.F. Les Franciscains – Un groupe de blessés dans le jardin (ca 1914–1918).
Courtesy of BNF / Gallica: https://gallica.bnf.fr

Research carried out over the past few decades has tended to confirm this idea of nature as a healer.[58] In 1984, an American scientist, Roger Ulrich, showed that patients who had had a surgical operation recovered better when their hospital window overlooked a natural landscape rather than a brick wall! More generally, other studies have underlined the anti-stress and reinvigorating qualities of natural spaces or simply the sight of vegetation.[59] We can better understand why therapeutic gardens are increasing in number in all health care institutions particularly over the past thirty years. In Alsace alone there are several examples of gardens designed for sight-impaired and blind children, such as the fragrance garden in Mulhouse (1981), gardens for senior citizens such as the therapeutic garden in the Bethlehem retirement home in Strasbourg (1996) or the garden for those in long-term care at

58 See, for instance, Anne Monjaret, 'Les vertus du jardin à l'hôpital', in Marie-Jo Menozzi (ed.), *Les Jardins dans la ville, entre nature et culture* (Rennes: PUR, 2014).

59 See the CNRS animated video : http ://www.cnrs.fr/cw/dossiers/dosbioville/bioville.html

Hœhnheim, created in 2001, the latter two aiming to stimulate aged people intellectually and physically.[60]

The study done by *Plante & Cité* then showed the more properly environmental functions of urban nature. For example, it plays a pivotal role in the reduction of heat from the urban heat island effect – a powerful vegetal presence can bring down the temperature of a town by nearly two degrees. Abundant vegetation in the streets and on buildings (roofs and walls) also allows better energy management. The effects on air quality are real but more diffuse and sometimes offset by allergic reactions. Nevertheless, innovative experiments have been undertaken, such as the high-rise car park at Lyon-Perrache train station where the vegetalised inside walls help contribute to atmospheric depollution. Along with this treatment of the air, mention must be made of the depollution of water: vast peri-urban wetlands are useful for naturally purifying water supplies. Since 2009 in the Hérault department a water treatment plant has been associated with one and a half hectares of wetland that host 48 different plant species chosen for their ability to absorb certain pesticides, heavy metals and medical waste.[61] Nature in the city can also help in the regulation of water, which is important in case of flooding: the Bois de Boulogne and the Parc André-Citroën in Paris as well as the wet zones upstream from the city would help to limit damage caused by excessive flooding of the river Seine.[62]

Finally, *Plante & Cité* reminds us that green spaces contribute to the attractiveness of a region and in particular of a town, as we saw at the beginning of this chapter.

These considerations explain that thinking about urban planning is not reduced simply to nature in town but is also about the nature that surrounds *towns*. This is an important change in scale, and one that had already been recommended by Jean-Claude-Nicolas Forestier, although he had reasoned solely in terms of aesthetics and hygiene. This time it is a question of more globally merging the town into its natural environment, thereby making it as ecologically 'neutral' as possible in order to get to that point which Caroline Mollie nicely called the 'town-landscape'.[63]

60 See Catherine Kern's paper, 'Du jardin d'Hildegarde de Bingen aux jardins thérapeutiques contemporains en Alsace', at the first symposium of the Association Jardins et Santé, 'Jardins à but thérapeutique en milieu hospitalier et médico-social', 23 May 2008, available at http://www.jardins-sante.org/2008/80-symposium-jets/symposium2008/253-s2008-deroulement

61 See http://www.cnrs.fr/cw/dossiers/dosbioville/bioville.html

62 Ibid.

63 Caroline Mollie, *Des arbres dans la ville, l'urbanisme vegetal* (Arles: Actes Sud, 2009), p. 230.

Urban marketing

Ascribing all the virtues to the vegetal is of course, on the other hand, allowing public authorities to take advantage of their greening policy. Such a phenomenon is not new and we saw it in action as early as the nineteenth century at least. But it has recently taken on a completely different dimension as the fashion for greenery in town is leading to a real instrumentalisation of nature as an element in the burgeoning discourse of urban marketing. The town today must be attractive and this is particularly true for those with aspirations to become or to remain regional metropolises. It is also the case for towns of lesser size which seek to revitalise their activity and for Paris, which is threatened by worrying and repeated pollution alerts. A study carried out in 2004 showed that in the capital 35 per cent of those questioned stated that the proximity of a green space was really a determining factor in the purchase of property.[64] The arguments about environmental quality – size of green spaces but also increasingly biodiversity, balanced management, valorisation of the local flora, etc. – have increased visibly in the advertising strategies of *towns*, echoing the classifications of green towns regularly published in the press and frequently associated with wellbeing. There was a great deal of discussion following a classification done in 2014 by the association UNEP – *Les entreprises du paysage*, (Landscape companies) showing Angers, Nantes and Limoges as the greenest towns in France.[65] This development is notable in Lyon where it was only at the beginning of the 1990s that political power began to examine the question of green urban spaces, improving parks, squares and gardens. If, of course, from the outset, these actions were used to enhance the actions of the city council, it was only from about the 2000s that a more or less sincere ecological commitment gave way to an instrumentalisation of nature in a context of urban marketing.[66] In May 2015, a festival of roses, which prolonged the seventeenth World Convention of Rose Societies, successfully led to the floral decoration of the city and led to thinking about making this kind of event more permanent with the organisation of a rose

64 Sylvain Lefebvre, Romain Roult and Jean-Pierre Augustin, *Les Nouvelles Territorialités du sport dans la ville* (Presses de l'Université du Québec, 2013), p. 90.

65 See the ranking of the 50 largest towns in France made by the association UNEP – *Les entreprises du paysage*, that uses five criteria: green patrimony, investment in favour of vegetalisation, biodiversity, green waste management, promotion of plants. http://www.entreprisesdupaysage.org/document/telechargerDocument.php?id=26829_56862

66 Paul Arnould et al. 'La nature en ville: l'improbable biodiversité', *Géographie, Économie, Société* **13** (1) 2011: 62–64.

biennial. In a similar vein, the unwavering success of the Towns in Bloom competition shows the same drive towards greenery to which town councils have to submit. At the start of the twentieth century, the Touring Club de France, a social club devoted to travel, was the first to encourage the floral decoration of train stations and hotels and inaugurated the 'Pretty Villages' competition in the 1920s. After the Second World War, following fresh ideas from the Touring Club, and in collaboration with horticultural associations, in 1959 the minister in charge of tourism, Robert Buron, launched a national competition for the floral decoration of towns and villages.[67] The original aim was very clearly to promote tourism in France but the committee's demands were gradually modified. In order to win the title of 'Ville Fleurie' (town of flowers) and one of the famous awards showing one to four flowers – or the highly coveted 'grand prize' – they had to meet quantitative requirements in terms of enhancing the town with many plants, aesthetic criteria, and also commitments to sustainable development practices: sustainable management, biodiversity, etc. Anyway, the slogan became a 'quality of life label' and the competition website reminds us that 'in a growing context of competition between different areas our label is an opportunity for towns to offer a favourable image and environment attractive to tourism, residents and economic activity'.[68] There is no mistake about this as 12,000 local communities take part in this competition – nearly a third of all towns and villages in France!

***

For four centuries, the vegetal has increasingly imposed itself at the heart of thinking about urban planning, accumulating functions in decoration, physical and moral wellbeing and ecological balance. It also leaves an imprint on urban space which continues to bear its sometimes-vanished memory as nature still makes its presence felt in many ways. The toponymy bears witness to this and a number of streets or places remind the pedestrian of the traces of past vegetation and gardens long gone. The pretty name of *rue du Bois-d'Amour* (Wood of Love Street) in Reims is thus a reminder of an eighteenth century plantation, destroyed in 1845, where lovers used

67 Bernard Reygrobellet, *La Nature dans la ville, biodiversité et urbanisme*, Report of the Conseil économique et social, 2007, pp. 67–68.

68 http://www.cnvvf.fr/un_peu_d_histoire-53.html (accessed 1 Sept. 2014).

to stroll;[69] in Le Havre in the nineteenth century the name of the *rue du Beauverger* recalls the gentleman named Verger but also the orchard (*verger*) of a convent located on this site in the sixteenth century; and what more needs to be said, in this same town, about the *rue des Prés* (Fields Street) or *rue du Champ-des-Oiseaux* (Field of Birds Street), a souvenir of the restaurant and dance venue *Le Chant des oiseaux* (The Song of Birds), about its gardens, its lawns, its flowers and the meadow next to it.[70] Sometimes, as in today's single-storey suburbs the language of plants is deployed where there is no historical reference but simply out of bucolic and poetic reinvention: who has never crossed over a 'rue des Lilas' (Lilac Street) or a 'rue des Tilleuls' (Limetree Street) but not seen the shadow of these eponymous trees?

The memory of urban nature is sometimes more subtle. In the centre of Paimpol there is a commemorative plaque which is a reminder of the planting of an 'arbre de la liberté' (a Liberty Tree) in 1792. In Paris, the elm tree in front of Saint Gervais church was a regular meeting place in this neighbourhood in the Middle Ages. It was replaced over the centuries and cut down, probably in 1794,[71] before being replanted in 1914. It lives on in the design of the balcony ironwork of the building adjacent to the church and, inside, on four choir stalls. The venerable tree has even become the sign of a toolmaker.[72]

This persistence of the vegetal, even in the memory of the places where it lived, is another proof that the town would not exist without it. Its implantation in the mineral world of the city is nonetheless subject to the determined and wilful intervention of a few particularly green fingered individuals.

69 https://sites.google.com/site/lavieremoise/l--les-rues-de-reims-memoire-de-la-ville

70 Charles Vesque, *Histoire des rues du Havre* (Brionne: Monfort, 1876), 3 vols.

71 Or at the beginning of the *Restoration* period (1815): dating this event is difficult.

72 Rodolphe Trouilleux, *Paris secret et insolite* (Paris: Parigramme, 2002), p. 30.

2.

GREEN FINGERS: ACTORS IN THE VEGETALISATION OF TOWNS

Arrested in November 1831 for night-time disturbance on his return from an evening party, Gérard de Nerval was obliged to spend several nights in the Saint-Pélagie prison in Paris. In 'Politique', a second-rate poem written on this occasion, he complained that in his jail '*pas une herbe ne pousse, / et pas un brin de mousse*' (no grass grows, nor a sprig of moss), and so he called on the winds and birds to bring him grasses or dead leaves. One would not, however, be happy to have just these contributions to greening the town. It is not that the town is resistant to nature – far from it – but it is characterised increasingly by a nature that is *sought after*, *desired*, owing nothing to chance - and it is expensive. It is estimated that today French *communes* spend some 2.5 billion Euros per annum on creating and maintaining green spaces. Highly touristic *communes*, such as Thonon-les-Bains, devote more than six per cent of their budget to this.[1] Customised vegetalisation of one's town requires great effort and effective collaboration: private individuals, professionals and public authorities all have to do their bit.

Private individuals

> Whose responsibility is it to beautify a town if it is not that of the residents who enjoy in it all that wealth and pleasure can furnish for man? ... The king, through his magnanimity and love of his people would like to contribute to making his capital worthy of himself. But he is no more king of Parisians than he is of the inhabitants of Lyon or Bordeaux. Each city has to come to its own assistance. Does a private individual require a council's decree to modify his house?[2]

In 1749 Voltaire called on townspeople to involve themselves more in the beautification of their town, rather than leaving it solely to the actions

1 Bernard Reygrobellet, *La Nature dans la ville, biodiversité et urbanisme*, Rapport du Conseil économique et social (2007), p. 68.

2 Voltaire, 'Des embellissements de Paris', *Œuvres complètes de M. de Voltaire*, vol. 38 (Paris: Delangle Frères, 1837), pp. 42–54.

of royal authorities. Essentially, he was addressing the social elites from the ranks of privilege, those with the means to do something to the fabric of the city, to straighten a facade or introduce a green breathing-space. The seventeenth century was in many ways the 'century of gardens', during which this vegetalised form rooted itself lastingly in the French urban space, continuing to prosper in the next century. Supplying food, medicine and spiritual comfort, the closed monastic garden never did so well as in times of Catholic reform. Revalorisation of the regular clergy attracted to the cloisters men with vocations who were often well-born and wealthy. Religious communities were great consumers of space and they invested massively in towns, contributing in some cases to fossilising urban land to their own benefit: in Laon for instance, during the course of the seventeenth century, they bought the equivalent of 150 houses. The model of the *hôtel particulier*, the private house, also contributed greatly to increasing the vegetal presence in the town: enshrined among its French-style parterres, the noble residence is shown at its best by the perspective play of long straight alleys lined with majestic trees.

Pleasure gardens like this are nonetheless distinguished by their private character, sometimes fiercely defended, if one thinks, for example, of the importance which the strict observance of the female cloister has for the Church. They are to some extent markers of a privileged topography reserved to the elite. Moreover, this patrimony of private property, including religious houses, is relatively fragile and liable to be eaten into over the course of time, according to how far it depends on the economic situation and the great pressure on land in the *Ancien Régime* town. In Lyon, from the end of the seventeenth century, a number of religious congregations were faced with financial difficulties that obliged them to cede to the city land that had not been built on in exchange for funds. In fact, major works extending the town ordered by architects (Perrache for the Presqu'île, Morand in the Brotteaux neighbourhood) did not advance quickly enough in the view of the contractors and the municipality, who put pressure on religious proprietors within the city walls. Between 1723 and 1769, the Abbey of Ainay lost the greater part of its gardens, which were promptly filled with dwellings. After 1789 the dismemberment and dividing up of former clerical property accelerated; the hill of the Croix Rousse was the scene of dense building on the site of former ecclesiastical gardens, transformed into buildings several storeys high to accommodate silk workers.

Did more modestly situated townsfolk play a part in the vegetalisation of towns? In view of the lack of extensive direct witnesses, we need to turn to police regulations and deduce from them the significance of everyday practices. The governing principle of straightening facades entailed the disappearance of balconies facing the street. Residents compensated for this loss of space by decking out window-sills with 'flower-pots and planters where they grew flowers and shrubs, which was very dangerous because they could fall and kill someone'.[3] There is another pointer to gauging how widespread this sort of practice was, and that is the proliferation of guides to gardening and horticulture advising the inexperienced on making indoor gardens. Hyacinths seem to have been particularly popular: 'they can be placed on balconies or terraces, in windows, or even inside apartments when they are flowering'.[4] But one also finds carnations, violets and basil, and sometimes tomatoes as ornamental plants. Marjoram seems to have worked so well as to become proverbial: lovers *awaken marjoram in pots* with their serenades, and lovely ladies *awaken marjoram* when they open their windows to water it and to flirt.

In both large and small towns from the eighteenth century on there was a proliferation of municipal decrees forbidding hanging pots or boxes of flowers on windows giving on to the public street.[5] This was to prevent buildings getting blackened by water (in the case of such prestigious buildings as Les Invalides in Paris, for example),[6] to avoid accidents and wetting passers-by.

This proliferation of regulations in no way stemmed the multiplication of window-gardens in an ever-denser urban space. It is, on the contrary, evidence of a growing need for greenery among even the poorest townspeople who, seeing their town industrialising and becoming more built-up under their very eyes, no longer had access to the smallest piece of land or little garden. These measures were therefore little heeded, at times probably through simple ignorance of the law, and it fell to police officials to act preventatively by having dangerous pots removed – not always in time if one is to believe Daumier...

3 Edme de La Poix de Fréminville, *Dictionnaire ou Traité de la police générale des villes, bourgs, paroisses, et seigneuries de la campagne* (Paris: self published, 1778), p. 35.

4 Jean-Paul de Rome d'Ardène, *Traité sur la connoissance et la culture des jacintes* (Avignon: L. Chambeau, 1759).

5 Société centrale des architectes, *Manuel des lois du bâtiment* (Paris: Moral, 1863), Title I, Article 3, General Order of the Municipal Police of 16 Feb. 1860, pp. 83–84.

6 Règlement général sur l'ordre et la discipline qui doit être observée dans l'Hôtel, du 9 août 1731, article XXVI.

Figure 7.

Honoré Daumier, 'Il faut semer de fleurs le chemin de la vie' ('The path of life must be sowed with flowers'), *Le Charivari*, 2 February 1840.

This resistance is explained by the growing fashion for window gardens, highlighted by press illustrations and fostered by the guides that appeared in the middle of the nineteenth century and multiplied from the 1860s onwards.

If one is to believe them, a need for nature prompted everyone to plant as and where they could: hence the water-carrier who cultivated a garden in the cracks in some old clogs, and the bootmaker growing flowers in the leg

Figure 8.

Cover of *Pêle-Mêle*, 14 October 1906.
Source: Authors' collection

of a boot.[7] The guides are at pains to explain, usually to women, presumably thought to be most interested, the best way of cultivating flowers and plants in windows, balconies and apartments. These gardening guides are in the end little different from ours today, which are abundant; at most, they differ by being more moralising and gendered in approach, more digressive and prolix, and rather less light-hearted than more recent writing. Otherwise, there are the same recommendations for preparing containers, choosing flowers – with choice a bit more restricted than nowadays – places and times for planting, etc.

Such prompting of the individual cultivation of plants is often accompanied by genuine philanthropic movements and undoubtedly one of the most successful of these concerns windows with flowers, which became 'Jenny's garden'.[8] Competitions for window flowers occurred from 1889 in Lille and 1900 in Bordeaux. It seems that in 1901 a Mme Challamet, inspired by a Scottish example, decided to give free flowers to the poorest women in Paris to decorate their homes.[9] On 21 March a distribution of seeds (nasturtiums, fuchsias, geraniums, mignonette) took place at the headquarters of *la Coopération des idées* (the Cooperation of Ideas), accompanied we are told by a homily on the benefits of beauty for the morals and health of townspeople… A competition was established: two months later a panel of poets and artists would choose the most embellished and flowery window, and a savings bank account would be opened for the happy winner! Complementing – or superseding? – this movement, in 1907 the 'Jenny's Gardens' movement was launched on the initiative of a celebrated publisher of *La Belle Époque*, Eugène Figuière. The idea was the same, to enable poor women to improve their lives by giving them flowers which they could grow at home on their attic room window-sills. The name comes from a well-known popular tune of the nineteenth century, the song of Jenny the worker: its refrain describes, up there on her window-sill '*le jardin de Jenny l'ouvrière / Au cœur content, content de peu ; / Elle pourrait être riche et préfère / Ce qui lui vient de Dieu*' ('The garden of Jenny the worker / Happy at heart, happy with little; / She

7 Maurice Cristal, *Le Jardinier des appartements, des fenêtres, des balcons et des petits jardins* (Paris: Garnier, 1863), p. 95.

8 Information on this issue is very patchy and sometimes contradictory. See 'Jenny qui n'avait qu'un jardin aura sa maison', *La Presse,* 2 July 1919 ; 'Le jardin de Jenny', *Revue de la Solidarité Sociale*, Feb. 1911: 168–169.

9 But other sources suggest 1904 for the first flower window competition in Paris. See Philippe Rivoire, *Fenêtres et Balcons Fleuris. Causerie faite le 4 juin 1905 à la séance de la Société d'Horticulture du Rhône* (Paris: Librairie Horticole, 1905).

Figure 9.

Jenny l'Ouvrière. Postcard from the authors' collection.

could be rich but prefers / What she receives from God.') For all the working women in Paris to be as generous, friendly and happy as Jenny, it seems that all they needed was flowers!

Figuière teamed up with a friend who was a nurseryman, and he agreed to give some seed and compost to any shopgirl who came along with an order signed by Figuière. Helped by the success of this, Figuière set up a committee, made an appeal for donations, and in 1911–12 the organisation really started to grow big. On 28 April 1912 between 25,000 and 30,000 rose plants were given out in the Square Saint-Médard, at the foot of the Rue Mouffetard, which is in a very ordinary area of Paris. The activity went on and was only suspended during the First World War. In May 1913, 50,000 plants, 2,000 statuettes and 2,000 theatre tickets were distributed; at Christmas that year, 30,000 Dutch flower bulbs, 3,000 statuettes, a similar number of theatre seats and 10,000 assorted plants were given out. Both social action and aesthetics were intimately linked in what Figuière called a flower festival. It was a real success, as is borne out by photographs from the period in which crowds of people are hurrying towards the carts distributing flowers and gifts by the handful. Newspapers calculated that 300,000 windows were filled with flowers during the pre-war period thanks to this activity.

This was of course a rather particular course of action, and there were other ways that private individuals introduced flowers into towns in the twentieth century. If it is not a balcony embellished with flowers, or an interior being decorated with floral arrangements and plants, then it is a garden being tended, a kitchen garden being looked after, or just a lawn mown and at times dug over. The expansion of towns fostered the multiplication of private gardens: in housing estates everyone has their own little bit of land to be improved according to desire and budget. In 2015 nearly ninety per cent of French people had access to a piece of ground for gardening associated with their main dwelling, and of them seventeen million had a garden. And along with this has come a massive use of phytosanitary products: 2,600 tonnes of pesticide were used by amateur gardeners in 2008.[10] Nowadays an attempt is being made to check this tendency through appeals for responsibility, awareness campaigns about biodiversity, and more trenchantly by a law of July 2015 which forbids the use of phytosanitary products by private individuals from 2019 onwards. This movement is accompanied by the promotion of biodiversity, particularly in densely packed towns where private green spaces are more rare.[11] The most recent and novel of these initiatives seems to be pavement gardens or MIF, *micro-implantations florales de trottoirs* (micro-planting of flowers on pavements):[12] this is a matter of planting, or allowing to grow, on one's pavement, some of the 240 vegetal species able to colonise French towns by themselves.[13] This spontaneous flora (or spontaneous encouraged by a few seeds) can be discovered in all the cracks in the tarmac. In Lyon and Villeurbanne since 2006 townspeople have been using grinders to cut little ditches in footpaths in which to plant, or to let plants grow. And towns have very quickly gone along with these movements emerging from civil society: Lyon has made ditches for planting available to residents who want them under the heading of 'floral micro-implantations', Strasbourg has launched a campaign called '*Verdissez vos façades*' ('Turn your house-fronts green'), Lille has developed linear gardens, etc. At Rennes the operation called '*Jardinons*

10 Union des industries de la protection des plantes (UIPP), ministère de l'Agriculture, INRA, CEMAGREF 2005, studies Ecophyto 2006 and Jardivert 2010.

11 See, for example, Marie-Jo Menozzi (dir.), *Les Jardins dans la ville, entre nature et culture* (Rennes: PUR, 2014), part 3.

12 For the example of the gardens of the Guillotière district in Lyon, see Laurent Denis, *Du jardin partagé au jardin de trottoir, Nature de quartier et éco-citoyenneté à Lyon*, Master 2 dissertation, Muséum national d'Histoire naturelle, 2010.

13 Nathalie Machon, *Sauvages de ma rue* (Paris: MNHN, 2012).

nos rues' ('Let's garden in the streets') has been such a success since 1999 that the municipality has set up a convention for managing street gardens in cooperation with private volunteers who wanted to be involved.[14]

The voluntary sector often extends purely individual action to make townspeople's desires for greenery better understood. Today more than ever, countless associations press for the development of nature in towns, and even for the management of green spaces. In Cognac alone there are now two societies dedicated to preserving examples of urban natural patrimony (the Portail wood and the Francois I Park) and two others aim more generally at raising awareness about the protection of nature (the associations *Perennis* and *Antenne, Nature, Loisirs et Patrimoine*). For the creation of the La Bruche urban natural park in Strasbourg, a participatory approach aiming to define the guiding principles was constituted in 2010 bringing together some thirty residents and association members. But, as this last example clearly shows, one cannot leave the responsibility for introducing nature to the town and defending it to private individuals alone: they have to be able to rely on the support of professionals and public authorities.

The professionals

While anyone, as long as he has the means, can grow a few plants on a balcony,[15] making a real garden in a town or anywhere else is an undertaking involving great aesthetic, logistical and practical problems (see the next chapter). It is not surprising that this has, in the course of time, become a profession.

From gardener to landscaper

The *Ancien Régime* in France did not have a term specifying the designer and creator of a garden. From the beginning of the eighteenth century, when the landscape designer or landscape gardener won his spurs across the Channel by contributing to the aesthetic success of the English-style garden, there were in France only 'gardeners'. The *Dictionnaire de l'académie française* (Dictionary of the French Academy) indicates the breadth of the term's meanings: the

14 Cédric Ansart and Emmanuel Boutefeu, 'Sous le pavé, les fleurs', *Métropoliques*, special report *Nature(s) en ville*, Feb. 2013. http://www.metropolitiques.eu/Nature-s-en-ville.html

15 It is also worth noting the emergence today of a new profession of gardeners, urban landscapers, specialising in the greening of small areas and first of all balconies and windows, offering the most suitable plants, ready-to-go vegetable gardens, original compositions where herbs and artichokes rub shoulders with grasses. See the companies Urban Green, Le Vert à Soi and Les Mauvaises Graines for example.

fourth edition states that a gardener is 'one … whose job is to work in a garden; it may also be one who understands the management, cultivation and beautifying of gardens, and who designs them'. Creating gardens is not the work of a well-defined profession. From the Renaissance on, architects worked as much with stone as with plants. However, they did not have a monopoly on making gardens, which were just as interesting to engineers, artists, enlightened amateurs (often large landowners from the aristocracy), and of course the 'technicians' themselves, practical gardeners who combined the skills of the cultivator with a conceptual and aesthetic approach.

During the two last centuries of the *Ancien Régime* there was a proliferation of treatises on the art of gardens, and on the art of cultivating them well, with a much more technical approach grounded in the transmission of agronomic practices and know-how. Gardens had become a real publishing genre, which also points to the tensions and re-ordering taking place in the world of professional 'gardeners'. In 1802, in an era of post-Revolutionary reconstruction, the architect François-Joseph Bélanger (1744–1818) imagined a 'gardener' who would be simultaneously an artist, engineer, architect, botanist, and a bit of a doctor (able to 'select a healthy, productive and pleasant site', to 'enrich his neighbours' and supply them with 'promenades suitable for exercise'.[16] This 'gardener' who seeks to distinguish himself from the mass of agricultural 'gardeners' is the product of two centuries of active promotion of a profession that did not yet exist. During the *Ancien régime* the organisation of gardeners as a profession was very indeterminate; in towns throughout the kingdom they did not belong to the regulated trades, where the completion of a masterpiece admitted one to the highly coveted status of 'Master'. As market-gardeners or servants, most gardeners shared the fates of the urban poor. One who did attain a desirable appointment working for a town or a botanic garden might be dubbed 'master gardener' so as to reposition himself in the social hierarchy. But in truth it was royal or aristocratic patronage that did most to move the boundaries, by making gardeners recognised as both artisans and artists. Gardeners had a model, André Le Nôtre (1613–1700), gardener to Louis XIV, and also a ruling dynasty in the Richard family, gardeners to Louis XV and to Louis XVI at the Grand Trianon.

None of the great gardeners were self-made men; all were the product of family strategies over several generations, manipulating the lever of princely

16 Speech delivered in 1802 before the Athénée des étrangers, in Jean-Claude-Nicolas Forestier, *Bagatelle et ses jardins* (Paris: Librairie horticole, 1910), p. 58.

favour. Le Nôtre was the son and grandson of ordinary gardeners for the king at the Tuileries Gardens. Thanks to his family's social influence, his education went beyond that professional horizon. He had the benefit of courses in drawing, geometry and architecture with such great artists as Vouet and Mansart. It was as a garden designer that he began his career in 1635, carrying out many projects in France, and in England as well. He accumulated commissions in the service of the royal family, great aristocrats and government ministers like Nicolas Fouquet, who entrusted him with work on the gardens of the Chateau de Vaux-le-Vicomte in 1656. This added to his fame; after Fouquet's fall, he entered the service of Louis XIV, making the Versailles and Tuileries gardens for him. So, was André Le Nôtre, ennobled in 1675, made a member of the Royal Academy of Architecture in 1681, and on his death leaving a fortune estimated at one million *livres*,[17] still just a 'gardener'? No doubt the amazing trajectory of his career can be partly explained by his family, his personal skills and his good fortune at court; but his training as an artist was also fundamental.

To make an impression, the creative gardener has to distinguish himself from both the plantsman and the architect, with both of whom he has similarities. As Jacques Boyceau de la Barauderie declared in 1638 when listing the skills that had to be mastered: the gardener must learn 'to read and to write, to portray and to design, for from portraiture comes knowledge and judgement of beautiful things and the essentials of all mechanics ... it will be necessary to rise up to geometry for plans, divisions, measures and alignments, and even ... to architecture.'[18] This training distinguishes the gardener from the simple cultivator, whose knowledge is wholly empirical, who cannot draw up a proper plan and who is incapable of abstract thought. D'Argenville, author of a celebrated *Théorie et pratique du jardinage* (*Theory and Practice of Gardening*) (1709) deplored the fact that 'even the lowliest of gardeners will drop their hoe and their rake to give their opinion on garden design when they know nothing at all'.[19]

The gardener also seeks to free himself from another influence – that of the architect. This is rather harder, as the skills are similar. Le Nôtre fired

17 The *livre tournois* was an account currency used under the *Ancien Régime* in France, which was replaced by the franc in 1795.

18 Jacques Boyceau de la Barauderie, *Traité du jardinage* (1638), quoted in Michel Racine (dir.), *Créateurs de jardins et de paysages en France du XIXe au XXe siècle* (Arles: Actes Sud, 2002), p. xv.

19 Antoine-Joseph Dezallier d'Argenville, *La Théorie et la Pratique du jardinage* (1709), in Racine (dir.), ibid., p. xv.

off this Parthian shot to Louis XIV who was showing him the Colonnade grove at Versailles designed by Hardouin-Mansart: 'You have made a gardener out of a bricklayer; he has served you up his trade on a plate.' The distinction began to become formalised during the eighteenth century. More and more, and particularly through the influence of English gardens, the gardener was seen as an artist, and the garden as a painting or a theatre set. In his famous poem, *Les Jardins ou l'art d'embellir les paysages* (*Gardens or the Art of Beautifying Landscapes*), published in 1782, Abbé Delille declared, 'Un jardin, à mes yeux, est un vaste tableau / Soyez peintre' ('A garden in my eyes is a vast picture / Be a painter.') A few years later in 1776 one finds in Jean-Marie Morel's *Théorie des jardins* (*The Theory of Gardens*) one of the most thorough articulations of this view. Attacking the symmetrical French garden, he also takes up arms against those he believes to be its principal inventors and defenders – architects.

> As soon as Architects took to making gardens it was to be expected that, confusing the principles of two different arts … they would try to draw a mutual correspondence between the building, their principal object, and the garden, to them just an accessory … They wanted to subject Nature to their methodical combinations, and thinking to improve nature, they disfigured her.[20]

Morel's case is particularly interesting in that his education did not predispose him to make such attacks. He was actually trained in the *Ponts et Chaussées* school (school of civil engineering – bridges and highways) at Lyon before joining the *Bureau des dessinateurs du roi* (Office of the king's draughtsmen), established in 1747 and later to become the *École des Ponts et Chaussées* (1775) in Paris. Typically for one who was involved in modifying the lie of the land, he got himself a sound training as an engineer. In 1760 he became *architecte-intendant général* (architect in chief) for buildings to the Prince de Conti. In the course of his career he constructed chateaux and parks at the same time, the most famous being those of Ermenonville (1764-70) and Malmaison (1802–05) for the Empress Josephine. The ambiguity of this relationship between two occupations, which was to be progressively formalised, is to be found in the nineteenth century name for those who made gardens, 'landscape architect'. For Michel Racine, this tension was permanent, and one finds it again for instance in the period between the wars: not having been invited to the *Exposition internationale des arts décoratifs* (International Exhibition of the Decorative Arts) in 1925,

20 Jean-Marie Morel, *Théorie des jardins* (Paris: Pissot, 1776), pp. 4–6.

landscape architects with a training from the *Société nationale d'horticulture de France* in 1932 published *Jardins d'aujour d'hui* (*Gardens Today*) demonstrating their skills in creating modern gardens.[21]

It is nonetheless undeniable that the status of the creators of gardens was transformed during the nineteenth century. While there had long existed families or individuals who were specialists in that area, it then became a true profession, particularly from the Second Empire (1852–70) onwards.

This was a time when, following Haussmann's works, a strong social call for gardens and parks emerged which encouraged the development of numerous occupations. And going along with this, a programme of training gradually came into being.[22] Treatises were published by the great names in landscaping. Édouard André's *L'Art des jardins. Traité général de la composition des parcs et jardins* (*The Art of Gardens. A General Treatise on the Making of Parks and Gardens*) (1879) became a standard work and could be seen as among the acts of the profession's creation. It details everything that is specific to the activity whose title – landscape architect, or just landscaper – was becoming generally acknowledged. André begins with a history of gardens since Antiquity. Such historical considerations were already to be found in Gabriel Thouin, for example, but they did not become a requirement until after the constitution of a French school under the leadership of Alphand. This was already a sign of the awareness of a professional and national specificity that a study of the past should illuminate. Two chapters are devoted to aesthetics and to the feeling for nature in painting and in literature: this is a reminder that the landscaper must also be an artist and a man of taste. There follows a typology of parks and gardens, private and public, for pleasure or for use. This shows very clearly, as Luisa Limido has pointed out, how we have moved on from 'a landscaper of agricultural space' to 'a landscaper of urban space'.[23] Three quarters of the book are then devoted to practicalities. Here, André details all the stages in the creation of a garden, beginning with ... the choice of an architect, henceforward subordinate to the landscaper! How to draw up a plan, follow the levels, prepare an estimate, how to get the work

21 Racine (dir.), *Créateurs de jardins et de paysages*, Introduction.

22 On this issue, see in particular Monique Mosser, '"Cette aimable manifestation de l'esprit humain": Édouard André et l'histoire des jardins', in Florence André and Stéphanie de Courtois (dir.), *Édouard André, un paysagiste botaniste sur les chemins du monde* (n.p.: Éditions de l'imprimerie, 2002).

23 Luisa Limido, *L'Art des jardins sous le Second Empire. Jean-Pierre Barrillet-Deschamps* (Seyssel: Champ Vallon, 2002), p. 225.

done – everything is explained in what is like a real manual. This approach to the terrain is the great innovation in the work of André, who demonstrates that his profession requires three kinds of ability, as engineer, as architect and as artist. There is the same intention – and a very similar format – in Armand Péan, who published from 1878 *Parcs et jardins, résumé des notes d'un practicien* (*Parks and Gardens, a summary of a practitioner's notes*) which he also turned into a manual in 1886 under the title *L'Architecte paysagiste, théorie et pratique de la création et décoration des parcs et jardins* (*The Landscape Architect, the Theory and Practice of Creating and Ornamenting Parks and Gardens*). The publication of these works is contemporaneous with the creation, at the instigation of the agronomist Pierre Joigneaux, of the *École nationale d'horticulture* by a law of 16 December 1875, established at Versailles in the *Potager du Roi* (Royal kitchen-garden).[24] The aim was to train professionals able to plan and maintain parks. The teachers, prestigious and experienced in the business, were Ferdinand Jamin, nurseryman and vice-president of the *Société nationale d'horticulture de France*, and Auguste Pissot, director of nurseries in Paris. A chair of garden and greenhouse architecture was created, to be filled illustriously by Edouard André in particular and his son René-Édouard, who in 1926 would include in his teaching questions bearing on urbanism, a convincing sign of both the persistent interest in having nature in towns, and the increasingly technical side of the training.

The professionalisation of the landscaper's trade can also be explained by market requirements. Since the desire for urban parks and gardens was ever growing, the offer became more diversified and, in order to differentiate oneself and to make a mark, it became necessary to develop an expertise that would attract customers. The know-how could manifest itself in various ways. First, this was done by giving the profession and the occupations associated with it more and more structure. Nurserymen, for example, indispensable suppliers, proliferated and at times specialised – landscapers in Lyon made fun of them, citing the sonorous names they gave themselves according to what they produced, from the pomologist to the orchidophile or the dianthologist (for carnations).[25] Their vegetal offer grew more extensive, and in so doing stimulated the creativity of their customers. Some great nurseries had existed since the seventeenth century, like that of the Carthusian monks in Paris,

24 Chiara Santini, 'Promenades plantées et espaces verts : un regard historique sur la ville de Paris', *Démeter* (2013): 216–218, http ://www.clubdemeter.com/ledemeter.php?demeter=2013

25 A. and F. Rouillard, *L'Art des jardins paysagers dans la région sud-est de la France* (Lyon: Adrien Effantin, 1902), p. 38.

who were engaged in a very lucrative business.[26] At the beginning of the 1650s, the traditional monastic kitchen garden, with its orchard and nursery, took on a quite different aspect under the guidance of a former nurseryman from Vitry who used the professional name of Brother Alexis. His successor, Brother François Le Gentil, was the author of a gardening treatise published in 1704 under the title of *Le Jardinier Solitaire* (*The Solitary Gardener*), a best-seller in the genre in the eighteenth century. In the space of two generations a nursery was established producing 4–500,000 plants and bringing the monks a substantial revenue up until the Revolution, supplying all Paris with carefully selected varieties. Customers could choose from a catalogue of 'fruit trees' (peach-trees, pear-trees ...) in which the Carthusians specialised. Also for sale were ornamental plants (such as the thuya (cypress), nicknamed 'the tree of life' in the 1775 catalogue), or exotic species requiring particular care, or even the use of greenhouses. Other, lay, commercial establishments expanded in the same period, such as that of Jacques-Martin Cels (1743–1806), an enlightened amateur botanist and collector who devoted the income from his lucrative employment as a tax-farmer to his passion; when the Revolution stripped him of income, he established his nurseries in the plain of Montrouge. Amateur botanists and collectors gathered there, wishing to study or cultivate the rare and precious specimens presented there, which had been collected on all the continents by the dozens of travelling naturalists among Cels's correspondents. His connections were particularly strong in the Anglo-Saxon world, and a large part of his collection came from North America: 'An ash found in Kentucky … a juniper found around Hudson's Bay … a pavia from California… a rhododendron discovered in 1786 at the source of the Savannah river…', without mentioning 'several new species from Peru, the Cape of Good Hope, the East Indies, the South-Sea Islands, etc.'[27] But such businesses were still quite small compared with those that appeared and flourished in the nineteenth century. Among the most emblematic of that century – and of our own! – one can name Truffaut, whose first establishments were formed in 1834, and who already cultivated rare fruits and vegetables in their greenhouses. They lasted right through the nineteenth century and passed from father to son, and then in 1905 moved to new 70,000 square metre premises in Versailles. This was so successful that a first shop was opened

26 Jean-Marie Pelt (dir.), *Un jardin de chartreux. Les conseils de jardinage d'un chartreux de Vauvert: histoire, patrimoine, savoir-faire* (Grenoble: Glénat, 2004).

27 Étienne-Pierre Ventenat, *Description des plantes nouvelles et peu connues, cultivées dans le jardin de J.-M. Cels: avec figures* (Paris: Crapelet, 1799), n.p. (Preface).

in Paris in 1927 and a factory established in Avignon for sending seeds and fertiliser more quickly to customers in the south. After World War II the business had four shops as well as branches in Cherbourg, Bordeaux, Reims, Montauban, Toulouse, Angers, Amiens, Melun, etc.

Furthermore, working alongside the landscaper, new trades appeared or arose from specialisation, including landscape entrepreneurs who made and maintained gardens, navvies, even garden designers and artists responsible for plans.[28] Their 'reports', or to use Claude d'Anthenaise's fine expression, 'gardens on paper',[29] were a seductive and convincing factor aimed at future clients. Expertise is also a product of technique: the methods of transplanting plants, and trees in particular, become more exact and the tools (mowing machines, watering, greenhouses, etc.) multiplied, becoming more efficient and bearing witness to the industrialisation of their production. It is not surprising then that the great workshops were set up to respond efficiently to demands. This is why some names always stand out when one studies the great landscaping projects in the whole of France in the second half of the nineteenth century: Édouard André, Jean-Pierre Barillet-Deschamps, the Bühler brothers, etc. All of them could claim a training experience, particularly in the Gardens and Promenades department of the City of Paris which gave them an international aura they could exploit. They were thus active worldwide, going as far afield as Latin America in Barillet-Duchamps' case, for example, consolidating impressive networks for themselves. Techniques and knowledge were propagated among amateurs and professionals by means of such journals as the famous *Revue horticole*, edited from 1882 by Édouard André.

This state of affairs has changed little since the nineteenth century. The organisation of the profession has continued: the first international congress of garden architects took place in 1937 at the time of the Universal Exhibition in Paris, and generated a manifesto calling for better collaboration between architects, town planners and garden-makers. The term 'landscaper' truly established itself after 1945, recognised by a government diploma. The chair in the architecture of gardens at the *École nationale d'horticulture* (National School of Horticulture) at Versailles became first the *Section du paysage et de l'art des jardins* (Section of landscape and the art of gardens) and later in 1976 an institution in its own right, the *École nationale supérieure du paysage*

28 Limido, *L'Art des jardins sous le Second Empire*, p. 230.

29 Claude d'Anthenaise, 'Jardins de papier', in Catherine de Bourgoing (dir.), *Jardins romantiques français* (Paris: Les musées de la ville de Paris, 2011), p. 23.

de Versailles (Versailles higher school of landscape). Once the war was over, the need arose to train professionals capable of 'considering the totality of public buildings, stadiums and whole towns, of transforming the natural context to create a green framework that would be not only beautiful but of value at the level of health ... and to contribute to the huge reconstruction made necessary by war damage'.[30] However between the inter-war period and the 1970s there were scarcely any workshops as prestigious as those already cited. But today, by way of such landscape personalities as Michel Corajoud and Gilles Clément, practices are being retrieved (although with very different styles and intentions) that were in vogue a century ago. Gilles Clément, for instance, one of today's most highly regarded landscapers, first published *Le jardin en mouvement* (*The Garden in Movement*) (1991), a landmark theoretical work, and the basis of his celebrity. Besides developing his thinking in many other publications, he has also led to many creations, in France and abroad, first alone and then at times in collaboration with other landscapers, architects and actual workshops. Among these are Coloco, founded in 1999. Bringing together architects and landscapers such as Miguel and Pablo Georgieff, this workshop aims at developing improvement projects 'favouring urban diversity' by involving a wide range of actors.[31] This is perhaps the most fundamental difference from the training of landscapers such as André or Barillet-Deschamps. Since the 1920s, with the surge in thinking about town planning, landscapers have incorporated this dimension more directly, often from the time they are training: one thinks about the whole town and its future before one thinks of a park or a garden.

Doing the vegetal work

This professionalisation not only affects the creators: it extends also to those who look after urban green spaces. Once a vegetalised space has been brought into being, it falls to municipal authorities to be responsible for its regular maintenance and to take charge of replanting when necessary. Given how popular public promenades and gardens are, there is a lot at stake in the field of good practice in managing urban space.

While certain municipalities, such as Lyon from the middle of the seventeenth century, could establish direct management by recruiting one or

30 Quoted in 'L'émergence internationale du paysagisme (1940–1970)', in Hervé Brunon (ed.), *L'Art du jardin, du début du XXe siècle à nos jours* (Paris: CNDP), p. 28.

31 http://www.coloco.org/index.php?cat=COLOCO (accessed 16 Apr. 2014).

Figure 10.

Harvesting the fruit, in Jean-Baptiste de La Quintinie, *Instructions pour les jardins fruitiers et potagers* (1690). Courtesy of BNF / Gallica: https://gallica.bnf.fr

more gardeners, most often towns delegated the work to private enterprises: there were many invitations to tender, and in the eighteenth century there are exact contracts stating the work to be done. This was essentially a matter of removing caterpillars, and pruning and watering trees in courts and promenades. The professionals employed on these tasks were designated by the generic term 'gardeners' which, as was said earlier, covered different occupations. In some towns, such as Tours, gardeners took away urban night-soil, which they reused in their own husbandry.[32] The gardener could be a cultivator, a garden creator, or appointed to maintain recreational green spaces. In Lyon, gardeners formed a socio-professional milieu particularly characterised by social continuity. Families stayed rooted in a single place, very rarely being well-to-do enough to own their own land, and rarer still

32 Béatrice Baumier, *Tours entre Lumières et Révolution, pouvoir municipal et métamorphoses d'une ville (1764–1792)* (Rennes: PUR, 2007), p. 44.

were those who found a position in the municipality`s service. While they were easily identifiable in social terms, these Lyonnais gardeners were in an indeterminate legal situation regarding their conditions of employment. They may have belonged to a single brotherhood, attached to the Saint-Nizier church, and some bore with pride the title 'Master', but they did not truly belong among the trades governed by statutes of corporation. The status of gardeners in Paris was also very complicated. In theory, since 1599, they exercised a sworn profession and were obliged to conform to the rules of their professional body, which stipulated that only master gardeners had the right to sell their products in markets. Even so, at the end of the seventeenth century this right of production and sale was extended to companion gardeners and to any market gardener of self-appointed bourgeois status, the masters keeping only the privilege of choosing the best locations in the Halles market and bigger selling opportunities. From the end of the seventeenth century, gardening was thus in the process of becoming a free profession that anyone could exercise outside the framework of the corporate body, which was already divided by the conflict between master gardeners and market gardeners. It did not survive the liberalising offensive led by Turgot. He suppressed the corporate framework instantly in 1776. On the eve of the Revolution, which finished the task of freeing work from privileges and monopolies, there were to be found in the centre of Paris, and particularly in the Saint-Marcel neighbourhood, real gardener-entrepreneurs, adorned with the title 'master gardeners' who maintained great public gardens, and private gardens, such as those of religious houses. They commanded large teams of up to fifty workers belonging to different professions and trades including gardeners of course, but also masons, labourers and journeymen come to give a hand.[33]

Up until the middle years of the nineteenth century, towns could have recourse to the services of such entrepreneurs. Thus, at Annecy in the 1860s the mowing and harvest of the Champ-de-Mars and Clos Lombard were put out to tender every June.[34] But it seems that the municipal authorities mistrusted the entrepreneurs, who were also often vigorously criticised by the townspeople. Contracts put out to tender became ever more specific in order to avoid abuse. At the beginning of the Restoration period, one even

33 Haim Burstin, *Le Faubourg Saint-Marcel à l'époque révolutionnaire. Structure économique et composition sociale* (Paris: Société des études robespierristes, 2012), pp. 236–237.

34 Michel Bizet and Alain Meyrier, *Annecy côté jardin*, *Revue Annesci* **31** (1990): 44.

finds the specifications for the circumference of branches which were not to be cut, and that of trees to be planted if others died and the exact conditions for doing this. The point was that the wood cut off belonged to the contractors and it was feared that they might get a bit heavy handed,[35] or simply would not do their job and would let trees die so that they could take them: hence there was a new specification in the contracts that dead trees belonged to the town, not to the contractor. The municipality watched the contractor closely, often by way of an inspector. Yet, however strictly these contracts were framed, they remained nonetheless attractive. In Nantes at a public auction on 1 March 1798, three gardeners were competing for a contract: the sum of 1,400 francs was proposed, but that was eventually lowered to 1,048 francs and so, as long as the successful bidder was reliable, the town hall got a bargain.[36] Probably because of the abuses that have been mentioned, and because towards the end of the nineteenth century local authorities had more funds available, the use of municipal employees increased. There were of course big differences between small *communes* employing one or two gardeners, sometimes poorly trained, and big towns whose imposing parks, squares, public gardens and promenades called for large, experienced teams.

Annecy is an interesting case, coming in between the two. In the first third of the twentieth century the town had just 17,000 inhabitants. However, like a number of French towns, under the Second Empire, in 1863–65 it made its own fine public garden with 650 trees around the lake for nearly 20,000 francs. An annual budget of 1,000 francs was envisaged for maintaining it, 700 francs for a gardener and 300 francs for equipment and planting. Furthermore, the tasks expected of Henri Inversin, the first gardener, recruited in 1863, were heavy and detailed. He was to keep the forty garden baskets flowering from May to October with dahlias, carnations, verbena, bouvardias, etc. He had to maintain the fertility of the land: sixty cubic metres of compost covered the lawns in January, and sixteen cubic metres of manure were to be dug into the flower beds. Lawns were rolled and cut regularly, four times over the summer, and the borders were trimmed to keep them neat. The aeration and fertility of the soil around trees and bushes was maintained by hoeing in the

35 Stendhal makes a quick reference to the pruning of the plane trees at the Fidélité in Verrières: 'The local liberals claim, but they exaggerate, that the hand of the official gardener has become much stricter since M. le vicaire Maslon got into the habit of seizing the mowing products'. (Stendhal, *Le Rouge et le Noir*, (Paris: Librairie Générale Française, 1983 [1830]), p. 18).

36 Nantes, Archives municipales, 'adjudication de la taille et de l'échenillage des arbres pour trois ans au profit du Citoyen Cronier', 1O16130.

Figure 11.

The public garden in Annecy. Early twentieth-century postcard in authors' collection.

springtime and by adding manure. Watering had to be done and each year forty cubic metres of gravel had to be raked and spread on the alleys to fill in holes and keep them even, plants had to be protected from excessive heat or cold (the most delicate plants were winterised, and greenhouses built for winter cultivation), and lastly the park had to be patrolled, as Inversin was also the parkkeeper.[37] Today the town's green spaces service comprises almost one hundred personnel, who maintain more than 110 hectares, and an extra 400 hectares of woodland, with a budget in the region of four million euros.[38]

This movement from auctioning contracts to establishing services for green spaces in many towns bears witness to the ever-increasing involvement of municipal authorities, and public authorities more widely, in urban greening.

37 Michel Bizet and Alain Meyrier, *Annecy côté jardin*, *Revue Annesci* **31** (1990): 65–66.

38 Information kindly provided in Jan. 2014 by Mr Christophe Ferlin, Director of the Annecy Green Spaces Department.

Public authorities

In the twentieth century, considering the urban landscape in its entirety and thinking about the way in which green spaces and the built environment articulate together over the whole city now goes without saying for urban planners. However, during the *Ancien Régime*, the issue of planning the vegetal in town and the place to be set aside for nature and green spaces in the urban fabric did not exist on its own as a category of urban development. It was always subordinate to other questions linked to the flexible category of 'town enhancements', and these, as we have seen, were far from being driven by simply aesthetic motivations. These urban developments did not depend on one single authority but on several actors whose fields inevitably overlapped. Town council minutes reveal the vital role played by municipal authorities in decision making and in managing urban works. To take Lyon as just one example, from the beginning of the seventeenth century the Consulate responsible for the administration of the city undertook projects for embellishment and in 1628 a planted promenade was laid out along the quays of the Rhône, running from the Saint Clair rampart to the Grand College; and French style parterres showcased great public buildings such as the Hôtel Dieu. However, the famous intendants, as representatives of royal power, also had to be taken into account for they enjoyed powers that were extended during the eighteenth century in order to guarantee the safety and the prosperity of the populations of the *généralités* (fiscal and financial regions). They had the funds needed for large scale public works, for developing infrastructure, installing equipment in case of natural or sanitary disaster and promoting projects for the enhancement of urban space that the whole population could enjoy. In Bordeaux, the intendant of Guyenne, Louis-Urbain-Aubert de Tourny (1743–1757), claimed with some boastfulness that it was his idea to lay out the Jardin Royal, a plan much anticipated by the economic elites of the city. He wrote of this project in a letter dated 2 July 1746 to the government minister d'Argenson:

> I would confess to you, sir, that it was I who had the first idea, among the very many for the embellishment of the city of Bordeaux, and this idea met with such delight from all the inhabitants that each one ardently desires its realisation. In truth, besides the fact that it will be a great pleasure for them and will be no small contribution to their health, one must, in a trading city, deem such a garden necessary or, at the least, extremely useful to commerce, as merchants often need to meet together to conclude their business, and it would thus be a second Exchange, or an evening Exchange.[39]

39 AD33, C1185, Letter from Tourny to d'Argenson, 2 July 1746.

In *pays d'états* regions, the provincial assemblies also had the power to intervene in towns. Since they had tax-raising powers, the provincial states could mobilise the funds necessary for major works and they made their staff available to oversee these projects. Actors in public life were not the only ones who could propose projects. The drive could also emanate from important figures from the social elites or religious authorities who were likely to use their own personal credit and activate their networks to influence public action. A case in point is that of Archbishop Loménie de Brienne in support of urban renewal in Toulouse during the last thirty years of the eighteenth century. While towns may have had a considerable margin for manoeuvre in the management of their vegetal heritage, they also had to take into account other significant actors, and in particular the monarchical state, who meddled in their affairs, either in the creation of parks properly speaking or else in the topic of vegetal supply. Such purchases always counted for more in public spending, since it was a matter of meeting citizens' taste in urban promenades and gardens and responding to the growing demand for trees to line roadways. Moreover, changes in the French vegetal landscape had to be taken into account, for this had become more complex because of the introduction of many plants and trees from outside Europe. Towns reacted by creating their own municipal nurseries, like the one at Wacken in Strasbourg in the 1740s.[40] A century and a half later, professionals were still praising this management that was closer to the area of operation:

> The preparation of plants in the municipal nurseries is carried out in the most favourable conditions. Various species of trees which will flourish the best in the city are nurtured there; saplings are prepared methodically and no effort is spared in transplanting so that, each year, there is the quantity of plants needed for replacements and even for less important new plantings.[41]

But these measures could only ever concern the wealthiest and the most extensive towns which explains the early intervention of the central powers able, from the seventeenth century onwards, to call on nurseries that had been set up to maintain the gardens in royal residences and which were managed by entrepreneurs under contract. In the Île-de-France region these establishments were located mainly around Versailles but also in the Saint Antoine du Roule district of Paris. During the first decades of

40 *Parchemins et jardins. Les jardins strasbourgeois du Moyen Âge à nos jours*, Archives de la Ville et de la Communauté urbaine de Strasbourg (Strasbourg, 2004), p. 52.

41 Georges Lefèbvre, *Plantations d'alignement, promenades, parcs et jardins publics: service municipal* (Paris: Vicq-Dunod, 1897), p. 37.

the eighteenth century, the monarchical government took very seriously mainstream arguments that evoked the old fear about the exhaustion of French forest stocks under the combined effects of climate change and urban and industrial needs. Besides taking extra measures for the protection of the forests, a decree made by the King's Council in 1720 promoted the spread of plant nurseries. Each *généralité* should equip itself with a royal nursery, placed under the supervision of the intendant and managed by a gardener paid by the state. These establishments were designed to be reserves of fruit trees, route-lining trees and exotic ones. They were supposed to make an active contribution to the vegetal restocking of the kingdom by supplying public works sites and by distributing plants free of charge to those private individuals who requested them. The functioning of the first royal nurseries was chaotic; it took several decades and two further decrees from the King's Council, in 1724 and 1767, for the system imagined in Versailles to be put in place. In 1788 the royal nursery in Lyon located outside the ramparts, held 43,000 plants. The inventory carried out in 1791 shows that priority was given to big ornamental trees and to road-lining trees while fruit trees were in the minority: 750 peach, apricot and almond trees as opposed to 2,920 chestnuts, 3,450 ash, 4,930 sycamores, 5,100 elms, 11,9000 walnuts …

State intervention facilitated the vegetalisation of public planning inasmuch as towns and cities were no longer wholly dependent on private supply circuits when obtaining trees destined for the enhancement of a public space. At the time of the Revolution and of the Empire, the state stepped up its interventionism in the vegetal domain by mobilising the learned societies of the *Ancien Régime* and their personnel, whose skills were recycled. The stakes were considerable as much in the field of management of public space (routes, urban planning…) as in the field of science, in industry in particular and especially in agriculture (plant growing innovations, acclimatisation of colonial plants, selection of the best performing varieties…). Between 1811 and 1813 a network of departmental nurseries was structured and expanded, within the boundaries of the Empire. Their functioning was closely linked to the major Parisian scientific institutions which were themselves joined to the web of metropolitan and colonial botanic gardens. The Jardin des Plantes in Paris, the Roule national nursery and the nursery at the Luxembourg Garden acted as seed banks, distributing seeds and genetically improved specimens.[42]

42 Ambrosoli Mauro, 'Marcher la nuit sans lanterne, c'est cueillir chardons pour luzerne…', *Études rurales*, 151–152 (1999): 77–102.

Any mayor who wished to diversify the vegetal range in the public gardens of his town could contact the nursery in his department to take advantage of this distribution.[43] In the bigger towns, elected officials also took advantage of gigantic nurseries associated with the new green spaces. Thus it was in Lyon that Denis Bühler convinced the imperial authorities of the interest in having a nursery with 16,000 trees, spread over 1.5 hectares specifically to serve the Tête d'Or park that he was laying out. He thereby hoped to ensure the quality of the produce and to get the trees at a lower price having calculated that he could save 10,000 francs.[44] This logic was pushed to its most extreme in Paris because of the gigantic requirements of the new landscaped developments of Baron Haussmann.

This was how, in 1855, Alphand and Barillet-Deschamps set up the Jardin de la Muette in Clos Georges, at Passy, where three greenhouses supplied the Bois de Boulogne and the Square de la Tour Saint-Jacques, which was being laid out, with 600 tropical plants which were then returned to over-winter there. This garden was reserved for decorative plants and it expanded continually: in 1865 it supplied the city with nearly 900,000 plants and it had 24 greenhouses and 3,000 cold frames with glass surfaces totalling over 10,000 square metres. These housed around 2,000 palm trees and 250 camellias and in cellars set up in former limestone quarries were 200,000 canna lily tubers. This establishment was completed by four branches. One occupied about 50,000 square metres in the Bois de Vincennes. It was an extension of the Muette garden and as soon as it opened in 1865 it produced over 400,000 plants. Two nurseries installed in the Bois de Boulogne, towards Longchamp (1856) and Auteuil (1859), and a third one at Petit Bry sur Marne (1859) completed this arrangement for supplying Paris with trees and deciduous shrubs, resinous trees and road-lining trees respectively.[45] This was a veritable plant factory and it met a triple challenge closely linked to the aesthetic of Parisian parks such as it was expressed in the art of Barillet-Deschamps: to have a supply of new and exotic plants virtually unavailable in shops and

43 While in the 20th century departmental nurseries were able to play the game of plant artificialisation, in connection with research conducted by INRA in the field of genetics, since the 2000s, most of them have been reclaiming an approach of environmental sustainability. So-called organic crops are favoured, without recourse to phytosanitary products, and the species distributed to populate public spaces are selected for their adaptability to the urban environment.

44 Louis-Michel Nourry, *Les Jardins publics en province* (Rennes: PUR, 1997), p. 90.

45 See article by A. Brongniart, *Journal de la SICH* (1867): 189, in Daniel Lejeune, *Édouard André* (Paris: Société Nationale d'Horticulture de France, 2009), p. 48; see also Limido, *L'Art des jardins sous le Second Empire*, p. 91.

which could be acclimatised in order to decorate public gardens; to ensure the constant replacement of trees and flowers all year round; to have available plants whose size and shape were adapted to the landscaper's artistic choices when they were planted.

The nineteenth century therefore appears to be a transition period during which the framework for public action became progressively more refined as urban planning experiments were undertaken in towns. On the advice of the medico-social sphere, public actors were clearly taking more pains with the greening of the cities. With the development of health and hygiene theories at the end of the eighteenth century and in the next century, with obligations that were social and sanitary and to do with the prestige of a town, the authorities, particularly at a municipal level, felt they had a duty to act and to bring gardens and parks and tree-lined roads to French *communes*. At the beginning of the nineteenth century, Strasbourg had a succession of 'green' mayors such as Jean-Frédéric Hermann and especially Georges-Frédéric Schutzenberger (1837–1848) who the citizens dubbed the 'Baïmelé maire' ('mayor of the shrubs'). He threw himself remarkably into the development of numerous promenades and planting for cemeteries.[46] Although the mayors acted in this way, they did so before the twentieth century with no real legal framework specific to the issue of nature in the town, a situation that was deplored by a number of social reformers and landscapers.[47] In fact, starting with the example of Paris, many bemoaned the fact that, since Haussmann, there had been no forward planning for the future needs of a constantly expanding population. This was one of the main arguments of the architect and landscaper Jean-Claude Nicolas Forestier in his 1908 book *Grandes villes et systèmes de parcs* (*Major Cities and Park Systems*). In a startlingly modern manner, he criticised the fact that no-one had done any serious or general urban thinking about the future of the capital, or about the places set aside for green spaces or about links with the suburbs and neighbouring *communes*. It was imperative, in his opinion, that the plan of the city, should be completed by his idea of a system of parks at an intercommunal level or even at the level of the province or the department. In the National Assembly, Charles Beauquier and Jules Siegfried, who were both members of the Social Museum, introduced bills in 1909,

46 Christelle Strub, *Assainir et embellir Strasbourg au XIXe siècle: étude sur la municipalité de Georges Frédéric Schützenberger (1837–1848)* (Strasbourg: Société académique du Bas-Rhin, 1998). This mayor had trees planted in every cemetery in the city.

47 For this whole paragraph, see Stéphane Frioux, 'Des espaces libres aux espaces verts, 1908–1952', seminar communication, ENS-LSH, 4 Mar. 2008.

aiming, as Siegfried said, at 'the rational development' of towns. These became the Cornudet law of 14 March 1919 which was the first to oblige cities with over 10,000 inhabitants to set up a development plan for embellishment and extension, and therefore to think about the place of green spaces in the urban fabric. This, then, is the bedrock of national legislation for the greening of French cities. The application of this law was sometimes hesitant and often awkward but the main idea was established: green spaces inscribed in law, and thinking at a local level about the future of each municipality. For example, in 1926, according to its chief engineer, Brive la Gaillarde had barely one per cent green space in its territory, which was extremely insufficient. This explains the requirement, in the proposed project, for a multiplication of gardens, parks and squares in a careful hierarchy so that every citizen should be no further than 500 metres from a corner of nature. The city itself should be girded by great parks 'resembling the countryside as much as possible, as places for long walks and Sunday excursions'.[48]

After the Second World War, this legislative base should have been made more specific and the powers of public actors better defined. But the demographic explosion of the baby boom, the strong growth of the *Trente Glorieuses* post-war years, everybody's accession to modernity with the automobile and travel, urban sprawl and many, often hasty, building schemes, delayed decision making. Public orders for greenery were reduced to a bare minimum and were often limited to the installation of green spaces in the interstices, with no global thinking beforehand. It was not until 8 February 1973 that Robert Poujade, the minister responsible for the protection of nature and the environment, sent a circular to prefects and established a regulatory text entirely dealing with green spaces, a notion that he helped to popularise. A goal was fixed: ten square metres of urban green space per inhabitant. This rose to 25 square metres per inhabitant for weekend green spaces (tacking into account urban forests and peri-urban spaces). Still today, this quantitative objective is a reference for town councils. If political leaders contributed to the greening of cities through this kind of regulation, they also contributed by public orders, whether national or more often local, particularly after the decentralisation measures of the 1980s. Thus it was that in 1971 that the first national landscaping competition was held in Seine-Saint Denis for the redevelopment of the peri-urban park at La Courneuve. The symbol of this

48 AD Corrèze, 3O 1022, quotation of the preliminary draft in Mr Boudy's report of 1931, quoted by Stéphane Frioux, ibid.

renewed interest was, however, the international competition launched in 1982 by the French state to create a park at La Villette. This drew over 500 candidates and the movement began. Municipal officials were encouraged by a growing demand for greenery from citizens and they now turned their gaze to the possibilities offered by the vegetal in town.[49]

This interest was expressed in particular in new legislative texts, which were themselves driven by major changes at an international level during the 1990s. Following the 1987 Bruntland Report, which popularised the term 'sustainable development', the Earth Summit that was held in Rio in 1992 adopted Agenda 21 which set action by towns at the heart of sustainable policies. From that point, two avenues opened up.

On one hand there was the slow adoption of these objectives into French national legislation. Different legislative documents with abstruse acronyms – *Solidarité et Renouvellement Urbain*, known as SRU (the law on Solidarity and Urban Renewal in 2000 for example) – guarantee the place for green spaces in all urban planning projects by integrating them variously, from the level of the *commune* to that of the region.[50] Moreover, since 2003 a national strategy for sustainable development has been supposed to help coordinate these strategies.

The other path taken to apply the Agenda 21 recommendations was done directly by local authorities themselves for they had not always waited until there was a national - or even an international – impulse to start concerning themselves with the role the vegetal played in their territory. According to the website of Comité 21, since 1993 1,012 territorial authorities have adopted Agenda 21.[51] The city of Nice, for example, did so in 2001 with a five-year environmental charter. These local authorities have set up networks which are national and European (with, for example, the Aalborg Charter in 1994). One of the most original and the most real is doubtless that of the association Plante & Cité, set up in 2006 in Angers to respond to the need for experimentation and the pooling of sustainable management techniques for green spaces. It organises working groups and on its website provides a very rich database on the actions carried out by its partners; its originality is that it combines research centres, practitioners and political

49 'Enjeux de l'espace public (1970-2010)', in Brunon (ed.), *L'Art du jardin*.

50 See Bernard Reygrobellet, *La Nature dans la ville, biodiversité et urbanisme*, Rapport du Conseil économique et social (2007).

51 http://www.agenda21france.org/agenda-21-de-territoire/index.html (accessed 17 Apr. 2014).

decision makers. In 2013 it referenced 172 towns, five department councils, two regional councils, 118 horticultural firms or landscape gardeners, twelve research establishments, etc.

The aridity of these institutional constructions should not belie their importance. They are often essential not just as the trigger for a coherent policy but also as a facilitator for its implementation. As a case in point, a 1971 project called *Métropole-jardin* (Metropolis-garden), launched by OREALM, a state-sponsored group set up in 1968 – the *Organisation d'études d'aménagement de la Loire moyenne* (Organisation for development studies in the Middle Loire) – was supposed to make the Orleans-Tours route a structuring axis for the development of these towns, with particular attention being paid to the natural heritage and the maintenance of green belts within the urban sprawl. Because there was no sustained political will and doubtless also because there were no institutional levers of action, this project lost its way but was partly relaunched in 2006 with an agreement signed by the main conurbations (Tours, Orléans, Le Mans, Blois, Saumur, Chinon, etc.). Above all, it established the idea, which has never been denied, of preserving the natural heritage, and particularly all that is vegetal, of this urban ensemble.[52]

Over the past ten years or so we have witnessed a different kind of incitation on the part of public authorities regarding a different approach to the greening of the city. In fact, one of the accompaniments to the 1992 Rio summit was the famous European Union 'Habitats' directive which determined the establishment, at a European level, of the ecological network 'Natura 2000' made up of specially protected zones. While most Natura 2000 sites are located outside actual towns, the great novelty at the beginning of the millennium was to no longer consider green spaces in towns as urban fittings but as total ecosystems.[53] This new thinking has been translated in a variety of regulatory manners. Thus, the idea of establishing ecological corridors (green and blue lines) to link together all the green spaces in the town and these in turn with peri-urban nature, little by little imposed itself on public authorities.[54] This received a boost with the Grenelle Agreements

52 *Revue urbanisme,* special report: *la Ville durable en question(s)* 363 (Nov.–Dec. 2008).

53 Lotfi Mehdi, Christiane Weber, Francesca Di Pietro and Wissal Selmi, 'Évolution de la place du végétal dans la ville, de l'espace vert à la trame verte', *VertigO* **12** (2): (Sept. 2012).

54 The idea of the ecological corridor is not new in itself: as early as 1976, there was talk of a green grid in the Paris region, while the Nord-Pas-de-Calais region, in the 1990s, was trying out biological corridors. The department of Seine-Saint-Denis, for its part, has become a pioneer

on the environment (2007–2009). This agreement specifically launched a plan named 'Restoring and Valorising Nature in the City'[55] one of whose main themes emphasises the shared governance of urban nature.

This last point demonstrates a new awareness that the participation of citizens is necessary and, more generally, that concerted action from all the actors interested in the vegetal in the city is needed.[56]

***

Professionals, private individuals and public authorities made the greening of the city their business but these multiple interventions made conflict inevitable. Expectations are not necessarily the same, nor are the methods, and the greening of the city must be seen as a non-linear process that is conflictual and sometimes erratic and as an arena for stakes that have been as much political as cultural or economic.

So it was, for obvious reasons of public order, as we have seen, that private citizens were constrained regarding the floral decoration of their apartments and residences: one could not put a pot of flowers just anyhow, anywhere on a pavement or a corner. Over the past ten years, there has been an increasing number of good practice guides for city dwellers who grow flowers in their gardens or on their balconies. They are discouraged from using phytosanitary products and told to choose local flora rather than imported varieties. In Toulouse, for example, a whole communication strategy has been aimed at involving citizens in the development of urban biodiversity. On the other hand, landscaping choices made by local councils regarding vegetalisation may be questioned by residents. This was the case, in particular, when it was a question of abandoning horticultural models in towns in favour of reintroducing wild plants. Very frequently town councils have needed to adopt a pedagogical attitude in order to explain that the city hall is not overlooking pavements, roundabouts and so on, where 'weeds' spring up but that they are managing green spaces differently and in particular without phytosanitary

in terms of environmental policy: to link the 1,550 ha of green spaces scattered throughout the department, a 60-km-long 'park path' has been set up - part of which became the first 'Natura 2000' site located in an urban area in 2006.

55 http://www.developpement-durable.gouv.fr/Plan-nature-en-ville.html, accessed 17 Apr. 2014.

56 On this subject, see the results of the survey conducted by the Centre d'études et d'expertise sur les risques, l'environnement, la mobilité et l'aménagement (CEREMA), *Implication citoyenne et nature en ville*, Bron, Éditions du Cerema, 2016.

products. Matthieu Tétard shows how in Caen and Toulouse these misgivings were expressed, particularly because it was feared that these tall grasses and weeds would encourage rubbish dumping, encourage the spread of ticks or increase the risk of fire, etc.[57] Thus, the greening of the town is not obvious and the conflicts of interest or expectations that we have just mentioned are just some of the many challenges to be faced.

57 Matthieu Tétard, *Le Sauvage dans la ville*, Master's dissertation, Toulouse IEP, 2012.

3.

TURNING THE TOWN GREEN: A CHALLENGE

Public authorities, town planners, architects, landscapers and amateur and professional gardeners have a tricky task in freeing up the space needed to introduce the vegetal into the mineral heart of the city, to get it to grow there and flourish. The question also arises of what species one wants to see growing in the town; since the seventeenth century much accumulated experience has demonstrated clearly the limits of humanity's will to manage nature, despite the technical innovations that can be brought to bear. The vegetal forms part of a complex urban environment, which functions as a system, where the modification of one element may have unforeseen and even undesirable effects on the whole. Trees and plants can resist gardeners' wishes, despite all the care taken in nurturing the nature one wants to grow in a town. Grenoble had bitter experience of this kind in the latter half of the eighteenth century. One of the tree-lined public promenades, the Cours Saint-André, established nearly a century before, saw three successive types of planting in less than twenty years. In 1760 the town council decided to replace the obsolete poplars from the previous century with elms, which was the least risky thing to do according to the agronomic knowledge of the time. And it was reasonable to expect a good price for the felled timber when the elms matured. Sadly, however, the death of the young trees, planted at a cost of some 30,000 *livres* to the public finances, seemed inevitable. Three contractors in succession were sacked when they proved incapable of restoring them to health. In 1776, and war-weary, the decision was taken to uproot the moribund elms and incur the expense of replacing them with Dutch limes and sycamores. Faced with disease and attack by parasites, the only solution the experts ended up agreeing on was to give up trying to treat urban trees like a forestry asset from the countryside and to diversify the species being planted. Turning the town green thus involves facing a number of challenges but also means adapting to the unpredictable character of nature in an urban setting.

Make way for greenery!

The land challenge: the garden will succeed the garden

The decision to introduce a natural space into a town always works against any argument for maximising the profitability of land, where it would be preferable that plots of land should be dedicated to more fruitful building operations. From the seventeenth century on, French towns were faced with significant population growth. The intramural space, within the city walls, became scarce and expensive. Plots of land formerly abandoned to nature or devoted to market gardening were steadily built over, when they did not belong to ecclesiastics or urban elites. These categories alone had the means, thanks to patrimonial strategies, to preserve green spaces for their own benefit, or, in the case of the most fortunate of all, to create new ones. The general rule was that only a garden should take the place of a garden, or at least that it should not be swallowed up by building growth. As we stated in Chapter One, one of the issues in seventeenth- and eighteenth-century town planning was explicitly to counter the effects of densification by improvements aimed at enabling the town to breathe. From the seventeenth century on, the urban vegetal landscape was enriched with artificial forms suiting citizens' expectations. While the urban population was not insensible to the embellishment of its surroundings, the people saw in this above all new spaces for recreation and socialising which were not the preserve of the elites alone and which could host the leisure moments of one and all, as we shall see further on. Greening operations were not, however, easily undertaken: landowners almost always stood in the way of projects involving expropriation, even if it was a matter of the wellbeing of all citizens. Lacking legal instruments which would have facilitated urban planning, public authorities in the *Ancien Régime* had to come to terms with private interests and to begin by bringing municipally-owned land into play, or land which the town could pre-empt without spending too much. Thus, very steadily, French towns gave themselves public gardens, often associated with sites of authority or with major public buildings, and these were an addition to the kaleidoscope of private gardens. Avenues, pathways and boulevards unfolding their perspectives and greenery in the urban landscape also formed part of the public space. At first associated with the limits imposed by a town's morphology (a river, old ramparts, fortresses and bridges...) planting ended up joining the urban skeleton, to mark where two neighbourhoods met, to emphasise a view, to extend the town beyond its city walls or ancient ramparts towards the flat land beyond.

While they might be a major obstacle to the greening of a town, it was nevertheless the straitjacket of ancient or medieval ramparts which defined a town as a legal entity imbued with privileges. The introduction of natural spaces goes hand in hand with the transformation of the closed town of the *Ancien Régime* into an open town. Some towns in France lost their ramparts in the first third of the seventeenth century on the order of a monarchy anxious to destroy inclinations to revolt among the great nobles, or to prevent Protestants establishing places of safety which could become a 'state within a state'. After the Fronde,[1] Louis XIV brought the rebellious towns to heel; for instance, in 1666 without any prior consultation with the municipal authorities, he had the ancient ramparts of Marseille knocked down, thereby indicating that he intended to favour the interests of the trading bourgeoisie at the expense of the pro-Fronde nobility. By the end of the seventeenth, century ramparts had lost all their strategic importance: thanks to the work of Vauban, the network of frontier fortifications, especially in the north and east of the kingdom, should stop any enemy invasion, while the royal navy, reorganised by Colbert, protected the Atlantic and Mediterranean seaboards. From now on, ramparts were thought of as an obstacle to urban expansion. A town could either break out of them spontaneously by expanding its suburbs, or the intervention of royal power accelerated the fall of city walls. However, for local reasons, in some towns the ramparts remained well into the eighteenth century and local authorities had to come to terms with the military architecture in making a space for the vegetal. This was the case in Nîmes, where the very real demand for fresh, airy public spaces had long been frustrated by the maintenance of fortifications. In this town, whose growth was due to silk manufacture, the density of the intramural population in the seventeenth century exceeded 370 inhabitants per hectare, and close to 2,000 near the arenas![2] The urban fabric was very dense, wholly made up of three or four storey buildings. Several peripheral suburbs developed outside the walls, taking in ancient rural towns. In the 1680s, the town threw off the medieval straitjacket of ramparts that hindered traffic between the centre and the new neighbourhoods. But Louis XIV imposed the construction

1 The Fronde is the name given to a series of armed conflicts between 1648 and 1653 in which the government of King Louis XIV (still a minor) was opposed by groups who were against the strengthening of royal power, including great aristocrats, part of the bourgeois elite and urban and rural working classes.

2 Line Tesseyre-Sallmann, 'Urbanisme et société: l'exemple de Nîmes aux XVIIe et XVIIIe siècles', *Annales. Économies, Sociétés, Civilisations* **5** (1980): 965–986.

of an extended perimeter of fortifications whose key was a new fortress, Fort-Vauban, built in 1667–1668. Nîmes remained a closed town. It was not until 1774 that the town council was able to decide to do away with the defensive works, and dismantling them took till the eve of the Revolution. Yet, despite the continued military constraints, from the end of the seventeenth century, perspectives transforming the urban space were opened up, thanks to the introduction of paths planted with trees, gardens and grassed areas for leisure-time. The medieval city walls, which had just been razed to the ground in 1688, were in part transformed into a large tree-lined public promenade, the Cours. Half a century later, the network of promenades was extended further, linking the old centre with the famous La Fontaine gardens, which took their name from the development of a spring supplying the town through a system of aqueducts. The design of these gardens had been devised in 1745 by the king's engineer in Languedoc, Maréchal, to make the most of the remains of antiquity discovered there. They were extended by a noble Grand Cours designed to create a direct perspective for the new suburbs. Travellers were stunned by the linking of the vegetal with water, as evidenced by the princess Marie-Louise de Gonzague-Nevers for whom Montpellier and Nîmes both had 'promenades which could ornament a capital city. That of Nîmes is particularly enchanting: it is like the island of Paphos. There are ancient Roman baths, whose design has been retained but which are most ingeniously transformed into gardens. The garden is in a lovely island surrounded by a canal of clear water enhanced by architecture and sculptures.'[3] In the *Belle Époque*, the Garden of the Fountain was still charming tourists who had come to enjoy the delights of the Mediterranean.

The greening of towns in the eighteenth century was firstly the result of their overspilling the ramparts, a spreading-out movement progressively absorbing the suburbs as the population grew. Town limits became fuzzy and they spread with a perimeter carrying the mark of a countryside that had become the melting-pot of all possibilities. Less dense building, relaxed constraints on land, speculators hungry for new residential areas, and the energy of improvers shaping the town's future – so many factors concurred in more or less ambitious town-planning projects all following the same strategy.

However, the simplest solution for getting round the land problem was to reinstate or adapt open spaces that had for centuries been consecrated

3 *Lettres de Madame la Princesse de G**. Écrites à ses amis, pendant le cours de ses voyages d'Italie, en 1779 & années suivantes* (Gênes: Yves Gravier, 1789), vol. 2, pp. 189–190.

Figure 12.

The Jardins de la Fontaine, in Nîmes. Autochrome, early twentieth century. Library of Congress: https://www.loc.gov/pictures/item/2001698496/

to recreational activities. This was the case with the Parc du Contades at Strasbourg.[4] In the sixteenth century, this shooting range devoted to training arquebusiers and crossbowmen lay outside the ramparts by the Porte des Juifs. In 1764, it was transformed into a promenade and planted with lime trees. In 1768 there was a proposal to establish a pleasure garden there. Even though this did not happen, the area remained determinedly devoted to leisure. By the end of the eighteenth century, the limes had come on so well that it was even possible to construct a dance floor between the branches of one of them! This dancing in the air did not, however, survive the revolutionary wars, when the promenade became a defensive buffer zone. At the start of the nineteenth century, the creation of the Parc du Contades on this struc-

4 *Parchemins et jardins. Les jardins strasbourgeois du Moyen Âge à nos jours*, Archives de la Ville et de la Communauté urbaine de Strasbourg (Strasbourg, 2004).

ture was really a re-creation, encouraged by successive mayors anticipating their townsfolks' desire for greenery. Limes, planes, horse-chestnuts, elms, maples, hornbeams, acacias, robinias – the old promenade was replanted with varied species that have been appreciated since the eighteenth century, as well as more exotic species whose identity was explained to the public by way of informative plaques. These modest improvements helped to secure the popularity of municipal administrations without overloading their budget, as they did not involve buying land.

During the following centuries, greening procedures did not change fundamentally, except that public authorities were henceforward able to control the development of the urban space thanks to planning tools, and they could act on a city-wide scale. One either freed up space in order to introduce the vegetal into built-up areas, as in the great Second Empire upheaval in Paris, or towns expanded outwards to gain space. There are nonetheless two notable differences, especially from the second half of the twentieth century onwards. The first relates to the rate of this urban overspill, which accelerated along with peri-urbanisation and suburban sprawl, far exceeding the growth of the population. Agricultural land around towns especially got swallowed up ever more quickly: 54,000 hectares a year between 1982 and 1992, and 86,000 hectares in 2010. Thus agricultural or forestry land is transformed into building plots and gardens: one form of nature displaces another and now remodelled space occupies almost ten per cent of the national territory, and this creates its own urban and environmental problems, as we saw in Chapter 1.[5] Another difference from past centuries relates to the ways in which town centres are greened, and this has been evident for only the last thirty years or so. The density of construction and population in town centres, along with citizens' growing call for nature, has fostered planting wherever possible (reclaimed river banks, as in Lyon, the edges of pavements, wasteland, etc.), to the extent that the vegetal is used as an indispensable adjunct of certain improvements: the tramways that have proliferated in various towns over at least the last twenty years (Strasbourg, Bordeaux, Orléans, Paris, Reims) all have areas of green grass and sometimes rows of trees. Line 1 of the Orléans tramway, dating from 2000, is ornamented along its eighteen kilometres with 1,200 trees and 5,000 shrubs.[6] The most spectacular and innovative feature is, however, taking gardens into

5 André Torre, 'Introduction générale', *Natures urbaines : l'agriculture au cœur des métropoles? Demeter* (2013): 100–102.

6 Ann-Caroll Werquin and Alain Demangeon, *Jardins en ville, nouvelles tendances, nouvelles pratiques* (n.p, Dominique Carré, 2006).

the third dimension: far from just being lodged on the horizontal earth they establish themselves vertically on walls, spread themselves over roofs, and even become wanderers! The vegetalised wall was perfected in the 1980s by the botanist Patrick Blanc who subsequently experimented with it at the Fondation Cartier in Paris, at the Musée du Quai Branly and the Square Vinet in Bordeaux, which since 2005 has featured the largest vegetalised wall in France (400 square metres). Many others have followed in his footsteps, proposing various ways of covering a vertical surface with vegetation, and hymning the merits of doing this in terms of sound and temperature insulation, of biodiversity, and of aesthetics of course. Paris now has more than 9,000 square metres of green facades covering more than a hundred walls. And in 2015 Paris also boasted 5.6 hectares of vegetalised roofs: this is another increasingly prominent way of fostering the introduction of the vegetal into towns, for insulation and biodiversity again, but also for the management of rainwater. Again, to augment the presence of the vegetal in towns, we do not hesitate to, in a sense, deracinate it: it should be mobile. It is so when planted in pots, of course, and this practice is still used. But some innovative undertakings go further. Thus, in Lille the Saprophytes, a 'poetico-urban collective' of architects and landscapers, are developing urban projects of all kinds – tiny or ephemeral spaces, furniture construction workshops, etc. - and they incorporate into these the principles of guerrilla gardening by establishing mobile kitchen gardens in shopping trolleys.

These various initiatives are going to evolve, but they cannot yet replace a garden or a park on the ground. Always, and above all, greening is expensive.

The financial challenge: When green is worth gold

In fact, creating a promenade or a garden is not just a matter of freeing up enough land, taking into account the restrictions of the terrain, but also about taking into account the cost of improvement that the public finances can bear, and this was as true of the *Ancien Régime* as of more contemporary times. This was the challenge which Louis-Urbain-Aubert de Tourny, Intendant of Guyenne, (1743–1757), took up in pursuing the policy initiated by his predecessors of beautifying Bordeaux. Despite Bordeaux's economic success the budget allocated to the Intendant was meagre, just a few thousand *livres*. But happily for Tourny's project the obstacle represented by the amount of land taken up by the Chateau Trompette turned into an advantage, because part of the reserve of land that it represented could be used at minimal cost. While there was no question of purely and simply demolishing the citadel reinforced by Vauban, the royal power was in no way opposed to it being invaded by peaceful planted pathways, to serve as promenades.

The idea emerged in 1746 of a garden linked to them, the first public garden in Bordeaux, taking the Tuileries as a model. Tourny sought the co-operation of Jacques-Ange Gabriel to design a French garden in the great tradition of Le Nôtre. In order to convince the municipality to support this ambitious project he took care to approach the issue of the land by way of a number of real estate transactions involving only the town, which sold land on the esplanade in order to buy a part of the glacis, then planted with vines and market gardens. Tourny promised economies, even anticipating using earth from the old promenade terracing to fill in the garden. He had not, however, foreseen that to secure the perfectly rectangular form desired by the architect (or something like it!) would take almost a decade in the law courts to overcome the resistance of a handful of owners implicated by expropriations around the boundary. These procedural vexations and the cost over-runs generated by prestigious improvements (terraces, porticoes, a pond) exacerbated the tensions between the Intendant and the municipal authorities and besmirched his popularity, despite the garden's scenographic effect.

Even if taxpayers were increasingly persuaded of the benefits of such public improvement, it was still necessary to spare their wallets as far as possible. New solutions gradually emerged, attaining maturity during the nineteenth century. The Englishman Joseph Paxton showed the way to economy, and was masterfully followed by Alphand in Paris: Baron Haussmann could justifiably boast of having achieved great natural improvements to the capital at minimal cost. This was the case for instance with the Bois de Boulogne: in the end Paris only disbursed 3.5 million of the fourteen million francs it had cost, the balance being absorbed by a state contribution towards the racecourse and by the sale of surrounding land that had been expropriated. The same pattern is found everywhere: land is rebought or expropriated and part is made into a park. The rest is built on, resold or rented. The presence of the park improves the area, the price of real estate rises, and fine gains are made. The most indicative example of this practice concerned the Parc Monceau, which was bought in 1860 by the city of Paris from the state and the Orléans family for a little over nine million francs. Of the original nineteen hectares, just 8.5 were made into a park. The remaining ten or so were sold to Émile Pereire for eighteen million francs – and he undertook the division of the land to construct private houses and blocks of flats some of which he could certainly sell for between two and three million!

What style of greenery for the town?

The aesthetic challenge: Veiling and revealing urban space

Introducing the vegetal to the town of course also raises questions of the aesthetic kind. Private individuals in particular are often constrained by the smallness of plots when planning a new garden. How can expectations of harmony, calm and space be fulfilled on just a few dozen square metres? How can the countryside be presented in the heart of a town? In 1820 in his *Plans raisonnés de toutes les espèces de jardins* (*Well Reasoned Plans for All Kinds of Gardens*), Gabriel Thouin described the challenge of city gardens like this: 'They have to offer an easy walkway for exercise, greenery to rest and rejoice the eye, as well as flowers that attract and charm, and scents to captivate the nose, and fruit to satisfy one's taste; and essentially, pure and balmy air able to counter the air one breathes in stuffy apartments and the cess-pit of most streets.'[7] In a lecture a century later, the architect and landscaper Achille Duchêne, creator and renovator of some 6,000 gardens, repeats these constraints and offers some solutions:

> The chief problem is to lend some character and originality to the urban garden. This can only be done if the garden's perimeter is planted with trees and bushes high enough to mask all the houses and walls that often surround it. Sometimes one can plant grown trees eighteen metres tall. When one has to make do with smaller trees, trellises and planters containing ivy or other evergreen climbers can be placed against the walls of neighbouring houses, which can be given a greyish colour to make them less salient ... If the garden is much too small it is best to keep the central part as sand or tiles, and to plant only the perimeter, while leaving adequate grassy surfaces.[8]

It is also worth mentioning here the services offered by professionals to private individuals able to afford a landscaper. The ordinary man in the street who has a garden will have to settle for the plentiful advice offered by landscape designers and their followers in publications which still flourish today. Guides like Albert Caussin's *Un jardin en ville* (*A Town Garden*) show how enduring this preoccupation is. The back cover[9] tells us that it is not just a matter of planting some vegetation and a lawn, but of creating a garden with its 'own character' that can 'give an impression of comfort and relaxation'.

7 Gabriel Thouin, *Plans raisonnés de toutes les espèces de jardins* (Paris: Lebègue, 1820), p. 7

8 'Wireless', lecture by Achille Duchêne, 7 June 1936, in Jean-Christophe Molinier, *Jardins de ville privés, 1890–1930* (n.p., Ramsay de Cortanze, 1991), pp. 47–48.

9 Albert Caussin, *Un jardin en ville* (Alès: Nature et Progrès, 2009).

Aesthetic requirements have varied over time. They are central from the seventeenth to the nineteenth century – with varying dominant styles. In the twentieth century, the idea of green space became more functional than aesthetic, and tended to marginalise somewhat this second aspect, at least in public creations, but private gardens still tended to bear witness to their owners' personalities. The gradual abandoning of this narrow, utilitarian view of the garden over the last thirty years has reintroduced an aesthetic dimension into landscape creation, even if it stresses decorative spectacle less than the re-creation of a 'natural' nature.

In any event, the relationship with the surrounding urban space remains central. As a refuge from urban uproar, an escape-hatch for townsfolk worn out by the hustle and bustle of streets and crossroads, the garden's place in the modern city is that of somewhere closed off, separate. It must help one to forget as far as possible the surrounding town, and this has been so since the end of the nineteenth century, which saw an unequalled growth in the discomforts associated with industrialisation and the transport revolution. Thus, Haussmannian squares are ringed with trees and bushes to lessen noise

Figure 13.

The square of the Batignolles during the Second Empire. Jean-Charles Alphand, *Promenades de Paris* (1867). Courtesy of BNF / Gallica: https://gallica.bnf.fr

and pollution and from these open-air drawing-rooms all the sundry annoyances that could disturb are cast out.

While one might look to keeping oneself away from the immediacy of the town, there is by contrast nothing against viewing it *from afar*. In keeping with theories of the picturesque that have been fashionable since the end of the eighteenth century, landscape designers do not hesitate to respond to the expectations of a public that demands viewing points – looking over the countryside, over particular monuments, even over the urban space as a whole, as long as it appears in the distance. Basically, it is parks which, by virtue of their size, make this duality of attitudes possible. The fine, high and often elaborate grilles surrounding these spaces have a vital role in this regard: they are unlike walls in that they do not totally eradicate the town though marking a clear division between one space and another.

The park cannot be reduced to a self-sufficient closed space: it also makes a link with the urban space, as with the costly Royal Garden in Bordeaux which harmoniously joins the old town with the economically important neighbourhoods of the Chartrons and Saint Seurin. Iconographic heritage shows that the architecture of park and garden entrances was a favoured subject, inspiring artists and enabling them to work both on ornamental details and on the art of perspective.

Highly ornamental park entrances have to attract walkers and so be open onto the town, but at the same time they must ensure both the easy dispersal of the crowd and the calm they seek. In the Parc de la Tête d'Or, in Lyon, while the main entrance was awkwardly placed at the junction of two streets, space was freed up to make it both majestic and welcoming. And more specifically, in the Parc du Thabor in Rennes, the French garden seems to overflow into a new housing estate by virtue of a planted pathway that extends it; from the greenhouses one has a panoramic view over the garden proper, and more distantly over the valley of the river Vilaine. In Béziers at the Plateau des Poètes, one can look over the town from a restful terrace. More contemporary parks have at times to deal with settings that are less conducive to calm and that offer little in the way of pleasant viewpoints. For instance the Parc du Chemin de l'Île, opened in 2006 at Nanterre, has to come to terms with a motorway, an RER railway line and the Papeteries de la Seine paper mill! Covering fourteen hectares beside the Seine and closing the axis between the Louvre and the Grande Arche de La Défense, it cannot rid itself of the chaotic, grandiose urban environment surrounding it; at best, it is able to make the Seine the unifying element in its design. Aquatic plants have been chosen to create an effect of profusion in architecturally designed ponds; a walkway planted with ornamental cherry trees introduces a line of warm colour. The aesthetics of an urban landscape comprising the mineral and the vegetal also derives from the vegetal forms and species that have been preferred in order to create an effect of perspective, to make a palette of colours and to offer seasonal variety.

The challenge of selection: a short review of vegetal fashion

What plants should be planted in town? This is not a new question and was already a preoccupation for elected officials and gardeners in the *Ancien Régime*. Making a choice can be particularly difficult and sometimes polemical with regard to trees which are required to last and therefore to fashion the look of the town over the long term. Should a variety be selected from an economic viewpoint or should a choice be made based on aesthetics? How should plants arriving from distant lands be handled? They may falsely appear to be fragile and sometimes turn out to be a particularly invasive species. The idea that contemporary citizens had of such or such a plant weighed as much in the balance as biological constraints which had nevertheless to be taken into account so that costly plantings did not perish.

The grass lawn was an invention of the *Ancien Régime* in a response to demands for the beautification of prestige spaces. A lawn is a living carpet whose quality depends as much on its composition as on its preparation, which requires the gardeners' whole attention. In the eighteenth century, in a context of widespread enthusiasm for *parterres en broderie*, where lawns and vegetal architecture alternated, lawn maintenance was part of the know-how dealt with in specialised texts. In order to obtain a smooth and even green sward the grass must be cut once a week 'and beat it or else roll it often with wooden & stone rollers as they do the flower beds in England'. The problem also lay in the choice of grass seed: 'It should be noted that a lawn type must be chosen that contains no weeds nor woven roots, but only a true grass that normally sheep graze.'[10] In fact, all through the eighteenth century, agronomists and botanists worked on the art and the manner of composing artificial meadows made up of mixtures of seeds according to whether the aims were economic or recreational. The recipe

10 André Mollet, *Le Jardin de plaisir, contenant plusieurs dessins de jardinage, tant parterres en broderie, compartiments de gazon, que bosquets et autres* (Stockolm: H. Kayser, 1651), chapter XI (not paginated).

for 'France's chosen lawn', which was much appreciated as a 'pleasure lawn' at the beginning of the nineteenth century, bears witness to this development in knowledge about the vegetal:

> Sow fifty to sixty pounds of seed which is a natural mixture coming from meadows, in which one finds, after sifting several times in order to set aside unwanted plants and just leave the following, in fair proportions, *Lolium perenne* or *ray-grass* (English lawn), *Holcus lanatus* or holcus, *Avena elatior* or tall oat-grass, *Poa patensis*, *Medicago lupulina* or black medick, a few *Festuca* ... Add six to eight pounds of small clover, with yellow or white flowers, four to six pounds of red clover and about twenty pounds of sainfoin.[11]

Today, ready-made lawns belong to this long tradition, while they are still the subject of technical innovations which mean they can be adapted for all kinds of functions. Bernadette Lizet studied the rolls of turf ('*enkagazon*') that cover the sides of the pyramid of the Paris Bercy Arena Sports Hall. The pyramid walls are reinforced with a kind of plastic trellis to take the pressure placed on them by the enormous rolls of turf, which are positioned by cable. The regular replacement of these strips of turf requires extensive and complex logistics as cranes and hydraulic winches are needed! Maintenance is not easy either: for the grass to stay the same shade of green, it is heated from beneath, watered with fertiliser and cut regularly, all on a 45 degree slope which requires special equipment, etc.[12]

While the lawn is a good example of artificialised vegetal composition that has made a place for itself in the urban space, one of the more visible consequences of the greening of towns from the eighteenth century onwards nevertheless remains the advancement of the tree.[13] Up until then trees had been regarded with some wariness and were considered to be sources of humidity and therefore insalubrity, so kept away from dwellings.

In the eighteenth century, the works by Bonnet and Duhamel du Monceau on plant respiration showed that, on the contrary, they helped to renew the air. The tree thus became the object of reintegration into urban planning in its own right. Apart from its symbolic significance, the practical implica-

11 Charles-Nicolas-Sigisbert Sonnini de Manoncourt (ed.), *Bibliothèque physico-économique, instructive et amusante : contenant des mémoires & observations-pratiques sur l'économie rurale, sur les nouvelles découvertes les plus intéressantes*, A.2 T.2 (Paris: Buisson, 1804), pp. 293–294.

12 Bernadette Lizet, 'Théâtres végétaux dans la ville : jalons pour une ethnobotanique urbaine', in Francis Hallé and Pierre Lieutaghi, *Aux origines des plantes* (Paris: Fayard, 2008), vol. 2.

13 For a British perspective on this question, see the novel approach of Paul A. Elliott, *British Urban Trees. A Social and Cultural History, c. 1800–1914* (Winwick, Cambridgeshire: The White Horse Press, 2016).

tions were not negligible, since using trees for recreational purposes implied planting dozens or even hundreds of them. The multiplication of trees in the public urban space in the seventeenth and eighteenth centuries made their potential pathologies all the more visible and problematic. A tree is not a column of age-old stone, and replacing a population that is damaged or ageing on the scale of the town represents a considerable investment.

Until the middle of the eighteenth century, therefore, preference went to varieties that were known to be robust but also because they were economically viable – since it was the practice to carry out clearcutting when the trees were mature with the money made from the sale of the wood paying all or part of the cost the new trees planted. The elm (*Ulmus*) was the preferred choice; had not Sully, ever pragmatic, recommended their systematic plantation alongside the roads in the kingdom? It is a great all-rounder, sturdy, exceptionally long-living and may be grown anywhere from cuttings; it provides wood that can be worked as appreciably well as oak. Lastly, it is particularly suitable for planting in staggered rows or in straight lines which means it is easily adapted to the urban space. The elm, in short, should be prioritised in decorating promenades and malls. Sometimes it is ousted in favour of other more local varieties, such as the lime tree in eastern France and the hackberry in the south, or more heavily symbolic ones such as the oak or the olive tree.

Despite the great voyages of exploration and the botanical discoveries thus made, which from the eighteenth century onwards allowed a certain renewal of vegetal fashions in parks and gardens, tradition still carried the day over experimentation. In the nineteenth century, although landscape gardeners spoke about being able to choose from between fifty and a hundred varieties for lining the streets and boulevards, in practice this was reduced to just a few species: above all, the plane tree, the chestnut, always the lime tree, the sophora in the north and still the hackberry in the south. The plane tree in particular, which grows rapidly and whose shade is much appreciated,[14] spread everywhere in the nineteenth century to such an extent that, a century later, in the 1980s, it represented between seventy and eighty per cent of urban French trees. The development of the Promenade du Gravier in Agen, along the banks of the Garonne, is fairly typical. This

14 In Provence, a whole imagination about the shade of trees can lead to favouring certain species over others. The shade of the plane tree is particularly appreciated, as well as that of the hackberry or fig tree. On the other hand, one must be wary of the lime tree, which can make you lose your voice, or of the poplar and walnut, which are considered too humid and harmful. See Caroline Mollie, *Des arbres dans la ville. L'urbanisme végétal* (Arles: Actes Sud, 2009), p. 74.

walk was established in the seventeenth century and a century later it had 185 elms. At that period they were replaced for the first time by other trees of the same species. They were finally cut down in 1867 and this time they were replaced by plane trees – only one elm remained.[15] This primacy of the plane tree was not always very well accepted, as shown a few years later in a little controversy in the town of Montmorency. In 1898, some of the town's residents proposed planting cherry trees on the newly laid out market-place, as a symbol of one of the region's most famous crops. In vain:

> There was the beginning of a subscription fund, petitions, songs and even a consultation among the highest placed members of the French National Society for Horticulture. But the town councillors, most of whom were not native to the region and did not share its history or its reputation, had plane trees planted, like in Paris, because they feared that children would be forever perched in the trees eating the cherries. In vain was it argued that the hundred eyes of Argus in the shape of the shopkeepers on the square were there to keep watch, that the flowers would be charming in the springtime, that the fruits would be sold in the summer and, finally, that the red leaves of the cherry trees would be more pleasant to gaze upon than the immense plane leaves littering the ground …. Enemies of the picturesque, ignorant of the history of the area, they were unrelenting![16]

In fact, over and beyond the plane tree, the choice of tree bears witness to the effects of fashion. The mulberry tree, for example, had its glory days in the seventeenth century – King Henri IV had 15–20,000 planted in the Tuileries Gardens! Following the advice of the agronomist, Olivier de Serres, and with the blessing of Sully who kept a close eye on how the king's money was spent, the king intended to cover the kingdom with mulberry trees in order to compete against Italian silk production. In the eighteenth century, intendants who wished to reinvigorate provincial economies may have been attracted by the prospects shown in the development of silkworm farms: in Auch, in 1755–56, Intendant d'Étigny installed a nursery of 20,000 mulberry saplings along the road to Agen and 6,000 were planted at the town gates. The nursery was a cunning mix of industrial business and a promenade: supervised by a guard in the king's pay, it was divided all along its length by a grass path, bordered on both sides by mulberries, between which were flower beds.[17] Devoid of any economic interest but bathed in an exotic aura,

15 Académie des Sciences, Arts et Lettres d'Agen, *Revue de l'Agenais* (1875): 49–53.

16 Julien Louis Ponsin, 'La cerise de Montmorency', *La Tribune de Seine-et-Oise*, v. 1900, Municipal archives of Enghien-les-Bains (D 221, Montmorency), published by Valmorency. http://www.valmorency.fr/102.html#sdfootnote16sym

17 Maurice Bordes (ed.), *Histoire d'Auch et du pays d'Auch* (Roanne: Éd. Horvath, 1980 (?)), p. 82.

the cedar tree greatly enhanced aristocratic parks and gardens in the eighteenth century after Bernard de Jussieu planted the first specimen in French soil in 1734. The famous cedar of Lebanon in the Jardin des Plantes in the capital, whose offshoots have been sent to the four corners of the kingdom, still spreads its branches under the Parisian sky.

> In the nineteenth century, the acacia met with less unanimity and had as many defenders as detractors. M. Durieu de Maisonneuve, a member of the Linnaeus society of Bordeaux, became very irritated about the fad for the acacia in an 1853 speech on the imminent opening of the city's botanical garden:
> Everywhere people are making hedges of them; there isn't a single sloping bank where acacia is not used; it is frequently planted in coppices, providing no shade and with no prestige, where ladies may not venture without having their dress torn to shreds. It seems to me then, that we have had enough of the acacia and that after having met it everywhere in our countryside we will not find pleasure in seeing it again on our public promenades.[18]

As these comments show, the choice of urban vegetals must answer to many expectations, notably social ones. This is particularly true in the case of exotic plants which form part of the visual identity of certain tourist resorts and there consist in a first-class asset to the point of really supplanting local vegetation and recreating a whole other environment. Excellent examples of this are the towns on the Côte d'Azur which were overwhelmed by the arrival of the railway, in 1861 in Cannes and 1864 in Nice. Tourists flocked there in the winter to enjoy the sun, restore their health, rest and relax or else party. From that time on, a real décor was created for them, architectural, of course – splendid villas sprang up, casinos were built, the number of promenades multiplied – but also vegetal. Many residents became keen on exotic plants: they first proliferated mainly in private parks which were given over to the same follies as seen in Parisian glasshouses. As early as the seventeenth century, the botanical garden of the Toulon Navy enabled people to find rare plants, come from the far-flung colonies; by the nineteenth century, the railway and the good care provided by nurserymen permitted all kinds of vegetal fantasies. Hyères in particular saw the expansion of these new gardens: that of its mayor, M. Denis, in 1865; that of Baron de Bonstetten, which contained plants from Australia and the Cape of Good Hope especially; and above all, though a little outside the town, the garden of the *La Blocarde* villa which was a true, private, botanical garden. Its owner

18 Michel Charles Durieu de Maisonneuve, *Le Nouveau Jardin des Plantes* (Bordeaux: Justin Dupuy, 1853), p. 11.

Figure 14.

Hyères, view of the Promenade des Palmiers in the nineteenth century.
Courtesy of BNF / Gallica.

Hippolyte Dellor became nationally renowned, even putting the municipal Jardin d'Acclimatation, an 1872 annexe of the one in Paris, in the shade.[19] The list is endless and is strung out along the coast…

This fashion for the exotic ended up influencing the public space, as in this description of the public garden in Cannes, created in 1856:

> All the rarities of the tropics, always green and perfumed, have been brought together there and mixed in with local species. The high-forest trees, from oaks and local pines to cedars from Lebanon and the Himalayas, from the magnolias from Carolina and Virginia to the acacias and bitter orange trees of Asia, all vie with shrubs from Brazil and Japan, the Canaries and New Holland, from China and La Plata.[20]

19 B. Chabaud, 'Les jardins de la Côte d'Azur', in A. Robertson-Proschowsky, G. Roster and B. Chabaud, *La Résistance au froid des palmiers* (Marly le roi: Champflour, 1998), pp. 176–178.

20 Robert de Souza, *Nice, Capitale d'hiver*, [1913] (Nice: Serre, 2001), p. 76.

These new possibilities as well as the wish to respond to tourists' expectations by always providing green vegetation – and so avoiding deciduous plants – brought about an upheaval in the landscape in this region which we barely realise today,[21] the eucalyptuses planted for the first time in France in Toulon in 1802; the mimosas introduced in the south during the Second Empire; the bougainvilleas, though collected by Bougainville as early as 1767, only really becoming acclimatised in the 1820s; and, even more emblematic, the palm trees which have colonised this territory and profoundly changed its appearance.[22] These last trees, of which only two varieties are native to France, were acclimatised in the famous 'floral garden' of M. Filhe, in Hyères, around 1820 and the first catalogues were published in 1834. But they only began to spread in an almost industrial manner from the 1860s onwards, giving the promenades of the towns on the Côte d'Azur the appearance that they have today – sometimes arousing annoyance because of the way they multiplied.[23] The identification of this region with palm trees is sufficiently strong, however, for the recent threats that they faced from the spread of the red palm weevil to have caused quite some concern. The town of Antibes had to destroy several dozen of its palm trees and there are fears for the 17,000 palm trees in Nice. Mandelieu la Napoule is also affected. In 2015, *Le Figaro* painted a terrible picture of the future: 'Imagine the Promenade des Anglais without its legendary palm trees! And beyond, the whole of the Mediterranean arc, from Nice to Perpignan, deprived of these majestic trees, synonymous with holidays and sunshine.'[24]

These infatuations are so strong that sometimes they allow a place to be dated by the vegetal varieties planted there: the red/green combination of an *Acer negundo* maple and a *Prunus pissardii* is for example typical of the period 1975–1985.[25] While fashionable trends are not extinct today (there are olive trees everywhere), the move is more towards the diversification of species and a revived interest in indigenous species, in particular to avoid the spread of afflictions which wipe out entire plantations, such as the box tree moth, for which there is no treatment.[26]

21 Ernest J.-P. Boursier-Mougenot and Michel Racine, *Les Jardins de la Côte d'Azur* (Aix-en-Provence: Édisud-Arpej, 1987).

22 Yves-Marie Allain, *D'où viennent nos plantes ?* (Paris: Calmann-Lévy, 2004).

23 Robert de Souza describes the palm tree as a 'feather duster' (*Nice, Capitale d'hiver*, p. 82).

24 'Il faut sauver les palmiers du midi de la France', *Le Figaro*, 23 Oct. 2015.

25 Romaric Perrocheau, director of the plant garden in Nantes, during an interview in April 2014.

26 For all these considerations on the choice of urban trees, see Mollie, *Des arbres dans la ville*, pp. 91–92.

This new preference for home-grown plants instead of non-indigenous ones can be seen, for example, in the advice given for the vegetalising of roofs. Bodies such as the *Muséum National d'Histoire Naturelle* stress the possibilities offered by this new way of greening the environment, encouraged by public authorities in order to increase biodiversity in town. And to do so, the planting of local or native species is encouraged, especially as they are better adapted to the regional climate and thus require less maintenance (particularly concerning watering). The diversity of an ecosystem will also allow it to live longer, for it will resist external constraints better.[27] Finally, such advice aims at limiting the risk of invasive animal or vegetable species spreading, to the detriment of local ecosystems. In this regard, the attitude towards Japanese knotweed is striking: highly prized for its ornamental qualities when it was introduced into Europe in the nineteenth century, today it is considered as an invasive plant that is disastrous for local biodiversity.

Conquering the hostility of the urban environment

The challenge of planting

In 1760, the agronomist and botanist Henri-Louis Duhamel du Monceau (1700–1782) published an illustrated compilation entitled *Des semis et des plantations des arbres et de leur culture* (*The Sowing and Planting of Trees and their Cultivation*), which was aimed more at private individuals. This compendium of knowledge of the period nevertheless allows us to follow the gardener and nurseryman step by step in his practices. He had a fairly short time window for planting large populations of generally between fifty and 200 trees. The success of the operation depended to a large extent on previous preparation of the soil. Before planting, between November and March (when it was not freezing) various tasks had to be carried out which included earthwork, digging trenches where the young trees would stand and improving the quality of the soil by adding good earth to it. Depending on the climate, particular arrangements might have to be made for the drainage of the soil. Gardeners delved into a tradition of empirical knowledge about plants and traces of this can be found in town council minutes. For example,

27 Observatoire Départemental de la Biodiversité Urbaine de Seine-Saint-Denis, Natureparif, Plante & Cité, Muséum National d'Histoire Naturelle, *Réaliser des toitures végétalisées favorables à la biodiversité*, October 2011, accessible online: http ://www.natureparif.fr/attachments/Documentation/livres/Toitures-vegetalisees.pdf

the entrepreneur responsible for planting the avenue which links the historic centre of Nîmes and the Jardins de la Fontaine was instructed to give these pathways a curved shape in order to evacuate rainwater down the sides so this would water the road-lining trees.[28] Another condition for successful planting: the species chosen had to adapt to local soil conditions. If planners did not take this into account, then they would be laying themselves open to painful experiences. Alphand thus reveals that two thirds of the resinous species planted in the sandy soil in the Bois de Boulogne did not survive!

More generally, the particular conditions that the town had to offer to plants had to be taken into consideration and these were often very far from favourable to their growth. The urban environment seemed to become more and more hostile to the vegetal, as ways of life and the environment became more artificial over the nineteenth century. People were told to beware of plants growing too close to walls, which reflected light, or the 'perfidious' rays of the setting sun; city dwellers (and their pets) also seemed to take liberties with plants, for example, by relieving themselves against or at the foot of a tree... And yet, much more serious were the soil and the atmospheric conditions that towns could offer the plants.[29]

The soil was the first to be incriminated: insufficiently rich, composed of gravel and debris, it had to receive an addition of good earth and be well loosened. But sometimes there was not enough room for the roots to develop, they also found themselves severed during roadworks or else struggled to extend themselves when the trees were planted too close to one another. Moreover, so that the water can penetrate the soil properly, care must be taken to avoid the earth being packed down by the comings and goings of pedestrians. In order to do this, from the Second Empire on, metal grids of one or two metres diameter were systematically installed around trees and sometimes they were even linked up by means of intermediary grids. But despite this, tarmac, asphalt and paving stones nevertheless reduced the watering of the lateral roots which move away from the trunk: to keep them humid, sometimes an elaborate drainage system was installed, linked to the drains in order to carry away excess water. Dryness is still one of the

28 'Arrêts du Conseil, et devis pour la construction des nouveaux canaux et bassins de la fontaine de Nîmes et pour l'embellissement de ses avenues. Années 1740-1747', in Léon Ménard, *Histoire civile, ecclésiastique et littéraire de la ville de Nismes avec les preuves* (Paris, H.D. Chaubert, 1744–1758), vol. 7, pp. 191–192.

29 Société d'horticulture, années 1820, Archives Nationales, F13, 868-870, in Marie-Blanche d'Arneville, *La France des jardins et des espaces verts de 1789 à 1870*, Ph.D. at Paris-Sorbonne University in 1986 under the supervision of Jean Tulard, p. 109.

major problems today as regards the healthy state of trees in town. This, for example, was the conclusion of a study carried out in Saint Quentin en Yvelines at the end of the 1980s: of the 15,000 trees studied, the study concluded that the plantation fail rate was twenty per cent (that is, the death of the tree and the need to replace it), and this was explained above all by lack of water – even though the study also highlighted other problems, such as poor preparation of the soil (which explains a fail rate of 44 per cent in city parks!), a lack of follow-up on the trees, a policy of going with the lowest bidder, leading to the supply of poor quality plants, etc.[30] It also happens that the soil is polluted. In the nineteenth century fumes from gas lighting were particularly singled out. In the second half of the century, public lighting in towns was provided by gas lamps which were supplied by unreliable gas pipes (in London it was estimated that thirty per cent of the gas was lost either in the earth or else into the atmosphere). Gas companies were then obliged to wrap their pipes in tubing or add pebbles for drainage and to install their connections in such a way that they gave onto the outside world – the smell of gas would thus make it possible to detect a leak. If the soil was too contaminated, there was no hesitation about removing it, aerating it and then replacing it. In the middle of the 1850s in Paris it was estimated that 200 trees a year fell victim to gas.[31] Still today, gas leaks can asphyxiate trees by the roots. Finally, different products thrown on the roadway can harm a tree – early use of salt for removing snow is the most common example and the most criticised (plane trees which stock the toxic ions in snow-removal salt poison themselves by spreading these around their young organs during growth phases); and the same is true of weedkillers.

If the elements have to be battled in order to make the soil more adapted to the growth of magnificent trees, then one also has to be mistrustful of the atmosphere in cities which does not always do trees any favours either, even if its effects are far from being as important as those of the soil. Apart from town gas fumes, already mentioned, the smoke from different factories also had to be reckoned with for it causes vegetation to wither – an 1896 treatise spoke of 'sulphurous' acid as being the most harmful of all and thus recommended moving trees away from insalubrious establishments. More

30 Claude Guineau, 'Saint-Quentin-en-Yvelines. Le comportement des arbres en ville nouvelle', *Metropolis (urbanisme, planification régionale, environnement)*, special issue *L'Urbanisme végétal* (1992) 96–97.

31 Alexandre Jouanet, *Mémoire sur les plantations de Paris* (Paris: Imprimerie Horticole de J.-B. Gros, 1855), p. 61.

generally, the amount of dust borne in the air and its dryness were often mentioned as limiting factors. In the twentieth century in France, and until the 1980s, dust and SO^2 were the main sources of urban pollution and were caused by central heating oil and coal. Their impact is double: the destruction of lichens which have disappeared from urban spaces and the weakening of trees, which then become more sensitive to other aggressions by the town. Thus, French poplars fell victim in 1985 to a disease known as *witches' broom* (the topmost branches wither while the lower branches multiply) caused by bacteria whose proliferation is linked to pollution and to drought. After the 1980s, urban pollution has been caused above all by automobiles. Carbon dioxide is not in itself particularly poisonous to trees but high concentrations caused by certain meteorological conditions are much more harmful. Their impact depends on the species but globally it has been shown that high doses of ozone slow the growth of poplars and cause necrosis of the leaves of the most exposed specimens. This has been noticed in particular in some towns in the south of France during the summer period.[32]

Faced with such unfavourable atmospheric and rainfall conditions the first line of defence and also the oldest, remains the selection of species according to where they are going to be planted. As Duhamel du Monceau explained, each plant, or shrub or average tree destined for use in fencing or for tall growth must receive appropriate treatment which differs from one species to another according to the amount of space allotted to it (a pathway, park or garden). As it is not a question of sowing trees, the choice of plants in the nursery is vital: trees for tall growth must be about eight to ten feet (about 2.5 to 3.5 metres) with a diameter of seven to nine inches (seventeen to 24 centimetres) which proves that they are already several years old. Moving the trees is a delicate undertaking: the longer the transport, the more the root system risks drying out. It is always possible to keep the lump of earth around the roots, to preserve the most expensive trees, but the cost of the operation reflects this for they have to be carried upright, in a box. More common trees are bundled together in groups of half a dozen or ten or so then loaded horizontally on beasts of burden or in wagons. They have their tops cut off beforehand to avoid damaging the branches during transport. Once they arrive at their destination the trees are raised on the spot prepared for them inside a trench. The most fragile plants have to be raised with the help of lifting devices

32 On the health of urban trees, see Louis-Marie Rivière (ed.), *La Plante dans la ville* (Paris: INRA, 1997), third part ('La plante dans la ville : sujet de recherches') and particularly André Vigouroux, 'Les dépérissements d'arbres en ville', pp. 249–265.

In the nineteenth century these logistical challenges were all the more daunting, since the creation of parks, gardens and green spaces had now become inscribed in the framework of public action and concerned huge surface areas. It was truly a case of *bringing* nature to the town: the promised parks had to be at maturity on the day they opened – at least in the main outlines and the masses; people could not wait for ten years to see a tree grow when it had been planted in the middle of a lawn that it should embellish. But plants and especially trees, long-living perennial and cumbersome, required care, speedy action and tools adapted for their transport. The breadth of works carried out during the Second Empire required faultless organisation and ground-breaking innovations. Public actors can always make a deal with nurserymen, who are numerous throughout the land, with specialisations according to the regions. But to keep costs down, a system of municipal nurseries began to spread, particularly in large cities, as we saw in the previous chapter.

Once the supply of plants had been assured, then it was a question of transporting them. One would be wrong to think that a park or garden is a place of stable, continuous plantations. In fact, they change all the time: new flowers are planted to replace those that have faded and in winter the fragile and precious plants are placed in greenhouses and brought out when the weather turns fine. There is therefore a constant circulation of plants in the city, between the parks and the municipal glasshouses.

This movement requires a few adjustments in order to take care of the plants. Édouard André tells us that, to decorate the interiors of public establishments and ministries, 'a special service of closed and heated vehicles has been organised for the transport of indoor plants during the cold season'.[33] In his famous *Promenades de Paris*, Adolphe Alphand describes the three kinds of carts invented for this purpose and used when decorating the Bois de Boulogne. They varied in their cost and their robustness, from 700 to 8,500 francs! Seven to nine horses could thus haul trees that were about twenty metres tall.

Some trees, because they had a symbolic value, received special attention when they were moved. This was the case for one of the great magnolias in Bordeaux which was moved from the old botanical garden to the new public garden opened in the city in 1857. It was carried on a specially built railway, two kilometres long. Sixty men and thirty horses were needed to

33 Édouard André, *Revue Horticole* (1882): 459, in Lejeune, *Édouard André*, p. 50.

Figure 15.

Transporting a tree in the Bois de Boulogne, at the beginning of the twentieth century. Courtesy of BNF / Gallica: https://gallica.bnf.fr

dig it out and transport it in front of a crowd which gathered along the rail track. This adventure lasted six days, from 30 April to 5 May and cost the city 10,000 francs – and the magnolia is still there.

While curiosity is normal for particular events like this transportation, most of the time these technical exploits just became commonplace and part and parcel of the perpetual upheaval in towns during the Second Empire, particularly in Paris. A blasé contemporary was thus able to comment in 1861:

> as things are at present, they'll plant a fifty-foot chestnut with no more fuss than if it were a Chinese rose. It's a bit more expensive but that's all. But for the practice, it's an everyday occurrence. You're visiting one of your friends who dwells quietly on the third floor. Suddenly, you see a tree go past the window: it's some modest remains of an old boulevard that's been razed to the ground that's on its way to settle in a new avenue. What do you expect? Paris is being so turned upside down that the trees are obliged to move.[34]

Taken to an excess, this logic of the objectification of the tree might lead to what Caroline Mollie has named the 'vegetal kit': against all urban planning or botanical logic, the transport and installation of adult trees to fill in all the gaps in the town: hence centuries-old Spanish olive trees are reduced to a tenth of their crown and travel in pots around Europe from grove to stand or from pavement to garden. This 'ready-to-plant' is particularly well illustrated by the highly controversial *silvarium* (forest under glass) of the French National Library.[35] In order to plant within this place of learning 'a part of the forest of Fontainebleau' in accordance with the wishes of the architect Dominique Perrault, it was necessary to find Scots pines about fifty years old and about twenty metres tall. They could not be found in nurseries so were removed from the state-owned forest at Bord (Eure), a site which was to be cleared of trees. In 1992, 130 pines were uprooted with their clumps of soil and received special care out of the ground for about two years. During all the autumn of 1994, it took no fewer than forty special convoys to bring these venerable trees to the 13th arrondissement where a crane installed them behind their (last) glass home. Like in the Second Empire, the transport turned out to be the most expensive: each tree cost 50,000 francs, of which just 350 francs was the price of the tree…[36] The arguments about this thirty

34 F. de Lasteyrie, *Les Travaux de Paris, examen critique* (Paris:Lévy frères, 1861), pp. 35–36, in Limido, *L'Art des jardins sous le Second Empire*, p. 57.

35 Mollie, *Des arbres dans la ville*, for the two phrases 'vegetal kit' and 'ready-to-plant'.

36 Pierre Alphandéry and Olivier Nougarède, 'Le silvarium de la Grande Bibliothèque', *Courrier de l'environnement de l'INRA* **24** (1995): 59–66.

million franc 'forest' have continued ever since and the most critical comments emphasise the poor rooting and almost total lack of growth of these trees, which are still harnessed by guy ropes.

The ailing vegetal: looking after it and caring for it

Since the urban vegetal is often conceived as decor and because plants are set in an environment which is not very favourable to them, they must be looked after on a regular basis. They cannot be left on their own. One of the most complex problems is undoubtedly that of watering. This is not just a necessity for flowers: trees need it in their compacted city soils, lawns need it in order to stay green and even dusty pathways require it for the comfort of those who stroll there. Watering by hand is not always possible, so, as early as the seventeenth century, to water pathways they used wagons pulled by horses and on these they set barrels holding a cubic metre which were pierced with holes from which the water could trickle out. The system was perfected by a tube dragged behind the cart, two metres long and punched full of holes. The procedure was costly, slow and required a great deal of water: just over a kilometre was covered in an hour and the barrel was refilled three times! In the 1850s a more mobile and less cumbersome watering machine was invented and gardeners used it to water pathways and lawns without inconveniencing passers-by.

But it was not until the works of Alphand and Haussmann were carried out in Paris in the Second Empire that perfected watering systems were installed on a large scale, using piping buried underground and with over 1,600 watering points in the Bois de Boulogne alone. However, not being able to make use of rubber, the watering hoses were made of leather and then of tin plate to reduce costs. Several sheet-metal tubes, tarred on the inside for water-tightness were thus linked together by leather nozzles over a length of more than twelve metres.[37] In 1895, the Lumière brothers film *Le Jardinier (The Gardener)* (better known by the title *L'Arroseur arrosé / The Sprinkler Sprinkled)* shows these pipes assembled together. From the beginning of the twentieth century, the widespread use of rubber joined up with metal grids that were more and more extensive made watering easier in both urban and rural environments.

Nevertheless, the water problem remained an important challenge for those who managed green spaces, particularly in the south of France where water is

37 Adolphe Alphand, *Les Promenades de Paris* (Paris: Rothschild, 1868), pp. 18–20.

Figure 16.

Jeannot, 'Rond Point of the Champs Élysées. L'arrosage', *Topographie de Paris* (1882). Courtesy of BNF / Gallica: https://gallica.bnf.fr

scarce. The minutes of a meeting held by the Academy of Agriculture reveal that in the 1970s manufacturers of watering equipment began suggesting techniques that would help to save water. In 1975 note was made of 'the progress made in the methods and the watering equipment that make it easier to use or is even automatic. This trend has continued and in fact research and projects into the use of drip irrigation have already responded to the concern about tackling waste which has already been highlighted.'[38] Since that time there has been a growing awareness about the issues around water, to the extent that cities have adopted measures for its rational use which their communications departments send out to all residents. At the present time, any extravagant deployment of water will only shock people and offend potential voters. The climate context and repeated heatwave phenomena, in particular during the summer of 2015, have continued to raise more public awareness about the question of water. To try to solve such concerns, the city of Montpellier, for example, has over the past few years set up a very sophisticated system which limits water consumption. First of all, in certain spots, in particular on roundabouts, there are floral arrangements of local plants which need no watering, or very little. Also, 37 kilometres of drip irrigation have been installed, as well as over a thousand timers, plus rain gauges which can help to measure the water need of large areas, and also systematic computerised monitoring of the weather, etc.[39] Watering is not the only care required by vegetation in town: plants also need to be pruned and receive fertiliser, the soil around them needs to be hoed and dead leaves and branches removed. If, despite the care it receives, a plant dies, it can often be replaced: the operation is easy in most cases, except of course when it is a tree – which by its very nature belongs to the long term. However, even when planted in favourable conditions and chosen because it is resistant, the tree in an urban environment is subject to many kinds of aggression. Numerous animals, cars and passers-by brush past, touch and bang into such trees, more so than in a less artificial location and they damage them and weaken them. Various systems of protection have been thought up. As early as the seventeenth century, the design of promenades and public gardens included the issue of how the space should be divided up for different uses. It was planned to make rows of ditches and little walls or other barriers, or even just plain stone benches, which would guide those moving round the garden either on foot or on horseback or in a carriage.

38 Académie d'agriculture de France, *Comptes rendus des séances de l'Académie d'agriculture de France* (Paris: Académie d'Agriculture de France, 1975), vol. 61, p. 399.

39 Gaëlle Aggéri, *Inventer les villes-natures de demain. Gestion différenciée, gestion durable des espaces verts* (Dijon: Educagri Éditions, 2010).

Figure 17.

An area reserved for walking: 'Vue du cours à Marseilles'. Eighteenth-century engraving. Courtesy of BNF / Gallica: https://gallica.bnf.fr

As these provisions were not sufficient to protect the trees, especially the young saplings which were more fragile, individual harnessing was deployed. The trunks were matched with a stake and tied to it by entwining iron wire and thorny branches (hawthorn, blackthorn) up to a height of about 1.7 metres from the ground. This technique of using thorns was practised until the middle of the nineteenth century as it was supposed to discourage animals from eating the trees, as well as human maliciousness.

This technique was not very aesthetic and was gradually replaced by a corset made of nine to ten branches two metres high, painted green and strongly curved at the foot, then brought together by circular hoops. This system did not prevent the tree from growing protected it while not offending the gaze. Other ingenious systems were aimed at helping old trees that had been replanted to recover by protecting them from the heat of the city: their whole height was swathed in a layer of foam rubber at the top of which a zinc goblet let water trickle slowly down in order to provide constant humidity.

On a more general scale, trees have to be cared for. If they are planted too close to houses, not only does this have a negative effect on their growth but it is also known that residents whose view is blocked will damage them.

Regular pruning is also often necessary to contain the volume of the crown of the tree: its ornamental role in lining a route, for example, requires such treatment and, moreover, traffic movement sometimes comes into conflict with unlopped trees. For its wellbeing, the tree itself requires a balance between the volume of its roots – greatly reduced in town – and the size of its crown, or else it will rapidly wither.

Similarly, efforts are made to protect trees against certain insects which may harm them, and in particular caterpillars. A 1732 decree from the Paris parliament, renewed in 1786, ordered private citizens to remove caterpillars from their trees and hedges and to burn the cocoons before the month of March or else face a stiff fine. This measure, which was reissued later by the Paris police prefect, did not seem to be well obeyed, so that public plantations near gardens were quickly attacked in turn by these very same caterpillars.[40]

The issue of the health of trees and vegetation in the city is, as we have seen, not a new topic. Under the *Ancien Régime* their decline alarmed public officials and the gardeners and scientists who were called on to help. These worries were all the more justified as, far from being invulnerable, the elm which had been believed to be so vigorous and had been planted everywhere since the seventeenth century, turned out to be particularly sensitive to attacks by parasites. In the second half of the eighteenth century the elm was being ousted by trees from other continents that were nevertheless perfectly adapted to European soils and climates. They were appreciated more for their ornamental qualities than for any economic use and finished by taking the lion's share of urban space, as we saw earlier. The biological factor of vulnerability or otherwise to disease of certain species has thus contributed to the development of fashions in vegetation.

Faced with an ailing plant, scientists seemed as ill-equipped as gardeners and nurserymen, which does not mean that they gave up imagining answers based on accumulated observations about the way nature worked. The work done by Duhamel du Monceau, who discovered the mechanisms of sap circulation in 1744, helped stimulate professional and amateur botanists in their interest in plant physiology. The archives from the Royal Academy of Sciences and provincial academies bear witness to the vitality of research into combatting tree diseases. The Academy of Toulouse nearly used this topic in a competitive examination: it was 1787 and the elms in the city were withering visibly. The foliage that was the pride and the pleasure of strollers had changed into skinny twigs and

40 Alexandre Jouanet, *Mémoire sur les plantations de Paris*, p. 57.

only drew pitying gazes. The public authorities were alerted and undertook an estimation of the damage: 4,250 elms planted along the city's promenades, boulevards and quays were potentially affected by a disease whose causes had not been identified. Everyone applied his skill, one suspected the quality of the soil, another criticised the tree-pruning practices, someone else pointed to the three years of drought and the vegetation suffering from lack of water. Picot de Lapeyrouse, an eminent amateur botanist was consulted on the subject by the Capitouls (magistrates) and in August 1787 he delivered his judgement in a paper addressed to the Academy of Toulouse.[41] He had discovered the guilty party in the world of entomology and revealed the identity to the public: it was a small insect, the elm leaf beetle, whose larvae, hatching beneath the bark of the tree, fed on its leaves. The scientist thought that the drought had been an aggravating factor and he suggested two solutions to save the elms on the promenades: remove the damaged bark or else water the foliage at night using fire pumps to knock off the larvae. In neither case was the remedy easy to apply on a large scale and they were both fallible. The uncertainty surrounding these solutions did not prevent agronomists, gardeners and enlightened amateurs from continuing to experiment with techniques and formulas that were the topics of a multitude of treatises published on keeping plants healthy. At the end of the nineteenth century, some of this empirical knowledge would be considered obsolete following the general spread of phytosanitary products produced by the chemical industry, which were effective, apparently, but whose use would prove to have serious consequences for the ecosystems.

Another aspect of research into plant health dealt with the artificial improvement in this area. Empirical efforts to 'make' a more resistant plant or one that was bred for very specific uses, date back to the birth of agriculture. However, innovations in the field of agronomy accelerated from the sixteenth century onwards: techniques that helped improve the most useful or the most appreciated species were refined, as was famously the case with tulips. Until the mid-twentieth century, apart from the careful selection of varieties, the principal concern was dealing with the external envelope of the plant, for example by grafting. However, by the end of the nineteenth century, knowledge about the microscopic structures of plants made a leap forward: from 1880 plant chromosomes were under study. The work of agronomy engineers turned towards genetics and in the 1970s they were able to modify

41 M. de Lapeyrouse, 'Mémoire sur la mortalité des ormes dans les environs de Toulouse', in *Histoire et mémoires de l'Académie royale des sciences, inscriptions et belles-lettres de Toulouse* (Toulouse: D. Desclassan, 1788), vol. 3, pp. 197–218.

the genome of plant species to respond to specifically targeted issues. For example, following the damage done to French elms by Dutch elm disease, a disease carried by a fungus, scientists at the INRA (*Institut National de la recherche agronomique* – French National Institute for Agricultural Research) created resistant hybrids that were physiologically and aesthetically adapted to the urban environment. These genetic manipulations, more effective and less harmful than large-scale chemical treatment, were also carried out on plane trees to strengthen them (with less success) against attacks from the cerastocystis platani fungus, which in the 1970s devastated several colonies of trees between Marseille and Lyon and which is still active today. Thus, in the twentieth century, the issue of plant pathologies was the subject of hyperspecialised research that was highly technical but did not exclude ethical thinking, particularly with regard to the controversial use of GM crops.

An identical movement is developing around the daily care of urban plants: the subject is too important for the agents whose mission this is not to be fully involved and for this task to be carried out without the benefit of new technologies. Before the Second Empire, municipal authorities always had the possibility of cancelling agreements with private contractors who did not provide satisfaction; such a recourse has become more delicate because public administration has become so much more complex since the second half of the nineteenth century. During the three decades of the *Trente Glorieuses,* in most French towns, the 'green spaces departments' routinely carried out drastic tree pruning to make room for new buildings or to ease traffic flow. To use André Vigouroux's choice expression,[42] trees ended up being viewed as 'urban furniture' in the continuation of the hubristic technicality in vogue since the nineteenth century. In fact, the spectacular growth in scientific knowledge during this period and the accompanying ideal of world domination led to thinking that possibilities were infinite: in the long run, any combinations of plants seemed possible in the imaginations of landscape gardeners and urban planners; there was no obstacle that could not be overcome. It was only in the 1980s that this supposition came to be questioned. The enquiries then carried out into the health of urban trees were alarming: there were many whose pitiful state meant that they needed to be replaced. In Castres, for example, thanks to a phytosanitary diagnosis, it was discovered in 1988 that half of the 500 planes in the town centre

42 André Vigouroux, 'Les dépérissements d'arbre en ville', 262.

were impaired![43] The consequences were worrying enough for the Ministry of Works, and then the Ministry for the Environment in 1982 to launch a programme for the protection and promotion of decorative trees, under the leadership of Caroline Mollie, in the context of a landscaping programme.

Tree pruning methods in particular have been the subject of innumerable debates, right up to the present, following the thinking of landscape gardeners who questioned mindless lopping that did not take into account the specific nature of each tree. In fact, since the 1970s, there has been a reaction to the excessive 'objectification' of the vegetal and a new scientific discipline has emerged, that of 'vegetal architecture', which seeks to understand how trees develop and what the processes that determine their shapes are. Understanding the mechanisms of regeneration after trauma, for example, helps to guide thinking about pruning methods but also to determine the tree's state of health. Recent research has thus shown that architectural styling which is often specific to towns (curtain shapes, canopy, cat's head) is beneficial to trees as long as they are regularly cut. It is vital here to be constant, for brutal changes in the way a tree is treated can only damage it.[44] To these theoretical reflections of the past thirty years are now added the possibilities offered by the digital age. In most towns, over the last few years, an almost personalised monitoring of each tree has been set up and they sometimes have a veritable digital identity card. This is the case in Greater Lyon, for example, where the data base 'Dryade' receives over thirty parameters for each of the 54,000 route-lining trees of a hundred different species within the urban community.[45]

These modifications reveal deep changes in the expectations of city dwellers regarding green spaces, which have created new constraints on the greening of the city. In fact, municipal authorities have found themselves facing imperatives that are sometimes difficult to reconcile: people want green spaces that are 'clean' and tidy, almost artificial in their perfection, as well as demanding more eco-friendly management of these same places,[46] in the context of ever more urgent claims in favour of a healthy environment and sustainable towns. Confronted with this

43 Corinne Bourgery, 'Castres, le renouvellement des arbres urbains', *Metropolis (urbanisme, planification régionale, environnement),* Special issue *L'urbanisme végétal* 96–97 (1992).

44 Claude Hedelin et al. 'L'architecture végétale dans la conduite des arbres urbains', and Gérard Bory et al. 'L'arbre et les opérations de taille', in Louis-Marie Rivière (ed.), *La Plante dans la ville*, pp. 187–205.

45 Emmanuel Boutefeu, *Composer avec la nature en ville* (Paris: CERTU, 2001), p. 172.

46. On the birth of the ecological management of green spaces, see Gaëlle Aggeri, *Inventer les villes-natures de demain* (Dijon: Educagri, 2010).

challenge, responses have been diverse ever since the first experiments took place in the 1980s in Rennes and Orléans; the most common has been 'differentiated management' which today has been adopted by about 200 French towns: each space is treated differently according to what is expected of it. Thus, in Caen in 2005, the environment and quality of life department decided on differentiated treatment of 'weeds': 'prestige' public spaces, scattered throughout the town (and not just in the city centre as is often the case) are systematically weeded but by non-chemical methods (hoeing, hot water, flame-guns). The other spaces are mown and weeded less regularly so that flora can develop and grow spontaneously. The result has been spectacular: between 2005 and 2010 the phytosanitary products used have dropped by seventy per cent The city has also been a pioneer in the fight against harmful insects by using other insects, for example by raising ladybirds in the 1980s to attack greenfly. The difficulties with this kind of management, in which a space is expected to be both 'natural' and domesticated, are not just technical ones. They also arise because of city residents' reticence when it comes to seeing some spaces virtually abandoned, or even from gardeners themselves who have to adapt to new methods and conceive of their profession differently.[47] In Nantes, in April 2014, the city's parks department received calls from residents who were furious on seeing that hollyhocks that they had planted in front of their houses, following an initiative by this very department, had just been destroyed by road maintenance personnel who simply saw them as weeds. This is but one example of the difficulties in adjusting behaviour, in reconciling expectations and in responding to the specific constraints of the city.

***

This expansion of the vegetal in all its forms, from the most constrained to the wildest, could engender a final challenge: how to master this phenomenon? Is there not a critical threshold beyond which the vegetal, free, moving and transient, will smother the town? Recently there have been warnings against the obsession with the indiscriminate greening of cities by political decision-makers. In the long run, will we not lose the very essence of the city? This is a location which in fact, above all, is conceived as being anti-nature, a place of artifice. Augustin Berque reminds us that it needs to exist in *contrast* to what it is not – countryside, forest, etc. This is where, like Christian Calenge, he sees the danger of the spread of towns and peri-urbanisation for they create an in-between space, neither nature nor city: 'there is a great

47. Matthieu Tétard, *Le Sauvage dans la ville*, Master's diss., IEP de Toulouse, 2012.

risk of seeing urban space being diluted to the point where, stripped of any density, it could no longer claim to be a town'.[48] The phenomenon of *edge cities*, which so far is typically American, is the incarnation of this dilution – and paradoxically these are turning out to be anti-ecological. The increase in distances, intensive watering and use of phytosanitary products, both of which are necessary to maintain immaculate lawns, have ended up creating a model that is a great consumer of natural resources... The town has been criticised for wanting to offer everything: wild nature, agricultural spaces, recreational parks, etc.[49] While one might be wary of greenness, it is of course not a question of excluding it from the town – for the city could not exist without nature in its widest sense (earth, air, water, animals), which makes it possible for it to exist in the first place, or without plant life in particular. But this should not be done at the cost of forgetting what fundamentally a town is, nor at the cost of losing public space where the heart of the *polis* beats.

> Is this not just a retrospective vision of defunct forms. Maybe not, if we observe the dual rise of ecological concerns and landscape issues in our societies. The first of these, sooner or later will oblige us to distinguish between the point of ecosystems (and the global interest of the biosphere) from that of the indefinite pursuit of exurbanisation. As for the second of these, this will imply that, more and more, the town, the countryside and the forest are turning towards their own image: for the town to be urban, for the countryside to be rustic and the forest wild.[50]

Michel Vernes, one of the founders of the School of Architecture at Paris-La Villette, traces this crisis in urbanism back to the eighteenth century when the break between nature and town was conceived, or even to the nineteenth century when the town became a place of damnation. According to Vernes, the perception of the vegetal as a remedy, the indiscriminate greening of the town to blur its misdeeds and to try literally to forget it in an abundance of leaves, trees and flowers, transforms nature into a device for erasing the past, for the sterilisation of urban space, in short, an element of 'disurbanism'. The city would lose its soul therein and gardens would 'rise up' against the town,[51] whereas they had originally been conceived as incarnating a particular order of the urban world.

48. Christian Calenge, 'De la nature de la ville', *Les Annales de la Recherche Urbaine*, Special issue *Natures en villes* 74 (1997): 19.
49. Lise Bourdeau-Lepage and Roland Vidal, 'Nature urbaine en débat : à quelle demande sociale répond la nature en ville ?' *Démeter* (2013): 195–210.
50. Augustin Berque, 'Des toits, des étoiles', *Les Annales de la Recherche Urbaine,* Special issue *Natures en villes* 74 (1997): 10. See also Augustin Berque, Histoire de l'habitat idéal (Paris: Le Félin, 2016).
51. Michel Vernes, 'Les jardins contre la ville', *Temps libre* 9 (Spring 1984): 47.

4.
VEGETAL THEATRE

> As urban areas are extended and peopled, the need to breathe a purer air and to enjoy the sight of the sky and of greenery is ever more deeply felt. The mood of society and the taste for open-air entertainments have prompted the establishment of large areas where the public can gather. [Public gardens and promenades] have become a necessity in recent times, especially for those living in temperate zones.[1]

Contemporary observers themselves recognised that introducing nature into a town in an orderly way answers to what was called 'the spirit of society' in the eighteenth century, the social practices and other relationships that bring together the diverse constituents of urban society.[2] Like other urban public spaces – squares, streets and cafés for instance – parks and gardens are places of meeting and sharing, and of exclusion and hierarchy. Nature is thus the stage-set for an ever-replayed theatre of appearances, in the context of the social order desired by authority. But the play of distinctions is not conveyed only by the use of urban greenery as a stage backdrop: in the case of private gardens, with their often exotic or rare vegetation, the use of greenery can be the vehicle of an assertion of social identity.

Living together in urban nature

Open air salons

In the eighteenth century, many natural spaces were public or semi-public. At busy times silence abandoned the shaded pathways of gardens, streets and promenades. The historian Arlette Farge set about using Parisian police archives to reconstruct a complex world of sound generated by the wanderings and doings of a mixed crowd of townspeople, all ages and classes mixed.

1 Antoine Chrysostome Quatremère de Quincy, *Encyclopédie méthodique* (Paris: Veuve Agasse, 1825), vol. 3, p. 218.

2 Katia Béguin and Olivier Dautresme (eds), *La Ville et l'esprit de société, actes de la journée d'études du 27 mai 2002* (Tours: Presses universitaires François Rabelais, 2004).

> The sound of different voices, of feet scraping on the gravel, the rustling of fabrics against each other, of people blowing their noses, coughing, spitting: all this made such an incredible racket that even if you spoke loudly it seemed that you were only speaking in your ordinary tone.[3]

Distinguished from the speech of ordinary people, laced with provincial accents and diction, were highly accentuated aristocratic voices, scrupulously articulated with tortured phrasing. There were also the international accents of visitors come from all over the world to be part of Parisian high society. And one has to imagine as well the cries and the movements of those playing ball or skittles or shuffleboard, people going past greeting and quizzing each other at a distance, the banter of schoolboys and students, the calls of lemonade-sellers, flower girls and town criers shouting for custom. As the day goes on, laughter becomes more raucous under the influence of drink, followed by quarrels and outbursts.[4]

To make all this meeting and talk possible, some arrangements had to be made – and if these had a bearing on urban greenery, they risked provoking keen dissatisfaction, for some plant specimens were real markers of urban identity. Intendant Tourny had bitter experience of this when he was setting about reorganising the quays in the port of Bordeaux. The town plan envisaged sacrificing an old elm tree remarkable for its great girth and for the attachment which merchants and seafarers felt for it.

> ... from beneath its shade
> The happy trader, scanning the water surface,
> Sees his ships returning home.
> And old men say that contracts made
> Beneath that calming shade
> Were ever just and true ...
> Bordeaux's fate is with its fate entwined.[5]

Faced with a rebellion from both the urban bourgeoisie and the aristocracy, led by the Duchess of Aiguillon, Tourny had to give way. The 'Duchess's elm', as it was called thenceforward, was preserved and could go on sheltering conversation and commercial deals.

More prosaically, organising green spaces where one could talk also im-

3 François-Marie Mayeur de Saint-Paul, *Tableau du nouveau Palais-Royal, première partie* (London: Maradan, 1788), pp. 134–135.

4 Arlette Farge, *Essai pour une histoire des voix au XVIIIe siècle* (Paris: Bayard, 2009).

5 Claude Carloman de Rulhière and Pierre-René Anguis, *Œuvres de Rulhières, de l'Académie française* (Paris: Ménard et Désenne, 1819), vol. 2, pp. 372–375.

plied somewhere to sit: chairs could be rented. These had featured in public gardens since the end of the seventeenth century: in Paris it was often Swiss Guards who were allowed to hire them out, and they already had the privilege of distributing drinks. From 1760 on, it was one of them, who was already in charge of policing the area, who held this privilege on the Champs-Élysées; when his successor, who was also a Swiss Guard, died in 1777, the Office for Buildings, under the command of the Count of Angiviller, took the opportunity to reorganise not only the policing of this promenade but also the commercial privileges authorised there. The financial interests at stake were substantial: Messieurs Bertoi and Pierlot, who from 1777 were authorised to hire out chairs on the Champs-Élysées, had nine-year renewable titles and each had to pay the king 3,350 *livres* a year![6] Renting several chairs for one's use was a way of advertising financial status. It is surprising that this did not lead to more friendliness with customers. In fact, opportunities for a bit of fiddling being plentiful, hirers of chairs – both men and women – were, like park superintendents, among the most redoubtable figures in public gardens. Some years before the Revolution, the regulars at the Palais Royal entertained themselves with an instructive story about defeating one of these local tyrants. A child's nurse quite properly seated on a hired chair ill-advisedly took a mind to use a second chair the better to change the baby in her care:

> The hirer of the chairs came to remonstrate with her; this made the nurse angry in return, the more so as the hirer of the chairs had roughly pulled away a chair she was resting her feet on. When the nurse refused to pay for the second chair ... the hirer had struck her. There was a nasty scene, and everyone blamed the hirer of the chairs, who was taken away to the guard-room.[7]

It is not surprising that in these conditions, and in step with the opening of parks and their much increased use, at times by very ordinary citizens, benches were thought of: the idea was sufficiently novel for d'Argenville to make an article out of it for the *Encyclopédie*, declaring that 'nothing is so necessary in great gardens as benches: one would have them at the end of every pathway. They have dedicated places, such as turning points and niches in arbours, the ends of walkways, terraces and viewing points.' It is very likely that, up until the middle of the nineteenth century, the only benches

6 Laurent Turcot, 'Former une promenade publique: les Champs Élysées au XVIIIe siècle', in Daniel Rabreau and Sandra Pascalis (dir.), *La Nature citadine au siècle des Lumières* (Bordeaux: Arts & Arts, 2005), pp. 53–54.

7 François-Marie Mayeur de Saint-Paul, *Tableau du nouveau Palais-Royal, deuxième partie* (London: Maradan, 1788), p. 101.

in towns were installed in gardens, before they colonised streets and squares.[8]

Once each one was installed, the space buzzed with news and rumours about politics and the economy, exchanged when people met and chatted for a while. The public garden in the eighteenth century was a new forum, where citizens served their political apprenticeship.

In Paris, the Luxembourg Garden, the Palais Royal and the Tuileries became the 'theatres of news'. On the gates journals and gazettes were to be read, both French and foreign, for a modest fee. And within the gardens, opinion formers had their meeting places. At Palais Royal, politicians gathered in the main walkway around the famous Krakow Tree,

> so-called because Polish affairs were passionately debated there. It was there, like Kings, that they decided the interests of the Great. They determined everything, and pronounced imperiously on all that happened; nothing escaped them; and a General in the army would have got the upper hand if he could have heard and followed the advice of the sublime politicians of the Krakow Tree.[9]

Those who made fun of the readers of the *Gazette de Leyde* and the *Courrier de l'Europe* called it derisively the 'Crackpot Tree'. To the chagrin of the news-merchants, the tree did not survive the great works undertaken by the Duke of Chartres to extend the Palais Royal leisure complex between 1781 and 1784. The beautiful minds took themselves off to the Feuillants terrace in the Tuileries to continue discussing the world's progress, and the farewell of the toppled Tree to its public was represented in a bit of doggerel:

> Farewell famous newsmongers,
> Who, cane in hand, on the ground
> Traced near my dusty trunk
> The Channel or the States lost by England.

In the course of the next decade, the gardens of the Palais Royal recovered their political vocation, to the point of being rechristened 'gardens of the Revolution' after the fall of the monarchy. From the time of the Estates General, they became a meeting place for Third Estate partisans who came for news, and contributed to sustaining public excitement. As the epicentre of agitation in Paris, the gardens, cafés, restaurants and performance spaces of the Palais Royal were suffused with rumours conveyed by word of mouth and by spontaneous orators as well as by printed leaflets and other posters contributing to the shaping of public opinion. Eventually, while the authori-

8 As suggested by Pierre Sansot, *Jardins publics* (Paris: Payot, 2003).

9 Mayeur de Saint-Paul, *Tableau du nouveau Palais-Royal, première partie*, p. 4.

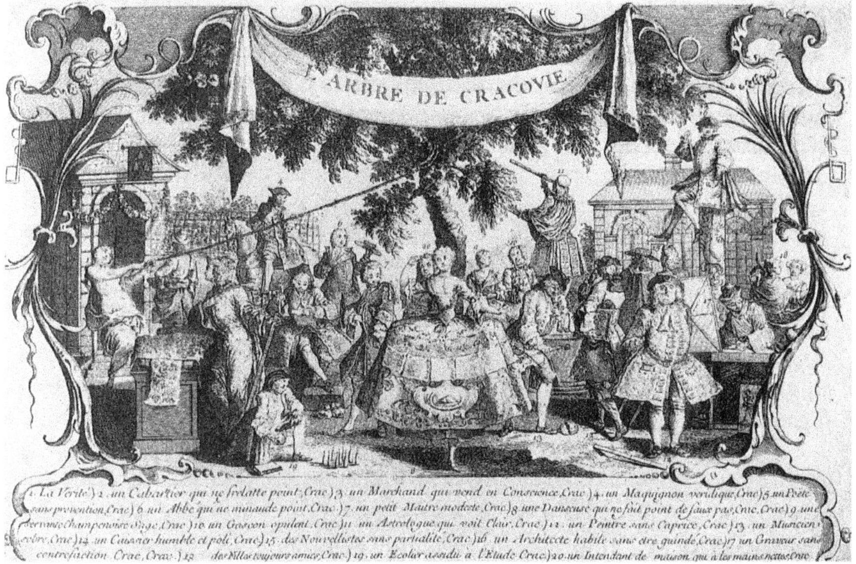

Figure 18.

'L'arbre de Cracovie', a seventeenth century etching, reproduced in *L'Illustration* (14 January 1933). Source: Authors' collection.

ties were trying to restrict intemperate gatherings, the public garden lost its character as a forum in favour of other places devoted to politics such as clubs and factional centres. The Napoleonic regime forced opponents and plotting partisans into the intimacy of secret meeting-places.

During the nineteenth century, natural spaces in towns found their bourgeois and orderly character strengthened, which left hardly any place for political usages. Significantly, they were neglected at times of revolutionary happenings, such as major strikes, when the priority lay in taking over the streets. Political socialising took place increasingly openly in cafés, or even factories, or in party or union offices. Parks and gardens nevertheless retained, as they do to this day, a role in sociability, expressed in fetes, or sporting activities (see next chapter), in taking children to the playground, meeting friends or in Sunday walks. It is telling that benches in public gardens in general face the paths rather than turning their back to them, the general idea, particularly for those installed in the nineteenth century, being to keep everyone in public view, a kind of mutual social monitoring that made for social harmony and even, who knows, encounters. The squares designed by Haussmann and Alphand were explicitly devised as small open-air drawing-rooms. They did function like this, but somewhat less than their designers wished.

In fact, it was a growing individualism in behaviour that partly overcame these original intentions. The use of green spaces became more occasional, and more solitary, focused less on social meetings than on the practical, concrete benefit each person could derive from them. Céline bears witness to this for the inter-war years when, in 1932 in *Voyage au bout de la nuit (Journey to the End of the Night)*, he describes the Toulouse public garden where Bardamu goes to walk:

> An unfamiliar city is a fine thing! ... It's dream time. And because you're in a dream you can afford to waste a little time in the park. Still, after a certain age, unless you have gilt-edged reasons, people will think you've gone to the park to chase little girls like Parapine...

This discrepancy between the hopes awoken by the idea of the park and its actual use is reinforced some lines later by a description of the benches in provincial parks left empty on weekday mornings, and by this sardonic conclusion: 'In the corners of all parks there lie forgotten any number of little coffins engarlanded with dreams, thickets charged with promises, handkerchiefs full of everything. All a big joke.'[10] Revealingly, Léon-Paul Fargue himself, in describing the Paris of this same period, rather disregards parks and gardens and refers only to cafés as meeting-places for poets and artists...[11]

The *Trente Glorieuses* years and the tide of little housing estates that went with them reinforced this neglect of the social role of nature in towns. It has however come back strongly in the last thirty years, particularly as an attempt to address the problems raised by great buildings and difficult neighbourhoods. This is what lies behind the shared, or participatory, gardens that proliferate these days and offer to whoever wants it a little bit of land to cultivate – at times at the cost of several years delay before success is achieved.[12] In the Hautepierre neighbourhood in Strasbourg, for instance, two came into being between 2007 and 2009, the 'Garden of Dreams' and the 'Participatory Jacqueline Gardens'. In the minds of the local associations that set them up, this was clearly a question of reclaiming public space and of involving

10 Louis Ferdinand Céline, *Journey to the End of the Night*, trans. Ralph Manheim (New York: New Directions, (1983) 2012), pp. 310 and p. 312.

11 Léon-Paul Fargue, *Le Piéton de Paris* (Paris: Gallimard, 1932); 'Se réunir', *Refuges* (Paris: Émile-Paul frères, 1942).

12 Joëlle Zask, *La Démocratie aux champs: du jardin d'Éden aux jardins partagés* (Paris: La Découverte, 2016), also sees it as one of the places where democratic practice is reinvented and anchored.

all categories of the local population, particularly in terms of age, with the eldest rediscovering their social usefulness and transmitting their know-how to the youngest. These places are communally managed, giving rise to much discussion, which is exactly the point: encouraging contacts, solving problems by talking them through, getting to know each other.[13] At the beginning of the 1990s, in the Les Aubiers area of Bordeaux, gardens at the foot of large residential blocks were rethought and it was a topic of common enterprise to reorganise them, renew social links, valorise the collective surroundings and even restrict vandalism. Such initiatives do not always take place around large residences; they proliferate today in so-called popular areas, and usually throughout towns, with strong institutional support. In 1997, in Lille, an area of wasteland was taken over by the AJONC charity which, with the support of the regional authority, made a communal garden that has come to be used by 600 gardeners. The presence of just one of their number would have been enough for onlookers to come and learn.[14] The strictly social function fades away as it succeeds and gives way to the simple pleasure of conviviality, communal meals in the garden, and, from the beginning of the twenty-first century, self-sufficiency in fresh, organic produce.

While public, shared gardens are today retrieving a sociability function that they seemed to have partly lost, they are, however, lacking in the aspect of ostentation that was central under the *Ancien Régime*.

To see and be seen

> There are public places where people gather …
> There nothing stops our gaze wandering where it will;
> It wants to take in all this rich spectacle,
> The waving plumes, and pearls and rubies,
> Proudly dressed hair and sparkling dresses,
> Veils and fabrics and shiny material,
> Ever-changing images, and gliding grandeur …
> Each is an actor on this vast and brilliant stage,
> Entertaining, entertained, watched and watching.[15]

13 Barbara Morovich, 'Hautepierre: de l'espace conçu à l'espace vécu', in *L'Urbanisme à Strasbourg au XXe siècle* (Strasbourg: Ville de Strasbourg, 2010), available online www.strasboug.eu

14 Vincent Larbey, *Jardins et Jardiniers. Les pieds dans la terre, la tête dans les nuages. Une anthropologie du potager*, Ph.D. Diss., École doctorale 60 'Territoires, Temps, Sociétés et Développement', Université Paul Valéry – Montpellier III, 2013, pp. 57–58.

15 Jacques Delille, *Les Jardins ou l'art d'embellir les paysages, poème en quatre chants* (Paris: Levrault, 1801), p. 61.

These alexandrine lines from the epic which the Abbé Delille devoted to gardens in 1782 are a reminder that, under the *Ancien Régime*, natural spaces were an open-air theatre for citizens where they could freely see and be seen. The great people of the world paraded in the promenades, as did those who wanted to be them, or at least to look like them; what was natural and what was false were confused in these places where ostentatious schemes were played out in a natural, vegetal setting. Dress, jewellery, hairstyling and accessories were the subject of the most minute care. All the rituals of the promenade were pretexts to flag up markers of distinction and so to signify one's position in society, or the position one sought: never was seeming to be something so close to being it.

Manon Roland remembers her younger years and the importance of the culture of show in the bourgeoisie she came from:

> It seems that I heard people saying, for whose eyes, in the retiring life I led, was this elaborate toilette? Anyone posing this question needs to recall that I went out twice each week; and if they had known the habits of those known as bourgeois Paris in my time, they would know that there were thousands of them whose expenditure, very great in jewels especially, was directed at a few hours display in the Tuileries each Sunday: their wives added to that the pleasure of church attendance and of passing gracefully through their neighbourhood under their neighbours' gaze.[16]

A witness tells how at Palais Royal it was necessary to show off one's gold watch, at the risk of being robbed by skilled pickpockets: dandies gathered for this purpose in a part of the garden where the meridian of the Rue des Bon Enfants could best be seen, and waited till exactly midday before resuming the promenade, proud to have given such a demonstration of the precision of their timepieces and of their wealth.[17]

To soak up Parisian manners, strangers and provincials went to the Luxembourg Garden, where the true judges of good taste set themselves up, always in the same place, along a balustrade near the Parterre: 'It served as a support for those who went there as a matter of course to scrutinise, praise or damn the new styles in dress or jewellery for Ladies, the charms or shortcomings of those walking in the pathways.'[18] The wide perspectives and the arrangement of spaces in urban nature combined to form a true theatre of the vanities, making the spectator sport of this culture of appearances all

16 Madame Roland, *Mémoires de Madame Roland* (Paris: Baudouin Frères, 1827), p. 31.

17 Mayeur de Saint-Paul, *Tableau du nouveau Palais-Royal, première partie*, p. 7.

18 Claude-Martin Saugrain, *Les Curiositez de Paris* (Paris: Société d'encouragement pour la propagation des livres d'art, 1716), p. 238.

the more easy. One gauges, evaluates, admires and derides with more or less judgement and knowledge.

The beau monde, which set the tone for elegance, diligently frequented the Tuileries, Palais Royal, the Luxembourg, the Arsenal and the King's Garden, as well as some private gardens, chiefly belonging to religious communities (Sainte Geneviève, Célestines, place des Victoires). As these promenades were open to the public, ordinary people could draw near the aristocrats and admire their behaviour and finery from close up. Tour guides to eighteenth century Paris recommend that those seeking a bit of the high life should go to the Tuileries: 'For here one sees the great people of both sexes and even royal Princes and Princesses very often. One should go with some friend ... who can point out who people are. One approaches them and passes as close as possible, look at them as attentively as possible.'[19] Aristocrats and the bourgeoisie did not give those who were staring at them so much as a look, even if inwardly they felt smug to be making such a sensation.

It has to be said, though, that things of this kind changed very little up until about the First World War. The Promenade des Anglais at Nice, built in the middle of the nineteenth century, was particularly glittering in the winter months, especially January and February; one had to show oneself there after midday and notably between 2 and 4 in the afternoon. There one could admire a diverse crowd of all nationalities, all elegant. Fops, mature men, well-born young ladies, fashionable ladies of the town, European aristocrats, old stagers and wealthy bourgeois all squeezed in there: one could almost forget that those first attracted to the place were victims of tuberculosis who came for the cure.

There were similar practices in the Bois de Boulogne, especially after its reorganisation during the Second Empire. It was the great salon of Paris, the place to be seen, and where one went to admire or criticise the great world one wanted to join. The provincial young woman in Maupassant's *Une Aventure Parisienne (An Adventure in Paris)* particularly wants to see the women of ill repute: there one would find both the aristocratic and bourgeois elite and courtesans in plain view with their clients. The fair ladies paraded in carriages or on foot, each vying in displaying luxury and making the most of her charms and dress. Fine gentlemen could show off their horse-riding skills and their horses.

19 Joachim Christoph Nemeitz, *Séjour de Paris, c'est-à-dire, instructions fidèles, pour les voyageurs de condition* (Leyde: Jean Van Abcoude, 1727), p. 157.

Figure 19.

Allée des Acacias in the Bois de Boulogne, *L'Illustration*, 14 June 1915.
Source: Authors' Collection.

> All Paris goes on display there, great and small, rich and poor, pure gold and ormulu, a small number for pleasure, others to give the impression they are happy. What is the dream of the tyro speculator whose fortune is still just a matter of hope? To have a carriage and to parade in the Bois. The Bois is a human exhibition, it is a kind of Exchange, where an individual's worth is totted up, higher or lower according to how brightly or not he shines. It is natural that this little corner of the earth should be the focus for those who want to succeed, and the place of choice for those who have arrived.[20]

About three in the afternoon, but preferably not on Sunday, was the time to go walking there, and hence the Goncourts' cruel wish to see a hellish machine killing all the people found there then, who in their eyes embodied 'chic stupidity' and 'elegant idiocy'.[21]

Many amorous fates were stitched together there, an inexhaustible well of inspiration for nineteenth century romantic novelists, who all drew from

20 Édouard Gourdon, *Le Bois de Boulogne* (1861), quoted in Jean-Louis Cirès, *La Construction des jardins publics à Paris sous le Second Empire*, Master's thesis under the direction of Alain Corbin, Université de Tours, 1985, pp. 181–182.

21 Frères Goncourt, *Journal*, Mar. 1865.

Figure 20.

'Le banc des "populaires": une élégante vient de passer', *L'Illustration*, 14 June 1913.
Source: Authors' collection.

it. Proust tells us that it was around the Lake, along the Acacias path (today Rue de Longchamp) or that of Reine-Marguerite, that Odette, having become Madame Swann, goes to display the success of her marriage, and even to find some distractions. It is significant that this pathway in the Bois and the changes that the author discovers over time - motor cars superseding old carriages, and one fashion chasing out another - feature at the close of the first volume of *A La Recherche du Temps Perdu (In Search of Lost Time)* with the awareness already of the irremediable distortion between memory and reality.

It is true enough that old modes of behaviour were lost during the twentieth century, and the levelling of living conditions has made ostentatious promenades obsolete – one no longer goes to a park to see or be seen.

But if these areas of urban nature are to be shared, there still has to be at least a minimal agreement about how they should be used: the lifestyles of the elites do not harmonise readily with those of plebeians. Henceforth our minds need to be shaped by some sort of vegetal order.

Vegetal order

Learning proper behaviour

Conduct in respect of nature in towns thus followed, at least at first, an ideal of urbanity governed by codes of propriety, courtesy and civility. Buffon said, 'Savages know nothing of promenading, and nothing amazes them more in our behaviour than to see us walk in a straight line and then to return in our own footsteps several times in a row.'[22] It is true that etiquette was less exacting in gardens and boulevards than in town and, as Louis-Sébastien Mercier recalls, the Parisian was less punctilious in manners when walking than in the drawing room, not wanting to seem provincial! However, a gentleman versed in propriety greets his acquaintances politely, treats ladies respectfully and regulates his steps according to social hierarchies. When one is with a person of quality in a garden, 'one must place oneself on the left of the person and discreetly retain that place at each turn. [If] three are walking together, the place of honour is in the middle and belongs to the most qualified person; the right is next, and then the left is third.'[23] One should take care not to hamper the steps of one's companions with inappropriate movements, and one only sit down to rest when invited, and at the end of the bench. It is through mastery of bodily gymnastics that the walker adopts in all circumstances a posture and carriage of the head that reflect his quality as a gentleman. Seventeenth and eighteenth century artists contributed to standardising behaviour by representing parks and gardens with ladies and gentlemen of impeccable conduct walking there, as we saw in the engraving of the Cours Royal at Marseilles (see p.114). There was no joy for those who thought of defying clothing customs or the aesthetic commandments of the time, or of raising their position by extravagant expenditure: if they did so, they, and women particularly, exposed themselves to gibes, even outright harassment, from young fops who set themselves up as arbiters of elegance. In 1769 several occurrences of this kind in the Tuileries and Luxembourg Gardens induced the Prefect of Paris to punish infractions of the rules of civility in the royal gardens in Paris, the law deeming them disrespectful to the king and a danger to public order. The play of exchanging looks formed

22 Comte de Buffon, *Histoire naturelle* (Paris: Imprimerie Royale, 1769–1781), in Jean-Baptiste Vaquin, *Atlas de la Nature à Paris* (Paris: Atelier parisien d'urbanisme, 2006), p. 181.

23 Antoine de Courtin, *Nouveau traité de la civilité qui se pratique en France parmi les honnestes gens* (Paris: L. Josse et C. Robustel, 1728), pp. 158–159.

part of the implicit rules of the promenade as long as this did not transgress the limits of propriety.

The adoption of these limits was initially effected, in a sufficiently direct way, by the establishment of strict rules of behaviour enforced by a watchful keeper within a precise area marked by the park or garden gate. Regulatory practices of this kind were established in the seventeenth century. They were backed by the legal status of gardens open to visitors but belonging in the main to the crown, to the owners of large townhouses and to religious houses. The Royal Garden of Medicinal Plants was the first truly public garden in Paris. Louis XIII agreed to finance a structure initially intended for students at the faculties of medicine. From 1640 the public could attend botanical demonstrations conducted by professors, and in the eighteenth century the King's Garden became a much-appreciated promenade. In general, access to royal Parks and Gardens was among the freedoms citizens relished. There had been a question of limiting entrance more strictly to the court at the end of the seventeenth century, but Louis ultimately chose to make the gardens demonstrations of his glory, and so their gates mostly remained open, enabling Charles Perrault to represent himself as a victorious defender of Parisians' ambulatory pleasures.

> [Colbert] said to me, Let us go to the Tuileries and close its gates: the garden must be reserved for the king, and we should not let it be ruined by the people, who will utterly wreck it in less than no time. This determination seemed to me crude and unjust to all Paris. When he was in the grand walkway I said to him, Sir, you cannot believe the respect that everyone, down to the most humble bourgeois, has for this garden: not only do women and small children never think of picking a flower, they never even touch it: they all walk around here like reasonable people … It would be a public wrong not to be able to come and walk here, especially as, at the moment one cannot enter the Luxembourg or the Hotel de Guise.[24]

Colbert may have let himself be influenced, but access to the coveted shades was nonetheless not unconditional. Visitors were expected to behave like the king's guests in respect of conduct and good manners. The plant world was thought of as merely decorative, and not to be touched. Garden regulations reflected social norms. Access was restricted to elites, to notables and to the middle classes, the keepers having the right to refuse entry to any whose age, working clothes, tools or uniform categorised them as undesirable: schoolboys, domestic servants, small tradesmen, labourers, tipsy soldiers, prostitutes, beggars and social rejects… In the last decades of the eighteenth century, the rules were eased a little in some towns, as in Paris, where the

24 Charles Perrault, *Mémoires de Charles Perrault, de l'Académie françoise* (Avignon, 1759), pp. 186–187.

people gained access to the public walkways on Sundays and holidays,[25] not without forceful reactions from defenders of the old order. One M. de La Croix, an advocate in Parliament wrote in 1780,

> Gardens designed and ornamented with care, such as those that beautify the capital, are precious in the eyes of those who have a taste for beauty and for whom, being accustomed to luxury, art has been made necessary; but the people only need uncultivated woods, fields of grass and flowers. Knowing neither embarrassment nor restraint they trample on everything and tear it up: walkways should offer to their eyes neither statues, nor vases nor precious flowers … It is not giving the ordinary people any pleasure to grant them the freedom to traverse a Garden .. : they see themselves as in a place of contradictions; the presence of keepers watching them irritates them, and they quickly become bored or break the rules imposed on them. There are reasons for keeping the people out of royal Gardens, especially in heavily populated towns: they are not being deprived, and one is giving much to persons of a certain status, in providing them with the facility of a peaceful promenade, where decency, honesty and discretion reign.[26]

The revolution did not put a stop to this social selection. A regulation for the garden of the town of Pontoise adopted on 15 May 1822 stipulates that, to enter, one must wear clean and decent garments, wearing working clothes being forbidden. This requirement for 'decency' in clothing as in manners, which is met again in the rules for the Thabor promenade in Rennes in 1845 and 1865,[27] led to the exclusion (at the keepers' discretion) of categories of people such as beggars, tramps and labourers, who were deemed undesirable and therefore dangerous. Thus, natural spaces in towns become the showcase for a regulated or even circumscribed society, from which all ungovernable spontaneity is banished: 'In public gardens and populous places one should not make oneself noticed. Attracting attention by eccentric manners, loud behaviour, great shouts of laughter, calling out to passers-by or pointing to someone or something, are all vulgar actions which a young man should not allow himself.'[28]

In a subtler way, the very composition of the park follows the 'civilising'

25 Anne Béroujon, *Peuple et pauvres des villes dans la France moderne* (Paris: Armand Colin, 2014), pp. 180–183.

26 Joseph-Nicolas Guyot, *Répertoire universel et raisonné de jurisprudence* (Paris: Panckoucke, 1780), vol. 33, pp. 26–27.

27 For example, Article III of the regulation of 1865 states that 'the entrance to the garden [of plants] shall be forbidden to any person whose dress is not suitable'; as for children under twelve years of age and their governesses, they may only enter with the parents of the said children - no doubt the governesses are not adult enough to prevent children from damaging the plants … in Louis-Michel Nourry, *Les Jardins publics en province* (Rennes: PUR, 1997), p. 84

28 F.G.M., *Manuel de politesse à l'usage de la jeunesse: savoir-vivre, savoir-parler, savoir-écrire, savoir-travailler* (Paris: J. de Gigord, 1922), p. 97.

mission of these regulations. As Alain Corbin says in a preface to a very fine book by Louis-Michel Nourry,

> The public garden of the Second Empire was a space organised with distinction and ostentation. It demonstrates the reconquest of the city by social elites. It authorises pleasure in Order: order of the parterres, order in conduct guaranteed by a regulatory structure of multiple prohibitions, keepers who watch everything, and above all by boundary fencing protecting the park from disruptive invasion. It is at the same time a manifestation and a metaphor of social order.[29]

In fact, green spaces introduced into towns by the Emperor and his agents – mayors and prefects – are not just following reasons of public health; they also convey a truly bourgeois view of the world and a dominant code of conduct shared by the ruling power: the idea was not novel, but it was considerably strengthened under Napoleon III. It was a kind of attempt to civilise the working classes, who had become dangerous and who had to learn to behave properly in public and to conform to the rules of propriety. It is worth dwelling for a moment on that very common, and very French, injunction – Keep Off the Grass – grass which takes up, on average, half the surface area of parks and gardens. It is found in practically all regulations, with a few exceptions – the Tête d'Or park in Lyon or the Pré Catalan in the Bois de Boulogne which are open for picnickers' pleasure. The forbidden lawn is very significant: it is not there, despite its tempting green carpet, to be trampled on by bare feet, but to bring air to the composition of the landscape, to keep viewpoints free, to clear wide spaces. The whole organisation of a park, with its twisting walkways, often its lake, its structures and its striking plant species whose vernacular and Latin names are often signposted, is conceived with the single object of calm walking. Thus the park in the second half of the nineteenth century imposes a bourgeois and controlled management of public space: one behaves there, one walks slowly and decently dressed, and one relaxes the spirit with carefully contrived fine views; there are no excessive physical activities, and no contact except by sight and smell with the natural environment: this is a decor for the spectacle of respectability.

It is however sometimes troubled by those who, notwithstanding the attempts at control and education we have described, seem to be ignorant of the elites' good taste and proffer their own forms of sociability and the use of green spaces. The beau monde can do nothing but dream up strategies for avoiding excessive social mixing.

29 Nourry, *Les Jardins publics en province*, p. 10.

To each his park? The strategies of social avoidance

Avoidance strategies are of two kinds: spatial, when the people and the elites divide up the green spaces that they frequent; and temporal, when the same location is used at different times of day according to social rank.

Under the *Ancien Régime*, those who could not bear the indiscreet gaze of the public could choose, for example, to go on horseback or in a carriage, sticking to certain promenades reserved for the elites. In Paris, people took a carriage ride along by the Seine (Cours-la-Reine, the Champs-Élysées), or else along the boulevards to the north of the city where the trip could be extended through the forests at Boulogne and Vincennes. The Cours la Reine had always been crowded since it had been created in the seventeenth century and it had maintained a very aristocratic status which was reinforced by the gates which isolated it from the rest of the city: 'in summer and spring, when it is warm and dry, the carriages assemble there in such great numbers that we have sometimes counted over a thousand of them. These Promenades are frequented by persons of the highest distinction and by members of the Royal Family ... One makes the acquaintance in this Assembly of many people whom one hardly sees elsewhere.'[30]

Those who preferred to walk needed to be aware of the customs and know when it was judicious to appear on the promenade or when one risked finding oneself mixed up in an inappropriate crowd. In Parisian gardens, for example, midday was the time for energetic walkers, concerned for their health, whose walking sticks beat time on the ground. Friends and business acquaintances met up for open air conversations; the idle, the curious and the elderly dawdled. Elegant ladies showed off their finery and compliments followed in their wake: 'They always walk together two by two, and they walk quickly; they are always laughing, even out loud, although sometimes they do not wish to do so, but this is in order to get themselves noticed.'[31] The atmosphere changed in the first hours of the afternoon with the shouts, cries and babbling of little children and the motherly voices of the nurses and maidservants who kept watch over their games. After six o'clock in the evening, the children's hubbub faded away as the beau monde arrived along with all those who wished to enjoy a stroll.[32]

30 Joachim Christoph Nemeitz, *Séjour de Paris, c'est-à-dire, instructions fidèles, pour les voyageurs de condition* (Leyde: Jean Van Abcoude, 1727), pp. 165–166.

31 François-Marie Mayeur de Saint-Paul, *Tableau du nouveau Palais-Royal, première partie* (London: Maradan, 1788), p. 133.

32 Farge, *Essai pour une histoire des voix au XVIIIe siècle.*

Figure 21.

Louis Lincler, drawing representing flowerbeds surrounded by a semicircle path with strollers (Jardin du Luxembourg?), ca 1640. Courtesy of Musée Carnavalet (public domain).
Courtesy of Musée Carnavalet (public domain).

Before the Revolution, the authorities did not hesitate to intervene in order to maintain propriety in certain places. Towns were often very concerned, for example, to avoid any confusion between the world of shopworkers and craftsmen and those places for showing off reserved for urban elites who had to maintain the required decorum. In Aix-en-Provence, in 1748, a lemonade seller nearly caused a riot among the elegant crowd when he took the initiative of setting up a stall on the Cours d'Orbitelle which, it was rumoured, would in no time be transformed into a shop and would spoil the location. The town council rapidly made a decision about this affair to calm people's nerves and published a decree on 9 April 1748 reminding citizens that only cafés had permission to set up in business along the promenade, exclusive of any other kind of commerce.[33] More generally, the only shops tolerated along the

33 Charles de Ribbe, *Les Embellissements d'Aix et le cours Saint-Louis: il y a deux siècles* (Aix: A. Makaire, 1861), p. 58.

promenades and in the public gardens were those which helped to liven up the planted vegetal environment and to set off the town's embellishments, since they provided vital services for a well-off clientele.

With the increasing opening of natural spaces to the whole of the population and the democratisation of leisure all throughout the nineteenth century, avoidance strategies were stepped up.[34] The Parisian boulevards, for example, were carefully divided: the people to the east of boulevard Montmartre or boulevard Bonne Nouvelle, the elite on the other side, in particular towards the Madeleine. From the start of the Second Empire, the fine folk gradually forsook the Champs-Élysées, in favour of the Bois de Boulogne in particular, and this move to the west of the city, further from the populous east would, it was hoped, keep the vulgar crowds away. With the creation of squares that were frequented by the middle classes or the common people and the Bois de Vincennes, the popular equivalent of the Bois de Boulogne, an effort was made to consolidate this social division of natural spaces. The *Grand Dictionnaire Universel du XIXe siècle* (*Great Universal Dictionary of the Nineteenth Century)* thus took great care in detailing the frequentation of major Parisian squares. What a difference between the Square Sainte Clothilde, 'the most aristocratic of all. There one only encounters maidservants and nursemaids of the grand houses', and the Square des Innocents where the people 'are not very distinguished, there one only sees market women sleeping or resting, labourers sleeping off their wine or messengers snoring on the benches!'[35]

The avoidance could be spatially less marked: it might simply be the case of different circuits taken by each group around the same space. At the beginning of the 1860s, the elite, who were still frequenting the Champs-Elysées, showing off, thus strolled along the main thoroughfares under the admiring or indifferent gaze of the people who were restricted to the side paths. In *La Fortune des Rougon* (*The Fortune of the Rougons)*, Emile Zola describes Plassans, a fictional version of Aix-en-Provence, in the mid nineteenth century:

> The whole town repairs to the Cours Sauvaire on Sunday after vespers … Three distinct currents flow along this sort of boulevard planted with rows of plane-trees. The well-to-do citizens of the new quarter merely pass along … taking the Avenue du Mail on the right where they walk up and down until nightfall. Meanwhile the

34 For all issues related to spatial and temporal segregation, see Robert Beck, 'La promenade du peuple des villes (fin XVIIIe–XIXe siècles). L'exemple du peuple de Paris', in Philippe Guignet (dir.), *Le Peuple des villes dans l'Europe du Nord-Ouest* (Lille: Centre de Recherches sur l'Histoire de l'Europe du Nord-Ouest, 2002), vol. I, pp. 247–266.

35 Pierre Larousse, 'square', *Grand Dictionnaire Universel du XIXe siècle* (1866–1877), p. 1035.

> nobility and the lower classes share the Cours Sauvaire between them. For more than a century past the nobility have selected the walk on the south … the lower classes have to rest content with the walk to the north … the people and the nobility promenade the whole afternoon walking up and down the Cours without anyone of either party thinking of changing sides.[36]

Avoidance in terms of time was also reinforced during the nineteenth century: depending on one's social group, one did not go out for a walk at the same time as others. Under the July Monarchy it was unthinkable for society people to stroll about on a Sunday, which was the most popular day of all since it was the only day of rest for the lower classes. This explains the surprise felt by two aristocrats in Balzac's *La Fille aux yeux d'or* (*The Girl with the Golden Eyes)* when they meet in the Tuileries on that day – an affair of the heart being of course behind the breaking of this social boundary in 1815.[37] This repugnance was also felt in the provinces: in Dijon in 1834, the distinguished classes abstained from going to the park to avoid the invasion by the proletariat.[38]

The move from the July Monarchy to the Second Empire changed nothing in this regard; still in 1855 we find this disparaging statement in a guide to Paris:

> On Sundays, everything changes in the Tuileries, as is the case everywhere else … A vast crowd, coming from all corners of Paris, pushes, jostles and stifles, on the pretext of seeking shade and coolness under the chestnut trees which are astonished by this unceremonious invasion … Elite society has given way to the mob.[39]

But these avoidance strategies were, *in fine,* doomed to failure. It is true that in Paris, for example, some spaces kept a certain social tone up until the First World War: the Bois de Boulogne remained more distinguished than the Bois de Vincennes where, in 1900, 'on Sundays … the Parisian from Belleville or Menilmontant … eats with relish a garlic flavoured sausage seasoned with gaiety', surrounded by noisy children.[40] And yet, this was simply a question of acquired habits, of nuances which progressively faded as a democratic society put down its roots and as equality in social conditions, borne by the

36 Émile Zola, trad. Ernest Alfred Vizetelly, *The Fortune of the Rougons* (1898), online at http://www.gutenberg.org/files/5135/5135-h/5135-h.htm#link2H_INTR

37 The book dates from 1834.

38 Suzanne Voilquin, *Souvenirs d'une fille du peuple,* in Robert Beck, 'La promenade du peuple des villes', p. 248.

39 Paulin and Lechevalier, *Guide des Promenades* (Paris: 1855), p. 120.

40 A.-P. de Lannoy (pseudonym of Auguste Pawlowski), *Les Plaisirs et la vie de Paris. Guide du flâneur* (1900).

Third Republic, settled in from the end of the 1870s: with the limiting of the working day (the eight hour day came in 1919) and the generalisation of the weekly day off, the lush Paris boulevards henceforward welcomed a more varied crowd, ever more numerous, and this left little room for avoidance strategies. The social levelling due to two world wars further contributed to the revision of these practices of socialisation as much as those of social avoidance. A place for sporting exercise and of bodily renewal, the green space was no longer, properly speaking, a space for sociability, but one of an individualisation of practices: one no longer walked there but one went jogging…[41] Other social markers and other more private sites for sociability appeared. In fact, the social distinction was no longer located simply in the way in which one used green spaces: one was no longer simply seen *in* a garden, one might also want to be seen through the lens of the garden, that is, using urban nature as a stage-set where one shows oneself off but also as a means to make oneself stand out.

Narcissus in the city. Plant life in one's own image

A garden of one's own

The social significance of urban nature cannot be overemphasised, even though it must not be reduced to this function: at any point in time it reveals hierarchies, exclusions or identities, and the aspiration to superior refinement. To own a garden, in the confined space of the city, is already in itself the radiant proof of one's social standing and the bigger the garden, the more convincing this is. It is a place of one's own, which keeps others at bay as well as urban inconveniences, a place where one may receive and display simple or sumptuous hospitality, according to one's means. One could doubtless, like Denise and Jean-Pierre Le Dantec, suggest an evolution in this role of the private garden.[42]

Under the *Ancien Régime*, and probably more so than in the period that followed, a garden was first and foremost a privilege for the most comfortably off.[43] This is how Boileau paints the portrait of the capital:

41 Jean-Baptiste Vaquin, *Atlas de la Nature à Paris* (Paris: Atelier parisien d'urbanisme, 2006), p. 197.

42 See Denise and Jean-Pierre Le Dantec, *Le Roman des jardins de France* (Paris: Bartillat, 1998), pp. 222–223.

43 Though the poor had access to communal land which they shared, and were therefore not deprived of nature.

For the rich man Paris is a magic land:
He can be in the country without leaving the town:
In his garden full of green trees
He can harbour the spring in the middle of winter
And strolling among his sweet-scented flowers
Bid welcome to all his delicate dreams.[44]

It is probable that these gardens did not reflect an individuality but rather a position in the world. In fact, in the eighteenth century the boundary between the public and the private tended to be blurred; it was not rare for garden owners to open their gates to visitors that they might enjoy the shade and the works of art that pleased the eye. The French elite were willingly inspired by the practices of the Italian aristocrats whom they met during the classical Grand Tour. In any case, it is travel literature which allows us to measure this phenomenon and in particular those guides that multiplied throughout the eighteenth century and initiated visitors from over the English Channel or from across the Rhine into the delights of French cities. The testimony left by the English lady Mrs Cradock lets us guess at the existence of a clear hierarchy of the 'fine gardens' in Paris. The gardens of Marshal de Biron's townhouse, which covered nearly three hectares behind Rue de Varennes were among the most admired. Our tourist was attached to the romantic disorder of English style gardens and portrays herself as being at odds with common opinion:

> They are said to be the loveliest in Paris and it is rare to get permission to visit them. These gardens in the French style are sadly regular. The trees all in a straight line, close to one another; here and there the parterres are symmetrically framed with flower pots; some ponds with fountains and a statue in the middle; many orange and lemon trees in planters. To sum up, these gardens may be huge but they are dominated by a joyless uniformity.[45]

Visits to private gardens remained rooted in the sociability practices of the elite. Visits were made to distinguished society but also to fashionable people: to receive one's guests and visitors in a beautiful garden was the sign of worldly success. At the beginning of the 1790s, the famous actress and dancer Marie-Madeleine Guimard thus had a townhouse built in Rue de la Chaussée d'Antin, by the architect Ledoux. This 'Temple of Terpsichore', as the regular guests called it, contained a library, a collection of paintings,

44 Nicolas Boileau, 'Satire VI', *Œuvres* (Paris: Lefèvre, 1821 [1666]), vol. I, pp. 127–128.

45 *Journal de Mme Cradock, Voyage en France (1783–1786)*, trans. from the original unpublished manuscript by O. Delphin-Baleyguier (Paris: Perrin, 1896), jeudi 17 juin 1784, p. 49.

a theatre, a summer garden and a winter garden where rare plants bloomed. But competition was fierce among the demi-mondaines who rivalled each other in extravagant spending in particular on the gardens. Baron d'Oberkirch was staying in Paris in May 1782 and, on leaving the Palais Royal on the way to the Tuileries, he called in on another dancer and opera singer at the Opera, a kept woman who, at the age of fourteen was already beginning to upstage La Guimard and who boasted of her English style garden, full of wonders.[46] The garden went well beyond its residential function; it was a social marker in the same way as buildings were, and a consecration of the social rise of these ambitious women.

In the eighteenth century, the destruction of the ramparts, or their uselessness, along with progressive urban sprawl, made it possible for dwellings embellished with large gardens and affordable by those with middling or newly acquired fortunes to spring up in the suburbs. Thus, beginning in 1787, Beaumarchais had a house built on a 4,000 square metre plot close to the boulevard that was named after him half a century later. This was a private townhouse which possessed a magnificent garden with numerous extravagances: grottos, groves, rockeries, Greek temples and a Chinese bridge, all reached through a monumental entrance that took care to remind visitors that the trees were planted there 'in the first year of Liberty'.

These delights and fantasies also prevailed in the provinces, of course. In 1738, Barral de Rochechinard, an advisor at the Grenoble parliament congratulated himself on the acquisition of such a pleasing residence adjoining the town:

> In a word, everything there is felicitous, sight & smell are satisfied there, one finds oneself in Town & in the Country, there is only the River betwixt the two, and all pleasures are brought together there, the water features, the bocages, the Hornbeam mazes, the Statues, the orange trees, the flowers in each Season & a prodigious quantity of trees bearing fruits of all kinds, are a charming concomitance …[47]

Such gardens could thus prove to be most spectacular.

With the changes of the second half of the eighteenth century and the emergence of the individual, gifted with an interior life which the Romantics were pleased to reveal, the private garden ceased to be solely the affirmation of social status and could become the expression of a personality. One no

46 Henriette-Louise von Waldner, *Mémoires de la baronne d'Oberkirch* (Bruxelles: J.-P. Méline, 1834), vol 1, p. 192.

47 In Clarisse Coulomb, *Les Pères de la patrie. La société parlementaire en Dauphiné au temps des Lumières* (Grenoble: PUG, 2006), p. 190.

longer simply obeyed the rules of good taste and of fashion – even though these persisted, of course – one tried to make one's garden in one's own image, that of the same self that was revealed in autobiographical writings, in private diaries where each strove to reveal his or her soul, in short, in the egotistical affirmation liberated by the French Revolution. Appropriately, we can see the proof of this in the extraordinary nineteenth century development of a vulgarised horticultural literature which enabled each and every one to cultivate his or her own garden in their own way.[48]

Those who could, and there were increasingly more of them as the century progressed, affirmed at the same time their social eminence and their individuality thanks to a private winter garden which was an extension of the salon. One received guests there, held receptions, or simply just read or played cards. When, during the Second Empire, the Parc Monceau was redesigned, most of the new private townhouses surrounding it possessed such a room. Some of the winter gardens were sumptuous, like that of Princess Mathilde, Napoleon III's cousin, whose salon, until the end of the century, drew all the artistic and literary elite, including the Goncourt brothers who described it thus:

> These conservatory-drawing rooms have been a new luxury, no more than twenty years old, the taste for which recalls that of Mlle de Cardonville in Sue's novel, which amazed Paris at the time. With her rather wild taste throughout the greenhouse that ringed her mansion, the Princess had scattered among all the beautiful exotic plants, all kinds for furniture from all countries and times, in all colours and shapes. It was most strange, like pouring an antique shop into a virgin forest. There were lamps on banana-tree leaves, which seemed to be electric lights and everywhere the soft green of exotic plants was detached, carved out and spread against the dark purple of a red hanging, crumpled in great folds against the walls. [49]

While Eugène Sue undoubtedly had a part in the winter garden fashion because of the description he gave of one in *Le Juif errant (The Wandering Jew)*, Balzac himself also made a little paradise for his two leading characters in *La Peau de chagrin (The Magic Skin)* : 'While all Paris was still warming itself by cheerless hearths, the young couple were laughing in a bower of camellias and lilacs and heather. Their joyous heads were side by side among narcissus and lilies of the valley and Bengal roses.'[50]

But, as can already be guessed from the lovers' décor, the affirmation of

48 See Denise et Jean-Pierre Le Dantec, *Le Roman des jardins de France* (Paris: Bartillat, 1998), pp. 222–223.

49 Edmond and Jules de Goncourt, *Journal*, 1867, 25 December, Christmas.

50 Honoré de Balzac, *La Peau de chagrin*, trans. Katherine Prescott Wormeley (Boston: Little, Brown, 1899).

self of course varies considerably depending on one's means and above all is itself inscribed very often in fashion trends: that of the English garden at the end of the eighteenth century, that of Japanese gardens thereafter, that of floral mosaics at the end of the nineteenth century, that of pineapples and orchids, or even of ficus, succulents and vegetalised walls today. Only the extraordinary abundance of floral choices allows one, in this context, to escape uniformity somewhat.

But, of course, it is the layout of the garden that translates best each one's individuality, social image and intimate thoughts. Zola gives a striking vision of this in *La Conquête de Plassans* (*The Conquest of Plassans*), where three gardens each reflect the political opinions and the social class of their owners. That of Mouret is the archetype of the bourgeois garden: nothing is useless, a few trees have been cut down to make room for vegetables, which take up three of the four squares surrounded by box, while flowers nevertheless decorate the fourth bed. Only fruit trees remain. On a lower level is the plot belonging to M. Rastoil, a legitimist justice of the peace; the inspiration is English, nothing in it is of any use, only what might help towards wellbeing: a rotunda of trees, small pathways, little lawns, rustic tables and chairs. Above Mouret's garden is that of the sub-prefect, a functionary of the Second Empire: its majesty lies in its large central lawn, a few clumps of trees and tall chestnuts which practically make it a park.[51]

In the same way, some gardens can be conceived as the affirmation of a thought, of a vision of the world, almost as a political act. This is the case of the famous gardens created from 1894 by the banker Albert Kahn and the landscaper Eugène Deny in Boulogne. Kahn wished to promote universal peace and had, for example, created in 1898 the *Autour du Monde* (Round the World) society which, through a system of bursaries offered to agrégés, (those who succeeded in passing the *agrégation* examination) allowing them to travel for fifteen months, sought to advocate and share the cultures of the world's peoples in order to promote harmony. To reflect this ideal, his garden would be a garden of different stage-sets, incarnating the major landscaping practices of the world: thus English, French and Japanese gardens alternated there. But we also find a Vosges forest, a souvenir of a childhood in Alsace, traumatised by the 1870 war...[52]

51 Émile Zola, *La Conquête de Plassans* (Paris: Charpentier, 1879 [1874]), ch. 4.

52 See the Albert Kahn Gardens website: http://albert-kahn.hauts-de-seine.net/les-jardins/histoire-des-jardins

Finally the individualisation of gardens was manifested by what Manuel Pluvinage and Florence Weber have called the invention of gardening in a popular environment between 1860 and 1950.[53] Indeed, during this period, gardening slowly became a leisure activity.[54] Of course, there are multiple meanings for a garden and the activities pursued there: a place to restore oneself, a place for production and consumption and one of conviviality – it is all these at the same time. Here we are only considering the manner in which it is inscribed in the processes of distinction and ostentation.

The private garden first spread, and became more democratic, in the nineteenth century. This movement was greatly helped by the shift to the suburbs and then, from the end of the century, by the actions of the *Ligue du coin de terre et du foyer* (*League for a Plot of Land and Home*) which helped in setting up allotments, or workers' gardens. From the 1850s, the porcelain workers who came from the countryside to the suburbs of Limoges planted flowers and vegetables there. Above all, very progressively, these practices became more individualised. While allotments were originally strictly regulated and controlled and subject to the effects of middle-class moralising, they did eventually, in the inter-war period, become the gardens *of* the workers, breaking free from this tutelage. An enquiry by the Ministry of Labour carried out between 1920 and 1923 testifies to the practices allowed on these plots: firstly, it was above all adults, fathers and heads of the household, who did gardening, after work and at the weekend. At the end of the week, the whole family gathered there to cultivate the vegetables, of course, but also to play bowls or cards or to enjoy a drink. Reputations were made by the beauty of one's flowers or, more frequently, by the size, the originality or the flavour of one's fruit and vegetables. If the interwar period was thus a kind of golden age of the kitchen garden, this role of the individualisation of activities was taken over by bungalow gardens starting in the 1950s. They increased the properly demonstrative dimension of the individual garden by becoming 'more a place of self-expression than a demonstration of knowhow'.[55] These gardens were made up of different

53 Manuel Pluvinage and Florence Weber, *Les Jardins populaires : pratiques culturales, usages de l'espace, enjeux culturels*, research report for the Ethnological Heritage Mission of the Ministry of Culture (1992), p. 34.

54 For all this insight into the practice of gardening, see Alain Corbin, 'Les balbutiements d'un temps pour soi', in Corbin (dir.), *L'Avènement des loisirs, 1850–1960* (Paris: Flammarion, 1995), pp. 448–469.

55 Ibid., p. 466.

Figure 22.

Garden on the fifth floor, overlooking the Muette roundabout (Paris), *L'Illustration*, 23 January 1932. *Source:* Authors' collection.

spaces according to their use: the kitchen garden persisted was relegated to the bottom of the garden, out of sight; the very best site for appearances was of course the front of the house, with its rare plants, its carefully manicured lawns, its garden gnomes, etc.; at the back, a space was set aside for relaxing with the family or friends (meals, games, children's activities).[56] The way in which these spaces were laid out of course helped to pinpoint the owner socially; a specific kind of furniture came about, as this 1939 article from *Vogue* attests:

> to enjoy one's garden and to furnish it, one must choose seats which are comfortable and, if possible, harmonious in their design. At the Decorative Artists' Show we noticed … a sort of chaise-longue garden bed, an armchair and a table in varnished bamboo, with a moveable glass top … [The chaise-longue] being moreover fitted

56 Ibid., p. 467.

with a canopy which can be lifted off when desired, and places to set a glass and an ashtray being set into the arms.[57]

The *Trente Glorieuses* period saw the triumph of plastic furniture which was much less costly and affordable for all budgets – until teak and its imitations took over.

The quest for distinction: the rare specimen

If gardening could thus express social distinction and individuality, it was because it allowed this singularisation through the quest for exoticism, the rare and surprising specimen: enthusiastic amateurs, knowledgeable collectors and professional botanists little by little became rivals in the cultivation of these vegetal phenomena which so amazed people.

During the sixteenth century, species hitherto unknown, such as the hyacinth and the tulip, arrived in Europe from the Americas and Asia. The first idea was to get either agricultural or therapeutic benefit from them but, in the end, they became decorative plants which were all the more valued as they had been 'improved' by the gardener's hand. Collectors set up strategies for the selection and cross-breeding of varieties in order to choose the shape and the colour of the petals, for example. Innovations were mainly to do with the substrates feeding the plants and the production of hybrids. Europe in the *Grand Siècle*, the long seventeenth century, was struck by 'tulip mania' and demand drove increased research in order to obtain the most delicate hues: in the eighteenth century about 2,000 types of hyacinth were listed.[58] These lovers of rare flowers drew the public's curiosity and so, in the mid-eighteenth century, Jean de La Tour du Pin, Marquis of Gouvernet, passed for a respected specialist of flowering bulbs and carnations and a visit to his garden in Rue de Vaugirard in Paris was recommended.[59]

The thing to do in town and in the countryside was to offer flowers and fruits from one's gardens; it was a mark of friendship and a measure of distinction. In the 1770s, Mme de Genlis thus enjoyed gifts from Marshal Biron: 'he kept sending me figs, apricot-peaches (the first we have had in

57 *Vogue*, July 1939, p. 42.

58 Milena Rizzotto, 'Le amene mostruosità: coltura, selezione e manipolazione delle piante ornamentali nel XVII secolo', in Allen J. Grieco et al. (dir.) *Le Monde végétal, (XIIe–XVIIe siècles), Savoirs et usages sociaux* (Saint-Denis: Presses Universitaires de Vincennes, 1993), pp. 141–155.

59 Jèze, *Tableau de Paris pour l'année 1759, formé d'après les antiquités, l'histoire, la description de cette ville, etc.* (Paris: C.Hérissant, 1759), p.238.

Paris) and flowers from his magnificent garden'.[60] The fashion was also for Mediterranean citrus fruits, which were favoured in Versailles: the fragrant flowers, the acidic fruit and the harmonious habit of lemon trees, citrons and other orange trees were the pride of garden lovers. Their cultivation was all the more prestigious as they were considered to be very delicate, particularly in northern climes where it was necessary to provide arrangements (boxes and greenhouses) to protect the citrus trees from the rigours of winter. The philistines could fortunately take advantage of the advice proffered in numerous gardening treatises, such as that by M. de la Quintinie, director of the fruit and vegetable gardens for Louis XIV. Cultivating citrus fruit nevertheless remained an expensive occupation when the cost of a glasshouse was taken into account – this was also tricky to install in an urban space. For La Quintinie, a greenhouse less than five metres high remained 'affordable for all sorts of interested, honest persons' and would accommodate plants of a reasonable size. If, on the other hand, one wished to grow trees over three metres in height this supposed the use of larger-sized boxes, so one should plan a glass structure of seven or eight metres in height – something which very few people knew how to build – so that the trees could be taken in there with no trouble.[61] Also, the heating of the glasshouse in winter had to be considered. La Quintinie proposed keeping lamps and torches lit to ward off frost; as for the Dutch, they had invented hydraulic heating devices, which the great botanic gardens procured, but which remained out of reach for average folk.

Expeditions by naturalists all over the world had also revealed, particularly in the second half of the eighteenth century, the extraordinary floral wealth of the planet and these plants were conscripted in the service of Western societies. To do this, it was necessary to rely on greenhouses, the building techniques of which were improving. Of course, initially they were only used by professional horticultors or wealthy amateurs in the countryside. Princes, nobles and all sorts who possessed a fortune had them built in the parks of their chateaux in imitation of the extraordinary one built by the Duke of Chartres at Folie Monceau at the end of the 1770s. They were also to be

60 Stéphanie Félicité de Genlis, *Mémoires inédits de la Madame la Comtesse de Genlis* (Paris: Ladvocat, 1825), vol. 2, p. 131.

61 'I confess to you that this height frightens me, there are, it seems to me, few people who can manage to make such buildings. Hardly even city gates can be seen that have such an elevation.' M. de La Quintinie, *Instruction pour les jardins fruitiers et potagers, avec un Traité des Orangers, suivy de quelques réflexions sur l'Agriculture* (Paris: Claude Barbin, 1690), vol. 2, p. 461.

found, ever more numerous and more gigantic, in botanic gardens. It was only slowly that they left the countryside or parks and gardens to enter the town. In fact, the nineteenth century would appropriate these techniques,[62] these constructions and this floral abundance to democratise them all; it was a period of overabundance, in which faith in science allowed all kinds of excesses, all sorts of hopes. The plant world had to follow this movement and no longer be subject to any limit in space or time: the demiurgic will of each was applied with haste to reveal, beyond the effects of fashion, a botanic talent, a social and technical eminence. Did not Balzac dream of growing no fewer than 100,000 pineapples on his small property, Les Jardies, bought in Sèvres in 1837, in order to make his fortune?

This was precisely the role played by exhibitions of all kinds that punctuated the century, to showcase these distinctions in rank, this emulation which extended right down to hoeing and the handling of secateurs in order to get *the* largest specimen, the rarest, the most beautiful which would bring one glory, albeit fleeting. The horticultural exhibition held in Paris in 1855 gives a good glimpse of all this, with its 650 exhibitors, 250,000 plants on show, 300,000 visitors and 170 medals awarded. One of these was given to the Côte d'Or horticultural society which shown a thousand edible or ornamental vegetables, praised by Roher, the minister for Trade and Agriculture. Acclamatory newspaper articles contributed to departmental pride and to the region's prosperity since orders for plants and fruits increased after this. It is no surprise that, envious of Dijon's success, Caen, Bordeaux, Montauban, Cherbourg, Toulouse, Orleans, etc., also organised similar local exhibitions.[63] The aim of these exhibitions was to display the vegetal, and it was all a true spectacle, with the show being as much to do with the stands where fruits, flowers and vegetables were elegantly arrayed as with those to be found there – the exhibitors and their public. The list of amateurs in Côte d'Or (though professionals also exhibited, of course) is significant: lawyers, doctors, manufacturers, merchants, bankers, perfumers, landlords, retired military officers. In short, the full range of provincial notables, and most of them lived in Dijon. There one found oneself among people from the same world, all of whom sought to stand out as much from the public as from other exhibitors – often flowers

62 Bernard Marrey and Jean-Pierre Monnet, *La Grande Histoire des serres et des jardins d'hiver, France 1780–1900* (Paris: Graphite, 1984).

63 Société d'Horticulture du département de la Côte d'Or, *Revue horticole de la Côte d'Or*, no. 1 (Jan. 1856).

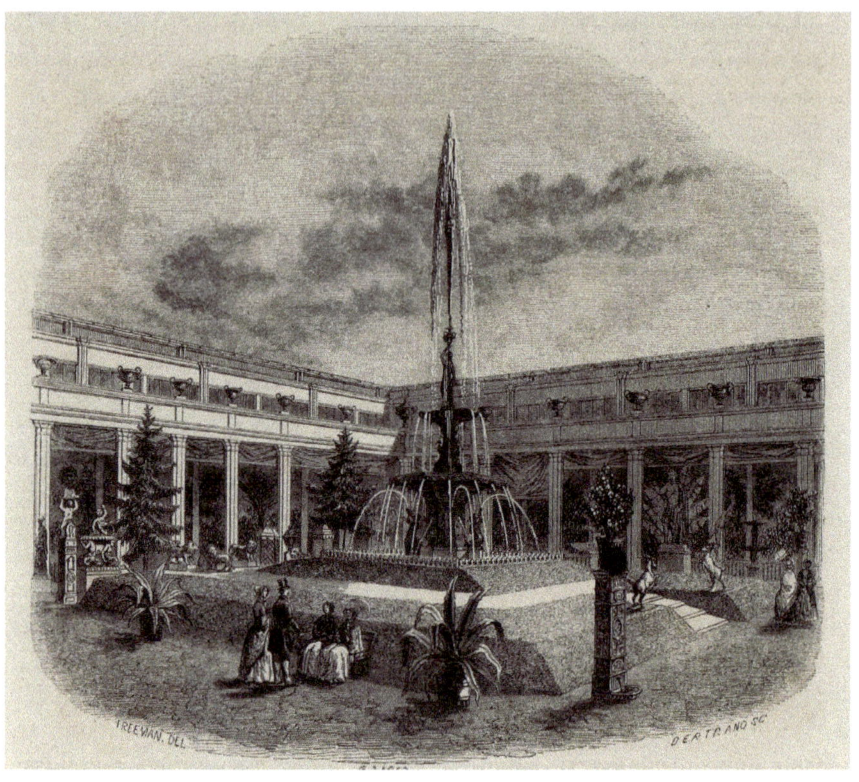

Figure 23.

Freeman, Exposition de l'Industrie en 1849. Cour réservée à l'horticulture. Gravure sur bois. Courtesy of Musée Carnavalet (public domain).

grown by these notables and those grown by workers and artisans featured in different categories.[64]

More poetically, probably, there was enthusiasm for floral novelties, unknown plants or simply those that were priceless. Marguerite Gautier would be the Dame aux Camélias, while Proust's Odette would be identified by her violets or her cattleya orchids. Renée's winter garden in Zola's *La Curée* (*The Kill*) is further testimony to the nineteenth century delectation for rare flowers, scientific and exotic names. Yet, some lamented finding in French parks and gardens only 'the products of cultivation, monsters obtained by a

64 Valérie Chansigaud, *Histoire des Fleurs* (Paris: Delachaux et Niestlé, 2014), p. 78.

hundred different tortures, grafts, mixtures of abnormal pollens' and seeing wild and local flowers completely disappear in the face of this fashion.[65]

This taste for the exotic and the singular grew stronger throughout the century and found its strongest expression in literature in Des Esseintes, a character in *À Rebours (Against the Grain).* Huysmans has him draw up a veritable social hierarchy of plants:

> He pleased his fancy by likening a horticulturist's shop to a microcosm wherein were represented all the different categories of society – poor, vulgar flowers, hovel flowers, so to speak, that are really in their proper place only on the window-sill of a garret, roots that are crammed in milk-tins and old earthen pots, the gilliflower for instance; pretentious, conventional, silly flowers, whose only place is in porcelain vases painted by young ladies, such as the rose; lastly, flowers of high lineage, such as the orchids, dainty and charming, trembling and delicate, such as the exotic flowers, exiles in Paris, kept in hothouses, in palaces of glass, Princesses of the vegetable world, living apart, having nothing whatever in common with the flowers of the street, the blossoms that are the delight of grocers' wives. [66]

This quest for the unusual and the bizarre led more than ever before to a blurring of the boundaries between nature and cultivation. Thus, Des Esseintes only wants in his home real flowers that imitate artificial ones, like the anthurium for example. Like all those of his era, he was also fascinated by orchids which require a heated environment to grow and so were only reserved to an elite. Such manias gave rise to incredible extravagances. This is how, a few years earlier, Théophile Gautier describes a very particular glasshouse as 'an artificial paradise':

> Once over the door step we found ourselves in a large greenhouse carpeted in plants and flowers, which to us at first seemed to be nothing out of the ordinary; except that no aroma came from these fresh plants, from these newly open flower heads. We told ourselves that in this century of strange progress some crazed horticulturalist had perhaps discovered a way of *purifying* a rose of its aroma; fragrance-free flowers! this challenge must have lured some anti-balsamic dreamer. Trying to garner a fine sprig of white lilac, as the proprietor invited us to do, we felt with our fingernail the hard resistance of a thin steel wire ... Everything was fake in this greenhouse, even to the very earth in which the plants plunged their lying feet.[67]

65 Louis Morin, 'Les fleurs', *Les Dimanches parisiens. Notes d'un décadent* (Paris: Conquet, 1898), pp. 61–67, in Limido, *L'art des jardins sous le Second Empire*, p. 44.

66 Joris-Karl Huysmans, *Against the Grain,* Dover, (New York: Three Sirens Press, 1951). Public domain translation – no translator's name given. http://www.ibiblio.org/eldritch/jkh/rebours.html

67 Théophile Gautier, *Moniteur universel*, 27 Oct. 1862, in Limido, *L'Art des Jardins sous le Second Empire*, pp. 47–48.

* * *

The twentieth century has seen the social role of green urban spaces wither and the primacy of respectability has been dropped in favour of freer and more individual relaxation. But since the 1980s, with renewed thinking about landscaping and the rise of ecological questions, topics such as aesthetic pleasure, the delights of the promenade and botanical curiosity are once again imposing themselves on park and garden designers. But nonetheless do we find therein the expression of a process of moral civilisation? Certainly, if we believe that ecological order has in some way supplanted social order. We no longer learn how to behave socially in parks and gardens – unless it is just on the basis of minimal respect arising from the wellbeing of each park user, though this hardly differs from the behaviour expected in any other public space – but we learn how to behave as ecologically responsible citizens, or at least as ones who are enlightened. Of course, urban nature is still, above all, a source of fresh air, for the enjoyment of the senses, for rest. But increasingly it is also the opportunity for public authorities to raise awareness around ecological balances, about the fragility of all plant life and the resources of biodiversity.

From a personal point of view, the vegetal is still a source of social distinction. For sure, the purchasing of plants has become widely democratised; but whether we find them in a garden, inside the home or on a balcony they continue to bear witness to individuality. What is more, access to a green space, be it private or public, remains a string social marker. Sociologists and geographers in fact continue to perceive and denounce what they call an ecological gap.[68] The 'gentrification' of inner cities where the greatest efforts in vegetal installations have been made has driven away the least favoured social groups towards the urban peripheries. Living close to a beautiful park or in a building that looks over a garden, is still reserved to a small number of people.[69] Thinking about the sustainable city tries to take these issues into

68 Jacques Theys, 'L'approche territoriale du "développement durable", condition d'une prise en compte de sa dimension sociale', Dossier 1/2002, online 1 Sept. 2002, http://developpementdurable.revues.org/1475 (accessed 31 Oct. 2014). See also Cyria Emelianoff, 'Pour un partage de la fabrique urbaine', *Revue urbanisme*, Dossier: 'La ville durable en question(s)', 363 (Nov.–Dec. 2008): 45–47.

69 Emmanuel Boutefeu, 'La nature en ville: des enjeux paysagers et sociétaux', *Géoconfluences*, 28 Apr. 2007, http://geoconfluences.ens-lyon.fr/doc/transv/paysage/PaysageViv.htm

account,[70] for it really is densely populated cities, where the highest and the lowest incomes both live, that are often the special target of sustainable development policies, to the detriment of peri-urbanisation. The construction of eco-neighbourhoods comes back to the same question: how, despite their high costs, can they be made accessible to the greatest number

70 Bernard Reygrobellet, *La Nature dans la ville, biodiversité et urbanisme*, Report of the Economic and Social Council (2007), pp. 113–114.

5.

WELLBEING, LIVING WELL

Since the seventeenth century, green spaces have been a site for festivities, merrymaking and diverse entertainments. The monarchy, with its parade of pomp, as it were invented the *garden party*, even if that expression, borrowed from Victorian social life, did not appear in France until the *Belle Époque*. Representing as it does harmony and happiness, vegetal adornment suits all festivities that bring citizens together, whether political, religious, social or even commercial. The many variations on the theme of festivity have diverse recreational forms, such as pleasure gardens and *guinguettes* (suburban cafés) whose vegetal extravagances have made a lasting mark on the collective imagination. But everyday green spaces are also essential to wellbeing in towns: there one can take exercise to stay fit, or relax, or cultivate one's mind, or let one's artistic sensibility have free rein.

Celebration greenery

Parade and decoration at festival time

The vegetal is associated with transience, for just the time that a festivity lasts, and contributes to reinforcing the urban social pact. Under the *Ancien Régime* secular celebrations were added to the feast days of the Christian calendar, commemorating events in a town's history, or connecting the king's subjects with great events in the life of him and his family and with the successes of his policies. The well-oiled mechanism of royal or princely visitations allowed towns to distinguish themselves by the grandeur of their welcome, offering to their sovereigns' eyes the spectacle of transient ornamentation that demonstrated their loyalty to the monarchical project. Nothing was left to chance in the ornamentation of such reinforcements for propaganda, remarkable for their symbolical and allegorical richness. Painted or sculpted artificial vegetation played a unifying role in the grammar of power, particularly the *fleur de lys* in all its variations. Less martial, and still marked with its rustic origins, natural vegetation was more incidental in town decoration in the seventeenth century. It could be that greenery would be strewn along already cleaned streets before the passage of some prestigious cortege; garlands of foliage on the town gates would evoke, where appropriate, the laurels of the victorious monarch.

Figure 24.

Detail of a print depicting the entry of Louis XIII in Paris into 1628.
Courtesy of BNF / Gallica: https://gallica.bnf.fr

Cities in the south of the kingdom opted for vegetal ornaments that testified to the rich productivity of their land. In 1701 Arles was preparing to receive the Dukes of Burgundy and Anjou in high style. The heir to Louis XIV's throne was making an inspection tour of the realm in the company of his brother and a highly ornamented train of courtiers. The route was decorated with great triumphal arches, and 'from the city gate as far as the lodging place of Messeigneurs the Princes, one passed between a double hedge of orange trees interspersed with armed Burghers'. The inhabitants were very vexed when, after they had gone to such expense and trouble, in the end the cortege turned away from their town as it was suspected of being the centre of a smallpox epidemic! At Aix, 'The first object that met the eyes of Messeigneurs the Princes was a forest of Orange, Lemon, Pomegranate, Palm, Fig and Olive trees laden with fruit & flowers, which interlocked and formed the first Arch, situated in the Avenue of the Faubourg des Cordeliers. These trees were ringed by a belt of Jasmines.'[1] As symbols of innocence and purity, fresh flowers more often decorated hairstyles and clothing and were associated with femininity and childhood. If ceremonial required offerings of flowers, young ladies and infants would bear the baskets, hand out bouquets and scatter showers of petals in the streets. Natural vegetal ornaments seem

1 *Mercure Galant*, Apr. 1701, vol. 1, pp. 115–116 and 127–128.

to have been appreciated more in the eighteenth century. Ceres and Flora had the advantage over Mars in the official rhetoric, which was now keener to stage peace and abundance. When she arrived in France in Spring 1770, Marie-Antoinette of Austria broke her journey at Soissons, where she was expected at the bishopric. 'The Intendant of the *Generalité* had had the three roads that led to the bishopric decorated with twenty-five-foot-high fruit trees; these trees, forming an arcade, were liked by ivy garlands wreathed in gold and silver gauze and intermixed with flowers, and lights in shades hung from them.'[2] This countryfied staging showcased a happy wedding, registering the hope then embodied in the Dauphin and Dauphine for the people of France who hoped for a new age of abundance.

After the Revolution, the representative of power, whether king, emperor or president, continued to be honoured with flowers. The vegetal remained central to ceremonial until quite a late date. The arrival of Louis-Napoléon Bonaparte in Paris on 16 October 1852, following his progress through the rest of France, was the occasion for a minutely organised celebration in the great tradition of royal entrances. The vegetal was very much associated with the decoration of buildings and triumphal arches specially erected for the occasion. In one of these near the Arènes de Lutèce, in Paris, two young women representing Renown were suspended, holding in their hands a crown of oak and olive leaves. Around the arch itself forty young women dressed in white scattered petals in the prince's path. Another regime, same flowers: the Republic did not scorn vegetal ornament when it came to flaunting its dignity, as was testified by the protocols surrounding presidential journeys and movements. In December 1888, President Carnot embarked on a real tour of France by rail, both to gauge its technical efficacy and to assert the loyalty of the peoples of France to the new regime. Receptions, banquets, toasts, troop reviews and exchanges with mayors and prefects followed one another, and in every town where he was received the President was awash with vegetal tributes, official bouquets and simple flowers that the townspeople rained down.[3] The ceremonials of the Third Republic also commemorated notable dates in the nation's calendar, harking back to the revolutionary past. From the end of the 1880s, mayoral banquets were deemed to symbolise the national unity proclaimed at the time of the Fête de la Fédération of 1790; those of 1888 and 1889 were given in the Palais de l'Industrie exhibition hall for 4,000 and 13,000 guests. Press photographs and drawings

2 *Gazette de Paris*, 25 May 1770.

3 Bertol-Graivil, *28 Jours du président de la République* (Paris: E. Kolb, 1889).

made of these celebrations show tables richly decorated with fashionable vegetal arrangements at the command of Adolphe Alphand, director of festivities for all of Paris society.[4] In 1900 23,000 participants were expected, more than any building could accommodate, and so the celebration was organised in the heart of the Tuileries Gardens under canvas in the open air decorated with Republican emblems mixed with ceremonial garlands of flowers.

The vegetal was not just the prerogative of ornament carefully managed to celebrate power; in natural or borrowed form it was present in many festive traditions dear to the heart of the urban population. There could be no gallantry without flowers and foliage; one charming custom specified that on the night of 30 April/1 May the besotted lover should plant flowering branches in front of the house of the beauty he was courting. It was also a custom for the residents of a neighbourhood to gather together for the ceremonial planting of a May tree, symbolising the renewal of the seasons, and of the generations, as it was then that young people sealed their betrothals.

> Tree of the month of May, favoured by fate,
> that we see crowned with garlands of flowers;
> planted to the sound of flutes and musettes,
> and the noise of drums and bright trumpets;
> peerless tree, drawing the eyes of all.[5]

Townspeople accorded a more or less complex symbolism to nature according to whether or not they had been introduced to a classical culture giving access to the keys of mythological reading, and according to how familiar they were with literary works between whose pages, from the eighteenth century on, a sensitivity to nature was born. At all events, everyone associated it with celebration, gaiety and conviviality. This was even more true on the occasion of religious festivals, when it was the custom to decorate not merely the church, but its surroundings as well. The ceremony of the branches on Palm Sunday at Easter is now a vestige of the vegetal present in celebrations that overflowed into the public urban space, up till the 1950s at least. Philippe L. de Vilmorin recalls that, in the nineteenth century, the month of Mary (May) was a boon for little florists selling white flowers – marguerites, dahlias, wallflowers, etc. More broadly, some particularly popular saints' days (John, 24 June; Peter and Paul, 29 June; Anne, 26 July;

4 Alain Corbin et al., *Les Usages politiques des fêtes aux XIXe–XXe siècles* (Paris: Publications de la Sorbonne, 1994), pp. 162–163.

5 *Mercure galant*, May 1700.

Louis, 25 August, for example) featured much buying of flowers, for a wish is not made without a bouquet: street sellers thronged to churchyards, and to the markets themselves, at least in Paris, and the markets on the Quai aux Fleurs were particularly busy at such times.[6]

At the end of the nineteenth century, social movements availed themselves of vegetal language to enhance their visibility in the public space. From 11 November 1934, patriotism was demonstrated by way of France's famous cornflower, admittedly often artificial, sold to support war veterans and their families. During the Occupation, the Pétain regime encouraged the sale of such flowers as mimosa in Annecy for the benefit of the *Secours National*, to come to the aid of the civil population. The lily-of-the-valley filled the streets from the beginning of May: a flower of the returning fine weather, and for centuries a lucky charm, it has probably only been associated with Labour Day in the Paris region for the last hundred years or so, replacing the red wild rose. It is only truly since the 1930s, and thanks to the government tolerating the sale of lilies-of-the-valley in the public street by private individuals on 1 May, that the tradition has taken root.

Since the *Trente Glorieuses* years (1945–1975) and the start of the dominance of plastic and electric decoration that could shine on into the small hours, times of festival and vegetal profusion are hardly ever associated. Spiritual flowers withdraw into churches, and the May Day lily-of-the-valley is purely commercial and void of all ideology, while since the end of the 1980s people have turned away from the big collectivist utopias; nowadays, fifty million sprigs are sold each year in France, most of them in just a few days. By taking part in Towns in Bloom competitions, local authorities are financing, often at great expense, the maintenance of terraces and permanent floral displays which make the vegetal just an element of everyday street furniture. This banalisation should not lead us to forget that, in the years after the war, festival times were marked by waves of flowers in the streets.

Flowers are at times the very substance of the festival, especially in the south-east of France where for centuries they have been linked with the benevolence of the climate and prosperity. This is the case with the celebrated competitions for flower-decorated floats[7] (sometimes called *corsos fleuris*) which originated on the Côte d'Azur.

6 Philippe L. de Vilmorin, *Les Fleurs à Paris* (Paris: Baillière, 1892), pp. 25–26.

7 Michel Conan and Juliette Favaron, 'Comment les villages devinrent des paysages', *Annales de la recherche urbaine*, 'Natures en villes', 74 (Mar. 1997): 51–52.

Figure 25.

Constitution of the 'French Militia in Annecy'. Sale of flowers for the benefit of the 'Secours national'.
André Carteron, 1er mars.
Courtesy of Photo archives Dep. 74, 7 Fi 703.

The first of these competitions took place in Nice, with the formalisation of the Carnival from 1873. From then on, popular initiative was supplanted by municipal organisation, which perpetuated the parades of floats and the battles of flowers. These parades were even organised outside the carnival itself, with competitions for children, motor-cars, bicycles, etc. It was necessary to pay an entrance fee and then to buy flowers to throw at the other participants. This model spread throughout France, to non-Mediterranean holiday resorts such as Aix-les-Bains and Luchon, and as far as Paris, where, from 1884, a parade took place on the very chic Avenue des Acacias in the Bois de Boulogne. Nowadays the town of Sélestat organises what is certainly one of the most famous parades in Alsace, inaugurated in 1929, and since 1954 organised around a particular theme variously interpreted by each float. The floral prodigality is always striking: at the end of the nineteenth century, some vehicles in Nice could use up to 2,000 bouquets! All sorts of flowers were deployed in the contests that often accompanied these parades: carnations, violets and peonies, for instance. Sometimes a town would specialise: Sélestat gave prominence to dahlias, easier to use in decoration and offering a fine range of colours, while Bormes-les-Mimosas made the most of its eponymous flower, but did not deprive itself of anemones, marguerites and gerberas for ornamenting conveyances. These fetes were very expensive, especially for those taking part. In Paris the 'Fête des fleurs' as it was called, which after its resounding beginnings had somewhat fallen out of favour, became fashionable again with the development of the motor-car. At the behest of the Automobile Club, Paris Society then hurried along to join the parade with finely decorated automobiles piled high with flowers thanks to the skill of the great florists, such as the Maison Lachaume, established in 1845 in the Rue Royale and supplying the elite - Marcel Proust got the orchids for his buttonholes there. In 1908, one of the winners of the competition, Madame Chiquita, spent 1,500 francs decorating her car. But what decoration!

> Under a dais of gauze topped by palm leaves of *Cocos Weddeltiana*, the artiste sheltered her Spanish elegance amid a flood of white Peonies and pure Lilies that made her dark beauty shine out. Garlands of *Mysiphyllum* mingled with blue Hydrangeas and *Cocos* palm leaves running here and there linked all parts of the car, whose contours they followed closely, from front to back; on the seat, on either side of the driver, was a magnificent sheaf of white Peonies and Hydrangeas, and the bonnet was buried under a superb profusion of green *Cocos* leaves, Peonies and Lilies whose artistic chaos enhanced the vibrant colours.[8]

The ladies were very prominent in these parades, and it was they who were awarded the prizes. It must not be forgotten that, while landscaping was a masculine business, along with natural history, horticulture and the kitchen garden, flowers were the province of the ladies, who, it was thought, shared their fragility and beauty. Flower festivals, open to the public at large and drawing all eyes to the magnificent arrays of high society, helped to make

8 'La Fête des Fleurs à Paris', *Le Jardin*, 20 June 1908: 180–182.

Figure 26.

Flower Festival in Trouville, summer 1922.
Courtesy of BNF / Gallica. https://gallica.bnf.fr

vegetal achievements commonplace: sumptuous floral arrangements were part of what good society expected to find wherever they took their leisure.

The theatre of ordinary entertainment

At the end of the seventeenth century and during the eighteenth, urban nature was organised to provide citizens with recreational space where they went for relaxation and entertainment. It is not surprising that public gardens, royal parks and boulevards then constituted a privileged context for festival/spectacles presented by towns or by the king as a show of munificence: they could entertain a large number of spectators and turn themselves into sumptuous decorations through the magic of illumination. The effect is even more interesting when it helps to valorise a seat of power. The reception organised in honour of the Dukes of Burgundy and Anjou in the gardens of the King's House at Marseille in April 1701 is an example of the prodigality the public authorities could display on the occasion of a princely entrance.

The garden of acclimatisation adjoining the Intendant's residence situated within the new arsenal built in 1665 was chosen for entertaining and feeding the company. At nightfall the vegetal world was transformed through the magic of lighting into fairy decorations: 'Everything was ringed by lights and outlined with lanterns, forming a thousand shapes … The Courtyard of the King's House was lit up, and above all a great Tree was raised right up and its lights showed up all its parts so well that for a long time it held the gaze of all those who had the pleasure of seeing this Fete.' At the end of the garden, a triumphal arch and temporary decorations blended kingly symbolism with glorious references to Greco-Roman Antiquity. In the walkways, lemonade sellers were busy in pretend shops giving out coffee, liquor, refreshments and other delights to the guests. The fete's finishing touch was a firework display in the garden, which the princes viewed from the balcony of the King's House. Worn out by the pace of the official visit the guests withdrew almost before the last rocket had fallen to earth, 'but those in the Garden did not wait until they had gone to pillage all the sweetmeats and bottles of liquor so that not even the coffee-pots were left'.[9] The ordinary people had not indeed been admitted into the princes' immediate presence, but they had been able to enjoy the spectacle and the profusion of food and drink symbolising the paternal and nurturing power of the king.

Besides this kind of exceptional event, the boulevards and some public gardens were still the theatre for ordinary entertainments accessible to all classes of citizens. In Paris, the boulevards and especially those to the north 'brought together all the facilities industry could produce to afford interest to the idle and relaxation to the busy, Spectacles of all kinds, charming & varied, fine Mansions and delightful Houses: there are the temples of Love; it is not only Cafés & Caterers with their music, garlands of flowers & shady groves who create an atmosphere of faerie and enchantment.'[10] For a few pennies, anyone could enjoy the living spectacles of fair-men and animal keepers, comic plays presented in the theatres, food and drink available in the cafés and restaurants, not to mention the lively market in love for sale, which was at its height (see Chapter 6).

In Lyon at the beginning of the reign of Louis XIV, the consulate licensed several lemonade sellers to set up wooden stalls in Place Bellecour, on condition that they were touching and aligned with each other to create

9 *Mercure Galant*, April 1701, vol. 1, pp. 115–116.

10 Jacques-Antoine Dulaure, *Nouvelle description des curiosités de Paris* (Paris: Lejay, 1787), pp. 71–72.

Figure 27.

Pierre-François Courtois, after Augustin de Saint-Aubin, *La promenade des remparts de Paris*, 1760. Courtesy of BNF / Gallica: https://gallica.bnf.fr

the appearance of a street, and that they should be dismantled at the end of the high season. In the spring and summer, welcome refreshments were offered to customers, such as 'rossoly', an alcoholic drink scented with roses and orange flowers much appreciated in southern Germany and Italy. In the public spaces devoted to leisure the beau monde mingled naturally enough with ordinary people, like them looking for entertainment. This festive atmosphere inspired many pictorial representations, and stage-plays too, such as *La Soirée des boulevards* (*An Evening on the Boulevards*) by Charles-Simon Favart, given in Paris by the Comédie Italienne in November 1758. 'The Theatre shows part of the fine Boulevards lit up; there are several tables in the background and to the sides, under the trees. Different people of all classes are sitting there; Catalans are making puppets dance on a board to the sound of oboes and bagpipes.'[11] The staging featured a mixture of witticisms and conversations caught between the tables; the matrimonial ambitions of

11 Charles-Simon Favart, *La Soirée des boulevards, ambigû mêlé de scènes, de chants et de danses* (Paris: Duchesne, 1759), p. 3.

a noble widow seduced by a schemer; the entanglements of a bourgeois torn between his wife and his mistress; the business of a knight and some smooth talkers, all intersected with the cries of the lemonade seller, the sweet-merchant and the ironmonger, and the songs and dances of folk from Savoy dressed as marmots. It all ended up with a patriotic representation of a situation, showing the celebrations enacted on the Boulevard in honour of a victory of Louis XV over Frederick II of Prussia on the battlefields of Hanover. This sort of cheap and unpretentious entertainment delighted both the workman and the aristocrat just come to have a good time. The play brought to life the little familiar world going on in urban natural spaces, as a response to the expectations of passers-by or as an inducement to them to spend money. While some commercial establishments were institutionalised and profitable, many of the small businesses in the boulevards and gardens were minuscule and brought only a few pence to those running them, such as the keepers of bears and dogs, acrobats and cake-sellers on the Champs-Élysées at the very end of the eighteenth century. Around 1830 we still find, on the same avenue, sellers of flowers or of blackcurrant juice, or those offering a kind of wafer called *les plaisirs des dames* (ladies' delights).[12] In the nineteenth century and up to our own times, attractions involving animals were particularly favoured by younger members of the public, and owners of more or less exotic quadrupeds could expect to make a bit of money. Thus, we find an owner offering rides on a donkey or in a cart to children visiting the Nantes botanic garden at the beginning of the twentieth century, or a mahout in the 1930s offering trips around the Jardin des Plantes in Paris on the back of an elephant.

It needs to be said that the Jardin des Plantes, in association with the Muséum national d'Histoire naturelle (National museum of natural history) of which we will say more in Chapter 8, owed something of its popularity to the magnificent zoo housed there from 1793 and drawing on royal collections.[13] Initially, scientists such as Bernardin de Saint-Pierre wanted to recreate the animals' original habitat as far as possible; in his turn Lacépède proposed designing an English-style park, bringing together the flora of the animals' countries of origin and giving them some freedom, each in its own space: enclosures for the herbivores, pools for the marine animals, caves for the big cats, etc. Landscaping projects were even developed to this end. But

12 John Claudius Loudon, 'Notes and reflections made during a tour through part of France and Germany in the Autumn of the year 1828', *Gardener's Magazine* (1830): 647.

13 For this whole section on zoos, see Éric Baratay and Élisabeth Hardouin-Fugier, *Zoos. Histoire des jardins zoologiques en Occident (XVIe–XXe siècle)* (Paris: La Découverte, 1998).

in the end, the scheme was adopted only for the most peaceful animal species, which grazed in an enclosure within an English garden (in distinction from the botanical school, which remained '*à la française*', French-style), while the more dangerous animals found themselves in pits or cages. Despite these modifications to the original project, it was nonetheless innovatory in respect of preceding menageries which were often private and of limited access, and which did not put their live collections on display. The term 'zoological garden' did not appear in France until the 1830s, and then yielded to 'zoo' in the first half of the twentieth century: semantics attest that at this period the space within which the animals were presented mattered as much as the species that lived there. What was wanted was a limited exoticism, an unthreatening escapism in the context of promenades whose highlight was the animals.

> The number of people walking in the Jardin des Plantes on holidays was not fewer than thirty thousand. And it was evident that these were all decent people; they were solid working-men, demure young ladies, often whole families, all prompted by a sound instinct to come to rest from the labour of the week and to seek calm and pleasant entertainment in this great temple of nature. Some surrounded the animal enclosures, others stopped in front of the cages of birds, marvelling at the sight of all their varied shapes and colours; and there were some, leaning on the terrace fences and studying delightedly the baskets of artfully arranged flowers and the rich, crowded flower-beds.[14]

Presentation in cages exemplifies what Éric Baratay called the encyclopaedic style: in the end it is a reproduction of the inventories of natural history cabinets, but this time with living beings. This enabled artists to draw often immobilised animals, especially the great birds of prey, who could not fly in aviaries that were too small. Public enthusiasm, however, steadily erased the scientific and the artistic interest in favour of mere spectacular presentation: this was the time of monkey and big cat 'palaces', devised more for the visual demands of the spectators than for the wellbeing of the animals. In Lyon, for instance, the bear cages, installed in 1865 and 1882 in the Tête d'Or park, were sited at the intersection of several pathways and surrounded by areas of grass inhabited by small animals, making the bears still more impressive. The great provincial cities, in fact, imitated Paris in this field: Marseille created its own zoological garden in 1854, Lyon established its own in the Tête d'Or park in 1858, Mulhouse set itself up in 1868 and Lille in 1877.

14 Michel-Charles Durieu de Maisonneuve, *Le Nouveau Jardin des Plantes, discours prononcé dans la séance publique d'hiver de la Société linnéenne de Bordeaux le 4 novembre 1853* (Bordeaux: imprimerie Justin Dupuy, 1853), p. 20.

As is shown in the words of this song, whose slightly ponderous punchline amused customers in bars in Lille at the end of the nineteenth century, a visit to the zoological garden did not give rise to melancholy: focusing on the spectacle of an exotic, unfamiliar fauna, the narrator and his companion forget the original point of their amorous meeting:

> When a native of Lille
> Sees his home town enhanced
> Seeing there a second Paris
> That really gives pleasure
> Nothing more magnificent
> Than a zoological garden
> …
> One day on a stroll
> I went in with my neighbour
> She and Me both stunned
> On seeing this paradise
> With baskets of flowers
> And birds of all colours.[15]

Pleasure gardens

In response to a pressing desire of the urban elites, a new kind of establishment appeared in the middle of the eighteenth century: the pleasure garden, offering various refreshments and diversions within its walls, which one paid to enter.[16] Paris in particular was the epicentre of this new fashion. From the 1760s onwards, Vauxhalls on the English model were being opened: these were generally circular buildings surrounding a central stage where spectacles were presented. They could be open or covered, with either a simple cloth or at times a rotunda. They were always surrounded by a garden, which played a more or less significant role according to whether it was a summer or winter Vauxhall. The first of these sites of pleasure in the capital was the Torré garden, which opened in 1764, followed the year after by the Ruggieri garden. Balls were given there, and firework displays; there were garlands and lanterns, and there were games, cafés, concerts, acrobatic shows and so on on offer. These enterprises were not always commercial successes; the Colisée,

15 Julien Grimonprez, *Une visite au jardin zoologique, chanson lilloise chantée par les Amis-Réunis, à l'estaminet du Petit-Guet, rue St Sébastien…* (n.p, n.d).

16 On the pleasure gardens, we have used Gilles-Antoine Langlois, *Folies, Tivolis et attractions: les premiers parcs de loisirs parisiens* (Paris: Délégation artistique à la ville de Paris, 1991).

which opened beside the Champs-Élysées in 1771, had to close ten years later; the Ranelagh, opened in 1774, did rather better, probably because in the middle of the 1780s it became a kind of private club for the elite. The most famous of these places of pleasure, and the one which gave a central role to its garden, was the Tivoli, whose name has since been taken up for pleasure gardens everywhere.

Created in 1771 by the wealthy businessman Simon-Charles Boutin in the Saint Lazare area, then Paris's northern limit, the Tivoli was in fact three gardens – French, Italian and English – on eight hectares of sloping ground. It drew in a varied public: Mme Vigée-Lebrun, or Marie-Antoinette, who spent the afternoon there the day before her flight to Varennes; a more popular crowd when it was declared a national garden in 1793, and after the beheading of Boutin the following year. Tivoli never stopped being reborn out of its ashes and transformed: there was even a great spectacle there for the coronation of Charles X in 1825. Here is an Englishman's description of the Tivoli in 1803:

> The place seemed to be raised by the magic touch of enchantment. We entered upon gravelled walks which were cut through little winding and intersecting hillocks of box; those which formed the sides were surmounted by orange trees which presented a beautiful colonnade; immediately after we had passed them, we entered an elegant bower of honeysuckles, roses and eglantines, which formed the grand entrance to the garden. Here a most animated scene of festivity opened before us. On one side were rope dancers, people riding at the ring, groups of persons playing at shuttlecock, which seemed to be the favourite, and I may add, the most ridiculous diversion; on the other side were dancers, tumblers, mountebanks; and parties all with gay countenances, seated in little bowers enjoying lemonade and ices. In the centre as we advanced were about three hundred people, who were dancing the favourite waltz.[17]

Pleasure gardens like this proliferated in the capital, each attempting to distinguish itself from its competitors by new extravagances. This is the foundation of today's amusement parks. The roundabout first appeared on the Champs Élysées under the Directory, replacing equestrian carousels where horsemen had to seize hold of a ring: a circular roof like a Chinese pagoda, fantastical animals, oriental people, horses, wooden admittedly, all put into circular movement by a mechanism activated by a number of men.[18] It was here too that the first roller-coasters were introduced, first as *Swiss mountains* and then as *Russian mountains*: in 1817 those in the Beaujon garden were

17 Sir John Carr, *The Stranger in France* (London: J. Johnson, 1803), ch. 13, p. 136.

18 Frank Debié, *Jardins de capitales* (Paris: éditions du CNRS, 1992), p. 152.

Figure 28.

Provost, Bal Mabille. Engraving, 19th century.
Courtesy of BNF / Gallica.

Figure 29.

Isidore Laurent Deroy, *Ancienne folie ou Chartreuse Beaujon. Rues Balzac, Berryer, Lamennais.* Engraving, 1819.
Public domain image from Musée Carnavalet.

the highest in Paris, reaching 25 metres high and plunging down at sixty kilometres per hour!

At Monceau, established at the request of the Duke of Chartres by Carmontelle in 1778 and then Blaikie in 1781, the extraordinary leapt out at all times: structures, decorative elements, often little buildings of oriental design calculated to surprise the visitor at every turn, multiplied across nineteen hectares. There was also a minaret, a drawbridge, a pyramid, a pagoda, a Greek temple, Gothic ruins, landscapes in a single colour, grottoes, an island, a desert, a wood, exotic vegetation, and so on. Of course, not all these places of relaxation and sociability were on this scale, and one finds little gardens, like the Frascati garden, a true sophisticated salon just twelve metres by 25, where every evening, for a fairly expensive entrance fee, you could hear serenades amidst illuminated acacias, orange and rose trees. If one were in a mood for dancing instead, one of the great fashionable places in the first half of the nineteenth century was the Grande Chaumière garden. Opened in 1783 in the Montparnasse neighbourhood it was famed for the beauty of the young women who went there, and it was frequented by young people of the Latin Quarter, artists and military men – Bonaparte lunched there the day after his marriage to Joséphine. A sort of prototype of the night club, it was one of the places students favoured for picking up girls; one waltzed around the house with its thatched roof, before the polka came along in the 1840s and then the cancan (which first saw the light here) took over. Even so, it had to close in 1853.

From the middle of the nineteenth century, town-dwellers could choose between the attractions of a pleasure garden in the open air and the comfort of gardens under glass, a novelty fostered by the triumphs of industrial architecture. Embodying progress in this technological century, huge glasshouses lent themselves to all kinds of vegetal extravagance, to enhance the leisure-time of the privileged. Once again, pleasure gardens created a sensation in seizing on these original and spectacular structures for commercial purposes: in Paris the most famous example was the aptly named *Jardin d'Hiver* (Winter Garden) on the Champs-Élysées which opened in 1846 and proved such a success – 40,000 visitors a month – that it was rebuilt in December 1847 even larger: a hundred metres long and above all eighteen metres high, unheard of in France.[19] In Lyon a similar establishment opened the same year, constructed by the architect Hector Horeau not far from the future Tête d'Or park. The public flocked into each of these, fascinated by these gigantic

19 Yves-Marie Allain, *D'où viennent nos plantes?* (Paris: Calmann-Lévy, 2004), pp. 119–120.

glasshouses, outstanding and magnificent constructions of steel and glass. Such places lent themselves to all kinds of diversions. One could dance there, certainly, mainly in the evening; by day, they could constitute a reading-room, with journals, magazines and botanical works available. One could eat there, but also buy bouquets of flowers, or flowers to enhance hairstyles or dresses. Here is a description of the Champs-Élysées garden some weeks after its opening:

> All fashionable Paris pours … into this Paradise at 12 degrees above zero. Palms, olive trees, luxuriant vegetation, spread out under this glass dome. Beds of camellias and the rarest of flowers line both sides of the pathway, to which the payment of twenty sous will allow you access … Birds from all four corners of the world, fish of all colours, bouquets and pots of flowers are yours to choose, from 50 cents to 100 francs.[20]

For unassuming, and doubtless less staid, entertainment in the nineteenth century, one made one's way to *guinguettes*, of which there were many in the villages around Paris, made famous by artists and literary Bohemians. Like pleasure gardens and winter gardens guinguettes were entertainment businesses using vegetal décor, but the cost of the many attractions on offer there was lower and made for a democratisation of this kind of leisure activity. From 1848 the *guinguettes* of Plessis became very popular thanks to a bar owner called Joseph Gueusquin who established a restaurant lodged in a huge chestnut tree which he named '*Au Grand Robinson*', alluding to Daniel Defoe's hero. It was so successful that many other bars, restaurants and all sorts of places of entertainment sprang up roundabout, and the hamlet took the name of 'Robinson' from then on, linking it to that of Plessis in 1909. Gueusquin's idea was taken up by competitors, and notably by the *Grand Arbre* (big tree) *guinguette* on the other side of the road: the *Grand Robinson* then became the *Vrai Arbre* (real tree) in 1888. On this postcard from the early twentieth century, one can see how crowded it was on the Rue de Malabry where these establishments were concentrated.

The guinguettes did not really survive World War II. Those at Plessis kept going until the 1960s, sometimes at the cost of surprising metamorphoses: the *Vrai Arbre* abandoned the myth of Robinson for the Wild West and Johnny Halliday. But the establishments were closing one after the other before their disappearance in 1976. They had nonetheless played a vital role in the development, popularity and features of the *commune*, which from being a village became a town in 1918 with the arrival of garden cities and *Habitations à Bon Marché* (affordable housing).

20 'Jardin d'hiver, Champs Élysées', *L'Indépendant*, 13 Jan. 1848.

Figure 30.

Competition from guingettes at Le Plessis-Robinson in the 1930s.
Courtesy of Plessis-Robinson Municipal Archives.

Nowadays there are hardly any equivalents of pleasure gardens or *guinguettes*. The mechanisation of roundabouts, roller-coasters and bumper cars, ever larger and more spectacular, omnipresent electric lighting and sound systems in fairs and urban amusement parks, have driven the vegetal context into oblivion – insofar as there is one, all the structures usually being sited on car parks and other concreted surfaces. Some theme parks and holiday villages have picked up the principle of a garden under glass, presenting covered swimming pools and other play ponds within highly artificial tropical vegetation. However, shortage of available land means that these establishments are usually sited on the outskirts of towns, or even in the heart of the countryside. Much the same can be said of zoos: fewer people are visiting city zoos, favouring instead rural ones whose larger grounds make them more able to offer visitors a real immersion in a natural environment. There is no denying that a taste for zoos persisted throughout the twentieth century. However, the increased prominence of defenders of animal causes and the dissemination of a now widespread environmental sensibility have contributed to a transformation of old zoos – which were more like prisons than 'animal gardens', as they were called in the nineteenth century – into ecologically correct establishments. Henceforward it has been less a matter of exhibiting mastery of nature than of allowing visitors to get close to it, to observe the behaviour of animals in a natural context that approximates to that of their life in the wild. The apes' rock in Vincennes zoo is characteristic in this respect. This movement, which began in the inter-war years, became stronger after 1945, and certainly promoted the development of places which offered animals other conditions of captivity. People were becoming aware that the vegetal, just like adequate space, was as crucial to the wellbeing of animals as it was to that of humans.

Time out in nature

We have described the emergence of a strong social demand for public recreational spaces as one of the factors explaining the greening of towns from the seventeenth century onwards. They became even more vital for town-dwellers with the development from the eighteenth century of a leisure civilisation that democratised time for oneself. As places suitable for both relaxation and physical activity, for creation and recreation, natural urban spaces fostered the wellbeing of both body and mind.

Exercising the body

Natural spaces in town are still favoured places for letting off steam physically: one can dance there, yes, but one can also give oneself over to physical games and activities. Since towns have existed, the inhabitants have been used to finding some free space within the urban fabric to practise energetic games in the open air, in pursuit of both enjoyment and health. At the beginning of the seventeenth century, people enjoyed games of skill, games with skittles, throwing games with pucks or balls, other ball games, and games with weapons such as bows and crossbows, gradually becoming rather more sporting than military. All social classes played games, but it was a given that the plebs did not mingle with the elite; it was also and exclusively a male kind of sociability. Open-air activities helped towards keeping some spaces not built upon, where nature could exercise at least some of its rights; for instance, land dedicated to shooting or ball games may have been meadows that stayed grassy because they were liable to flood. While some games such as skittles or shuffleboard could be arranged spontaneously on a street-corner or in a square, others needed bigger spaces and more or less important specific arrangements. The popular game of '*courte boule*', a kind of bowls or shuffleboard, required a '*bouloire*' (a bowling alley) with a wooden floor where the player threw his bowl by hand. It was relatively easy to fit private gardens with this kind of equipment. By 1630 the fashion for *courte boule* was such that Louis XIII authorised the commercial exploitation of 1,500 such structures. The cost of taking part was quite modest, about two *sols* for each ball thrown. In the case of '*mail*', an ancestor of croquet played with balls and a mallet, the spatial requirement was much more considerable. Much favoured by Henri IV and the young Louis XIII, this somewhat aristocratic game was played in Paris on two pitches lined with elms beside the Porte de Montmartre or on the mall of the Arsenal beside the Seine, an old quay that Henri IV had made into a tree-lined promenade.[21] In Nîmes the enthusiasm for *mail* was such that parties spontaneously organised in the streets were accused of disturbing the traffic and hindering the smooth flow of business, as well as attracting complaints from locals about the damage done by stray balls. In 1636 the municipal authorities gave permission to the lieutenant of the diocesan provost to construct a pitch for *mail* on land he owned in the Saint Vincent quarter near the old ramparts. In the eighteenth century this pitch was a matter of pride to the townspeople: it was 'one of the finest that there is in France, both by the extent and beauty of its two great pathways, and by the singularity of those which cross and intersect these two along their whole length in the form of a labyrinth'.[22]

When there was no provision of this kind, boulevards and promenades, intended for well-regulated walking, were taken over. On the Champs-Élysées, games of *jeu de paume* (real tennis) and groups playing ball or '*barres*' prompted the keeper to intervene and he harangue the players, without much success. A report from April 1779 shows how determined the players were not to let this recreational space be taken from them: 'these little jokers, who are almost all lads from shops or school, soon restarted the same game, shouting out on all sides in defiance of the Keeper. When he appeared they just stood still. As they split up, they shouted to each other: See you on Sunday, four o'clock, game of *barres*.'[23] In the Age of Enlightenment the 'jokers' in

21 Élisabeth Belmas, *Jouer autrefois : essai sur le jeu dans la France moderne (XVIe–XVIIIe siècle)* (Seyssel: Champ Vallon, 2006), p. 114.

22 Léon Ménard, *Histoire civile, ecclésiastique et littéraire de la ville de Nismes avec les preuves* (Paris: H.D. Chaubert), vol. 6, p. 10.

23 Arlette Farge and Laurent Turcot, *Flagrant délit à la promenade des Champs-Élysées, les dossiers Ferdinand de Federici, 1777–1791* (Paris: Gallimard, 2008).

question came from the lower classes. From the end of the seventeenth century, well-born young men forsook team games, devoting themselves to exercises with a military origin, such as fencing and riding, and to dancing – all activities requiring strict physical discipline.

In the eighteenth century, however, physical activities were the subject of renewed interest among the social elites, under the influence of Neo-Hippocratic medical discourse – as testified by the numbers practising the rapid walking recommended by Doctor Tronchin, described in Chapter 1. The public was quickly convinced of the health-giving value of physical activities.

> It is certain that of all the Games involving exercise *Mail* is the most enjoyable & best for the health; it is not at all violent and one can at the same time play, chat & walk in good company. There is more movement involved than in an ordinary walk, and the stimulus you derive from pushing the 'Boule' from place to place does wonders for the transpiration of the humours, & there is no rheumatism or similar malady that cannot be prevented, or cured, by this game, played in moderation when good weather and circumstances allow it.[24]

Medical discourse also promoted the positive effects on the body of real tennis right up until the last years of the nineteenth century. One finds hygienist arguments in the promotion of tennis by certain doctors, such as Doctor Lagrange, author of an 1891 essay on *'la longue paume'* (early version of lawn tennis). It particularly recommends the curative effects of tennis for women, for strengthening their abdominal muscles.[25] In a style that was doubtless more eye-catching, journalistic writing of the time shows laughing couples bursting with health exchanging shots in a romantic context of lawns enclosed by protecting hedges. The first tennis courts did not appear until after 1880.

Despite the continuance of playing games, during the nineteenth century *Ancien Régime* games became transformed into sports with codes of rules and, gradually, specific equipment and clothes. This evolution can be explained by a conjunction of external factors (social preoccupations, hygienic theory and the discourse on the 'improvement of the races' in a context of international competition, and the introduction of physical activities into the school system); and developments in the preferences and practices of sportsmen themselves. Up to the 1870s, the French sporting landscape was

24 *Nouvelles règles pour le jeu de mail. Tant sur la manière d'y bien jouer, que pour décider les divers événements qui peuvent arriver à ce jeu* (Paris: C. Huguier, 1717), p. 2.

25 Jean-Michel Peter and Gérard Fouquet, 'Du jeu de paume au tennis, les discours des médecins aux XVIIIe et XIXe siècles', in Grégory Quin and Anaïs Bohuon, *L'Exercice corporel du XVIIIe siècle à nos jours* (Paris: Glyphe, 2013), pp. 61–80.

dominated by gymnastic societies, generally working class, offering both indoor and outdoor training, and also some more social events. In the Belle Époque, representatives of the elites, such as students, made English-style sports fashionable, sports played in defined spaces where the vegetal supplied the background or else the complete natural context. Establishing spaces reserved for sport in French towns proceeded very gradually in comparison with other European examples. In the 1870s and 1880s, enthusiasts of sports from over the Channel, such as running races, had to negotiate use of public spaces.[26] Members of the runners' Club des Coureurs met on the Cours-la-Reine, and those of the Racing Club used the Tuileries before obtaining from the City of Paris a concession to have tracks constructed in the Bois du Boulogne. Footballers and cyclists were in the same predicament: to hold championships and races they set up temporary places with trees serving as markers and even forming curves to be negotiated! Before the building of Lyon's first velodrome in 1893, cyclists invaded the walkways of the Tête d'Or park, or even the Place Bellecour, which was the setting for a race in 1887. However, the sophisticated spa towns set the tone by fitting themselves out with such structures as racecourses that were indispensable to the pleasures of the elite. The Jockey Club was founded in France in 1833, and while there were only around thirty branches in 1845, on the eve of World War I there were nearly 450. It was on the grassy grounds of racecourses, where leisure events were almost systematically organised, that good society initiated itself into such new sporting activities as lawn tennis, and even motoring. By the end of the nineteenth century, these new sporting practices were absorbed into public policy, with specialised structures beginning to proliferate, and so they became much more democratic. For instance, from 1913, the architect Tony Garnier was tackling the construction of a veritable sports plain at Gerland, associating the famous football stadium with running tracks, games fields, a gymnasium, a swimming pool and a restaurant. By 1936 there were already 149 sports complexes of this type and 589 stadiums.

In this sort of highly functional space, artificialised nature accommodates itself to the requirements of sporting performances: we have already described in chapter 3 the techniques of preparing grass, and one could also cite the case of golf courses, whose structure, with obstacles, stretches of water, 'roughs' and mathematically exact greens, is devised to make the player deploy all his skills to make good shots. None of this inhibits the organisation of events in

26 Philippe Tétard (ed.), *Histoire du sport en France, de la Libération à nos jours* (Paris: Vuibert, 2007).

Figure 31.

Postcard of the Pommery stadium in Reims.
Source: Authors' collection.

traditional gathering places, such as public parks, as, for example, the now ritualised arrivals of the riders in the Tours de France.

Through the twentieth century, sport in fact established its hegemony in western society as both a practice and a spectacle. At the level of nation states, it need not be said that the power of a nation is measured in part by the yardstick of its sporting achievements in such great international meetings as the Olympic Games, whose political importance is no secret from anyone. It was following the lamentable Rome Olympics of 1960, where French athletes did not exactly shine, that a very proactive and youth-oriented public policy came into being. In the context of civic planning that manifested itself particularly in the construction of large entities, the state financed, in the framework of legal programmes, hundreds of thousands of sports installations whose management was left to municipal authorities. This enabled whole generations to be introduced to competitive sport, and also contributed to the dissemination of leisure sport. Leisure sport is a creature of post-modern industrial civilisation: at the same time as labour law granted more free time, households' rising purchasing power enabled a greater part of people's time to be devoted to leisure activities. Since the

1970s, the manufactured sports products industry has exploded. In 1970 there were 5.3 million licence holders with membership cards allowing them to take part in sport, and by 2003 there were 34 million.[27] In the 1970s, the three most widely practised activities were jogging, swimming and football; twenty years later football continues to attract men's attention, while cycling (with 18.1 million participants) and walking (with 12.6 million) have come to top the list of mixed activities. While competitive sport keeps its followers in a more professional context, we have also seen an explosion in membership cards issued for leisure activities and free activities, regulated and otherwise. Sporting activities nourish everyone's daily life, for individual motives – relaxation, wellbeing, health, friendship or excelling oneself. Developments in relations to the ideal body during the 1980s – an efficient body whose slenderness and tone symbolise social success, a body conforming to the aesthetic canons laid down by the media – have contributed to promoting new activities, like body-building, aerobics and jogging. The law of 1984, promoting the practice of an active physical regime for everyone, helped to establish these new social norms, which were passed on in the discourse of schools and associations. The period embraced the made-to-measure and the extreme individualisation of sporting practice, everyone being obliged to find what suited them. Besides, one does not practise just in the collective space devoted to such-and-such a sport. Leisure sport has invaded the public spaces of towns, just as it has invaded natural spaces more broadly. Rambling and its related activities, like Nordic walking, always have their enthusiasts who can also, if they wish, choose what are called 'soft' modes of travel, like roller blades or bicycles, all the more so since many towns offer very liberal renting arrangements. Running races attract more and more city-dwellers, both women and men. Many are not satisfied with a bit of peaceful 'Sunday jogging'; they run to train themselves to take part in the official races staged by large towns in particular, which see their own dynamism reflected in them (marathons in Paris, Lyon, etc).

Lastly, some sporting activities are linked to young and sometimes dissident urban subcultures, such as skateboarding, rollerblading and BMX, which use the features of urban structures as the canvas for their acrobatic demonstrations. In Lyon, in the 1990s, Place Louis Pradel and Place de l'Opéra were the top places to go for urban sliding sports: the arrangement of the Place, giving onto the steps of the Pentes de la Croix-Rousse, the access

27 Ibid.

ramps, the monumental décor and the strips of grass, all lent themselves to the performance of manoeuvres both spectacular and widely publicised, given the large number of people there.[28] Skate parks and other all-terrain circuits set up for practitioners to avoid conflicts of use in public spaces do not deter enthusiasts of urban sliding sports from performing in other spaces. This demonstrates how sporting and physical activities of all kinds are central to the town and how they reject being segregated into sites dedicated to sport or to suburban recreational areas dreamed up by the designers of a purely functional town-planning. A recent manual with the subtitle 'The town, your sports hall' clearly illustrates this development: it suggests adapting benches, steps, park gates and walls into body-building aids; the proposed illustrations systematically show sportsmen interacting with the vegetal either under their feet or present as a backdrop.[29] It should be noted too that, in order to counter gender stereotyping and to enable women to reoccupy the places which they tend to avoid as darkness falls, like parks, gardens and unlit or poorly lit walkways, there is a proliferation of night-time activities intended for them (like walking, either in races or for exercise). Since the 1980s and 1990s another trend has, to some degree, helped to hand back to women a town shaped as masculine, especially where traditional sporting provision is concerned, particularly stadiums. The fashion for personal development goes along with a rise in physical activities taking place close to nature[30] and predominantly favoured by women. Tai-chi, qi gong and even some kinds of yoga take place in gardens and public parks, individually or in groups, as exercises in physical and mental balance.

Cultivating the spirit

At the end of the eighteenth century, the philosopher Condillac identified himself as belonging to the humanist tradition in reminding us that 'Exercising the body is necessary to the spirit too …' Natural spaces in which the body is exerted are also places of spiritual exercise: 'For those who can think, walking is an exercise for the faculties of both body and mind … One thinks,

28 Éric Adamkiewicz, 'Nouvelles pratiques et sports autonomes dans la ville. Création de nouveaux types de relations à l'urbain. L'exemple lyonnais', in Christian Vivier and Jean-François Loudcher, *Le Sport dans la ville* (Paris: L'Harmattan, 1998), pp. 303–313.

29 Walig Chartrain and Nicolas Fonteneau, *Entraînement urbain, exercices et circuits au service de votre bien-être. La ville, votre salle de sport* (Paris: Amphora, 2015).

30 Bernard Andrieu and Olivier Sirost, 'Introduction à l'écologie corporelle', *Sociétés* **3** (125) (2014): 5–10.

as one dreams, alone, and one lets one's thoughts reach out to whatever attracts them. When we are with others we converse, and are enlightened, and nature becomes a kind of book we are studying that conversation teaches us how to read.'[31] In *Ancien Régime* towns, subject to an ideal of measure, symmetry and harmony, nature promoted order in the body and the spirit. This topos of a civilising nature is rooted in several traditions: the mystical and courtly gardens of the Middle Ages, as well as the academic garden of ancient Greek philosophers, rediscovered in the Renaissance.

Christian heritage links the closed garden with spiritual elevation of the soul. Furthermore, for motives that are as much practical (production of fruit, vegetables and herbal cures) as religious, since the eighth century the garden has had a central place for all orders of the Christian monastic tradition.[32] In Cluny and at Cîteaux the garden is sited within the cloister and within the life of the community, while among the Carthusians it is individual, with each monk duty-bound to cultivate the patch of land extending the area of his cell. From the loss of Eden to the New Testament narratives, the garden resonates with meaning in the Scriptures. Nature is not dwelt upon for its own sake but for its symbolic dimension and what it reveals of Creation and the divine. This tradition of the mystical garden was given new life at the time of the Catholic Reformation, from the end of the sixteenth century. The most devout sectors of Catholic society were then infused with an ideal of sanctity which led them to seek out the individual impulse of the soul towards the divine. The hagiography of Catherine de Montholon (1568–1650), who helped to found the community of Ursulines in Dijon, describes her 'holy walks' in the garden of the convent: 'picking the flowers that she loved so much, she rose up to Him who had made them so beautiful; their scent, variety and colour represented for her the perfections of her God, & seeing Him in everything, she delighted to see Him in carnations and lilies, where it seemed He had wanted to portray Himself.' Through prayer and meditation our devout nun transforms the cloister garden into an open-air church: 'Her companions ... seeing her so carried away, left her alone to give her all the freedom possible to converse with God.'[33]

31 Étienne Bonnot de Condillac, *Œuvres de Condillac* (Paris: C. Houel, 1798), book 13 (vol. 5), pp. 40–41.

32 Étienne Grésillon, *Une géographie de l'au-delà ? Les jardins de religieux catholiques, des interfaces entre profane et sacré,* Ph.D. in geography, Paris-Sorbonne University, 2009.

33 François Senault, *La Vie de madame Catherine de Montholon, veuve de monsieur de Sanzelles, maistre des requestes, et fondatrice des Ursulines de Dijon* (Rouen: L. Gy, 1653), p. 96.

While their missions during the century (teaching, health, aid…) relegated contemplation, congregations that emerged during the seventeenth century in the context of Catholic reform remained attached to the model of the monastic garden. This was even more the case with nuns who, whatever their engagement with the world outside might be, were nonetheless bound by the obligations of the cloistered life. New religious houses, mainly established in towns, had to adapt their architecture to a limited urban space. Despite the land issue, gardens were far from disappearing from the urban religious landscape, especially as the phenomenon of suburbs spreading outwards absorbed old monasteries formerly sited outside the walls, and often with extensive possessions. An instance is the Charterhouse of Vauvert: founded in the middle of the thirteenth century at the gates of Paris under the patronage of Saint Louis, it was reabsorbed by the urbanisation of the Saint Michel district at the beginning of the seventeenth century, when Marie de Médicis had the Luxembourg palace built in its immediate vicinity. At the end of the eighteenth century, this Carthusian enclosure comprised 26 hectares of semi-rural land right in the heart of Paris. While members of the order were hidden from public view in their individual cells their domain was generally open to visitors. At the beginning of the seventeenth century, it was a great spiritual centre, with such major figures of the Catholic reformation as Cardinal de Bérulle and Madame Acarie, grouped around the learned scholar Dom Richard Beaucousin. Later, the religious influence of the Carthusians over the urban elites became more tenuous. If people went there less for spiritual encounters, the cloisters and gardens were still a walking place much valued by men (the rigours of the rule of St Bruno excluded women from these places). At the end of the eighteenth century, the sophisticated set, the curious and foreigners doing the Grand Tour were keen to go there, intrigued by an austerity that seemed to them anachronistic in the capital city of the Enlightenment. But men seeking calm and introspection could still be found there: 'Silence almost always presides in this vast solitude where one can readily give way to one's thoughts, without those who have chosen to dwell there coming to interrupt you.'[34]

A secularisation of the contemplation of nature came about under the influence of the writings of enlightenment philosophers. Rousseau's solitary walker is mindful above all of the aesthetic emotions his experience arouses

34 Jean Bardou, *Histoire de Laurent Marcel, ou L'observateur sans préjugés* (Lille: Le Houcq), vol. 2, p. 206.

Figure 32.

A solitary reader in the cloister of the Carthusian monastery in Paris, drawing by Michalin, engraving by Duparc, aquatint, 1850.
Courtesy of Musée Carnavalet (public domain).

in him, and is inattentive to the Christian interpretations the landscape might prompt. This does not imply that the spiritual function associated with some natural spaces in towns disappeared, especially as it was in the nineteenth century that care was taken to vegetalise cemeteries, which were planted up with trees: these would simultaneously purify the contaminated air and lend beauty to places destined to become resting places for both the living and the dead, and hence the choice of certain species, yews, to be sure, but also cypresses, poplars and willows.[35] This was the time when visiting cemeteries housing the tombs of loved ones became common practice, as did taking offerings of flowers. Thus, the largest and finest of them, like Père-Lachaise in Paris, Saint-Charles cemetery in Marseille, Bellecroix in Metz and the Chartreuse in Bordeaux, having become true gardens for the

35 Jean-Baptiste Vaquin (ed.), *Atlas de la Nature à Paris* (Paris: Atelier Parisien d'Urbanisme, 2006), p. 215.

dead, are mentioned in tourist guides from the 1830s and 1840s as places to visit, with pathways to follow to admire the monuments. At the same time (probably a bit earlier in Paris) a funerary tourism was established, with flesh and blood guides to show the tombs of celebrities and picturesque spots.[36]

While it did serve to continue a contemplative tradition, nature in cities was not destined to turn in on itself, very much the opposite in fact, as it was there that the 'social spirit' discussed in Chapter 4 flourished. Within a society locked in classical culture, the theatre retrieved its place in the life of the city from the seventeenth century on. There was a real mania for theatre in the eighteenth century: prestigious theatres, like the Comédie Française, where the privileged companies played, were now joined by very many theatres in fairs and on the boulevards, without forgetting the playhouses in pleasure gardens. During the nineteenth century, many public gardens and squares were fitted out with 'theatres of greenery', to use the favoured term, devoted to open-air spring and summer shows. Such shows might be educational, or even edifying, for an audience of families or children, or they might continue in the light entertainment tradition of boulevard shows. In the Bois de Boulogne, the Theatre of Flowers had its glory years in 1850 to 1870, creating wonders for generations of children:

> the proscenium was jasmine, the boxes were honeysuckle and the stalls were violets; a bush of roses that sank into the earth formed a backdrop and venetian lanterns took the place of chandeliers ... On stage were conjurers, balancing acts or even the Mendez or Dolores senoras, fiery-eyed Spanish ladies, 'dancing the cachucha'.[37]

While some of these theatres were very chic, like the Pré Catalan which succeeded the Flowers in the Bois de Boulogne at the beginning of the twentieth century, other 'theatres of greenery' were by contrast very much open to the ordinary public. To go to the premiere of the comic-opera *Mireille* on 9 July 1932 in the Square des Épinettes in the seventeenth arrondissement of Paris you would have to pay ten francs to sit in the stalls, but only two francs (the price of a kilo of bread) to go in and listen to the lines from a distance. Some allotments could also turn themselves into theatrical spaces in summer so that families could come along and broaden their literary and artistic culture: in June 1915 at Bicêtre the company *Théâtre de verdure des Jardins ouvriers* (The Green Theatre of the Allotments) gave an edifying performance of

36 Madeleine Lasserre, *Villes et cimetières en France de l'Ancien Régime à nos jours* (Paris: L'Harmattan, 1997), pp. 197–202.

37 George Cain, *À travers Paris* (Paris: Flammarion, 1909), pp. 353–355.

Geneviève de Brabant. Many cultural performances in the nineteenth and twentieth centuries aimed to combine recreation and instruction, in order to immerse all social classes in the crucible of civilising nature.

While it was endorsing theatre as a mode of expression in public spaces, *Ancien Régime* urban civilisation was shaping another ideal: the garden as an open-air drawing room, a space favourable to conversation and a quite separate site of culture. Fed by their reading of the classics, townspeople from the educated elites had in their heads the Platonic model of the gardens of the academy in Athens, where the philosopher would converse with his pupils. It was deemed that urban nature, with all its organised harmony, formed a framework conducive to intellectual banter and verbal swordplay. In the view of the artist and art critic Roger de Piles (1635–1709) the Tuileries garden particularly lent itself to select conversation, thanks to 'the lawns, which induce people to relax and to talk of things they love'.[38] One might converse there while strolling along the pathways, or sit without any fuss on the lawns. In good company, speech matches the body language: it accommodates itself to the rules of good taste. This civilised discourse excludes facetiousness and pedantry, ranting and slander. Besides, moralists berated the domination of witty sallies and facile chatter that made court society so superficial. According to La Bruyère, 'The pleasure of society between friends is bred of a similarity of taste in matters of morality, and some differences on science: thus one's feelings are reinforced, and one is exercised and instructed by disagreement.'[39] To warrant interest, time spent in a garden should be dedicated to select conversation on subjects that will raise the spirit, turning on the arts, letters or the sciences. Such aspirations are to be found in the model of the bourgeois promenade in the nineteenth century, even if there may have often been a wide gap between the ideal and reality. Accordingly, Maupassant in his cruel novella *Un fils* (*The Son*) (1882) portrays a senator and an academician who start to speculate chillingly on the consequences of incidental affairs they had imposed on young servant girls and sundry kitchen maids when they were young: 'They talked first of politics, exchanging opinions; not on ideas but on men, personalities in this regard taking prominence over Reason.' To hear utterances on a higher plane than the pontificating tattle of worthies, one could go to public lectures on

38 Roger de Piles, *Conversations sur la connoissance de la peinture, et sur le jugement qu'on doit faire des tableaux. Où par occasion il est parlé de la vie de Rubens, & de quelques uns de ses plus beaux ouvrages* (Paris: Nicolas Langlois, 1677), p. 3.

39 Jean de La Bruyère, *Les Caractères ou Les mœurs de ce siècle* (Paris: J. Delalain, 1878), p. 79.

Figure 33.

Poetry reading in the Luxembourg Gardens for Verlaine's birthday, 1922. Courtesy of BNF / Gallica: https://gallica.bnf.fr

literary works. For instance, in May 1922 the Amis de Verlaine group met around a statue erected in the poet's honour in the Luxembourg Garden and made speeches in his honour.

After 1901, many associations of lovers of literature organised this sort of event in the setting of urban nature. Cultural practices, however, have a tendency to become more based on the individual. In the nineteenth century, access to public education greatly extended the number of readers and potential readers, while changes taking place in the world of publishing contributed to the diversification of what was on offer. In poor weather the reading desks of the winter gardens filled up with customers: in the Champs-Élysées for just twenty sous 'you have the right to read all the newspapers in Paris and the departments', the advertising leaflet announced.[40] With the return of fine weather readers could cheer themselves up again in the natural spaces in the open air. If there was a theme that seized the imagination of artists,

40 'Jardin d'hiver, Champs Élysées', *L'Indépendant*, 13 Jan. 1848.

it was that of reading in the garden.[41] The reader will very often be shown deep in a newspaper on a bench in a public garden, which is an image of urban reality, for the bourgeois classes at least: Charles X for instance had the pathways in the Tuileries provided with cloth pavilions where one could obtain the day's papers. By contrast, female readers preferred to stay within the flowery bounds of a private garden, as propriety demanded that respectable women should not appear more than necessary in public places, especially if they were alone. Young ladies were invited to read on quiet mornings in the family garden; it was up to their mothers to put useful and select works before their eyes, rather than sentimental novels condemned by the Church. These rules of conduct of a bourgeois morality tended to become more relaxed in the first decades of the twentieth century; at this time, parks and public gardens were equipped with furniture prompting one to read – benches and, more particularly, light moveable chairs, and even deck chairs, enabling one to choose a place to sit, and exposure to the sun.

In her *Mémoires d'une jeune fille rangée* (*Memoirs of a Dutiful Daughter*), Simone de Beauvoir describes her recollections of how, as a young Parisian who devoured all the books she could get hold of, including 'the prohibited Balzac', sometimes on the balcony of the family apartment, sometimes in the Luxembourg when the weather was fine, 'I walked in the sunshine in a state of exaltation around the pond repeating phrases that I liked.'[42] While one encounters as many readers today in natural spaces in town, pages of paper alternate with the screens of tablets and mobile phones. In summer 2015 at Chambéry the 'transats and wifi' event in the Verney public park, made up of sundry performances by various artists, was a decided success.

Another kind of screen had become commonplace earlier in the twentieth century, the cinema screen. Cinematography as such came into existence in the 1900s and extended the tradition of performances and theatrical shows given in the open air since the seventeenth century. Before cinema theatres became widespread, the first films, silent and lasting only a few minutes, were projected elsewhere by itinerant showmen on circuits from town to town. If French towns did not yield to a passion for the American-style drive-in cinema, emblematic of the *Trente Glorieuses* period on the other side of the Atlantic, then open-air cinema still attracted many enthusiasts at summer festivals, the most famous being that held at La Villette, which started in

41 Jacquie Pigeaud and Jean-Paul Barbe, *Histoires de jardins, lieux et imaginaires* (Paris: PUF, 2015).

42 Simone de Beauvoir, *Mémoires d'une jeune fille rangée* (Paris: Gallimard, 1958), p. 186.

1900. The public is invited to come to the comfortable lawns at the foot of the screens to enjoy the show. Family gardens that have replaced allotments also try to revive the desire to cultivate both the soil and the mind: open-air film shows play their part in an array of events, from educational leisure to exhibitions, organised for the dissemination of cultural creations.

The vegetal between art and artifice

The seventh art was thus the last to be invited into the garden, which had welcomed all the muses from the seventeenth century onwards, hosting in turn theatre and ballet scenes, in a space dedicated to literature and poetry. A piece of vegetal jewellery, the garden itself was a work of art at the same time that it was a space conducive to creation.

Nature is an inexhaustible source of creation for artists, who have borrowed its simplest forms (flower, fruit, leaf) and created the most complex compositions based on a true vegetal grammar.

Because the vegetal is associated with prosperity, peace and moments of joy, it has been given pride of place in classic urban landscaping either living or else cast in stone. Under the *Ancien Régime* the elites wanted to make nature a civilising principle that contributed to the reinforcement of monarchical order in towns. Since the seventeenth century, they thus intended in their leisure time to enjoy nature ennobled by the art of the garden. All of the vegetal kingdom was mobilised to this effect, through the representations which the arts provided, in order to express a harmony based on the respect of social hierarchies. Learned culture seized for itself the symbolism associated with the vegetal, omnipresent in the urban landscape. Associated with rhetoric, poetry and also memory, the vegetal thus spoke the language of concord. It contributed to the stability of the social edifice, like those great, remarkable trees which defy the centuries and preside over the fates of generations of city dwellers, and which are inherent to the town's past. To continue in the register of the symbolic, the first edition of the *Dictionnaire de l'Académie française* (1694) associates with the word 'flower' the figurative sense of 'decoration, embellishment' and also 'what is the best, the most excellent'. The kingdom of Flora remained an endless source of inspiration for artists. Epic crowns, Virgilian garlands, patrician paintbrushes; the inspired vegetal fictions of the aesthetic canons of Antiquity added to the organisation of the mineral decoration of the town.

Since the sixteenth century, vegetalised spaces have also been a special exhibition place for statues and sculptures, particularly in French-style gardens where constrained nature dominates and is treated like a material for sculpture by the art of topiary. When he stayed in Paris in 1766–1767, the young painter Joseph-Henry Costa de Beauregard appreciated the staging of works of art in the royal gardens.

> As I passed by, I saw the Thuilleries garden which is the most beautiful thing in the world. The trees which form these grand alleys cross their heads and in summer give impenetrable shade; it is decorated by a great number of statues by the greatest masters. There are six which depict a faun, seated and playing the flute, a Hamadryad, a flower, two Nymphs and a young man returning from the hunt, and they all border the terrace which dominates the length of the Palace. Near a pool, which is the closest are four groups in a beautiful composition and beautifully crafted.[43]

The young man came from a noble family in Chambéry and thus far had been happy to conscientiously visit the most illustrious collections in the capital in order to complete his artistic education, and he became aware that art is to be found in the garden as well as in the museum. The vegetal showcase, crafted by the hoe and the shears, but perishable and fragile, the muse of budding artists and amateurs who never miss an opportunity to visit and to be inspired, must enhance the mineral creation.

Nature in town could not be conceived without art. Of course, wild vegetation was often the uncontested winner in the nooks and crannies and is the sovereign of wasteland and uneven paving. But the malleability of vegetalised spaces, even the most modest, owes nothing to chance: whether they spring from the fertile imagination of the artists or from a commonplace design office, they are inscribed in the aesthetic canons of an age. The *Ancien Régime* and the nineteenth century have consecrated the mode of the artificialised vegetal, and broderie style parterres are perhaps the most extreme model of this. Up to the beginning of the twentieth century, this French style had not totally vanished despite stiff competition from supposedly more natural English-style gardens. The 'mixed' style defended by Édouard André, for example, continued to be requested in orders for urban gardens while, with the stimulus of nationalism, the merits of the national heritage were expounded through the works of the landscaper Achille Duchêne. Moments of glory for vegetal mosaics came at the turn of the nineteenth and twentieth centuries, in the main Parisian parks like the Luxembourg Garden, for example. The First World War brought about profound social, economic and cultural transformations and these changed the conditions

43 Joseph-Henry Costa de Beauregard, *Journal de voyage d'un jeune noble savoyard à Paris en 1766–1767* (Villeneuve-d'Ascq: Presses Universitaires du Septentrion, 2013), p. 53–54.

for artistic creation. With inspiration coming from elsewhere (Spain, Italy, the United Kingdom, Japan from the 1860s) and the Modernist movement, French garden creativity lost its national links but still kept very fixed ideas about the vegetal: in the very clean, very geometrical lines of the Véra brothers – their La Thébaïde garden at Saint-Germain-en-Laye after 1920, for example – or in those almost Cubist works by Gabriel Guevrekian – the garden at Villa Noailles in Hyères – this is a nature marked with a chalk line and subjected to the same constraints as the prevailing stone.

Works of art thus have a place expected of them there, since, basically, in the way they are treated, they are not distinguished from the nature surrounding them, as was well exemplified in the garden of water and light displayed by Guevrekian at the international decorative and industrial arts exhibition in Paris in 1925. This garden was presented as a picture by Delaunay, coming close to abstraction therefore, and above all playing around with flattened effects and contrasts in colours. This spectacular reduction of the vegetal to an inanimate material was to be found in unfortunate avatars, as we have seen, in the green spaces which flourished after the war during the *Trente Glorieuses* period. They continue to host, in a kind of poor showcase, works of art, more or less inspired, more or less respected by passers-by. Talented landscapers like Bernard Lassus, however, play with any such interferences in their works: the hanging gardens that he designed in 2000–2001 and 2005–2007 for the head office of the Colas company at Boulogne-Billancourt are dominated by metal plates cut out in the shape of trees and plants.

However, it is in *the other direction* that the nature-culture scrambling seemed to operate in the 1970s. During the period that we are examining here, we have, in a way, moved from an artificialised nature to a naturalised nature.[44] This transformation reflects the spirit of the age and anticipates the ever-stronger desires for nature felt in our society. For over forty years, the ecological demand and the attention paid to biodiversity have helped to promote gardens with more diversified plants, which are more local and freer, inspired by the cottage gardens of Gertrude Jekyll and William Robinson at the end of the nineteenth century. If we add to that a revival in the art of the garden and of landscaping activities plus an artistic modernity which, since the beginning of the twentieth century, contested the very principle of the work of art in its unity and its eternity, we understand better the

44 For this entire sub-section, we have relied in particular on Hervé Brunon and Monique Mosser (eds), *L'art du jardin. Du début du XXe siècle à nos jours* (Paris: Canopé-CNDP, 2011).

advent of a kind of ecological aesthetic. Gardens, now as little artificialised as possible, lend themselves undeniably, in their creation, to movement and the ephemeral. They are conceived as a process rather than an end product. Thus, art becomes a gardener, in a way. *Land Art*, which from the outset integrated the temporal dimension into the artistic creations made around natural materials is, of course, the best representative of this trend, but the attention paid to the site very often removes it far away from the towns themselves. Nomadic arts and gardens are nevertheless exhibited in various urban settings. One of the most famous sites is definitely the Hortillonnages in Amiens. In the Middle Ages, a community of market gardeners, the *hortillons,* settled in the Saint-Leu neighbourhood and created gardens from the marshes around the town by extensive drainage works and raising the level of the land. Their crops were of exceptional quality and were sold in the Amiens markets. In 1900 this particular vegetal space, adjacent to the town and then absorbed by it, covered 300 hectares and was worked by a thousand *hortillons* gardeners. It dwindled away during the twentieth century: today only seven people work it and it only covers thirty hectares. But these days it is protected and since 2010 the area has become an exhibition space to encourage young artists.[45] Seeing how successful this reconversion has been, the festival has continued and become more widely known and more international. Today it draws 30–40,000 visitors to admire the work of landscapers, visual artists and architects. The works exhibited must, of course, respect the place they are in and be ephemeral; they may be gardens or installations and often the boundaries between the two are undetectable.[46] The same ambiguity is to be found in Bitche, a smaller *commune* in Moselle, where since 2003 a 'Garden for Peace' located at the foot of Vauban's citadel hosts horticultural creations. The whole town is taken over during the 'Jardins en Troc' festival. Here, again, the plants mingle with creations in crystal, glass or wrought iron, as in the meteoric garden imagined by Arsène Kremer and Jean-François Frering, a sort of circular chamber, illuminated by light filtered through 170 discs of blown glass made in the neighbouring village of Meisenthal, which is famous for its glassworks.[47] Henceforward, it is the gardens themselves that are on display.

45 Michel Conan, 'Les hortillons', in Michel Racine (ed.), *Créateurs de jardins et de paysage*, vol. 2 (Arles: Actes Sud, 2002), pp. 64–69.

46 Gilbert Fillinger, *Art, villes et paysage. Hortillonnages Amiens* (Amiens: Éditions trois cailloux, 2014).

47 Sonia Lesot and Henri Gaud, *Les Jardins en troc de Bitche* (Moisenay: Éditions Gaud, 2009).

* * *

Today, art's descent into the garden seems to be widely accepted, even when it is not part of the politically correct discourse of 'culture for all'. Eye-catching urban marketing imposes this and often features world-famous contemporary artists such as Jeff Koons or Anish Kapoor, who are invited to present their creations in the gardens of the palace at Versailles. As for the gates and railings of urban parks, a new purpose has been found for them and these days photo exhibitions are hung on them, as at the Luxembourg Garden in Paris or the Jardin Public in Bordeaux. The welcome the public gives to some works does not always match that of the buyers at the FIAC (International Contemporary Art Fair) and this sometimes poses a problem, especially when acts of vandalism damage the integrity of the work. In autumn 2015 Anish Kapoor's 'Dirty Corner' was vandalised and covered in anti-Semitic graffiti. In the artist's own words, this work, dubbed 'The Queen's Vagina' was intended to disrupt the classical balances in Le Nôtre's gardens at Versailles: the objective was achieved a hundred times over. Even more recently, in December 2015, photographs by Olivier Ciappa depicting 'imaginary couples' on the railings of the Grand-Rond garden in Toulouse were covered in homophobic messages. Works of art disturb, cause scandal, provoke unexpected reactions and even break the law: these affairs are a reminder that public parks and gardens are not museums, under close surveillance, and that the vegetal can also be disorderly.

6.

THE URBAN JUNGLE? PLANT LIFE... WILD LIFE

On 31 March 1787, Nicolas-Joseph Belamy, secretary of the municipality of Besançon, signed a decree that began:

> The care and effort employed in making promenades in this city, the money that was spent on them and is spent daily in looking after them and keeping them so fine as to arrest the attention of both citizens and visitors, and to furnish them with all possible amenities for tranquillity, utility and attractiveness, requires of us a constant vigilance to maintain order, decency, calm and safety, and to anticipate and hinder everything that would damage them.

The decree related particularly to the Chamars promenade, whose luxury layout bore witness to the commitment of the municipal authorities to the wellbeing of their citizens. There were already two promenades in existence in the seventeenth century before the conquest of Franche-Comté by Louis XIV. The gradual demilitarisation of the fortifications of Besançon after

Figure 34.

Promenade de Chamars, watercolour by Jean-Alexis Cornu, circa 1785.
Courtesy of Departmental Archives of the Doubs, Gérard ANTONI, ref. 1Fi1602.

1755 made it possible to join them together. The freed-up earthworks were transformed by the architects Longin and Bertrand into planted pathways bordered with lawns and flowered terraces, palisades with bowers, aviaries with rare birds, and not least great pools stocked with ornamental fish that so fascinated the public, as is seen in this print from a gouache by Cornu.

We saw in earlier chapters that the vegetalisation of towns was a manifestation of a social, symbolic and even political order, as the decree bears witness. In it, Belamy described the delights of the walkways provided for the townspeople by the authorities, and the pleasure they gave; but he also favoured order and decency, that is to say a certain way of being in the spaces, of using them. So, in the heart of the city, gardens and parks offered a space for civility, a model of civilisation; paradoxically, nature in cities was thought of in some ways as also a site of urbanity where, in the centre of a town that was always susceptible to serious unruliness, behaviour might be controlled. But there is a large gap between such aspirations and reality, as natural spaces are also experienced by some of those who use them as places of liberty, far from the constraints of the town: Belamy's decree, following on from two others of 25 November 1778 and 14 April 1781, made this quite clear.

Beyond the regulated orderliness of the park, this chapter is drawn to discover the urban jungle, where nature can be wild and ungovernable: it can bring back in undesirable or uncontrollable plant species, it can incite uncivilised behaviour, and even constitute a political challenge.

Unwelcome plant life

Domesticating the bad seed

If nature is to be a feature of the urban it has, by definition, to be policed: it is unthinkable to conceive of a town drowned in ungoverned vegetation. A garden, especially in a town, cannot accommodate nature in the wild: it is the opposite of that, it is a kind of civilised nature, even if it can sometimes give an illusion of spontaneity, hiding the hand of the man who constrains it. Parks and gardens, public and private, classical or English, have always been, down the centuries, places of control: flowerbeds, lawns and groves are framed, restricted and managed by gardeners. Weeds are rooted out: these 'wild' things are as unwanted in a town as individuals threatening the social or political order, whether royal, imperial or republican. When a large concentration of working people in great cities like Paris and Lyon generates fear of new revolutionary upheavals, it is all the more vital to be in control of all aspects of the urban space. Industrialisation in the nineteenth century brought a step change to this concern: the development of asphalt road surfacing (particularly with the introduction of the motor-car at the beginning of the twentieth century) as much as the perfecting of pesticides, especially after World War I, have enabled greater eradication of any remaining undesirable and all-invasive plant life.

However, if you chase out nature it will come galloping back: it is in any case a difficult or impossible thing to do in a town where all uncultivated ground, all gaps, all half-forgotten land are there for any kind of plant to grow in.

> There is no crumbling wall
> Nor bare earth, nor small corner
> Where some humble daisy
> Does not reclaim the rights of summer
> Pull them up, place stones
> In heaps on their frail hues,
> They will open their eyelids again:
> You cannot eliminate flowers.[1]

The words of the poet Albert Mérat are confirmed by the lists of plants in towns that were made in the second half of the nineteenth century. They belong in the canon of flora of the environs of towns which proliferated in the eighteenth century, thanks to the enthusiasm for botany that was shared by experts and amateurs alike, inducing them to go walking *extra muros* in search of remarkable specimens. Plants growing freely within towns escaped their attention because they found enough material for their investigations in botanical gardens, and maybe also in public promenades. The impulse to make botanical observations was only unleashed at the city limits, around the gates and ditches of the ramparts. The botanist Jean-Louis Thuillier, author of *Flore des environs de Paris (Flora of the Environs of Paris)* (1790) observed that Dendroids were to be found 'only in the Bois de Boulogne, a gun-shot from the Obelisk, going in by the Porte Maillot'. As for *Sisymbrium vimineum* it could be seen 'on the edge of the vines before you get to the Porte Saint Mandé' and it 'is also found in the flower-beds of the Pont Tournant in the Tuileries'.[2] It was not until the 1850s and 1860s that an interest in plant life *intra muros* became widespread among botanists.

1 Albert Mérat, 'Terrain vague', *Poèmes de Paris* (1880).

2 Jean-Louis Thuillier, *Flore des environs de Paris* (Paris: Veuve Desaint, 1790), pp. 184–185 and 318.

The second edition of the *Flore des environs de Paris* by Ernest Cosson and Germain de Saint-Pierre (1861) offered some observations specific to Paris, for example the presence of white cress on the walls of the Luxembourg Garden. More methodically, in 1862 in his *Flore d'Alsace* Frédéric Kirschleger drew up a precise table of plants growing on old churches, ruined buildings and the walls of fortifications, in Strasbourg particularly; fifty species of plants had established themselves between the stones of the Bridge of Cats, there were 85 species in 1855 in the courtyard of the imperial palace, left untouched for two years while work was being done on the buildings. The first study specifically devoted to an urban flora is however Joseph Vallot's *Essai sur la flore du pavé de Paris limité aux boulevards extérieurs (Essay on the Flora of the Pavements of Paris Within the Outer Boulevards)* (1884), which lists 209 species on the public roads alone.[3] Like Kirschleger, Vallot laments municipal practices tending to destroy this floral diversity. For the Strasbourg professor, the destruction of ancient walls, the strengthening of some of them with mortar, and the uprooting of the shrubs threatening to undermine them led to the disappearance of a specific mural flora. And for his part Vallot complains,

> Since the beginning of the century Paris has changed its appearance: there is not one corner that is not paved, tarred or macadamised. An army of workers, equipped with water jets and mechanical brushes carry out daily street cleaning, and if a little plant dares to grow between two paving-stones, some of them, mindful of the cleanness of the streets, rush to tear it out with special tools. The very edges of the quays do not escape this regime of regular clearing.

This concern was not, however, widely shared unless, of course, by the 'wild gardens' movement that developed in Great Britain around the landscapers William Robinson and Gertrude Jekyll, who tried to break away from the intensive horticulture and the formalism of their contemporaries. They both, Jekyll in particular, rehabilitated the local flora and add a touch of 'the wild' to their landscape creations. Of course, this was still a matter of putting together a garden, but doing so while affording more space for floral abundance, in simulation of the spontaneity of nature. Gaëlle Aggéri sees in this an anticipation of today's ecological practices.[4]

In the twentieth century, up until the 1970s and 1980s, a few rare in-

3 Bernadette Lizet, Anne-Élisabeth Wolf and John Celecia, *Sauvages dans la ville. De l'inventaire naturaliste à l'écologie urbaine* (Paris: MNHN, 1999).

4 Gaëlle Aggéri, 'Le sauvage dans les villes: du *wild garden* à la gestion différenciée', *Le Jardin et la Nature dans la Cité* (Besançon: Institut Claude-Nicolas Ledoux, 2002).

dividuals continued to show an interest in wild plants in towns. The most important was certainly Paul Jovet, who published two botanical articles in 1945 on plants found on certain Paris metro lines unused during the Occupation: some wheat and tomato plants, and peach trees which the workers dug up to replant elsewhere, and dozens of other species: there were some 100 different plants on the Combat-Envers line![5] In the 1950s he and his wife, both researchers at the Museum of Natural History, settled at Athis-Mons and collected plants there, seeking out wild specimens in the streets, and allowing nature to evolve spontaneously in their garden. In 1988 Paul Jovet and Bernadette Lizet devoted themselves to a particularly significant experiment, identifying the weeds in the Jardin des Plantes at Paris. Beyond the desired and cultivated flora of the Garden, they wanted to uncover the wild plants that had eluded the hoes and the endless vigilance of the gardeners or else were tolerated, and at times even nurtured discreetly.[6] This interest in the wild plant life of towns made the Jovets into pioneers and even plant smugglers, with a considerable influence on modern researchers as well as on major landscapers like Gilles Clément. Following in their wake, over some forty years Vincent Rastetter has counted up some 167 adventitious plants (come from elsewhere) within the limits of greater Mulhouse.[7]

Such activities were in the minority in the *Trente Glorieuses* post-war period, which saw the highpoint of a mechanistic and standardised approach to urban nature with the wholesale use of pesticides and impeccable lawns, both of which were fostered by the tide of housing developments that extended the town and impoverished plant-life. It was only movements like guerrilla gardening in the seventies, the emergence of the concept of biodiversity in the 1980s and the Rio Conference of 1992 that put this at the heart of discussion.[8] Spurred on by a renewal of thought in both town-planning and landscape design, there has been a change in our way of thinking about wild plants in towns. Following studies in both the United States and in Europe,

5 Paul Jovet, 'Végétation des lignes aériennes du chemin de fer métropolitain de Paris I', *Bulletin de la Société Botanique de France* 92 (1945): 92–97 and Jovet, 'Végétation des lignes aériennes du chemin de fer métropolitain de Paris II', *Bulletin de la Société Botanique de France* 92 (1945): 105–109.

6 Paul Jovet and Bernadette Lizet, *Les Herbes folles du Jardin des Plantes* (Paris: Muséum National d'Histoire Naturelle, 1990).

7 Vincent Rastetter, 'La flore adventice de Mulhouse et de ses environs', *Bulletin de la société industrielle de Mulhouse* 784 (1982): 55–67.

8 But as early as 1971 UNESCO launched the 'Man and Biosphere' programme, which conceived the city as an ecosystem.

we are also finding out about the potential biological wealth of towns,[9] which can often be greater than that of the intensively cultivated countryside that surrounds them. Many rare plants find a refuge in allotments, city parks or roadsides, as long as such places are not over-maintained: this is often a matter of some local flora that has somehow survived urban encroachments. Montpellier actually gives shelter to some twenty protected plant species in its parks and gardens.[10] The roof of the submarine base in Bordeaux, a kind of huge bunker built during World War II, has been enriched by way of some fifty spontaneous plant species (ash, micocouliers, rosetrees, ivy, etc.) which in 2015 were the subject of an exhibition of photographs happily entitled 'Improbabilis. Plants under shellfire'.[11]

A new urban regime is becoming established, very different from that of previous centuries. 'Ordinary nature'[12] is reassuming its rights to urban space, and in the context of a new style of existence that is both civic and city-dwelling. The gardens in movement theorised by Gilles Clément, inspired by uncultivated land, is a perfect illustration of this new regime.[13]

The shade of the tree

This rolling wave of plant-life in urban spaces, which seems to rather stun our elected officials, should not conceal the existence of resistance to introducing nature into towns, which goes back a long way indeed. There is general agreement about parks and gardens, but not single plants or in groups sited within the urban infrastructure and which might prove a nuisance in many ways. We have already described citizens' reservations about new practices in green-space management which leave a fair amount of space to minimally controlled wild plants: weeds strictly speaking have no right to be there as they give an impression of neglect… Green waste also has to be dealt with.

9 See the studies of Herbert Sukopp in the 1970s; see also *Quelle biodiversité dans la ville? Cahier Spécial de La Recherche* 422 (Sept. 2008). François Couplan counts more than 760 wild species in Paris, out of the 4,500 in mainland France, including purslane, sow-thistle, plantain, clover, dandelion, cyclamen, hops, chamomile, knotweed, snapdragon, sedum, St John's wort, rosehips, buddleias, etc. François Couplan, *Plantes urbaines* (Paris: Sang de la Terre, 2010), p. 13.

10 Philippe Croze, 'Étude de potentialité des sites sur la ville de Montpellier', in *Actes du colloque 'Vers la gestion différenciée des espaces verts'* (Strasbourg: CNFPT, AIVF, 1994), pp. 73–81, in Emmanuel Boutefeu, *Composer avec la nature en ville* (Paris: CERTU, 2001), p. 98.

11 Carine Caussieu, 'Sur le béton, les plantes', *Sud Ouest. Le Mag* 168, 20 June 2015: 38–39.

12 Bernadette Lizet, in Dominique Chouchan, 'Les citadins aiment-ils la biodiversité?', *La Recherche*, Cahier Spécial 'Quelle biodiversité dans les villes?' 422 (Sept. 2008): 14.

13 Gilles Clément, *Le Jardin en mouvement* (Paris: Pandora, 1991).

Nothing was really considered under the *Ancien Régime* except burying it or composting it, the latter still being the favoured solution in most parks. Some vegetable material does not lend itself very well to composting: up to the nineteenth century, dealing with the residue of tree lopping was normally delegated to the firms contracted to maintain the trees. More problematic was waste from private gardens; a dustbin can deal with small amounts, but sometimes more comprehensive solutions are called for. The case of Christmas trees is typical: for twenty years or so special operations have been in place to avoid the aftermath of the festivities encumbering the pavements. One can take the trees to collection points where they are reduced to chippings that can be used around the base of plants; towns like Annecy and Chambéry have introduced a picturesque system of horse-drawn carts to encourage this practice.

Even trees, the outstanding sign of urban vegetation, do not automatically receive the hoped-for enthusiastic welcome. They have not always got the decorative virtues attributed to them. Where the planting is poorly done, some scrawny and inelegant trees have scarcely any aesthetic value: in 1877 the director of the *Revue des Eaux et Forêts* (*Rivers and Forests Review*) complained about the negligence of some provincial towns that entrust engineers with no horticultural or landscape training with the vegetalising of their territory, which is limited to a few promenades lined with stunted and dusty lime-trees.[14] Even fine trees in good condition may be unwelcome if it is deemed that they too much obscure the harmony of a façade or architectural grouping. The Rue de l'Opéra in Paris was for this reason left free from all planting, the better to show off Garnier's creation. In Bordeaux the English-style garden in Place Gambetta, added in 1868–69 by a pupil of Eugène Bühler, offended those who found that it concealed the harmony of the eighteenth-century facades too much.

In addition to these aesthetic considerations one has to take practical issues into account: low branches can be troublesome to traffic, and many problems are caused by vegetable rubbish. Leaves make pavements slippery, and from the eighteenth century on they have been accused of blocking foul water drains and adding to the build-up of stagnant and fetid mud. Trees and bushes attract other nuisances: birds whose droppings compromise the cleanliness of streets, and insects and caterpillars with their dreaded

14 Amédée Bouquet de la Grye, 'Observations sur les plantations urbaines', *Revue des Eaux et Forêts* **XVI** (1877): 345–346.

destructive effect on cultivation and market gardening. As we have seen, a decree by the Parliament of Paris dated 4 February 1732 provided for a considerable fine on owners or tenants who failed to rid trees in Paris and its nearby suburbs of caterpillars.

These are minor inconveniences compared with the principal criticism levelled against trees: that they make too much shade. This complaint has been voiced constantly since the nineteenth century. So, were eighteenth century city dwellers insensitive to the loss of light caused by tree branches? People with power did not hesitate to require the elected authorities to cut back what was not wanted, like the Archbishop of Tours who in 1772 had the elms in the mall that ran beside the episcopal palace trimmed; but that was less because they took away the light than because they 'obstructed the view' from the windows.[15] Writings on rural living advise anyone buying a house in the country to take care that 'trees in the vicinity of the house do not make it too dark',[16] advice that would apply just as well to a private town-house. Even so, shade is not a subject to be found in police documents or records of municipal deliberations. It would have taken a proliferation of complaints to give rise to a regulatory acknowledgement of the problem; the threshold may only have been crossed with the multiplication of tree-lined avenues and boulevards in the nineteenth century, when the likelihood of having a tree opposite one's window became much greater for dwellings giving onto the street. A study of 1849 reveals that at Bar-le-Duc requests were often heard from people with houses on the street: the limes lining the south side of the Rue du Point du Jour were removed, as was every other poplar on the Quai des Gravières in 1840, and in 1846 all the line of chestnut trees behind them. 'They explain that these trees rob them of air and light and make their dwellings less healthy and more disagreeable.'[17] This argument against urban trees was particularly common in the first half of the nineteenth century and was based on widely held scientific and medical notions owing much to hygienist ideals: a healthy town needs air and light, whose circulation is inhibited by trees.[18] This is of course a clear deviation

15 Béatrice Baumier, *Tours entre Lumières et Révolution, pouvoir municipal et métamorphoses d'une ville (1764–1792)* (Rennes: PUR, 2007), p.44.

16 Louis Liger, *Œconomie générale de la campagne, ou Nouvelle maison rustique* (Paris: Sercy, 1700), vol. 1, p. 3.

17 *Études sur le budget de la ville de Bar-le-Duc*, 1837–1846 (Bar-le-Duc: Numa Rolin, 1849), p. 50.

18 See Paul A. Elliott, *British Urban Trees. A Social and Cultural History, c. 1800–1914* (Winwick, Cambridgeshire: The White Horse Press, 2016).

from the theory commonly favoured in the eighteenth century that trees absorbed noxious exhalations and gave out purified air. The *Mémoire sur la plantation des arbres dans l'intérieur des villes* (*Memoir on the Planting of Trees in Towns*) presented in 1847 by Dr Jeannel of the Royal Medical Society of Bordeaux is a good example of the construction of a new argument against urban trees. He first challenged the supposed cleansing virtues of trees planted in towns, on the basis of a disproportion ingeniously (if dubiously) calculated between their capacity to absorb carbon dioxide and the amount breathed out by Bordeaux residents. And this is without taking into account, he says, that trees slow down the movement and therefore the renewal of the air. Worse, not only do they not effectively cleanse towns, but trees are a factor contributing to unhealthiness: planted too close to houses they block out the sun and warmth; and furthermore, they take up rainwater and then by transpiration make the atmosphere humid which is seriously damaging to citizens' health. According to the good doctor, when all was said and done, the citizens were not fools, as was evidenced in frequent petitions to the municipality to remove such and such a row of trees making excessive shade for neighbouring dwellings.[19] While it is true that major onslaughts on the vegetal in towns were not frequent, they nonetheless revealed cracks in the claimed unanimity: it is indeed true that trees can improve the urban environment, and after all Jeannel does not deny it, but not under just any conditions. Possible contradictions between aspirations to beautification and those to hygienic improvement pointed to this, as did tensions between what municipalities wished to do and what certain citizens expected, tensions of which the author of the memoir on Bar-le-Duc was fully aware, seeing the opposition between the general interest (walkers for instance) and the particular interest of local residents.

There is a striking instance of all such reservations about trees in a petition to the mayor of Nantes around 1835 in which citizens complained about another kind of nuisance to which the branches of trees gave rise:

> The owners and tenants of houses on the Rue d'Entrepot in Nantes, to Monsieur le Maire of Nantes, Chevalier of the Legion of Honour, explaining that several years' experience has convinced them that the trees which were planted in front of their houses are now grown so large, they have become very prejudicial on several grounds:

19 Julien-François Jeannel, *Mémoire sur la plantation des arbres dans l'intérieur des villes* (Bordeaux: Émile Crugy, 1848).

> … When the wind blows strongly, the tops and branches of the trees knock against the walls and the windows with such violence that they cause damage and prevent people going near the windows.[20]

Although with the brilliant success of beautification works under the Second Empire, along with advancements in medicine and in the techniques of urban planting, strictly medical critiques had become less strident, angry outbursts against the shade which trees cause have not stopped – up until our own times, sometimes from owners of solar panels that have become less efficient. Nevertheless, new objections have come along.

Allergies to greenery

The issue of allergies first emerged in the course of the nineteenth century. Hay fever was hardly mentioned before that time, and only then did it become a subject of interest to the scientific community: deemed exceptional at the beginning of the century, it seems to have become relatively common a hundred years later.[21] It was only at this point that links between urban planting and allergies came to light, in the writing of Ernest Guinier, inspector of Waters and Forests. In his work *Promenades, Parcs, Jardins paysagers* (*Promenades, Parks and Landscaped Gardens*) in 1904 he issued a warning about the excessive use of sycamores in the streets of France, especially of Paris. There were 26,000 of them among the 100,000 trees ornamenting its streets. According to Guinier the combined action of the down on the leaves and the 'hairs of the fruit' of this tree could not only induce hay fever but could be harmful to people with chest ailments.[22] With twenty per cent of the population suffering from some degree of allergy, this issue has become a major element in public health policy, especially in towns, where atmospheric pollution increases both sensitivity to pollens and their allergenic potential.[23] In 1961 recording stations installed in Paris, Marseille and Briançon made it possible to establish the first pollen level calendars for these cities. National coverage was only made possible in 1984 by way of sensors set up under the aegis of the Institut Pasteur – a network which in 1986 became the Réseau National de Surveillance Aérobiologique (National Aerobiological

20 Archives municipales de Nantes, 1O16123, Petition to the Mayor of Nantes, c. 1835.

21 M. B. Emanuel, 'Hay fever, a post industrial revolution epidemic: a history of its growth during the nineteenth century', *Clinical Allergy* **18** (1988): 295–304.

22 Ernest Guinier, *Promenades, Parcs, Jardins paysagers* (Annecy: Abry, 1904), pp. 13–14.

23 Réseau National de Surveillance Aérobiologique, Végétation en ville: http://www.vegetation-en-ville.org/PDF/Guide-Vegetation.pdf

Monitoring Network), with 82 sites today. In addition to measures already taken, this association tries to keep citizens, elected authorities and professionals informed via its website about all matters related to urban allergies.[24]

Various strategies are adopted at the local level. Since 2003 the botanical garden at Nantes has featured a '*pollinarium sentinelle*' (watchdog pollinarium), a square of land on which some thirty allergenic plants grow. Because of the favourable situations in which they are placed they release their pollen some weeks before wild species – making it possible to anticipate allergy peaks and, in collaboration with the city's health personnel, to prepare suitable treatment for people concerned. In the town of Meyzieu in the suburbs of Lyon, the priority is the battle against ragweed, a particularly allergenic plant affecting ten per cent of the population of the Rhone valley. Because of its industries and its proximity to Saint-Exupéry airport, Meyzieu is particularly vulnerable to ragweed, which thrives in uncultivated land and along transport routes. The municipality takes great pains to keep residents informed, to clear communal land regularly and to identify infested private land in order to require owners to take action by destroying the plants.[25] More generally, countering allergies in towns implies consideration in advance of what species to plant in public places, and how many of them: fostering a degree of biological diversity reduces the concentration of the pollen of any one species and hence its allergenic effects.

Urban nature evades control by secateurs and pesticides, frees itself from the shackles of the border edgings and introduces disorder into towns; far from limiting itself to being an agent of social control, as elected authorities and elites would wish, it can equally excite ungoverned behaviour, within or sometimes against vandalised greenery. In every case, the initial order is profoundly disturbed.

Discipline and punish: Disorder in parks

From the freedom of the body to the transgression of social rules

Despite local authorities' regulatory efforts and however efficient their police, public spaces and especially natural spaces in towns are regularly

24 www.pollens.fr

25 Inès Méliani, Isabelle Roussel and Saïda Kermadi, 'Politiques et pratiques de la santé environnementale à travers l'exemple de la commune de Meyzieu', *Pollution Atmosphérique* 206 (Apr.–June 2010): 222.

the scene of practices which propriety would condemn, and even of actual attacks on public order and the law. The uncontrolled relief of bodily needs is, in the absence of facilities for such functions, one of the commonest of such offences, though of only admittedly minor seriousness. Literary texts, touching on this subject more lightly than police decrees, reveal that public hygiene became a growing preoccupation for public authorities from the eighteenth century on. Not unmischievously, Louis Sébastien Mercier describes a reorganisation of the Tuileries garden on the initiative of the Count of Angiviller (1725–1802), director of the king's buildings. In order to keep the promenade clean, public latrines were installed in the place of some yew hedges which had served in this role previously.[26]

Another solution was adopted against the 'unruly piddlers' at Palais Royal. This temple of consumerism and leisure, fitted out by Louis-Philippe Joseph d'Orléans (1747–1793) from 1781, comprised private housing and the famous gardens sheltered from the street by the galleries of the Palais Royal, which housed shops, bookshops, cafés, restaurants, theatres and gambling houses. 'You could not take a step into the garden without seeing men pissing against the pilasters of the galleries; this was very disagreeable to women. … It was useless to wash down the bases of the pilasters every morning; the smell became intolerable as the day went on. So benches were placed there and this kept the pissers at a distance.'[27] There were similar problems at Nantes where the municipal council met in 1796 to try to protect the town's promenades from citizens who 'against all decency every day do their business there, and especially in the quincunxes, not only making them foul but also ruining the healthiness of the air, especially when the weather is hot.'[28]

The body resumes its rights in this urban nature, which becomes to some extent a place where it is possible to evade social scrutiny and control. While it should contribute to making manners more civilised, urban nature seems, paradoxically, to offer a place for running wild, an outlet. According to the social and legal context, offences committed there are more or less tolerated. By providing somewhere both familiar and removed from daily life, natural spaces have always been the resort of lovers who go there to flirt, just as much in real towns as in novels. Gardens are a favoured site for

26 Louis Sébastien Mercier, *Tableau de Paris* (Amsterdam: 1785), vol. VII, p. 205.

27 François-Marie Mayeur de Saint-Paul, *Tableau du nouveau Palais-Royal* (London: Maradan, 1788), part 2, p. 99.

28 Archives municipales de Nantes, 1O16122, 25 Thermidor an IV.

Figure 35.

'Lecture du Journal par les Politiques de la petite Provence au jardin des Thuilleries', from an engraving by François Huot, late eighteenth century.
Courtesy of BNF / Gallica: https://gallica.bnf.fr

love intrigues, the sociable pathways being propitious for exchanging looks, and love-letters, even private conversations between young people, perfectly innocent because in public. Young ladies, appropriately chaperoned, go to the promenade and hope to be noticed, as Jeanne-Marie Philipon, known as Manon, who came from a middle-class Parisian family and was a diligent walker in the Tuileries and the Jardin du Roi, tells us in her Memoirs. One of her cousins tried in vain to arrange a marriage for her to an ambitious young doctor, more interested in the size of her dowry than in her person. 'The financial arrangements were made before I knew anything. The deal had already been done when they spoke to me of marrying a doctor. The married state attracted me, and promised me an enlightened husband. But it was necessary to know what he was like. A walk in the Luxembourg was arranged.'[29] But this ritual's magic did not work. Neither the interested parties nor the family were convinced, and the affair went no further. This instance

29 Madame Roland, *Mémoires de Madame Roland* (Paris: Baudouin Frères, 1827), p.171.

of the failed union of Manon Philipon nonetheless shows that under the *Ancien Régime* the margin of manoeuvre given to well-born young people, even in places noted for their freedom, was still limited by the exercise of a permanent social control.

The slow but sure individualisation of matrimonial choices, and the Rousseauesque identification of nature with purity, steadily turned green spaces into the very places for lovers' meetings. In the Romantic era, a garden was the ideal setting for tender conversations: there lovers attain a degree of intimacy in an environment felt to be propitious to the outpourings and tremblings of the heart. Bourgeois and masculine symbolism are reflected there: a flower among flowers, the young woman is *plucked* by her loved one; the purity of their sentiments is reflected in the innocence of the nature that surrounds them. The rendezvous may be more worldly and less naïve, but the park is still the favoured site for that. And if one is to believe Grimod de la Reynière, the aptly named pleasure gardens (see Chapter 5) were well suited to adulterous joys:

> Torches in earthenware pots along the walkways and in the bushes indicate the paths clearly enough to guide the unsure footsteps of the young and delicate lady-love, whose downfall they have also illuminated on occasion; and if one is to credit wicked tongues the many little green chambers have seen more than one sacrifice, and the setting-off of Fireworks is generally the moment for love to be consummated. More than one father, tutor or husband has been readily tricked in that propitious moment, unaware that the lovely one he accompanied to the festival tasted pleasures other than those for which he had brought her.[30]

Hedges and foliage form recesses favouring the intimacy of illicit meetings, and other monetised frolics. The free-living life of Paris at night in the age of Enlightenment stirred the imagination of contemporaries, virtuous moralists as well as lovers of literature and pornographic prints. The writer Restif de la Bretonne leads the reader of his *Nuits de Paris* (*Paris Nights*) through such scenes. He describes gardens and natural spaces which, properly policed at midday, mutate at midnight into sites of transgression where instincts and passions are given free rein. A fictional episode in the King's Garden brings the narrator into contact with a group of young blades, students of botany who, after bribing the guard, have come to have some fun with the ladies in the Labyrinth.[31] While one has to be wary of taking fantasies for what really went on, as evidenced in

30 Grimod de la Reynière, *Le Censeur dramatique*, vol. 3 (1798), p. 451.

31 Nicolas-Edme Restif de La Bretonne, *Les Nuits de Paris ou le spectateur nocturne* (London: 1788), vol. 3, p. 1224–1226.

Figure 36.

Walk of the Elegantes at the Palais-Royal, engraving by Louis Le Coeur, after a drawing by Claude-Louis Desrais, 1787.
Courtesy of BNF / Gallica: https://gallica.bnf.fr

police records for instance, the reputation of some haunts of debauchery was not unwarranted. The proliferation of municipal police regulations and royal commands to counter such phenomena indicates the public authorities' inability to control their citizens' behaviour. Despite setting up surveillance arrangements and employing guards, the royal gardens in Paris, led by the Luxembourg and the Tuileries, did not lose favour with commercial Venuses and Cupids. As for the Palais Royal, it had a special place in the capital's topography of places for monetised pleasure.[32] Day and night, the walks and gardens were a real hunting-ground for prostitutes who bargained their charms with the client before leading him to some room reserved for the purpose, or to complete their transaction al fresco. In the deep shade, the recesses and paths furnished with benches lent themselves very well to furtive encounters.

It was there that Napoleon found the way to lose his innocence in 1787. It was not until 1837 that prostitutes were banned from there, though it did not stop being a place for encounters.

32 Clyde Plumauzille, 'Le "marché aux putains": économies sexuelles et dynamiques spatiales du Palais-Royal dans le Paris révolutionnaire', *Genre, sexualité & société* **10** (2013), http://gss.revues.org/2943; DOI: 10.4000/gss.2943 (accessed 4 Aug. 2014)

Other green places were available for the illicit pleasures of Parisians, their popularity varying with the intensity of policing: until the Champs-Élysées were reorganised, it was not advisable to go there at night, and that remained the case until the nineteenth century. Not to mention the Bois de Boulogne, of course, whose steamy reputation began with the parade of courtesans at the end of the eighteenth century and lasts to this day. Smartly dressed Second Empire tarts were to be found there as well as poor girls, but at different times of day. Again, between the wars in the twentieth century, it was known as a place of night-time debauchery: when Catherine, one of the heroines of Aragon's *Cloches de Bâle* (*The Bells of Basel*) wanders into the Bois at night she is immediately taken for a prostitute by the police, who seek to arrest her. Significantly 'a couple of pederasts'[33] are arrested in the same round-up.

In fact, if homosexuality is sometimes associated with town life, for obvious reasons of anonymity, of networks and of refuge, it is interesting that often gardens, parks and promenades (though not exclusively) are places favoured for seduction, amateur or professional, by 'the third sex'. The chief meeting-places, in Paris at least, which is the most fully documented, were the great green spaces – which sometimes allowed furtive encounters when, like the wooded areas, they were less well-lit and less policed: the Palais Royal, of course, whose popularity lasted until the middle of the nineteenth century;[34] the Luxembourg and Tuileries gardens, especially in the eighteenth century; and, increasingly from the 1780s onwards, the Champs-Élysées, which remained up until the First World War the number one site for homosexual dalliance; and one can add to these the quays of the Seine and the great Boulevards.[35] This geography stayed much the same until 1914.[36]

While Cora Vaucaire may have sung in 1953 of the amorous and libidinous

33 Louis Aragon, *Les Cloches de Bâle* (Paris: Gallimard, 2010), pp. 249–251.

34 Michael Sibalis, 'The Palais-Royal and the Homosexual Subculture of Nineteenth-Century Paris', *Journal of Homosexuality* **41** (3–4) (2002): 117–129.

35 Thierry Pastorello, 'Sodome à Paris: protohistoire de l'homosexualité masculine, fin XVIIIe-milieu XIXe siècle', Ph.D. thesis, Université Paris-Diderot (Paris VII), 2009; Leslie Choquette, 'Homosexuals in the city', *Journal of Homosexuality* **41** (3–4) (2002) 149–167.

36 Régis Revenin, ‹L›émergence d›un monde homosexuel moderne dans le Paris de la Belle Époque›, *Revue d›Histoire Moderne et Contemporaine* **53–54** (4) (2006): 78–79. Michael Sibalis explains the frequency of outdoor sexual practices by the lack of real privacy in the dwellings themselves for a large part of the population. It was with the advent of the modern city, particularly under Haussmann, that such spaces were gradually established, and at the same time, public spaces were subjected to stricter and more constant control through lighting and patrols. See Michael Sibalis, 'Les espaces des homosexuels dans le Paris d'avant Haussmann', in Karen Bowie, *La Modernité avant Haussmann. Formes de l'espace urbain à Paris 1801–1853* (n.p., Éditions Recherches, 2001), pp. 236–237.

meetings that were possible in the 'gardens of Paris',[37] this was obviously not peculiar to Paris: throughout France and especially in big cities, gardens and parks remain the favoured sites for illicit encounters and prostitution, both male and female. This was the case in Marseille, for instance, where at the beginning of the twentieth century police regulations highlighted areas where commercial sex prevailed and forbade prostitutes to solicit in promenades and public gardens. It was similar in Lille, where the wood of the citadel, nicknamed the Bois de Boulogne of Lille, was known for prostitution at the end of the nineteenth century.

This was widely known, accepted by some and vainly resisted by others. On 26 August 1880 the newspaper *La Lanterne* expressed astonishment that some persisted in wanting to close squares and public gardens, especially at variable hours: 8.15 pm for the Luxembourg, but 10 pm for the Tuileries and Parc Monceau; would it not be more simple and consistent to leave them open all night?

> 'But what about public morality?' say the prudes, 'If the gardens are left open won't there be abuse?... men and women!...'
> This argument does not work: after a certain time we know perfectly well all the fathers and mothers of families have gone home. Only the lovers of flirtation are left. They will do what they want … A few park-keepers and rounds by the town's sergeant will be enough to prevent blatant disorder: that is the aim of the police … not to teach the citizens morals. They are there for one purpose, to stop some people's bad behaviour being a nuisance to others.[38]

Will this debate ever end?

Green spaces are far from answering all the expectations their planners and public authorities invested in them when they were devised; some people are disturbed by this and suggest ways of avoiding any deviation from good intentions. At the very start of the July Monarchy, the naturalist Pierre Boitard rejected the English style in favour of French symmetry,

> especially if the garden should be open after sunset, because then all the remote groves, the winding pathways and the mysterious recesses would draw in people with bad morals and inveterate rogues with no intention of giving themselves up to romantic reverie. Good conduct must be maintained in everything, never losing sight of the safety of walkers, who would never be comfortable in a garden of the irregular or picturesque style.[39]

37 'Les Jardins de Paris', song by Michel Vaucaire/Philippe-Gérard (1953).

38 'Les jardins publics', *La Lanterne*, 26 Aug. 1880.

39 Pierre Boitard, *Manuel de l'Architecture des jardins* (Paris: Roret, 1854 [ca 1834]), in Michel Conan, *Dictionnaire historique de l'art des jardins* (Paris: Hazan, 1997), p. 194.

This, however, was the dominant style and, through destiny or not, green spaces continued to escape from their creators as it were. They are reinvaded by the public who, in so far as the restrictions imposed on them enable it, take them over and adapt them to their needs. Park rules, which go on being formulated right through the nineteenth century, revealed undesired practices: linen hung out to dry, ropes hung from trees to swing on, sundry ball-games, kites, ice-skates in the winter, and so on. The park-keepers were on the watch, trying to constrain the people, acting as policemen – but new uses and practices were always emerging, and these sometimes required compromise. Children and vagrants were the most recalcitrant. How vagrants seized on green spaces is seen in Jean-Paul Clébert's striking narrative of his years of delinquency which he published in 1952 under the title of *Paris insolite* (*Unfamiliar Paris*). Here we find a post-World War II Paris still dotted with greenery, even if it is endlessly pushed away. It is not that there was a shortage of places to settle: abandoned railway lines invaded by grasses – especially what is now called the '*coulée verte*' (green corridor) – disused land on the embankments of fortifications, the Buttes Chaumont, or the Champ des Curés at the Porte d'Italie, the tall weeds of the avenue Romain Rolland and even the Père Lachaise cemetery where certain tombs, bigger than others, kept an acquaintance of the author out of the rain for several nights. It was always a matter, except for this last example, of free and accessible spaces with no specific function, though often closed with fences and gates. It was quite different in the gardens and woods of Paris. Early in the 1940s Clébert, still an adolescent, hopped over the wall of his boarding school to go and sleep under the weeping willows in the Bois de Boulogne. Several years later, when he had made his choice for a vagabond life, he complains of the impossibility of repeating this exploit because of annoying persons who wander there every night seeking impossible loves and furtive encounters – a problem he also finds in the garden of the Carrousel.[40] This situation has hardly changed in a half-century. For instance, the Bois de Vincennes has become a refuge today for the homeless: 270 of them were living there in 2010, especially in the areas devastated by the 1999 storm; these are now re-growing and offer a kind of privacy. A comprise has been reached with the managers of the wood: they interfere very little as long as the homeless do not impinge on the spaces that are really gardened. This is a flagrant divergence from Vincennes' original destiny.

40 Jean-Paul Clébert, *Paris Insolite* (Paris: Denoël, 1952).

Vandalism: from carelessness to maliciousness

While green spaces may be the object of unexpected or reprehensible practices, they are also at times subject to real vandalism.

One is bemused by the frequency with which the authorities are notified of damage. It is often due to ignorance of the harm that can be done to trees, or indifference to it: they are used for the needs of the moment, or for daily life, with no thought for the damage one is inflicting on them. Repeated regulatory injunctions change nothing. Thus, at Nantes in 1921 the oaks in the Place du Champ de Mars 'are covered in nails, some not used, others holding wires for hanging up laundry … And furthermore … several trees have been bound round with wire and rope.'[41] Similarly, at the end of the nineteenth century, some residents of the Boulevard Pasteur in Nantes got into the habit of 'throwing their domestic rubbish and household waste water over the feet of the trees. The debris ferments, rots and leads to the overheating of the roots and then the death of the trees.' Anyone trying to bring these people to reason finds himself 'rudely rebuked'.[42] These acts of stupid maliciousness, though at times simply the results of ignorance or indifference, are evidence of a rejection of the order in the streets that was sought by the authorities and elites who did not expect such uses of the vegetation, hoping for a different, more respectful, treatment.

At times it is hard to determine where the border lies between careless damage and vandalism. In 1666 the councillors of the town of Nîmes paid for the restoration of an old ball-games pitch by the Porte de la Couronne, which is extended by a planted esplanade. 'These improvements were only just finished when a gang of young people went in the night of Monday 8 March to cut down some of the newly planted trees and to disturb others.'[43] There is no interpreting the message conveyed by such action, if indeed there is one; was it a mad party going off the rails or a challenge to the social order as the municipality had employed the town's poor on the work? By the same token, how does one explain, for instance, on the occasion of Victor Hugo's funeral in Paris, the crowd seriously damaging trees in the boulevards Saint-Germain and Saint-Michel and in the Champs-Élysées? What does one say

41 Archives municipales de Nantes, 1O16127, Planting Service, Information Bulletin, 21 Nov. 1921.

42 Archives municipales de Nantes, 1O16127, The Inspector of Walks and Public Gardens to the Mayor of Nantes, 14 May 1893.

43 Léon Ménard, *Histoire civile, ecclésiastique et littéraire de la ville de Nisme avec les preuves…* (Paris: H.D. Chaubert, 1744–1758), vol. 6, p.180.

about schoolboys throwing stones and sticks to get chestnuts down? Or about the 'pranksters' and 'clowns' who, coming out of school, rip the bark off trees? Records often identify young people as principally responsible for damage. Is this a challenge to the established order or just adolescent games? In 1959 the mayor of Besançon asked the press to 'make their readers understand all the harm caused by youngsters, and sadly not only youngsters, when they systematically damage trees'.[44]

And of course, incidents of deliberate vandalism are not rare either.

Vandals can take advantage of exceptional circumstances to express themselves: in France successive revolutions, and especially that of 1789, gave rise to all kinds of damage, sometimes symbolic and targeted, and vegetation did not escape. In Montpellier for instance, a number of rare species were cut down and used for firewood, while kitchen gardens were apparently planted in the rich soil of flower beds.[45] As for the trees in the Tuileries, they were really wrecked, along with the Palace, during the 1871 Commune. Wars were not kinder than revolutions. The gates of Paris bristled with vegetal barricades in 1914: the trees of the boulevards were victims of the combat to protect the capital in case the front should be broken.

In World War II and during the Occupation, to install anti-aircraft batteries in the Jardin des Plantes in Montpellier, the Germans had hundred-year-old trees cut down, destroyed flower beds and made a great reservoir ruining the landscape.[46]

One does not always find reasons to explain this damage. In 1913 in Nantes, on the Boulevard Gambetta, 41 plane trees were slashed with a sharp weapon: suspicion immediately fell on men from a regiment of dragoons, but it seems they were quickly exculpated. In 1921 it was the turn of the Square Saint André to be the object of wrongdoing: some plants there were stolen and others wrecked: the report sent to the mayor states, 'some flowers were snapped off on the spot and others ripped up, proving that the motive is not theft alone, but a premeditated desire for vengeance or vandalism.' Was Nantes particularly liable to this kind of crime? That seems to be what the author of the report thought; he says he 'knew of scarcely anywhere but Brest and Nantes for organised pillaging! In Paris and in the East gar-

44 Musée d'histoire de Besançon, *La Ville en ses jardins* (Besançon, Catalogue of the exhibition at the Palais Granvelle, 8 Aug.– 24 Sept. 1984), p. 29.

45 Jean-Antoine Rioux, *Le Jardin des plantes de Montpellier* (Graulhet: Odyssée, 1994), p. 40.

46 Ibid., p. 92.

Figure 37.

Barricades at Porte Maillot in Paris, circa 1914–1915.
Courtesy of BNF / Gallica: https://gallica.bnf.fr

dens are respected.'[47] Whether or not this was Nantes' speciality in crime, repeated offences prompted a reaction from the authorities who, through the Tourist Office, addressed the population in the press on 16 June 1922. They deplored having to do away with floral decorations, so often targeted by thieves and vandals, and asked honest folk to incite punishment of the guilty whenever they could:

> The Tourist Office is keen to preserve everything attractive in our town … and implores all those who love their City to be watchful of its reputation, badly damaged by such acts of depredation. It urges teachers in particular to impress on children and young people that a population only truly deserves liberty when it uses it reasonably.[48]

47 Archives municipales de Nantes, 1O16127, The chief gardener at the town hall of Nantes, 3 June 1921.

48 Archives municipales de Nantes, 1O16127, Tourist Office, 16 June 1922.

Here one sees that the vegetal arrangements of a town are deemed to say something about it, its status and the respectability of its inhabitants, and why it is so important that the town hall manages to preserve them. And one also realises that education is needed so that everyone, and the young particularly, pays due respect to urban planting. Lastly, it is apparent that beyond appealing to the public and to teachers, very strict measures of vigilance and control are required if one hopes to put a stop to this blight.

Protecting the order of green spaces

Natural places in towns are not like other spaces: the many specific regulations concerning them which we have already described bear witness to that. Why this special treatment? Could one not simply employ the normal rules for conduct in public places? We are not surprised these days by this singularity, and yet it is not obvious. It derives from two characteristics of parks and gardens: their vegetal environment, which is more fragile than a stone building or pavement; and the freedom of space they seem to offer to townspeople, offering a range of possibilities that have to be rapidly contained. This escape from the town and its constraints is both what gives value to urban green spaces and what makes special regulations all the more necessary. The role of these spaces is to bring a breath of liberty, not to create disorder in the heart of the city.

This regulatory practice was established little by little as royal and municipal authorities took possession of and organised urban green spaces. In the seventeenth century, when the opening of parks and gardens was a royal activity, this could be interpreted as a manifestation of kingly liberality. As towns expanded, new grounds were recuperated and laid out by the authorities, who imposed their own regulations on them. In Paris the most representative example is still that of the Champs-Élysées, progressively 'civilised' through the course of the eighteenth century. A crucial stage was marked by the ordinance of 11 June 1777, passed by the Count of Angiviller, director and commissioner general of the King's Buildings, and by that title in charge of the land. Practices deemed prejudicial to the public's comfort and the maintenance of the promenade in a proper state were thenceforth banned: the number of stalls and shops was restricted, games such as boules and real tennis were herded into a circumscribed area; peddlers, vehicles and horses in the quincunxes were forbidden, as were the use of firearms and dumping rubbish. Any use of the land for agriculture or animal-rearing was outlawed: 'all private persons were forbidden to send oxen, cows, donkeys or other animals to graze there'.

(Article 10) Lastly it was forbidden 'to climb the trees, to shake them or to throw stones or sticks into their branches'. (Article 11) From the eighteenth century, French provincial towns readily equipped themselves with gardens and parks and adopted rules for policing them to control how they were used and to protect the investment made in the vegetal. The delicate and costly planting of botanical gardens warranted the authorities' particular concern. Picture postcards of the botanical garden at Nantes from the early twentieth century provide glimpses of barbed wire protecting plantings that were doubtless more vulnerable than others. This work of protection, especially in forming regulations, has continued through the centuries, with some modifications, up till the present day. At the beginning of the twentieth century, municipal decrees bearing on the Borély Park in Marseille classically forbade touching the plants, walking and sitting on the lawns, throwing objects liable to injure passers-by or make them dirty, and playing with kites or balls; there were also rules about the passage and parking of motorcars and bicycles.[49]

Order in green spaces sometimes had to be imposed by force, as we have seen. Guards were assigned to some *Ancien Régime* gardens, notably Swiss Guards. The Count of Angiviller assigned the soldier Frédérici as a guard to the Champs-Élysées and he left us valuable eye-witness evidence. Municipal police were not in the front line, not even later on. First in that role were inspectors of the promenades, responsible for oversight of the various town plants, and protecting trees especially, and for keeping order in parks, gardens, and squares. They were assisted by keepers (in Besançon in the ordinance of 1787 these are already 'promenade caretakers') whose appearance became progressively more uniform. In 1894, when the guardian of the Square La Monnaie in Nantes was insulted and threatened by some young people, the inspector demanded that the mayor swear him into office and allow him to wear the arms of the city on his helmet: it appears these were two ways of enhancing the guardian's authority and of limiting breaches of the regulations.[50] Added to this panoply of officials were police specialising in issues of morality. In 1715 two of them were responsible specifically for Parisian 'sodomites', and one of them was specially assigned to the Tuileries, a favourite place for meetings. Their job was not made easy by the fact that the garden was royal ground and they could not just act as they pleased:

49 Municipal bylaws of 13 Sept. 1904 and 13 June 1891.

50 Archives municipales de Nantes, 1O16127, The Inspector of Walks to the Mayor of Nantes, 9 Mar. 1894.

they used informers to lure suspects out of the garden, when they could be arrested. The moral police patrolled particularly in and around green spaces: in 1848 a police patrol mounted a nightly watch on the Champs-Élysées. Its actions were at times injudicious and unfair and in the second half of the nineteenth century the police earned a reputation for inefficiency and for encroachments on the freedom of the public, to the point where they saw their existence threatened in fierce discussions between 1878 and 1881.

Green spaces can be defended by singling them out with a statute that grants them supplementary juridical, and hence police, protection. The woods of Boulogne and Vincennes were respectively classified, by title of the 1930 law on the protection of natural monuments and sites, by a decree dated 23 September 1957 and a 22 November 1960 ordinance. By adding to the regulation of the parks and promenades of Paris, this classification strengthens the juridical coverage of such spaces: for instance, they cannot be modified without reference to the departmental commission for sites, views and landscapes and to the *architecte des bâtiments de France* (for listed buildings, etc.). The classification of these woods as 'natural and forest zones' under urban development plans increases even further the protection they enjoy, if this should prove necessary.[51] A notion of 'green heritage' is thus coming to light, even if it is still rather vague.

The importance the authorities give to their greenery can be measured by the severity of the punishment anticipated when it is attacked. In 1768 the Capitols (magistrates) of Toulouse condemned one Pierre Daydé, a chair bearer, to 'fifteen days in prison, with corporal punishment for repeated offences' for having stolen stakes and cuttings from trees in the Promenade on the quay, overthrown the parapet of that quay and having stolen iron ties. In the same era the 1777 ordinance on the Champs-Élysées included graded punishments according to offences: this was usually a matter of fines, for instance twenty *livres* per horse for those who let a vehicle enter the plantations and quincunxes. Or ten *livres* for dumping rubble or rubbish. Repeat offences, of course, increased the penalty, up to imprisonment. While physical punishment tended to disappear in the course of time, the law remained strict on any attack on urban greenery: at the end of the nineteenth century in Nantes for example there was no hesitation about prosecuting those who violated the regulations.

It was only a short step from freedom to disorder, and one which the

51 Jean-Baptiste Vaquin, *Atlas de la Nature à Paris* (Paris: Atelier parisien d'urbanisme, 2006), pp. 202–203.

welcoming lawns and the screens of vegetation tempted one to take: criminal behaviour, libertine activities or simple vandalism occurred in and on urban nature, despite the repeated efforts of the authorities deploying an entire legal and police arsenal to control excesses. But, beyond just moral disorder and criminal behaviour, assailing nature in the town may also have, as we might have guessed, a genuinely political aspect.

Vegetal battles

The apples of discord

Trees and gardens can be the subject of lively disagreement, between people and authority, or even between different authorities. They can become the object of emotional attachments, even embodiments of politics. The Luxembourg Garden in Paris has been a good example of this down the years.

Around 1715, the Duchess of Berry, daughter of the regent Philippe of Orleans, set about walling up all the gates of the Luxembourg except one, which she opened only rarely. The Duke of Richelieu explained this action by way of a verbal attack she and her friends had suffered, which could have gone further if the Swiss had not intervened. As for the people, now deprived of a place they had adopted and valued, it was more a matter of the duchess, said to be of loose morals, spending nights there, 'with a freedom that needed accessories more than witnesses' as Duclos neatly put it. A satirical song lampooned 'the closing of the Luxembourg gates':

> There's now just one way in
> To lovely Luxembourg;
> Venus, escorted by the devil,
> Has just played this trick on us.
> To punish the Goddess
> The hole had to be blocked
> Through which Cupid hurried
> To slip her his jewel.

It was only in 1719, after having given birth, that the duchess re-opened the gates of the garden, without being forgiven by the population.[52] The people demonstrated the same attachment to the 'Luco' a century and a half later when protesting violently against a project by Napoleon III that aimed

52 Émile Raunié, *Chansonnier historique du XVIIIe siècle. Recueil de chansons, vaudevilles, sonnets, épigrammes, épitaphes et autres vers satiriques et historiques, formé avec la collection de Clairambault, de Maurepas et autres manuscrits inédits* (Paris: A.Quantin, 1879–1884), vol. II, pp. 41–44.

at reducing the area by getting rid of a nursery garden in particular. This encroachment was decided by a decree dated 26 November 1865 and was for the benefit of streets and buildings, but it aroused a wave of indignation expressed with astonishing virulence against such an authoritarian regime as that of the emperor's. A first petition with 12,000 signatures (former members of parliament, French peers or ministers, lawyers, doctors, architects, artists, mothers, workmen, etc.) was sent to the Senate a week later by Adolphe Joanne, the author of famous guidebooks. The press took up this campaign, entitled 'Sauvons le Luxembourg' ('Save the Luxembourg') and on the whole supported the petitioners, as did the president of the Court of Cassation who judged that the decree was unconstitutional. According to him and most of the opponents, it needed not a decree but a law to expropriate a garden belonging in the public domain and therefore to the nation. This was, then, one of the most serious challenges to the Emperor's authority expressed during his reign since his adversaries took advantage of this to underline his anti-republican character. Much fun was made of this regime which, on one hand, turned Paris upside-down in order to provide the children and the poor with green spaces where they might unwind and grow in good health and, on the other hand, destroyed one of the most emblematic parks in the capital located, what is more, in a student quarter! At one point it was believed that a surprise visit by Napoleon III to the Luxembourg Garden in February 1866 might change everything, but the revised plan that he proposed still ate away all the south side of the garden. Indignation sometimes gave way to anger and to open defiance: on 17 March 1866 during the première of a play at the Odéon theatre, just by the park, the imperial couple were booed several times and welcomed with cries of 'Long live the Luxembourg!' and 'Long live the nursery garden!' It is worth noting that the last attempt to save the park was undertaken by women, in fact by mothers, who addressed the Empress to share with her their anxiety about the health of their aged parents and their children if the Luxembourg was reduced in size. Was that the right card to play? We do not know what finally convinced the authorities but a third plan was finally proposed and accepted, which limited the encroachments and transformed what was left of the nursery garden into an English style garden – bestowing on the Luxembourg Garden the look it still has today.[53]

53 Richard S. Hopkins, 'Sauvons le Luxembourg: Urban Greenspace as Private Domain and Public Battleground, 1865–1867', *Journal of Urban History* **37** (1) (2011): 43–58.

Protests of this type dot the history of French towns. Even in 2015 a wave of discontent motivated those who used the park at La Courneuve; a project for a 'French style Central Park' planned for a quarter of this 410-hectare park to be removed and for luxury housing to be built on the land. Local elected politicians, often from far-left or ecology parties, as well as many residents from the area signed petitions and took part in citizens' picnics to put pressure on the government, which seemed ready to backtrack: there is certainly no way that green spaces belonging to the people for several decades can be altered with impunity.

Vegetal space could also be the source of conflict about the legitimacy of two authorities – generally, between civil power and the army. In fact, the military, in particular in border towns, had their own logic regarding the use of unused spaces or those close to the city walls, a view which municipal authorities shared less and less as peace seemed to become a settled state of affairs. Nevertheless, the army planted a lot of trees on city walls,[54] an enquiry in 1761–1762 tells us that the ramparts and the citadel at Arras had 5,219 trees (including 5,068 elms) and there were 898 trees at Doullens. These plantations can be explained by four reasons. Firstly, they played a structural role because the roots helped to fix the raised banks of earth. Secondly, there were defensive motivations as they acted as a screen for the defenders. Their economic part was also vital: wood was a precious source of income and was indispensable in case of siege, used as arms and in defence. Finally, and this is the point where there might be some understanding with the town authorities, they ornamented the town. This, however, was of course of least concern to the officers but, on the other hand, was the prime concern for the town's residents and their representatives. So, this is where quarrels arose, for example over the choice of trees – town councillors in Lille had lime-trees planted in the place of elms, which the military preferred by far! It was because it was feared that the army would fell the trees when military exercises and the needs of the troops became pressing: when in 1765, 203 trees from the ramparts and the streets of the town of Châlons-en-Champagne thus came under threat, the municipal authorities became indignant and appealed to the ministry.

However, it was particularly in the eighteenth century that the reposses-

54 On the army and nature in the city, we rely here on Yoann Brault's fascinating chapter, 'Fortifications, esplanades et champs de Mars. Nature citadine et principes de contiguïté entre civils et militaires', in Daniel Rabreau and Sandra Pascalis, *La Nature citadine au siècle des Lumières* (Bordeaux: Arts & Arts, 2005), pp. 203–213.

sion of city walls and the land around them gave rise to sharp disputes with military authorities. In Besançon, for example, the laying out of the magnificent Chamars promenade was done by the continuous erosion of the army's prerogatives, from the end of the seventeenth century onwards. The army ended up giving way on all points, including breaking through the fortifications built by Vauban, the raising of land that was supposedly floodable thus making the town impregnable, etc. By an irony of fate, the destruction of this same promenade under the July Monarchy was partly carried out by the army: in 1835 an artillery school was set up there and a swathe of the land was ceded to the military command; in 1840 the botanic garden was destroyed in order to build the arsenal; in 1873 new agreements between the town council and the army signed the definitive death warrant of this exceptional park.

More subtly, as Yoann Brault clearly demonstrates, the creation of avenues at the foot of citadel esplanades, first in Lille, then in Cambrai, Arras, Montpellier, Chalon-sur-Saône, Strasbourg, Valence, Laon, Verdun and Perpignan, happened because of highly symbolic motivations: it was about diminishing the impression of the citadel's domination of the town by offering the town's residents a place for enjoyment and relaxation. These avenues thus became the link between the citadel, which was architecturally and often culturally detached, and the town itself. It provided a French model for leisure and promoted the merits of the occupier, softening the impact of domination by the very agency of their occupation and thus making it even more efficacious.[55]

So, plant life could thus be coloured with a political hue, properly speaking, symbolising the clash between two antagonistic orders. To each regime, its symbol: the lily of the Bourbons, the oaks and laurels of Bonaparte, the trees of liberty for the republicans, not forgetting the lilac which was to the liking of Louis-Philippe. On 1 May 1831, St Philip's feast day, he took part in a truly royal entrance into Paris where, acclaimed by the crowd, he bore in his buttonhole a lilac flower and in his hand a fragrant flowery branch, the symbol of springtime hope for the very new July Monarchy.[56] The practice continues to this day: if we think about Mitterrand and the roses he carefully laid in the Panthéon on the day of his investiture as the new socialist President on 21 May 1981, on the tombs of Jean Jaurès, Victor Schœlcher and Jean Moulin; or of Chirac's apples, offered by his supporters a few years

55 Brault, 'Fortifications, esplanades et champs de Mars', p. 207.

56 Alain Corbin et al., *Les Usages politiques des fêtes aux XIX*^e^*-XX*^e^ *siècles* (Paris: Publications de la Sorbonne, 1994), p. 98.

later; or even of Pétain's lime-tree, planted on 23 September 1941 during the Marshal's visit to Annecy.[57]

Two particularly striking examples seem to us to best embody this politicisation of the vegetal: that of the trees of liberty and that of guerrilla gardening.

The trees of liberty

Having overthrown the *Ancien Régime* and its symbols, the Revolution needed to set up a new symbolic order. Respecting the Age of Enlightenment passion for nature, the vegetal was in its proper place in the new political language, all the more so since green urban spaces remained the special place for great collective demonstrations. Since they were accessible to everyone, open-air ceremonies, commemorations and festivities staged the universal adhesion to the new order of things. Natural spaces in towns were associated with aims for the regeneration of society but also for the preservation of the revolutionary memory. Busts, columns and pyramids celebrated the great events or actors which were to be honoured. A ceremony was held where Marat's heart was on display on an altar in the middle of the Luxembourg Garden, while his remains were buried in the Cordeliers garden, depicted by some artists as a veritable natural temple.

At the beginning of 1790 a spontaneous popular movement became more widespread: 'trees of liberty' were planted with great joy during civic ceremonies celebrating the election of the first town councils to which the National Constituent Assembly had just granted new powers on a local scale (decree of 14 December 1789). Trees of liberty came from two symbolic traditions: the old maypoles and the new emblems of freedom used during the American and Dutch revolutions. The people were experimenting with a new political language able to express their aspirations while rejecting the symbolic order of the *Ancien Régime*. In 1792 in Paris, during ceremonies to commemorate the 14 July, the tree erected on the Champ de Mars prefigured the monarch's grave:

> At a certain distance from the Altar of the Nation … a great Tree will be raised, from the branches of which will be hung, like garlands, Crests, Helmets and the Trappings of banished Orders, intertwined with chains; at the foot of this Tree a Pyre will be built, covered with carpets, with all kinds of Crowns, Hoods, Ermines, Doctoral Hats, Titles of nobility and Brief-bags.[58]

57 Michel Germain, *La Vie quotidienne à Annecy pendant la guerre, 1939–1945* (Montmélian: La Fontaine de Siloé, 2005), p. 55.

58 *Commémoration nationale du quatorze juillet* (Paris: Dubosquet libraire, 1792), p. 7.

As early as 1793, Abbot Grégoire devoted an *Essai historique et patriotique sur les arbres de la liberté* (*Historic and Patriotic Essay on Trees of Liberty*), in which he argued for their highly charged symbolism and the expectations of revolutionary leaders, as well as giving useful advice to ensure the viability of these monuments. From this essay sprang the legend about the first tree of liberty being planted, with no roots, in Saint-Gaudet (Vienne) on 1 May 1790, whereas the first known mention of such a tree states that the first tree was at Gahard (Ille-et-Vilaine) on 16 February 1790. These plantings were originally spontaneous but they became increasingly encouraged and controlled by the new authorities. On 22 January 1794, a decree passed by the Convention thus obliged every town to plant a tree of liberty on its territory[59] and to replace it if necessary. In order to avoid the symbolically regrettable withering of the trees, it was better to make a certain effort in forestry.

In November 1793 a sub-committee in Agriculture was tasked with advising towns and disseminating the necessary agronomic and botanical knowledge. André Thouin, newly appointed professor of cultivation at the National Natural History Museum, saw in this a new mission for his institution: he wanted all of France to benefit from the resources of the Paris botanic garden.[60] In his 'notes on the planting and choice of trees to be dedicated to liberty', he set out a list of about sixty species likely to thrive in the three main climate zones and three major types of soil. At the same time, the question of symbolic plants was a topic for public discussion and exchanges were becoming very heated. It was an important issue, since it concerned the selection of trees as standard bearers of republican values, embodying the Revolution. A member of the sub-committee in Agriculture, Franck Hell, reckoned that the noble oak was the only tree worthy of being associated with freedom. Members of popular societies disagreed with him as they saw the oak as being too aristocratic and denounced its former links with the kings of France. Why not choose instead native species, such as the lime-tree, the elm, the beech or even better the poplar, whose Latin etymology evoked the *populus*, the people? Consensus was easier to find when it came to equality and fraternity: trees from America were recommended to pay homage to the people who pioneered revolution. At a local level, the trees of liberty also unleashed passions between the partisans of the regime and the rejected opponents of the Counter-Revolution. On 22 October

59 The name, which until then had varied (tree of fraternity, equality, concord, tricolour), is now fixed.

60 Pascal Duris, *Linné et la France (1780–1850)* (Geneva: Droz, 1993), pp. 110–111.

1792 a tree of liberty was planted on Place du Change in Avignon; a pine was selected for it was supposed to chase away 'the pestilential vapours of the aristocracy' and embody the triumph of the defenders of the Revolution over the counter-revolutionaries.[61]

Damage, bad faith on the part of local authorities sometimes, or simply trees dying because they were badly planted or at the wrong time, made new laws necessary and, on the 22 Germinal in year IV (11 April 1796) and the 24 Nivôse in year VI (13 January 1798), these laws specified the penalties for whoever laid a hand on these 'signs of liberty' and recalled the obligation to (re)plant them, in particular on the anniversary of the king's death, on 21 January. This was not a minor phenomenon: according to Abbot Grégoire 60,000 trees were planted in 1793–1794! In Caen alone, 31 liberty trees were planted in just the Revolutionary decade. This tradition, which died out somewhat at the turn of the eighteenth and nineteenth centuries, came back with some force during the revolutionary period of 1848, as the Second Republic recalled its links with the First Republic. In the former department of Moselle, about eighty trees were supposedly planted, mostly spontaneously, in the months that followed the February insurrection.[62] After that, the great events in French history, either republican (centenary of the Revolution in 1889, for example) or wartime (victories of 1918 and 1945) have often seen the resurgence of this symbolism, but never with the intensity of 1792 or 1848. In Moselle, however, the department's return to France was marked in 1919 by the planting of 'trees of deliverance'.

The symbolic load of these trees was therefore particularly strong and long-lasting and was manifested in various ways. Firstly, the planting was the occasion for a ceremony which was both festive and solemn. This is how the ceremony to be held in Le Havre in 1792 was planned, according to the council minutes:

> A new tree of liberty will replace the one that exists at present. The ceremony will take place the following day 'at mid-day'. All the citizens will be invited. The assembly will gather in the grand hall of the Palace of Justice. The procession will make its way to the Place de la Liberté with the Société Populaire leading it, carrying its banner, and followed by the General council. A second group will comprise the old and the

61 Robineaux, *Discours prononcé par Robineaux, substitut du procureur de la commune d'Avignon, lors de la plantation de l'arbre de la liberté à la place, dite du Change, le 22 octobre 1792* (1792).

62 Charles Hiegel, 'Les arbres de la Liberté dans le département de la Moselle', *Les Cahiers lorrains* 4 (Dec. 1999): 440.

> children – the hope of the nation. The third group will comprise the respectable crowds of citizens and citizenesses.[63]

There was a pleasure taken in the hope of unanimity – denied in the reality by the refusal or the exclusion of the anti-revolutionaries. Most of the time, young people were placed to the fore as they incarnated the new generation which could bear witness, in the shade of the newly planted tree, to the extraordinary events that they had lived through. It was also the younger citizens who had asked the town council in Metz for permission to plant a tree of liberty on the Place de la Loi. The ceremony was held on 20 May 1792 and it was sumptuous: a mass celebrated in the cathedral; a speech by the deputy town; an escort by the National Guard; and the judicial and administrative authorities, once the tree was planted, trooping round it and throwing handfuls of earth on the roots, followed by the other citizens; a Te Deum to close the ceremony, and at the end, a ball at the town hall to finish off the day in general rejoicing.[64] We find the same outline, more or less, for each planting episode in the decades that followed. At the most, one can point out, in 1848, the more marked presence of priests who blessed the young trees, and also of workmen: this is what George Sand wrote to her son on 28 March 1848: 'Every day, and in all spots, they plant trees of liberty. I saw 3 of them yesterday in different streets, immense pines, carried on the shoulders of 50 workmen.'[65]

Whenever possible, major national figures were called on: thus, on 2 March 1848, Victor Hugo made a speech on the occasion of the planting of a tree of liberty in Paris, Place des Vosges.

This official aspect is to be found in a commemorative picture depicting such a ceremony in Metz in 1848: the engraving is framed by the Marseillaise and a text in honour of trees of liberty. A commentary insists on the popularity of these plantations throughout France and the particularities which distinguish each region, especially regarding the choice of trees.

At the heart of these ceremonial practices the tree itself was, of course, the focus of all attention. Despite the debates mentioned, very often the choice of species fell on the oak, whose strength and longevity had a symbolic and

63 Summary of the deliberation of the council of the commune of Le Havre, 29 brumaire year II, in Pascal Guillot, *La Nature en révolution – de la liberté de la chasse aux arbres de la liberté*, Master's dissertation, Lille, Délégation Régionale à l'Architecture et à l'Environnement, 1989, p. 62.

64 Hiegel, 'Les arbres de la Liberté dans le département de la Moselle', 420–21.

65 George Sand, 28 Mar. 1848, in Jacqueline Lalouette, *Les mots de 1848* (Toulouse: PUM, 2008), pp. 16–17.

Figure 38.

Victor Hugo plants the Tree of Liberty on the Place Royale (in Paris) in 1848, watercolour by Hermann Vogel, 1892.
Public domain image from Maison de Victor Hugo.

useful weight, in particular for weak, budding republics. Unlike the '*mais*' (maypole) of earlier centuries, most of the time it was saplings that were chosen, so that they would take root and flourish. Generally, these were flanked by a whole series of symbolic elements, not least of which, during the revolutionary period, was the altar of the nation where public ceremonies were held (republican marriages or baptisms or proclamations of official notices, for example). Young women were encouraged to decorate the trees with ribbons and rosettes and usually they were topped by a Phrygian bonnet. To remove any ambiguity about the meaning of the tree, sometimes a placard or a notice was added. Thus, in Guéret on 17 May 1792 it was clearly stated that 'Citizens, friends of the Constitution and Equality have dedicated this tree to freedom and to concord.'[66] Finally, the site chosen was not haphazard. In villages, it was very often planted on the main square, even if less symbolically significant places were often chosen, being better adapted to the growth of a plant.

In town, the tree found its place in the heart of the urban fabric, in places loaded with meaning or that were just simply very busy. In Limoges, for example, the former Place Royale became Place de la République and on 19 March 1848 it hosted 15,000 people come to witness the planting of the tree. At Sarreguemines, as at Saint-Avold, during the Revolution, the Place du Marché became Place de la Liberté before it hosted the symbolic tree, which then became part of the 'urban furniture'. 'It completes the town by bringing to certain places a republican dimension. Its vegetal status only has meaning in the end because of the values it embodies', as Hugo said in 1848. 'Liberty has its roots in the heart of the people, as the tree has its roots in the heart of the earth; like the tree, liberty raises and unfurls its branches in the sky.'[67] It is not simply a tree, in the true sense of meaning that was planted during these ceremonies but also an allegory, although a living one.

It is precisely because of this strong symbolic meaning that the tree of liberty was contested vegetation. This was the case for all those authorities who did not align themselves with the political order imposed by the different French revolutions. As early as March 1816, a ministerial circular from the restored monarchy encouraged prefects to pull up the trees planted in the preceding decades. Similarly, in 1852, the Second Empire hurried to eliminate all the symbols of the overthrown republic. A circular from the prefect of the Creuse department thus asked mayors to pull up these trees, except for those that enhanced the streets and squares and which bore no symbols; but in 1853 his successor was less conciliatory and ordered the destruction of all the trees of liberty, without exception. In Moselle, the attitude was the same: a decree by the prefect, dated 12 January 1852, demanded

66 Mona Ozouf, *La Fête révolutionnaire* (Paris: Gallimard, 1989), note 83.

67 Victor Hugo, 'Plantation de l'arbre de la Liberté place des Vosges', speech of 2 Mar. 1848, *Œuvres complètes* (1880–1926), p. 171.

the uprooting of dead or dying trees of liberty and those which were 'an obstacle to traffic, or which hindered access to public places, or altered or spoilt the view of any monument'.[68] And once again, a reminder had to be issued a few months later.

The trees of liberty were not only threatened by reactionary powers but were also in danger at the time of their planting from opponents of the revolution. Individual acts of vandalism were frequent. We can cite the example of what happened in the town of Sarralbe where, on 21 January 1794, two policemen discovered a notice on a tree proclaiming: 'Tree of misery, bonnet of toil, ribbon of the brigand, you will not last long. I'll say it, like this, soon the patriot will sh** in his pants!' The bonnet (Phrygian) and the ribbon (tricolour) are thus closely associated with the tree which had become a republican symbol par excellence.

These actions, public or individual, which were quickly qualified as 'sacrileges', sometimes aroused very fierce reactions. To the walls and the railings protecting these symbols, to the repressive laws which multiplied in the last decade of the eighteenth century and punished these attacks with four months in prison, must be added popular feeling. In 1820 in Bayeux the prefect provoked a riot when he decided simply to cut off the branches of the tree. In Amiens, the martyred tree was covered in black crepe and was buried by 9,000 armed men.[69] Yet, despite popular vigilance, there are very few trees of liberty still standing today (such as the one in Bayeux); in towns in particular, they have disappeared, their symbolic presence being too obvious to be tolerated by the anti-revolutionary authorities.

Guerrilla gardening

If plant life has thus acquired a strong political dimension in urban environments it is because the town is the symbol of a particular relation to the world which seems to be opposed to nature or to build itself against nature (even though this may be a false idea as the main argument of this book is trying to demonstrate). Even if the town does become greener, until recently this has mainly occurred through a nature judged as being too artificial, too controlled by municipal authorities, reduced to the same shapes, concentrated in just a few places and excluded from most urban spaces. Against this presumed rarity of greenery in town and its domestication, protest movements have recently

68 Hiegel, 'Les arbres de la Liberté dans le département de la Moselle', 449.

69 Mona Ozouf, *La Fête révolutionnaire.*

sprung up and come together in what has been dubbed guerrilla gardening. The origins go back to the 1970s in New York when Liz Christy, an artist, set up a community garden in place of the wasteland next to her apartment block. Following that she undertook what she called 'Green Guerrilla', which was (peaceful) fighting to revegetalise urban interstices, all the abandoned spaces, whether public or private. The movement grew, particularly under the impetus of Richard Reynolds, a British man, who in 2004 set up a website and in 2008 published a book *On Guerrilla Gardening*, translated into French in 2010. The movement has now spread all over the world, thanks to social media in particular and has even launched its *International Sunflower Guerrilla Gardening Day*, which has been held on 1 May every year since 2007. On that day the idea is to plant sunflowers everywhere possible in towns. In France, there are guerrilla gardening groups in Paris, Bordeaux, Lyon, Lille, Toulouse, Blois, Clermont-Ferrand, etc. Each time it is about cultivating plants – flowers, vegetables, and all sorts of wild vegetation – in places where the town seems to exclude them. People act alone or in groups, at night or even in full daylight, gardening openly or setting 'seed bombs', made of clay and compost. A new kind of street art has been the spin-off of this illegal gardening: moss graffiti, and vegetal graffiti more generally. This consists in making designs out of moss applied to walls. The growth of the moss then ensures that the tag has its own life. People can cut out the moss shapes at home and then stick them on a wall, but the most common practice is to mix up a kind of daub made from moss and other ingredients which most of the time are beer and sugar. This can then be applied to the surfaces where you want to tag (see Figure 39).

The guerrilla gardeners are members of networks that are basically non-hierarchical, with libertarian tendencies, and they are driven by different motives. For the most part, those behind the movement have a discourse which is well constructed and basically about contestation. Reynolds presents his guerrilla activities as 'soft protest', as a 'struggle for resources, a battle against the rarity of the earth, the destruction of the environment and the wasting of opportunities. It's also a fight for freedom of expression and social cohesion.'[70] The statement on the French website is not so different and actually goes further in the political dimension. It places the movement within a long tradition of environmental struggles, from the seventeenth-century English Diggers to the Indian 'tree huggers' fighting against deforestation.

70 Richard Reynolds, *La Guérilla Jardinière* (n.p, Yves Michel, 2010), p. 15.

By recuperating public spaces in towns left in the hands of law enforcement agencies and municipal authorities, the guerrilla wants to engage in local democracy and aims at self-management by citizens. The guerrillas also demonstrate their refusal for land to be monopolised. Through gardening and the planting of seeds, city dwellers should be in a position to take back the town by bringing to it a spontaneity and variety which the monotony of standardised landscapes and a technicist vision of nature no longer allow.

Moreover, by relearning the gestures used in gardening, by becoming reacquainted with plants and especially vegetables, the guerrilleros are breaking with the usual systems of marketing and are rejecting market garden productivism in their wish to stimulate local production. Lastly, the actions carried out should encourage social contact and conviviality and give meaning back to urban living: basically, this is where the vegetal brings a new meaning to the town.

From such a conceptual base, the guerrilla gardeners have grown in number throughout France, dipping into this theoretical arsenal and taking from it what they choose. In Bordeaux, for example, a group has sprung up which does not burden itself with rhetoric and just aims simply at beautifying urban

Figure 39.

Activism in Lyon: moss tag inviting us to rethink the system in a more ecological way, spotted on 18 February 2016, rue Chevreul, Lyon II University buildings.
Courtesy of Julie Damaggio.

space for festive occasions or just for fun.[71] It is interesting also to note that, as quite often happens, protest groups can become institutionalised, thereby losing their subversive dimension yet all the while gaining in efficiency. As an example, one such case is the *Laissons Pousser* (*Let it Grow*) project,[72] launched in 2010 by two women in Paris, Hélène Binet and Emmanuelle Vibert. In the spirit of guerrilla gardening they created a wild, communal garden on a roundabout near the Gare de l'Est station. Backed by Paris City Hall and fifteen or so towns in the Paris region, they launched a campaign of collective sowing: 55,000 packets of seeds were handed out, of which 20,000 were for Paris. Everything was carefully planned: naturalists from Naturparif checked that these packets only contained local varieties of plants to avoid invasive species and the places available for planting were carefully chosen (at the foot of trees, communal gardens, etc). The project is still ongoing on *Green/Graine Day*, and about fifty towns participate, each one adapting it to local conditions. In Annecy, for example, the children all receive two packets each, one for planting in pedagogical gardens and the other to sow at home. Vegetal graffiti workshops were set up during 'FloraLille', held in the spring of 2014. The commercial world has picked up on the idea: *Mousse Graffiti* proposes the creation of high graphic quality tags for private individuals, schools or businesses for educational or advertising purposes. Doubtless, nature in the town has become too much an object of consensus to be the means of radical protest against the established order.

* * *

In a town at peace, plant life carefully set in the urban décor speaks the language of harmony, contributes to the civilising of behaviour and attracts the support of the greatest number to the cause of established social order. When troubles rear their head, or popular emotions or revolutionary events, then the vegetal changes sides. In the case of the trees of liberty, the original symbolic meaning was diverted towards the development of a new political language. More prosaically, in these difficult times when city dwellers are obliged to use any means available to them, plant life is no longer sanctified in parks and gardens which used to be so well regulated; it can even be enrolled in the fight against the old way of doing things. Witness and actor

71 See http://guerilla-gardening-france.fr/wordpress/

72 See http://www.laissonspousser.com

of the days of revolution in Paris in 1848, a republican democrat tells of the building of barricades in an incident in the February of that year when 4,103 trees were felled.

> The People, in revolt, descended into the street with their workshop tools for the meantime, while waiting to take up their guns later on. They cut down, alas! the fine trees on the boulevards ... And all we could hear were the blows of the axe and the noise of the trees and the crashing of their branches as they fell ... and soon the barricades were occupied and guarded by sentries; and we spied, around the sparking braziers, groups of men, crouching, making bullets and calmly smoking their pipes, in a strange encampment, in the middle of a great city ploughed up so that liberty could be planted there.[73]

73 Marc Caussidière, *Mémoires de Caussidière, ex-préfet de police et représentant du peuple* (Paris: Michel Lévy frères, 1849), vol. 1, pp. 47–48.

7.

THE ECONOMICS OF THE VEGETAL

Because of the almost continuous demographic growth cities have absorbed since the seventeenth century, they have become insatiable.[1] A profusion of food products floods into covered and open-air markets and excites townspeople's senses and imaginations. There are plentiful witnesses to the feverish activity prevailing in Les Halles markets in Paris, no matter at what period. An observer notes in the eighteenth century that,

> There is in Paris an unimaginably large trade in all sorts of fruit, flowers, vegetables, grasses, tree plants, grafts for vines, bushes, vegetable seeds, both annual and perennial plants, in fact all the products of the earth produced by the art of gardening. It is quite amazing what quantities arrive every morning at Les Halles in Paris and spread out from there into the town right up to the Rue Saint Honoré, and on Wednesdays and Saturdays to the old Vallée quay.[2]

A century and a half later, Zola embarked on a more poetic description of this 'belly of Paris' which has never stopped growing. The buildings at Les Halles being not big enough, the vendors spread outwards, filling the neighbouring streets, which were literally submerged, especially at dawn, by foodstuffs and particularly vegetables:

> the day [was] dawning over the vegetables. It was like an ocean spreading between the two groups of markets, from the Pointe Saint-Eustache to the Rue des Halles. In the two open spaces at either end, the flood of greenery rose even higher, submerging the footpaths ... The unloading continued; the carts discharged their enormous loads as if they were so many paving stones, adding their cascades to all the others which were now flooding across the footpaths opposite. And from the far end of the Rue du Pont Neuf fresh rows of carts continued to arrive.[3]

Far from merely being planted in the city soil, the vegetal circulates on a huge scale through the city streets, driven by a trade whose range of activity has grown ever bigger down the centuries.

1 Steven Kaplan, *Les Ventres de Paris : pouvoir et approvisionnement dans la France d'Ancien Régime* (Paris: Fayard, 1988); Reynald Abad, *Le Grand Marché. L'approvisionnement alimentaire de Paris sous l'Ancien Régime* (Paris: Fayard, 2002).

2 Jacques Savary Des Bruslons, *Dictionnaire universel de commerce, contenant tout ce qui concerne le commerce qui se fait dans les quatre parties du monde* (Waeberge: Jansons, 1732), p. 386.

3 Emile Zola, *The Belly of Paris*, trans. by Brian Nelson (Oxford: OUP, 2007 [1873]), p. 25.

Figure 40.

Léon Augustin Lhermitte, *Les halles de Paris*. Oil on canvas, 1895.
Public domain image from Musée Carnavalet.

The town, a great market for the vegetal

At Besançon, Place Neuve, the heart of the merchant quarter of the town under the *Ancien Régime*, was renamed Place de l'Abondance (the Place of Plenty) in the Revolution. This new name bore witness to the durability of an imagination ready to associate business and general prosperity. Up to the end of the nineteenth century, travellers were in any case used to gauging a city's vitality by the quality of its markets. An increasingly blossoming and varied offer was adapted to the ever-growing requirements of an urban population. Producers and numerous middlemen invested in this trade in the vegetal that vitalised the whole town through such nerve-centres as the markets and quays.

Flavours and aromas: the taste for the vegetal

From the seventeenth century, elites who settled in towns set the tone and contributed to the progressive normalisation of a profusion of vegetal products for consumption or ornament. At the end of winter, all townspeople hoped that Ceres would be generous and would fill the market stalls to overflowing with fruits, flowers, vegetables and grain. Among prestige foods, citrus and Mediterranean fruits had long held first place. At the end of the seventeenth century, early fruits and vegetables featured in shopping baskets, giving both visual and gastronomic satisfaction and contributing to the development of the art of the table.[4] It was a matter of who could first regale the eyes and the tastebuds of his guests with early strawberries, raspberries, gooseberries, cherries and apricots, without forgetting, among the vegetables, asparagus, peas and various beans, whose arrival on market stalls was looked out for from early spring. But the honest man, disinclined to favour luxury and its excesses, would have the good taste to keep such unnatural prodigies, said to be somewhat lacking in flavour, far from his table. Is it not part of the gustatory culture of people of quality to know how to appreciate the deliciousness and the aromas of the fruits of the earth? For Jean-Jacques Rousseau:

> Nothing is more insipid than forced fruits; a wealthy man in Paris with all his stoves and hothouses only succeeds in getting all the year round poor fruit and poor vegetables for his table at a very high price. If I had cherries in frost and golden melons in the depth of winter what pleasure should I find in them when my palate did not need moisture or refreshment? … A mantelpiece covered in January with forced vegetation, with pale and scentless flowers is not winter adorned but spring robbed of its beauty; we deprive ourselves of the pleasure of seeking the first violets in the woods, of noting the earliest buds…[5]

But purists who shared the opinion of the Genevan philosopher were uncommon and early fruit and vegetables retained favour with most townspeople.

In the nineteenth century, foods which had gratified the palates of high society descended to bourgeois kitchens, as recipe books and works by gastronomic critics testify. If one leafs through the *Manuel de la bonne cuisinière enseignant le menu d'une bonne cuisine bourgeoise moderne* (*Good Cook's Manual Teaching the Menu of Good, Modern Bourgeois Cooking*) of 1877, one notices that some fifteen pages are devoted to 'gardening', that is, to serving fashionable vegetables, and there are more than twenty on 'jams and preserves' made with

4 Florent Quellier, *La Table des Français, une histoire culturelle (XVe– début XIXe siècles)* (Rennes: Presses Universitaires de Rennes, 2007).

5 Jean-Jacques Rousseau, *Émile, or Education*, trans. by Barbara Foxley (London: J.M. Dent, 1911 [1762]), pp. 311–312.

cooked fruit.[6] Vegetables even abandon the table to go to the theatre, as Jacques Offenbach's comic opera *Le Roi Carotte* (*King Carrot*) testifies, in which the courtiers are pink and red radishes, turnips and beetroot... When Huysmans writes of the lavish offer displayed on the market stalls of *Belle Époque* Paris he evokes both abundance and the pleasures of the flesh. In his 1881 novel *En ménage* (*Home Life*) the hero André, torn between wife and mistresses, wanders around Paris, 'looking into the alluring window of the fruit and vegetable seller ... oranges nestling in tissue-paper like rounded breasts in a bodice ... and fruits so large and perfect they seemed fashioned by the hand of man.' Nothing is said, however, about the transformations in the economic sector enabling such beautifully presented delights to reach town after hours of train travel. From 1840 on, gastronomic magazines nevertheless celebrate the opportunities the railway provided for gourmets in the capital: 'If it is true', as Brillat-Savarin said, 'that a nation's destiny depends on how it is fed, what can Paris's destiny be, at the hub of a network of railways allowing its inhabitants to bring together in a single meal the early production of Normandy, Auvergne and Provence?'[7] In the same way, the train conveyed fresh flowers from where they were produced, abolishing distances and seasons.

It has to be said that there was no diminishing of demand among either high society or bourgeois families: for the better-off, the cost of flowers was part of the running expenses of the household. Interiors, and especially reception rooms, were invaded by vases and flowerpots which had to be regularly replenished with carefully arranged bouquets of flowers. Think of the imagination of Proust's Odette on the topic of floral decoration. And fresh flowers were to be found on the evening-dresses of ladies and in the breast-pockets of gentlemen's jackets. The Countess, heroine of a play by Alexandre Dumas fils, is eloquent about the cost of her prestigious life-style: 'As I had today all to myself, I looked over my unpaid bills from tradesmen: among other things, I owe 38,000 francs for hats and bonnets, 11,000 francs for gloves, 52,000 francs for dresses, 28,000 francs for flowers...'[8] However fantastical these figures may be, they nonetheless reflect practices of consumption thoroughly embedded in society. Young working girls, like Jenny in the song, would always grow flowers at no cost on their windowsills

6 *Manuel de la bonne cuisinière, enseignant le menu d'une bonne cuisine bourgeoise moderne, du nord & du midi de la France, etc.* (Avignon: A. Chaillot, 1877).

7 *La Gastronomie: revue de l'art culinaire ancien et moderne*, 26 July 1840, p. 3.

8 Alexandre Dumas fils, *La Question d'argent* (Paris: Charlieu, 1857), p. 14.

to brighten up their rooms, even if they could not live like grand ladies.

For the better-off, the nineteenth century town, increasingly well connected with the rest of the world, was as fertile as the female sower on the 'germinal' franc. Paradoxically, it was at this time of industrial revolution, when the great works of town planning were going ahead, that one can speak of a kind of golden age for vegetal products in towns. Found everywhere in the urban landscape, they attained unmatched qualities of aesthetics and taste, thanks to cultural innovation and selection upstream. However, from the end of the century, the increasingly systematic use of phytosanitary products and recourse to more or less objectionable preservation methods, fostered the steady uniformisation of vegetables and fruit and the artificialisation of flowers. This phenomenon reached its climax in the middle of the *Trente Glorieuses* post-war period. What was on offer was never so profuse, or so disconnected from the cycle of the seasons (everything could be found at any time of the year), without mentioning the almost universal use of plastic packaging and protective wax coatings, deemed to improve the durability of vegetables and fruit with no thought for their taste. The growing popularity of organic products from the 1980s on seems to have inaugurated a reversal of this tendency, as evidenced in the revival of interest in that ancient holy place of urban trade, the market.

On the stalls or under the counter: selling the vegetal under the Ancien Régime

Market places and halls were certainly the pre-eminent sites where townspeople obtained their everyday vegetal requirements. Since medieval times many towns have had their '*place aux herbes*' (plant place) devoted to the trade in 'plants for cooking' or 'herbs', the medicinal fruits and herbs which constituted part of most remedies as chemical medicine was only at the experimental stage under the *Ancien Régime*. The place-name may vary with local custom: in Paris the Marché aux Poirées (Chard Market) in the Les Halles quarter is particularly famous. 'In all seasons and every day they sell all sorts of herbs, medicinal as well as for the pot, and all sorts of fruit and flowers, so that it is like a garden where you can see the flowers and fruit of every season.'[9] This decor, so pleasant for someone strolling by, has

9 Jean-Aymar Piganiol de la Force, *Description de Paris, de Versailles, de Marly, de Meudon, de S. Cloud, de Fontainebleau et de toutes les autres belles maisons et châteaux des environs de Paris* (Paris: Théodore Legras, 1742), vol. 3, pp. 123–124.

however another side: the vegetal rubbish left there by the sellers. Every five years or thereabouts the local authorities, wanting to keep control of public spaces, would repeat formal warnings to both men and women 'Gardeners, Shellers of Peas, [who] leave Artichoke roots & leaves on the paving slabs and in the streets, and piles of Pea and Bean Shells, where there is a custom of throwing them away around the Pillory & other sites in the aforementioned public Markets.'[10] If there was no commercial specialisation, the same site could host several kinds of market according to the day of the week. In Lyon in the eighteenth century, fruit and vegetable sellers took over the Place de la Fromagerie in the parish of Saint-Nizier on Wednesdays and Saturdays, where some thirty stalls were available to them. The producers (gardeners and market gardeners, both from Lyon and elsewhere) had a stricter timetable for selling their fruit directly without paying fees, at cock-crow and at the beginning of the afternoon.[11] Some products such as fruit could be found, prepared and transformed to some degree for affluent customers, in the boutiques of confectioners, pastry sellers and sellers of liqueurs.

Quays formed other nerve centres for trade in the vegetal and its derivatives, until the railway came to compete with river and maritime transport. There were wharves that specialised in unloading corn and others specially for wood, which was the main fuel for domestic use before the use of coal became widespread in the nineteenth century. Supplies for Paris were mainly carried by water from a large Parisian basin. Logs were hauled and dried on the quays of the Seine at the two main ports for wood, the Quai de Grève and the Quai de l'École.[12] These were places teeming with activity, and their landscape was shaped by great hills of river-borne logs up to fifteen or sixteen metres high. In 1683 the corporation ruled that these piles should not be more than six metres high.[13] This was to reduce the risk of them slipping and endangering the safety of people nearby: loggers and day-labourers, rivermen, merchants, retailers, idlers and lookers-on, not forgetting the officials controlling this trade.

10 Châtelet de Paris, *Ordonnance de police portant défenses de laisser dans les rues, halles, marchés et places publiques aucuns pieds et feuilles d'artichaux ni écosses de pois ou de fèves. à peine de 50 livres d'amende et de confiscation* (Paris: Mariette, 1730).

11 Anne Montenach, *Espaces et pratiques du commerce alimentaire à Lyon au XVIIe siècle, l'économie du quotidien* (Grenoble: PUG, 2009), p. 46.

12 Jérôme Buridant, 'Flottage des bois et gestion forestière: l'exemple du Bassin parisien du XVIe au XIXe siècle', *Eau et forêt, revue forestière française* 4 (July–Aug. 2006): 389–398.

13 M. des Essarts, *Dictionnaire universel de police* (Paris: Moutard, 1786), vol. 2, p. 521.

The vegetal, like any other merchandise, was subject to regulations governing the production and sale of goods under the *Ancien Régime*. The tariffs applied at town entry points give exhaustive lists of vegetal productions traded within the walls. Some products could only be bought in the shop of a specified merchant. For example, dried plants, of obvious importance in inhabitants' daily lives, were the object of particular vigilance because they were potentially dangerous, for some could be poisonous if misused. The policing of commerce took place at the town gates first. At the Paris barriers the exotic Cardamom ('An aromatic plant from the Indies which produces in small pods a kind of Pepper also called the Seed of Paradise', used as a spice and in the composition of theriacs)[14] was three times more highly taxed than more common plants like Cardiac or Motherwort, 'a plant which grows around Paris: it has a strong odour and is a vermifuge', or Carline, 'a medicinal, aperitive and anti-hysteric plant which grows in the mountains'.[15] Not everyone could afford to go to the well-stocked apothecaries' shops where medicaments were prepared according to the instructions of practitioners whose services had to be engaged in advance. Inhabitants with less money turned to monasteries (like the Carthusians), known to distribute remedies unofficially to their spiritual clientele, or got the dried plants from herbalists in order to prepare medicines themselves according to recipes transmitted around their immediate social circle. In the eighteenth century the public authorities sought to restrict to qualified men the monopoly for prescribing plant-based remedies. The voice of the majority, influenced by the opinion of doctors declaring themselves to be on the side of the Enlightenment, tended to denounce the poor practices of herbalists, with no consideration for the so-called popular knowledge they embodied. The *Dictionnaire universel de commerce* (*Universal Dictionary of Commerce*) of 1712 defined them as 'poor women generally established in street corner shops, especially close to the best-stocked Apothecaries' establishments.'[16] In 1773, the Intendant for the Généralité of Lyon, Monsieur de Flesselles, lamented that 'the normal collection & sale [should] nowadays be abandoned to the lower classes who, having no exact knowledge of Botany, buy the plants from Country-folk, dry them badly, keep them in damp rooms, rarely renew them, & so sell

14 Theriacs are pharmaceutical preparations intended as universal remedies.

15 Ferme Générale, *Tarif général des droits dûs aux entrées de Paris sur les marchandises et denrées y arrivant par terre* (Paris: Lamesle, 1781), pp. 24–25.

16 Jacques Savary Des Bruslons, *Dictionnaire universel de commerce, contenant tout ce qui concerne le commerce qui se fait dans les quatre parties du monde* (Waeberge: Jansons, 1732), p. 348.

them altered, corrupted, & under the wrong names.'[17] Despite the efforts by public authorities to regulate a profession that was suspect because it was popular and feminised (a certificate in herbalism was required from 1790), in the eighteenth century herbalists remained the poor relations of medicine, especially since grocers and druggists sold medicinal plants in common use, such as healing plants used in dressings and plasters along with plants for tinctures and detergents.

Living or freshly cut vegetal material is more immediately evident in the urban space by virtue of the large quantities traded every day: one might then suppose that the trade would be easier to control. However, supplying large towns needed complex and shifting trading networks, involving local producers, major dealers importing products from distant regions, and a swarm of retailers. In the eighteenth century, when public health was the object of ever more attention from public authorities, the quality of traded commodities began to be controlled. A police ordinance in Lyon in 1788 forbade the sale of fruit and vegetables that were too green, which were considered to cause dangerous digestive trouble in consumers. It is true that applying such a measure raises questions. In theory, selling vegetal products was the province of well-defined trades in the corporate system: for example, in Paris this time-honoured right which had devolved to master gardeners (who numbered about 1,200 in 1740), was opened up to market gardeners, even to journeymen gardeners at the end of the seventeenth century. In the course of their life-cycle, fruit and vegetables changed hands between producer-sellers, and between intermediaries like merchant fruiterers, 'orange-sellers' and grocers, and were perhaps transformed at the end of the chain by workers preparing foodstuffs. The most recent historical studies have, however, clearly shown that a majority of such economic exchanges took place outside the controlling framework, which eighteenth century liberals considered to be out of date anyway. Complaints emanating from people in the trade cannot be simply traced back to the passion for chicanery readily attributed to them. They lift the veil on complex commercial transactions, both shifting and competitive.

In the pre-industrial town, vegetal products were effectively omnipresent. This was true whether one considers food for daily consumption or the market in the decorative vegetal, which was equally competitive and was present

17 *Plan de l'établissement d'un jardin de botanique et d'une école d'histoire naturelle. Arrêté par Monseigneur de Flesselles, Intendant de la généralité de Lyon* (Lyon: Delaroche, 1773), p. 3.

on every street corner in fine weather. The women who ran florists' shops in Paris, who in theory had a monopoly on the sale of flowers, were always complaining to the authorities about street sellers, who were nevertheless forbidden 'to gather on Bridges and Quays, or around Churches or near their Doors or in other places in this Town, under the pretext of offering Flowers and Bouquets for sale, and are barely fined fifty pounds'.[18] Regulatory endeavours were ineffective in the face of the strategies of wandering sellers who, with the minimal equipment of moveable stalls, carts or just a basket, inveigled a place for themselves in the urban space, relying on unquenchable demand from the inhabitants. These vendors with no legally acknowledged existence contrived to negotiate as it were a *de facto* tolerance by the authorities. While the established businesses paid municipal taxes, eyes were more or less closed to the informal activities of small-scale street sellers. Otherwise, was there not a risk of swelling the ranks of the poor shut up in workhouses. Besides, this small retail trade had the not insignificant advantage of allowing procurement at minimal cost of the basic household requirements of the least favoured part of the urban population. In Lyon in the seventeenth century gardeners, market gardeners and even peasants from the nearby suburbs bypassed the regulations in force to obtain a regular supplementary revenue from the direct sale of all or part of their production. That did not require a stall in a weekly market so they accosted customers in the streets. This was often the task of the family's womenfolk, who turned themselves into wandering street-sellers, risking featuring in police records when there were accidents or quarrels, or when they aroused the wrath of tradespeople who denounced the unfair competition they faced. From 1776 in Paris anybody could trade in 'fruit, vegetables, and herbs' in the markets or streets as long as they did not hinder free movement in the urban space: the police therefore had a job on their hands to shift out of doorways people openly displaying their green goods there. The Revolution endorsed the abolition of the system of privileges governing different trades, but even so sellers and dealers always had to yield to municipal regulations designed to grant them a well-defined situation in the urban space.

18 Châtelet de Paris, *Ordonnance de police portant défenses aux colporteuses de bouquets de s'attrouper ni exposer en vente des fleurs sur les ponts, près les portes des églises ni en aucuns autres lieux* (Paris: Mariette, 1730).

Trade in the vegetal, in the industrial town, between stall and display-stand

At the beginning of the *Trente Glorieuses* decades and despite the proliferation of food shops and grocery stores, going to the market was lodged deep in townspeople's habits and both private and professional people had their suppliers there. As we have seen, multi-coloured stalls overflowing with all kinds of products were an inexhaustible source of inspiration for poets and painters. Thanks to the railway, commercial networks were established over ever-greater distances, enabling all kinds of vegetal products to be brought in. In many cases Paris was the beating heart of this trade that had become national, and even international. Witness the renovation of Les Halles which, under the Second Empire, made it an unavoidable hub. The ten pavilions and covered streets designed by Victor Baltard were built between 1854 and 1874 and, from then on, they organised the 40,000 square metre central market of Paris. Each building was devoted to a particular kind of produce: fish, meat, flowers, vegetables, etc. In 1875, the Saint-Simonian economist Armand Husson estimated that about 400,000 tonnes of vegetables and 66,000 tonnes of fruit (of which two thirds were sold in or around Les Halles) arrived in Paris annually.[19] The need for short supply chains gradually diminished with the increase in the speed of transport through the century and with the establishment of refrigeration techniques from the 1880s, which also favoured centralisation in Paris. Even the most rural departments made efforts to capture the Parisian market. In 1887 producers in Vienne were behind an official request to the Ministry of Transport to open the Loudun-Châtellerault line earlier in the day in order to dispatch in time early produce destined to supply Les Halles in Paris.[20] Drawings, paintings and photographs preserve the memory of the flower market that brightened the tarmac in the nineteenth century with colours and scents. Such gatherings of merchants often became very large and literally took over squares and pavements: the flower market in Tours, established in 1856 on what is now the Place Gaston Pailhou, found itself so cramped by 1874 that it was moved to Boulevard Béranger, where it still is today.[21]

19 Armand Husson, *Les Consommations de Paris* (Paris: Hachette, 1875 (2nd edition)), pp. 435 and 518–519.

20 *Rapports et délibérations du Conseil général de la Vienne* (Poitiers: Conseil général, 1887), p. 498 (session of 31 Aug. 1887).

21 *Tours, Le Marché aux Fleurs*, leaflet published by Tours Town Hall for the 'Green Days', 27–28 Apr. 1996.

Figure 41.

The flower market of Tours at the beginning of the twentieth century.
Source: Authors' collection.

In Marseille at the beginning of the twentieth century one bought flowers between the Canebière and the Rue de Rome. But the effects of centralisation were such that it was still Paris that became one of the world's leading markets for cut flowers. As was appropriate, Les Halles became the nerve centre of this trade: in summer, the doors of the flower market were open from 3 a.m. There were some ten other markets too, supplied by train or by producers coming with handcarts or horse-drawn vehicles. These markets, usually open two days a week, shared between them the favours of the capital's customers, generally coming to buy flowers in pots. The most elegant was that of the Madeleine, opened in 1834, and the oldest that of the Cité, institutionalised since 1799 and receiving 200,000 plants a day in 1908. And we must not forget the merchants who went on foot, semi-beggars, with their baskets of flowers, and the greengrocers pushing their handcarts through the town, of whom there were still 6,000 in 1892!

Lastly, there were kiosks, often around churches, and flower shops, chiefly used by the elite.[22] Some florists were brilliantly successful, such as Alphonse

22 Philippe L. de Vilmorin, *Les Fleurs à Paris*, pp. 18–21 and 23–33.

Figure 42.

In the flower market - near palace of justice, Paris, France. Photograph, ca 1900. Library of Congress, https://www.loc.gov/resource/stereo.1s23921

Karr (1808–1890), who set up in Nice in 1853 to escape Napoleon III and successfully opened a shop in the public garden. There, often using flowers he had cultivated himself, he prepared bouquets that made his reputation in the town, and then throughout Europe, and he then exported them to England and to Russia. At the beginning of the 1860s it only took two days for a Parisian to receive one of these much-vaunted marvels, which cast the city of Genoa, then unrivalled for bouquets, into the shade.[23] Perhaps inspired by this exemplary commercial trajectory, in Paris, the number of 'florists' shops' multiplied by more than five times between 1870 and 1890, by which time there were several hundred.[24]

In the second half of the nineteenth century, this was a change which came to dominate and transformed the flower trade throughout France; Lyon, for example, experienced the same development.[25] When, between the wars, it was necessary to clear the streets to make automobile traffic easier, the flowers,

23 Daniel Lejeune, *Édouard André* (Paris: Société Nationale d'Horticulture de France, 2013), pp. 63–64.

24 Philippe L. de Vilmorin, *Les Fleurs à Paris*, p. 34.

25 A. and F. Rouillard, *L'Art des jardins paysagers dans la région Sud-Est de la France* (Lyon: Adrien Effantin, 1902), p. 34.

and also the fruit and vegetables, retreated behind the windows of shops, on display shelves conforming to the rules of what was not yet called marketing. From the start of the *Trente Glorieuses* era, vegetal products disappeared even more from the urban landscape, with the advent of supermarkets (3,000 at the start of the 1980s, and about 10,000 in 2005) and other large shopping centres, which deflected a majority of customers from traditional markets, grocery stores and other specialised shops. The transfer of Les Halles in Paris to Rungis, decided in 1962 and completed in 1969, was another symptom of this change. However, it is worth noting that, over the last two or three decades, town-centre markets have recovered a certain degree of dynamism. For reasons that are as much ecological as economic, many townspeople are reacquainting themselves with commercial practices characteristic of the pre-industrial city. People prefer to avoid middlemen, to get closer to the producers and to favour short supply chains and local agriculture.

Figure 43.

Immeuble Boulevard de la Villette n°128, Union Photographique Française, 1907.
Courtesy of Musée Carnavalet (public domain).

Producing the vegetal in town

The agricultural peripheries of towns act as an economic driving force throughout the period we are considering, but in a non-linear way. Up till the mid-nineteenth century, green belts were indispensable to supplying urban markets. Then transport infrastructure, the development of more effective preservation methods and, more importantly, the creation of a complex commercial network made it possible to bring vegetal products from much further away. Were market gardeners to become the obsolete witnesses to a lost past? The answer was, as we shall see, much more nuanced than that. While facing competition from outside and threatened by the spread of the built-up town at the expense of agricultural land, cultivation around towns or within them resisted and kept going, even benefitting from a social enthusiasm for 'the local product'.

The persistence of strong local production

Under the *Ancien Régime*, all towns of any size were ringed round more or less continuously with market gardens. This made it possible, with the aid of advanced technical skill reflected in books on gardening, to satisfy the urban demand for early produce, fruit and 'herbage' of the season. For instance, in the suburbs close to Rennes at the end of the eighteenth century, gardens were to be found growing onions, basil, thyme and rows of chard; others had endives, pumpkins and fruit trees.[26] In Paris, market gardens were known as '*marais*' (marshes), even if there was no connection with a drained wetland. The 'marais' certainly had nothing of the aristocratic or ecclesiastical leisure garden about it, no more than it could be mistaken for the traditional peasant kitchen garden designed to provide for the family table and to make some supplementary cash. It was a case of intensive cultivation occupying full-time one or several market gardeners noted for their know-how. To improve the soil, they used fertiliser and, particularly urban waste. The elite travel guides closed their eyes to this particular landscape, which formed a gradual transition from ploughing in the Île-de-France to the built-up capital city. By contrast, the public authorities were very well aware of what economic stakes the market gardens represented. It was clear that town planning operations could only be undertaken to the detriment of the green belt, even when it meant substituting one garden for other gardens, as

26 Catherine Laurent (ed.), *Histoire(s) de jardins, usages et paysages à Rennes* (PUR: 2009), p. 40.

when the enlargement of the King's Garden in 1782 put an end to a good number of kitchen gardens. However, the expropriated market gardeners could usually count on generous compensation: they had, for example, a six- year exemption from land tax on condition they took up their valuable activities somewhat further away.[27] Market gardeners were courted in this way because they had become indispensable suppliers to the tables of the ever more demanding elite. After the last frosts of winter, they had to be in some measure able to offer their impatient clientele early vegetables, at prices in proportion with their scarcity. The golden trick was to push back the limits of the natural vegetative cycle by way of innovatory techniques. One could then hope for returns on one's produce with plenty of added value because it was well in advance of the classical agricultural calendar. The cultivation of early produce came to a height in the eighteenth century, as the agronomic literature bears witness. Abbot Rozier explains that 'in and around Paris, where manure is very plentiful, one can sow in January under frames, and then prick the plants out in another bed as soon as the first two leaves sprout; then in March transplant these into a central bed, in a warm place sheltered from cold winds, under the protection of straw or furze ... the price of early produce recompenses the care and trouble.'[28] In 1780 one Fournier introduced the use of frames around Paris, and one of his colleagues, Quentian, had forced white asparagus in 1782 and green in 1800. Cauliflower forcing was achieved in 1811, and that of endives and romaine lettuce at about the same time, and then carrots around 1826.[29] Early varieties of cabbage, carrot, parsnip and leek were also selected. Some were cultivated as early varieties: cucumbers, onions and peas, which were much prized, the first deliveries of which drew a very high price. It is reckoned that in 1786 the supply zone of the capital covered the Seine basin to a radius of more or less 150 kilometres, while for fruits and vegetables average distances were reduced to 87 kilometres.

Vine-growing countryside was also on the horizons of most towns in France, including the most northerly, up until the end of the nineteenth century. All kinds of fiscal and administrative strategies on the part of towns were warranted by the added value of wine production. In the seventeenth century

27 Reynald Abad, *Le Grand Marché. L'approvisionnement alimentaire de Paris sous l'Ancien Régime* (Paris: Fayard, 2002), p. 627.

28 François Rozier, *Cours complet d'agriculture théorique, practique, économique et de médecine rurale et vétérinaire* (Paris: Libraires Associés, 1793), vol. 3, p. 250.

29 William Robinson, *The Parks, Promenades and Gardens of Paris* (London: Murray, 1869), pp. 469–470.

the municipal authorities in Lyon embarked on a legal battle to extend the perimeter of the town to include the vine-bearing hills to the north-east. The stakes in this move were nothing less than securing control of a strategic space for supplying the urban market.[30] Fourvière became part of Lyon without a shot being fired, and its inhabitants were prompted to go in for wine production by exemption from a licence, an advantage they enjoyed thenceforward. By contrast, the inhabitants of Croix-Rousse refused to be integrated into the urban space of Lyon, because the suburb would lose its status as a free area, allowing wine production to be marketed without taxes. At the gates of this suburb, bars, pubs and other duty-free drink outlets proliferated, and were frequented by an urban clientele; the inhabitants of Lyon used to go there to get cheap wine, which they drank on the spot, or took home illegally without paying the duty. Croix Rousse is a hillside that is as much wine-producing as ecclesiastical: the charterhouse of Lyon, proprietor of eighty per cent of the cultivated land, drew on the services of a gardener and four winemakers to work it. Many of the houses of the bourgeoisie of Lyon set up their more modest plots of vines there, which explains why, despite the presence of the austere monks, the suburb became a hub for the sale and production of wine. In any case, everyone was in agreement to multiply the appeals to the monarchical authorities, to such a point that at the end of the seventeenth century the town was requested to give up such claims. Whatever their administrative status, there was no abrupt break in the countryside between the wine-producing areas, and other surrounding market garden areas, and the town itself. Maps produced under the *Ancien Régime* clearly show, for Lyon and most French towns, that nature had a presence both outside and inside the city walls, a mingling accentuated by the progressive disappearance of walls in favour of boulevards and promenades, planted with trees and dotted with lawns and bowling greens.

Through the greater part of the nineteenth century, trade in the vegetal rested on local production: on the outskirts of towns, gardeners and market-gardeners cultivated their green goods and sent their daughters or wives to sell them at market. In the account of the journey he made in France at the end of the 1820s, the great Scottish landscaper Loudon describes cultivators in Rouen, probably living close to the outskirts of the city, though he does not state this. He encounters a large-scale market-gardener, Monsieur Berquier,

30 Anne Montenach, *Espaces et pratiques du commerce alimentaire à Lyon au XVII*[e] *siècle, l'économie du quotidien* (Grenoble: PUG, 2009).

quite a character at 87 years old, red-eyed and toothless, married to a 35-year-old woman, evidently mistrustful of this stranger questioning him so closely but unable to understand the careful answers that he gives him in his dialect… Through the year Monsieur Berquier cultivated leeks, cabbages, turnips, carrots, peas, artichokes, asparagus, gourds, celery, endives, cucumbers, lettuces and even melons. Pears, apples, plums, cherries, grapes and figs and a few blackcurrants, raspberries, gooseberries and strawberries rounded out this production. Loudon also visited numerous nurserymen around Rouen (not much different at the time from flower gardeners); the most striking among them is Monsieur Prévost junior, a local botanist belonging to numerous learned societies and possessing five or six hectares of land. There he produced many rare and remarkable plants: roses in profusion, peaches from Isfahan, sundry magnolias, maritime flax, fine hazelnut trees, quince trees from China, etc. The other nurserymen were less original and were satisfied with more usual plants, particularly roses, dahlias and, above all, orange trees, grown in pots throughout the kingdom.[31] Similarly at Troyes some thirty years later, right in the town, a nurseryman was to be found specialising in apples and pears, and there were also many small private gardens whose surplus was sold in the market, as happened almost everywhere.[32]

Thus we find the maintenance and even strengthening of market arboriculture and horticulture around large towns, very close to the consumers, thanks to the development of techniques and know-how for adapting the cultivation of even the most delicate plants to northern climates.

Towards a delocalisation of production?

In the course of the nineteenth century, however, and up until around the Second World War, a movement of disconnection began between sites of consumption and places of production – but it was an incomplete trend, as it only eroded local production, which resisted more strongly than expected.[33] Urban expansion continued and the construction of dwellings and industrial zones offered an often more lucrative alternative to the sustaining of agricultural activity. Also, the development of transport infrastructure, particularly the railway, brought endless, intersecting traffic in the vegetal

31 John Claudius Loudon, 'Notes and reflections made during a tour through part of France and Germany in the Autumn of the year 1828', *Gardener's Magazine* (1829): 371–378.

32 William Robinson, *The Parks, Promenades and Gardens of Paris* (London: Murray, 1869), pp. 619–622.

33 René Lebeau, review of Michel Philipponneau, *La Vie rurale de la banlieue parisienne* (1956), *Revue de Géographie de Lyon* **34** (1) (1959): 75–79.

- flowers, vegetables and fruit – not only within towns themselves, but between them, and even internationally: the central Halles in Paris became a genuinely national market, as evidenced by the passing of a law in 1896 regulating it. However, one must take care not to forget that the strong demand generated by the presence of a town sustained and even helped develop agricultural activities with high added value like horticulture and market gardening; and that the use of urban waste allowed farmers to benefit from many cheap fertilising agents. The erosion of local production was nonetheless a reality, but it took place slowly. In 1896, 82 per cent of the fruit and vegetable arriving at Les Halles came from the Île-de-France, from an average distance of 97 kilometres:[34] until the 1930s, market garden production around Paris or major French cities still partly set the pace for household consumption – the arrival of Thomery grapes or Montmorency cherries was impatiently awaited each year in the capital.[35]

A study by the secretary of the union of Parisian market gardeners in 1900 bore witness to this slow erosion, as well as to the resistance of the cultivation of fruit and vegetables around the capital; this was under endless pressure from urban expansion, but persisted on the urban edges. He described market gardens 'scattered among the factories and railways' at Aubervilliers and Saint-Denis, at Clichy and Saint-Ouen.[36] There were also a few market gardeners within Paris itself, mainly on the left bank, notably in the 15th arrondissement, the remains of the expansion of the town when it was decided in 1860 to annexe the neighbouring communes.[37] At the beginning of the twentieth century, the area of these Parisian 'marais' still comprised, despite everything, nearly 1,000 hectares.[38] Thus there was a strong persistence of local cultivation over two centuries even if its mass was eroded bit by bit. This can only be explained, given the rapacious tendency of towns to absorb land, by the continued presence of market gardening in urban interstices. However, a major change was coming by virtue of national, and even international,

34 In 2006, 70% of the capital's cereals and 50% of its fruit and vegetables still came from the Paris Basin. G. Billen, S. Barles, P. Chatzimpiros and J. Garnier, 'Grain, meat and vegetables to feed Paris: where did and do they come from? Localising Paris food supply areas from the eighteenth to the twenty-first century', *Regional Environmental Change* **12** (2) (2012): 325–335.

35 Christian Deverre and Jean-Baptiste Traversac, 'Manger local, une utopie concrete', *Métropolitiques*, 26 Oct. 2011, http://www.metropolitiques.eu/Manger-local-une-utopie-concrete.html

36 J. Curé, *Les Jardiniers de Paris et leur culture* (Paris: Librairie agricole de la Maison rustique, 1900), pp. 310–311.

37 Ibid., p. 265.

38 Ibid., p. 320.

competition: specialisation both in market gardening and in horticulture, which was to be seen to some degree nationwide.

It was manifested in the case of Montreuil and its famous peaches. In the seventeenth century, a fashion emerged for 'country houses', which allowed the elites to have a pleasure house to retire to when summer heat became too much, where one could devote oneself to rustic pleasures. These country houses were also sites of production, growing vines in the case of Lyon, as we have seen, and trees around Paris: the Montmorency valley was particularly celebrated for fruit production.[39] In the case of Montreuil, which was then just a big village, in the second half of the seventeenth century the cultivation was introduced of espalier peach trees, which La Quintinie had experimented with at Versailles. This was not the only venture, and Montreuil gradually made itself a name for various products, both horticultural (violets, peonies and wallflowers) and market gardening (cherries, gooseberries, pears and then apples, and the famous monk's beard lettuce, the commune's great speciality that disappeared at the beginning of the twentieth century in favour of the Belgian endive). Vine-growing survived for a long time and only disappeared around the time of the First World War in the face of competition from wines of the Midi (the south of France). Vine leaves were used for wrapping peaches. In the nineteenth century, peach trees came to dominate at the expense of other fruit trees, but without eliminating them, and this went in parallel with the demographic and industrial evolution of the town: 3,500 inhabitants in the eighteenth century, 13,000 in 1872 and more than 30,000 at the end of the nineteenth century. The commune then took on a distinctive appearance, with industries and enclosed gardens mingled together.

In the 1880s peach cultivation extended over 300 kilometres of walls and covered a third of the town's surface area, or 320 hectares! It was a way for the town to distinguish itself from imports from the South. In the Paris Halles, the 'Montreuil Square' had a very sound reputation. But the pressure for land and industrial requirements, the rise in the price of the plaster used to cover the walls repeatedly so that they would store heat, and, above all, fierce competition from produce from the Midi, led to the gradual abandonment of this highly specialised cultivation from the 1930s on, though some growers carried on into the 1980s.[40] Today, some measures

39 Florent Quellier, 'Le bourgeois arboriste (XVIIe–XVIIIe siècles)', *Histoire urbaine* **2** (6) (2002): 23–41.

40 *Montreuil, patrimoine horticole*, Itinéraires du Patrimoine, Inventaire général (1999) and http:// www.montreuil.fr/la-ville/histoire-de-la-ville.

Figure 44.

The Peach Walls of Montreuil, postcard, early twentieth century.
Source: Authors' collection.

have been taken in an effort to safeguard what is left of this very specific landscape of walls and gardens.

The specialisation in produce brought on by competition and the centralisation on Paris is also seen in the case of French and foreign horticultural production. At the very beginning of the twentieth century, Paris imported more than a million plants from Belgium, and millions of daffodil and tulip bulbs from Holland.[41] The main region for the supply of cut flowers was the South East, and in particular the Côte d'Azur. At the end of the nineteenth century in Paris you could see, especially in winter, mimosa, carnations, roses, wallflowers, marguerites, anemones, narcissi and hyacinths pouring in from Provence. There was a certain profit in this for the railway Compagnie du PLM (Paris-Lyon-Marseille) and they reserved special wagons on their express trains for the wicker and reed baskets specially devised for transporting these delicate products.[42] As for plants in pots, there were hydrangeas, camellias and

41 'Le commerce des fleurs à Paris', *Le Jardin. Revue d'horticulture générale illustrée* (1908).

42 Philippe L. de Vilmorin, *Les Fleurs à Paris, Culture et Commerce* (Paris: Baillière et Fils, 1892), pp. 47–48 and 52–54.

azaleas from Angers, oleanders from Orleans, hydrangeas and camellias from Nantes and the famous Brie Comte Robert roses.[43] But local production did not disappear, however, even in the Paris suburbs. Orchids were to be found in Avenue du Chatillon, bouvardias at Vanves and Grenelle, heliotropes and cyclamens at Glacière and stocks at Picpus. The suburban communes were also active: in the south, Bourg la Reine and Sceaux specialised in violets; Vitry gained a reputation for forced lilac, and Bagneux for lilies of the valley.[44] Such specialisation was necessary to confront the now international competition and it was only possible with increased glasshouse cultivation: in and around Paris at the end of the nineteenth century, there were 400–500 horticulturalists using between 2,500 and 3,000 greenhouses to supply the capital.[45] In 1908, the annual production of flowers in the Paris suburbs was worth not less than five million francs.[46]

Despite this resistance, the role of imported flowers in the national market grew throughout the twentieth century, above all in Paris – at the regional level, local producers still played a part, and Rungis had of course replaced the Paris Halles. Imports of cut flowers in France rose from 165 tonnes in 1960 to 900 tonnes in 1979 and 22,000 tonnes in 1984.[47] At the same time, the country's horticultural sector has remained large: in 2005 it employed 150,000 people in 45,000 SMEs, thanks to the 2.5 billion euros spent by individuals on their internal and external vegetation![48]

It was certainly the international opening up and the major industrial and urban development of the *Trente Glorieuses* years that led to a decline in local cultivation through the whole country, as is revealed in the decree of 30 September 1953 which instituted a network of Markets of National Interest to adapt to the modernisation of agricultural production and to regulate its commercialisation.[49] This period saw an unprecedented upheaval in the world of rural France, whose productivity was to be marked with the following characteristics: concentration, intensification and increased specialisation in

43 'Le commerce des fleurs à Paris'.

44 de Vilmorin, *Les Fleurs à Paris*, p. 42.

45 Ibid., p. 50.

46 'Le commerce des fleurs à Paris'.

47 Valérie Chansigaud, *Une Histoire des Fleurs* (Paris: Delachaux et Niestlé, 2014), p. 85.

48 Bernard Reygrobellet, *La Nature dans la ville, biodiversité et urbanisme* (Rapport du Conseil Économique et Social, 2007), p. 68.

49 Antoine Bernard de Raymond, *En toute saison: le marché des fruits et légumes en France* (Rennes: PUR, 2013).

products, development of agro-industry, super and hypermarkets, mechanisation of farms, export of products, amazing increase in production (between 1955 and 1965 the amount of fruit grown doubled, and the same for cereals between 1960 and 1990). While it may be a bit early to sound the death knell of the peasant farmer, and while specific culinary and agricultural practices remain vigorous in some regions, these profound changes have entailed a relative delocalisation of consumption: products come from everywhere and nowhere (the famous Kenyan green beans and Dutch flowers) and their relationship to the land is obliterated by commercial networks. And yet, this delocalisation began to be challenged as early as the 1970s, and all the more since there have been some major food scares – particularly the 'mad cow disease' crisis in the 1980s.[50] There is a marked contrast with the development of networks for flowers, whose intensive cultivation, particularly in developing countries, has at times had dramatic social and ecological consequences that scarcely trouble public opinion.[51]

Town cultivation today?

Developments over the last quarter of the twentieth century explain the emergence in the last thirty years or so of thoughts on what is now known as urban agriculture.[52] This is defined as agriculture sited in or around a town whose produce is mainly aimed at that town.[53] We have seen how the peri-urbanisation of the period 1970–1980 made the border between town and country more indistinct than before: beyond the suburbs one often finds a mix of bungalows, infrastructure, fields and a whole zone strongly linked socially and economically to the dominant urban pole, as can be seen in the Languedoc or in the Nord-Pas de Calais. So called urban agriculture is not negligible: in 2010 it was estimated that there were more than 36,000 urban farms, which is a little over eight per cent of the total of French farms, and to these can be added 110,000 in peri-urban zones.[54] Long neglected by public

50 Caroline Brand and Serge Bonnefoy, 'L'alimentation des sociétés urbaines: une cure de jouvence pour l'agriculture des territoires urbains ?', *VertigO* **11** (2) (2011).

51 Valérie Chansigaud, *Une Histoire des Fleurs*, pp. 80–87 and pp. 188–202.

52 Leïla Kebir and Bernard Barraqué, 'Éditorial', *Espaces et sociétés* 158 (2014/3): 9–12. See also the special issue of *Déméter* (2013): http://www.clubdemeter.com/ledemeter.php?demeter=2013

53 Christine Aubry and Jeanne Pourias, 'L'agriculture urbaine fait déjà partie du "métabolisme urbain"', *Déméter* (2013): 140.

54 Jean-Baptiste Traversac, 'Inventaire statistique: état des lieux de l'agriculture dans et à proximité des villes', *Déméter* (2013): 126.

authorities, urban and peri-urban agriculture is now, and particularly over the last fifteen years or so (SRU law in 2000: Solidarité et Renouvellement Urbain / solidarity and urban renewal), encouraged in various development plans (SCOT: Schéma de Cohérence Territoriale / Plan of Territorial Coherence; PLU : Plan Local d'Urbanisme / Local Town Plan, etc.) and even in the master plan for the Ile de France region, decided on in 2014 and giving a large place to agriculture, which occupies half the surface area of the region. Seven per cent of the land in Montpellier, for example, a town of 250,000 inhabitants, is agricultural space, basically devoted to durum wheat and vines. While the greater part of land like this is naturally located on the urban periphery, it is also found in the heart of the *commune*. But the forms of this urban rurality are significant: agriculture for the market is in decline, while non-profitmaking cultivation, both private and public (and especially allotments) is favoured.[55] Various movements are seeking to promote these changes: the organisation Terre en ville (Land in Town), for instance, founded in 2000, seeks to bring together local representatives and responsible farmers around Metz, Aix-en-Provence, Dijon and Lorient to encourage cooperation and the exchange of information on the joint development of towns and peri-urban agriculture. Les Associations pour le Maintien d'une Agriculture Paysanne (Associations for maintaining small-scale agriculture), originating near Toulon in 2001, similarly aims to foster short distribution circuits by bringing together small-scale producers and consumers. More widely, the aim of replanting urban space with consumable produce prompted the creation in 2008 of the movement called Incroyables Comestibles *(*Incredible, Edible*)*. British in origin, it aims to share fruit and vegetables, to encourage towns to be self-sufficient, to favour local agriculture and networks, and food diversity for children in particular, to plant vegetables everywhere, in planters in front of one's house or on vegetalised roofs, to do this alone or together and to allow anyone to use the produce without payment.[56] There are many variations on these initiatives. In Albi the local authority has allocated a whole public space for the cultivation of kitchen produce, aiming to achieve food self-sufficiency by 2020 by promoting urban agriculture. In Nantes, 'stations gourmands' (food stations) have been set up by the parks authorities: around wooden tables, trees and fruit bushes and

55 Pascal Scheromm et al., 'Cultiver en ville… cultiver la ville? L'agriculture urbaine à Montpellier', *Espaces et Sociétés* 158 (2014/3): 49–56.

56 'Plantez et mangez la ville, l'incroyable revolution', Blog Le Ventre Libre (*Le Monde*), 1 May 2013.

kitchen gardens are looked after by associations or groups of inhabitants; the products are free. Similarly, in public gardens such as the Crapaudine and the Fournillière, vegetable gardens are maintained by private individuals joining forces. Urban beehives like those in the Luxembourg Garden in Paris feature in this movement. These agricultural productions, especially the most symbolic, rarely get beyond the anecdotal. Only vines, because they are very ancient and have resisted the encroachment of concrete, constitute a significant urban agriculture. Besides the aforementioned instance in Montpellier, one might mention the famous Montmartre vine, the last trace of a once well-cultivated hillside; the vineyard of Bellet, one of the oldest in France, now incorporated into the commune of Nice; Bordeaux vines, at times squeezed into the urban fabric for even such great vintages as Haut Brion, and at times in the very heart of the city, like those at Place de la Victoire and La Béchade, both harvested and vinified.

Despite everything, the expectations associated with urban agriculture are many, and the role of actual production ultimately has only a very limited role. More often the aesthetic benefits and environmental functions are to the fore with this cultivated nature: urban agriculture is just one form taken by the strong social desire for nature in the town. Movements like Slow Food, which commend local production, traceable and non-intensive, may point to humanity's future, and urban farms may be the answer. And we can think about vertical farms with a production stage on each level, which would have the great virtues of solving the problems of the scarcity of land in cities, and of limiting the carbon footprint through the proximity of the places of production and consumption. But that is still a very distant prospect – or for some, indeed, an illusion pure and simple, with so many difficulties remaining (cultivation and plant-raising without earth yet still offering good environmental conditions, the issue of pesticides and the closeness of dwellings, etc.).[57] It is not very likely that towns can become self-sufficient in this way if one reflects that today it takes 0.3 hectares to feed each French person.[58] Besides which, the issue of the quality of fruit and vegetables produced in this way has been raised for a number of years. People are concerned about the way atmospheric and soil pollution can

57 Dickson Despommier, *The Vertical Farm* (New York: St Martin's Press, 2010).

58 Lise Bourdeau-Lepage and Roland Vidal, 'Nature urbaine en débat: à quelle demande sociale répond la nature en ville ?', *Déméter* (2013): 206. See also Roland Vidal and André Fleury, 'L'autosuffisance agricole des villes, une vaine utopie ?', *La Vie des idées*, 4 June 2010, http://www.laviedesidees.fr/L-autosuffisance-agricole-des.html

be detected in vegetal matter grown in towns. Particulate emissions from heating and motor vehicles are deposited on plants or on the soil where they grow and can alter their quality. It is calculated that plants growing less than fifty metres from a busy road are most affected. And as far as the soil goes, it is already not very suitable for agriculture, being compacted, stony and dry – not to mention often having been polluted long ago as a result of the city's industrial past. When this is so, heavy metals, lead, arsenic and notoriously dangerous elements can be found in vegetables grown there. French and European legislation has nothing to say on this question, and it is difficult for local authorities to take adequate measures: establishing the composition of soil is expensive, the effects of pollution on vegetal matter are still poorly measured, and the pressure of society, obsessed with climate warming and with a desire for nature, disregards these reservations. Problems arise particularly when municipal authorities try to put an end to longstanding practices, as was the case in Rennes for instance. The Prairies Saint Martin occupy 28 hectares in the centre of the town, on ground used in the nineteenth century as a tannery. Families have lived there for some fifty years, and family gardens were set up there in 1929. In 2011 the town hall announced that the gardens would be closed and the Prairies transformed into a park, because the soil was polluted and the risk of flooding too great. Vigorous resistance to this project showed the disbelief of the users of these gardens who demanded new studies to determine how polluted the soil was, suggested solutions (pollution-absorbing plants, etc.) and, universally, refused to stop the vegetable-growing activity they had practised for decades.[59] When new gardens are established, problems can be resolved more easily, but at a cost: large cities like Lyon and Paris systematically add new soil to the allotment gardens they set up. For the same reason the French government has forbidden market gardening on expansion zones in the Paris region since 2000, because of toxic material carried in urban waste.[60]

Apart from its role in production, other roles are attributed to urban agriculture - recreational, educative (teaching children where their food comes from and how plants grow) and even social. This last aspect is at

59 Paula Nahmias and Emmanuelle Hellier, 'La gouvernance urbaine en question: le cas des lieux de nature cultivée', *VertigO* **12** (2) (2012): 13–15 ; http://vertigo.revues.org/13109

60 On this issue of agriculture and urban pollution, see Christine Aubry and Jeanne Pourias, 'L'agriculture urbaine fait déjà partie du "métabolisme urbain"', *Déméter* (2013): 150–151; http://www.clubdemeter.com/ledemeter.php?demeter=2013

the forefront of projects in the new ecological municipality of Grenoble, apparently in accordance with residents' wishes.[61]

By a surprising reversal, the reintroduction of some urban market cultivation into commercial networks has been used since the 1980s as an instrument of social reinsertion: for example, at Tourcoing where the first workers' gardens were created in 1903, in 1996 there were 1,280 plots of land, one of the largest such zones in the country. Work in these gardens is undertaken in agreement with the local authority and with rehabilitation organisations to lead the way in the business of social reintegration for people in difficulty, such as the unemployed and drug addicts.[62] But more commonly gardens for reinsertion are set up outside the structure of workers' gardens. The greater part of these are openly directed at helping people who have not managed to find any economic or social activity by getting them back into a commercial network through market gardening, and so relieving their exclusion: they work, they keep to a timetable, they eat better and learn a trade and they socialise with other gardeners. It is the recovery of self-worth by work rather than just the social link that enables people to rebuild their lives. This is what lay behind the establishment of the Cocagne gardens, first set up experimentally in Besançon in the early 1990s: families join for a fee and each week receive a basket of fruit and vegetables grown by people in difficulty. It has to be acknowledged that such initiatives are not yet a complete answer…[63]

A garden of one's own

Far from the major commercial distribution networks, a solution is being sought in productions which are local, traceable or even private. On terraces and balconies and on window sills, a few herbs or two or three tomato plants testify to many city residents' desire to have products that they know well because they have cared for them.[64] This is the tricky and still marginal return to a lively habit that existed at least until the Second World War.

61 See the town magazine Gre.mag 1, Oct.–Nov. 2014: 19–21; http://www.gre-mag.fr/dossiers/cultiver-la-ville.

62 Béatrice Cabedoce and Philippe Pierson, *Cent ans d'histoire des jardins ouvriers* (Grâne: Créaphis, 1996), p. 97.

63 Vincent Larbey, *Jardins et jardiniers. Les pieds dans la terre, la tête dans les nuages. Une Anthropologie du potager*, Ph.D. in sociology supervised by Pr. Martine Xiberras, University of Paul Valéry – Montpellier III, 2013, pp. 53–56.

64 Jean-Baptiste Vaquin (ed.), *Atlas de la nature à Paris* (Paris: Atelier parisien d'urbanisme, 2006), pp. 249–263.

Kitchen gardens in town houses

Under the *Ancien Régime*, professional gardeners, market gardeners and nurserymen were not the only ones working the land inside the town or at its gates. There were many well-heeled garden owners inside the city limits whose delight was to produce fruits, vegetables and flowers of their own, for their own table, of course, but also because it was the done things to offer them to one's social acquaintances, as we saw in Chapter 4. Some products, such as citrus fruit trees in pots, were prized by seventeenth century urban elites to the point that their delicate cultivation required the complete attention of particularly competent gardeners. The gardener's know-how also helped in the evaluation of the master's social position, as an English doctor named Lister testified in 1698 when on a visit to the Pussort townhouse, belonging to a relation of Colbert and located along by the Tuileries:

> The gardener was a skilful man: he had a few fine plants in boxes which are to be found nowhere else, such as great tufts of rosemary, maritime cineraria, marum syriacum etc. The walls were well covered in espaliers. He had not yet pruned his peach trees; & when I asked him why he said that he had noticed that pruning after flowering improved the fruit, whereas doing the opposite overloaded them & spoilt the quality.[65]

If we set to one side the elite fashion of dilettante gardening, we should not lose sight of the vital importance of the kitchen garden and orchard resources for the middling citizens, still haunted by old fears: poor harvests, spiralling prices and cruel famines.[66] In the small and middle-sized towns in the kingdom, where urban developments remained modest and where the pressure on the land was less, the smallest houses in the centre kept their agricultural extensions in the form of gardens or yards, generally at the back of the house. There, people grew trees, both fruit trees and other varieties, vegetables and grasses, sometimes plants for grazing fodder, sometimes decorative flowers or even a small row of vines. It is easier to trace the possessions of the better-off through notaries' archives. In 1685 in Besançon one Luc Morel inherited a garden of fairly substantial size and the proximity of the famous Hotel de Montmartin justifies the detailed description made of it:

> The orchard covers half of the heritage mentioned and is planted with 17 pear trees, 12 apple trees, 13 plum trees, 26 apricot trees, and 12 dwarf trees … there are a number

65 *Voyage de Lister à Paris en M DC XCVIII* (Paris: Typographie Lahure, 1873), p. 171.

66 Florent Quellier, 'Le jardin fruitier-potager, lieu d'élection de la sécurité alimentaire à l'époque moderne', *Revue d'histoire moderne et contemporaine* **51** (3) (2004): 66–78.

> of rose bushes planted, some against the wall separating the said heritage from the Montmartin house and some on the other side of the pathway going alongside the wall ... also a trellis above the said heritage and as wide as it, and still to be found on the said heritage are 2 walnut trees and 6 cherry trees.[67]

The food that the better-off households could gather from gardens allowed them to make some savings, however small, on household expenses.

Every one tried therefore, whenever possible, to improve the daily lot by growing subsistence crops. In 1784 in Rennes, a small property owner who complained about the destruction in his garden caused by a fire in the neighbouring house was found to possess several vegetable beds, a vine and several fruit trees.[68] Once again, this was probably the case of a citizen without major financial worries. The humble were of course much more hard done by, particularly during urban densification which accelerated during the nineteenth century. In the industrial towns which developed at that time workers sometimes enjoyed the generosity of the factory owner and this might have included land for cultivation along with the rented lodgings. This was the case in Creusot in the middle of the century.[69] It was above all, from the 1880s onwards, in response to a 'social question' that had become pressing, that actions were multiplied to lend poor families plots of land that they could cultivate.[70] In 1882 in Chantilly, for example, the town council rented the Duke of Aumale 2.5 hectares of fields divided into plots and destined for the workers. In Sedan from 1899 plots of land were loaned to families in need. In Saint Etienne the tradition was to cultivate the land over the top of mines, sometimes on plots loaned by the mining companies.

Gardens to feed humble families

In 1894, a priest named Father Volpette decided to rent two hectares of land which he divided into thirty gardens that were made over to large working-class families in need. The idea took off in the years that followed with the support of the Houillères de Saint-Étienne (Saint-Étienne collieries). It spread throughout the impoverished neighbourhoods in the town: in 1920

67 Christiane Roussel, 'Besançon au XVIIIe siècle', *Histoire urbaine* **8** (2) (2003): 78

68 Catherine Laurent (ed.), *Histoire(s) de jardins, usages et paysages à Rennes*, p. 80.

69 François Portet, *L'Ouvrier, la terre, la petite propriété. Jardin ouvrier et logement social 1850–1950* (Le Creusot: CRACAP Écomusée de la communauté, 1978).

70 On workers' allotment gardens, we rely on the following book: Béatrice Cabedoce and Philippe Pierson, *Cent ans d'histoire des jardins ouvriers* (Grâne: Créaphis, 1996); as well as the website http://www.jardins-familiaux.asso.fr/histoire.html.

the Association pour le Jardin et le Foyer de l'ouvrier (Association for the Garden and the Home of the Worker) (set up in 1902 to guide and manage this initiative) had over a thousand gardens spread over thirty hectares! However, it was in the north of France that the workers' allotment gardens movement became truly organised,[71] upon the initiative of Abbot Lemire, a leading personality in the Third Republic.[72] He was a priest and also taught at the little seminary in Hazebrouck, and in 1893 he was elected as a member of parliament, serving for 35 years. He became the mayor of Hazebrouck in 1914. He defended terrianism, a political and social doctrine that wishes to maintain man's links with the earth in order to avoid the moral and physical decay of urban environments. With this in mind, in 1896 he started the Ligue française du Coin de Terre et du Foyer (French League for a Garden and a Home). This idea spread rapidly, and nationwide the League acted as a federator for the various ideas that shared the same goals. By 1907 the League was present in 63 departments and fifteen years later had over 47,000 gardens. Favourable legislation accompanied this development (the association was recognised as being in the public interest in 1909, recognition of family gardens in the rural code in 1952, etc.). The gardens were between 200 and 300 square metres in size and generally had a little shed at the bottom to store tools and to provide a space to eat.

The aims were ambitious. The reverse side of a League postcard at the beginning of the 1920s sums them up like this:

> In the Garden the worker finds:
> 1° A healthy occupation for his hours of leisure after his eight-hour working day (The garden kills alcoholism)
> 2° A means to combat high living costs: a 200 metre garden gives the worker 500 francs worth of fresh vegetables: the amount of his rent.
> 3° The chance to spend his hours of rest with his family: the garden and its complement the arbour are the worker's country house.[73]

The social channelling and the moralising ambition evoked in the first point are doubtless what motivated the philanthropists, the landowners, captains of industry, men of the Church, members of temperance societies,

71 The expression was coined by Dr. Gustave Lancry, Lemire's collaborator, who used the term in the journal *Démocratie chrétienne* in October 1895. After the Second World War, the expression 'allotment gardens' was more commonly used; in 1992 the league became the Fédération Nationale des Jardins Familiaux and in 2006 the Fédération Nationale des Jardins Familiaux et Collectifs.

72 Jean-Marie Mayeur, *Un prêtre démocrate : l'abbé Lemire* (Paris: Castermann, 1969).

73 Postcard published by the Ligue française du Coin de Terre et du Foyer, early 1920s, in Béatrice Cabedoce and Philippe Pierson, *Cent ans d'histoire des jardins ouvriers* (Grâne: Créaphis, 1996), p. 28.

all deep into terrianism, who covered France with these gardens. This partly explains the rules adopted regarding the distribution of plots of land. In Troyes in 1900 eight workers' gardens were created in the town centre. In order to get one, a family had to have at least three children (young couples who had no children within three years were considered barren and obliged to leave the garden …) and large families had priority. 'Reasons for excluding or refusing to allot a garden are as follows: ground poorly maintained, theft of vegetables, fighting, blows, drunkenness, marauding or poaching, selling smuggled matches, divorce, gardeners being too old.'[74] In fact, one had to show undeniable motivation because of course it was not the best plots that were made available to workers: heavy work was often required to prepare the soils, as in Ivry in 1938 where workers lent each other a hand to remove stones from the earth.

Nevertheless, the success of this initiative can be explained above all by working families' wish to have access to more varied and less expensive foodstuffs (and after the First World War this wish was shared by low ranking office workers and civil servants). Above all, it was about growing for oneself (the regulations limited the temptation towards commercialisation by forbidding monoculture and the sale of products): in general, priority was given to vegetables rather than flowers. With the diversification of the social origin of beneficiaries and thanks to the guidance of local committees managing the allotments, who lent gardening manuals, gave advice and handed out seeds and tools, production became more varied from the 1920s onwards and even more so after 1945 (the association's magazine explained in 1946 how to grow soya for example). With the *Trente Glorieuses* years these gardens had become more 'family' oriented and the leisure and relaxation dimension became more important. Today the association emphasises its role in sustainable development and biodiversity. The number of plots has nonetheless dropped significantly: in 1945 there were about 700,000 workers' gardens in France; by 1985 there were no more than 150,000.

A garden of one's own did not mean no sharing. This was already one of the ideas behind the workers' and the family gardens, suggesting sociability around sharing agricultural activity but also sharing its products, which are exchanged or eaten together. Shared gardens today aim for the same goal, as we have seen. The current trend for forgotten or exotic plants has reinforced this trend; it is about who will be the one to introduce others to such or such

74 Ibid., p. 94.

Figure 45.

Working-class gardens of Roubaix, potato harvest. Postcard, 1907. Courtesy of Médiathèque de Roubaix, CP_A25_L09_S1_004.

a forgotten or unknown vegetable, or variety of fruit on the edge of extinction (Pomexpo in Villeneuve-d'Ascq to taste the infinite variety of apples), and above all it concerns original ornamental plants. Exhibition-sales of rare plants began in France in the 1970s in the châteaux of Courson and Saint-Jean-de-Beauregard, and then started up in towns over the following decade; between 1985 and 1993 there were 170 of them. Of course, professionals sometimes show plants and town councils support these initiatives, but it is amateur gardeners who play the central part, and with real success. At Saint-Priest, an industrial suburb of Lyon, the socio-cultural centre held an exhibition in 1988 and since then the numbers of visitors has risen tenfold in a few years.[75]

75 Françoise Dubost, *Vert Patrimoine* (Paris: MSH, 1994).

When cultivation in town becomes a question of survival

As we saw, under the *Ancien Régime*, it was better to be one of those lucky urban garden owners who could meet any emergency that might arise in case of a subsistence crisis. During the Revolution new thinking and concrete suggestions appeared regarding the improvement of access of all to foodstuffs. When faced with war abroad and unrest at home, the *Convention montagnarde* (1793–1794) stood out because of its innovative measures to improve Parisians' daily life by getting all the resources possible out of the very soil of the city.[76] At that time, corn was the focus of very strict control while meat was scarce and the supplies of dairy produce, fruit and vegetables for city residents remained precarious. On 9 February 1794, the Convention and the Commune of Paris thus ordered that all public and private gardens in the capital should be cultivated under the supervision of the revolutionary section committees responsible for the 48 quarters of the city. While most citizens rejoiced at 'luxury gardens', as they were called, being transformed into kitchen gardens, some private individuals on the other hand complained about the zeal of the *sans-culottes* as is shown in this eloquent plea by Monsieur Georget from the North section.

> The commissaires of this section arbitrarily entered his garden and ordered him to pull up all the trees and the vegetables that were in there and then to sow the whole plot with potatoes and spinach ... It is doubtless not the intention of the Council to restrict the cultivation of gardens to two species, potatoes and beans, and to ban all other vegetables and foodstuffs useful in a household.[77]

In the end, the application of this measure to the whole of the urban territory remained fairly uneven, especially after Thermidor (the fall of Robespierre in 1794), and mostly concerned public gardens and the former properties of nobles or the clergy which had become national property.

The urban geography of the vegetal was even more changed by the great conflicts of the twentieth century, during which public authorities did everything possible to meet the requirement for feeding citizens, a first necessity. During the First World War, for example, several factors combined to modify the place that nature had in the town. The mobilisation of the French population, body and soul, in a conflict that for the first time was 'total'

76 Aurélien Larné, *Jean-Nicolas Pache, maire de Paris. Mouvement populaire et question sociale en l'an II*, Ph.D. supervised by Marc Bélissa, CHISCO, Paris-Ouest Nanterre La Défense University.

77 James Guillaume (ed.), *Procès-verbaux du Comité d'instruction publique de la Convention nationale*, vol. 4 (Paris: Imprimerie Nationale, 1891), p. 50.

war left little room for the maintenance of parks, gardens or promenades. The race-course at Longchamp became an animal compound, the gardens at Bagatelle were invaded by 10,000 sheep! Moreover, supply difficulties encouraged the cultivation of the slightest of plots of earth. Fortifications were also placed under cultivation, thereby becoming the place for a Sunday stroll.

As a contemporary put it: 'the *zone* (area outside the former ramparts) has lost its picturesque side but it has become the market garden of Paris.' Balconies and terraces were also pressed into service for small scale crops: 80,000 beans were planted in Avenue de la Malmaison in the latter years of the war. There was even a market garden set up near the Panthéon.

The Second World War saw a similar phenomenon. France was disorganised and isolated and Germany in fact carried off fifteen to twenty per cent of agricultural production for its own supplies. While in the countryside local cultivation allowed people to eat correctly, in the towns the situation was much more complicated. Ration cards appeared in September 1940. And of course the situation only got worse as the demands of the desperate Reich became more pressing. So, town councils organised themselves to try to limit hardships somewhat, though without managing to change things very much: *Cuisine et restrictions* (*Cooking and Restrictions*) by Édouard de Pomiane was the indispensable bestseller cookbook of the day. In Rennes, for example, the mayor made 46,000 square metres of council land available to the public to facilitate the food supply situation; teams of council workers even accompanied citizens in their agricultural labours by giving practical advice.[78] In Paris in April 1943 many green spaces, including the Esplanade des Invalides, the Luxembourg and the Tuileries, were ploughed up to plant potatoes, carrots and beans. In this, the Vichy Regime found the opportunity to exalt the return to the soil: a law dated 18 August 1940 obliged towns to give uncultivated urban plots to fathers of large families or else to make them over to workers' gardens associations. Large companies also played their part: employees of the SNCF were allowed to cultivate company land including the embankments of railway lines.

During the First and the Second World Wars, private individuals did not lag behind and planted cabbages, tomatoes and beans, as far as they could, in front of their houses.[79] Carrots, leeks and various root vegetables replaced flowers in their pots, cheek by jowl with rabbit farms .

78 Catherine Laurent (ed.), *Histoire(s) de jardins, usages et paysages à Rennes*, p. 84.

79 David Pryce-Jones, *Paris in the Third Reich* (London: Collins, 1981), p. 95.

Figure 46.

Gardening vegetables in the Luxembourg Garden in Paris during the Second World War. André Zucca, 1941. Public domain image from Bibliothèque historique de la Ville de Paris.

As stated in a famous song in 1941: 'There are swedes …' Magazines like *Rustica* or *L'Illustration* gave advice on growing Jerusalem artichokes, kohlrabi, New Zealand spinach and other forgotten plants. It is estimated that in the town and the countryside nearly three million gardens were cultivated in this manner in 1941. It was not just a question of cultivating plants in towns, for

Figure 47.

Cultures de guerre, satirical drawing by Robida, 1917.
Courtesy of Association des Amis d'Albert Robida.

they continued to circulate but in a new way: family and friends who lived in the country would send what they could in the way of foodstuffs unavailable in the towns. These agricultural, family parcels were limited by a decree dated 13 October 1941 to a maximum of fifty kilos (25 kilos from 1 July 1943). A maximum of ten kilos of fresh fruit and vegetables was allowed with no more than five kilos of asparagus or vegetable preserves; and these fifty kilo parcels could not include any potatoes or root vegetables. For the one year of 1942 there were apparently 13.5 million packages, representing 279,000 tonnes of merchandise![80]

* * *

Grids of cultivation for subsistence or for sale, of associative or private planting, thus mark towns and their margins: the urban vegetal has to be

80 On urban agriculture in the Second World War, see Éric Alary, Bénédicte Vergez-Chaignon and Gilles Gauvin, *Les Français au quotidien, 1939–1949* (Paris: Perrin, 2006), pp. 226–232 and 243–253.

worked and maintained, consumed directly or sold. Equilibriums appear: land use, social links and economic relations, commercial networks are set up, yet all of them can be troubled in exceptional circumstances such as in wartime, though not only in such cases. The winter is often a more common period of disturbance as regards the circulation of the vegetal, and of wood in particular.[81] Up to the start of the nineteenth century this was the main heating fuel but cold weather disrupted transport, particularly by river which was how such heavy loads mainly used to be carried. When periods of really cold weather lasted in towns fuel could be in short supply (country dwellers had easier access to small amounts of this fuel) at the time when it was most needed. Public authorities did what they could to avoid such situations but did not always succeed. During the siege of the Paris Commune in the winter of 1870–71 the residents suffered terribly. The national guard was mobilised to save some trees from destruction, as was noted in the Goncourt brothers journal: 'These women are helped in their destructive work by frightful kids who give each other a leg up on the trees in the Avenue de l'Impératrice where they break off what they can reach, and pull along behind them a little bundle, tied to a string which they hold in their hand thrust deep in their pocket.'[82] A few weeks later the authorities had to give way:

> On the Champs-Élysées, a rampart of felled trees, and before they can be hauled into trucks a crowd of children swarm over them, armed with hatchets, knives, anything that cuts, to hack off bits with which they fill their hands, their pockets and their aprons while in the hole left by the felled tree one sees the heads of old women busy with pickaxes, digging up whatever is left of the roots.[83]

These assaults were common practice in the terrible circumstances of famine, harsh winters or wartime attacks. The ravaging was indiscriminate as long as the vegetal could briefly relieve suffering and deprivation. One place particularly liable to such outrages was the botanic gardens, more precious than the other green spaces because of the unique riches that it contained: quite often the beating heart of naturalist science is to be found in the town.

81 François Walter, *Hiver. Histoire d'une saison*, Paris, Payot, 2014, p. 234 and p. 281.

82 Edmond and Jules de Goncourt, *Journal des Goncourt : Mémoires de la vie littéraire* (Paris: Bibliothèque Charpentier, 1892), pp. 164–165.

83 Ibid., p. 192.

8.

NATURE AND LEARNING

> Sire, I propose to your Majesty the construction of a garden for the cultivation of medicinal plants to which your subjects may have recourse if they are ill, where students of medicine may learn, or where practitioners may obtain what they need ... The garden I propose needs to be fifty acres at the most: the plants will not just be there in single examples for instruction but in profusion for use, and to furnish experience ... For, Sire, I assure your Majesty, that once established all the plants that can be accommodated to our climate, whether naturally or artificially, will be grown there.

In these terms the doctor Guy de La Brosse tried in 1625–26 to persuade Louis XIII to create a botanic garden in Paris. He explains the four functions such a space could have: cultivating plants, describing them to pass on knowledge, introducing new ones, and disseminating them.[1] Because towns are major centres of population, because they comprise sites of learning – home to universities, academies, sundry learned societies – and because political and economic activity is concentrated there, they offer an appropriate environment for harbouring learned gardens like this, despite the spatial constraints of the urban fabric. It is a surprising paradox, that one should learn better about nature in a town.

Sites of learning

Health through plants

Plant sciences made their way into towns as early as medieval times by way of doctors and apothecaries and through monks and nuns. A few carefully maintained herb beds allowed them to always have close at hand the vegetal products that made up remedies. While medicinal plants were certainly always cultivated within towns, their presence was unobtrusive and hard to locate as any owner of a garden could devote a little space to them. From the seventeenth century on, the demographic dynamism of towns contributed to the development of a market for health products. With more, and better qualified, doctors being required, medical faculties sought to silence detractors who, as in Molière, called their training into question: 'you have only to

1 Yves-Marie Allain, *Une histoire des jardins botaniques, entre science et art paysager* (Versailles: Quae, 2012).

Figure 48.

Botanical garden of Montpellier after two copper plates made by its founder Richer de Belleval, circa 1603. Courtesy of Bibliothèque municipale de Lyon.

hold forth; when you have a cap and gown, any stuff becomes learned, and all rubbish good sense … a beard is half the doctor.'[2]

So it is in this context that a new institution, already tried out in Italian and Dutch towns, appeared in the kingdom of France. The first botanic garden was created at Montpellier in 1593, thanks to the persistent efforts of Pierre Richer de Belleval and to the resources of his personal fortune.

This botanist-doctor, a teacher in the prestigious medical university, convinced Henri IV to lend his moral, if not financial, support to a project inspired by what had already been done in such other great European universities as Padua and Leyden. The botanic gardens associated with these places of learning were much more than herb gardens, even though in practical terms they supplied health institutions with fresh plants. Their pedagogical function was central: students, future doctors, surgeons and apothecaries could see the properties and therapeutic virtues of plants demonstrated before their own eyes, rather than having to content themselves with learning from books. What is more, the gardens allowed hundreds of plant species from the Orient and America, previously unknown in Europe, to become acclimatised, and it was hoped that most of them would be brought to the point where they could be identified, classified and described in detail. Such research helped to focus botanic expertise in the vegetal kingdom.

2 Molière, *The Imaginary Invalid*, trans. by Charles Heron Wall, Act 3, sc. 22. http://www.gutenberg.org/files/9070/9070-h/9070-h.htm

The botanic garden in Montpellier having somehow outlived its creator, more than half a century went by before public authorities looked again at this kind of urban provision. And this required another initiative, this time in Paris, but again coming from an urban medical background. Guy de La Brosse (1585–1641) was also concerned to improve the training of future practitioners by making use of an experimental space devoted to the vegetal realm. His project for a 'royal garden for cultivating medicinal plants', established at the beginning of the 1610s, had a social aspect as well: to give the needy access to treatment by providing them with the remedies prescribed by doctors at no cost. What is more, La Brosse wanted to escape the tutelage of the all-powerful medical Faculty of the capital, the only one entitled, along with Montpellier, to issue medical diplomas valid throughout the kingdom. Notorious for its resistance to any innovation likely to threaten its prerogatives, it had little time for botany anyway, deeming it a mere secondary discipline. After a long struggle, in 1626 La Brosse was authorised to establish the King's Garden, under the sovereign's exclusive patronage.[3] But because of pressure from the medical faculty, the institution was not permitted to issue diplomas. There were, however, demonstrators employed from 1640 to deliver courses to students. In the winter season they employed collections of herbs and drugs kept in a cabinet as teaching aids. In the garden itself an original arrangement was adopted on the model of Montpellier, for growing plants from different climates, including a pyramidal 'mountain' that was claimed to vary conditions of altitude and exposure to the sun!

Despite these vital innovations for learned botanists, in its early years the King's Garden was in the eyes of the great Parisian public not much different from apothecaries' gardens that already existed within the urban space, especially as it was established on the site of one of these. In the Saint Victor quarter, the king had in fact bought an 'apothecary's garden', also called 'the Paris pharmacy school', founded at the end of the sixteenth century by a philanthropical apothecary called Nicolas Houël; in accordance with his last wishes free courses in herbalism were given there. One garden then succeeded another, outside the walls and close to ecclesiastical properties and market-gardens; it was modest in size (about seven hectares, though by the eve of the Revolution it was close to 24 hectares), and of interest only to the small world of apprentice doctors and botanists. It did not come out of the shadows until

3 Alexandre Lunel, *La Maison médicale du roi, XVIe–XVIIIe siècles. Le pouvoir royal et les professions de santé* (Seyssel: Champ Vallon, 2009).

Figure 49.

Jean-Baptiste Hilair, *Jardin du Roy. La nouvelle serre prise du Jardin de Botanique*, drawing, 1794. Courtesy of BNF / Gallica: https://gallica.bnf.fr

the last quarter of the seventeenth century. Louis XIV's state was then pushing its policy of giving support and encouragement to arts, letters and science, particularly through the Academy system. In the 1660s, Colbert put an end to the medical Faculty's continued harassment of the King's Garden by way of opening, outside the Faculty's monopoly, a particularly innovative anatomy course examining the circulation of the blood and the human respiratory system: hundreds of students and other interested persons flocked to it.

New statutes helped to define the mission of an institution that was seen henceforward as vital and more complex, as it was opened up to medicine, surgery and, a little later, chemistry. From the seventeenth century on, botanic gardens, while retaining their initial therapeutic function and their connections with the world of medicine, more widely became tools for the knowledge of nature.[4]

4 Marie-Noëlle Bourguet and Pierre-Yves Lacour, 'Les mondes naturalistes: Europe (1530–1802)', in Dominique Pestre (dir.), *Histoire des sciences et des savoirs*, vol. 1, *De la Renaissance aux Lumières* (Paris: Seuil), pp. 255–281.

In the course of the eighteenth century, many towns in the French kingdom took their turn to equip themselves with a botanic garden. Study of the properties of plants was the main item of interest to medicine which, for instance, brought the use of new anti-fever plants (ipecacuanha and quinine) into practice. But applied botany was also of use to the arts and to industry, the textile industry in particular having recourse to dyestuffs. These scientific and economic interests explain the intensification of the networks of urban botanic gardens in France and throughout Europe. This sort of provision, which had the blessing of royal authority, was henceforward a byword for progress and modernity. In the middle of the Enlightenment, in the great cities of the kingdom and above all in Paris, several types of botanic garden coexisted. Added to the reinvigorated heritage of the gardens of universities, health institutions and apothecaries were new gardens founded by academies, learned societies or amateurs. And to these have to be added botanic gardens under the tutelage of the ministry for the navy and the colonies, and of military hospitals.

In 1763 the botanist Adanson enumerated, in addition to the King's Garden, twelve establishments that gave courses in botany, in Montpellier, Nantes, Toulouse, Bordeaux, Besançon, Pont-à-Mousson, Angers, Caen, Rouen, Reims, Nancy and Strasbourg.[5] This list is an indication of the efforts made by the old medical universities to modernise by furnishing themselves with botanic gardens linked to the network of the Republic of Sciences by way of their professors. The following decades saw the list grow, with Lyon, for example, Grenoble and Perpignan, which in 1759 devoted a large space in its botanic garden, which also comprised an arboretum, open to students of the university and also to strollers. If one excludes gardens of the 'colonial machine', expressly subordinate to the King's Garden, which will be discussed later, these foundations were not the work of the monarchy. They were the outcome of local initiatives and their success was closely tied to the cultural context on the ground. However, they benefited from a favourable dynamic, in that the greater part of French towns, including those of only average size, endeavoured in the middle of the eighteenth century to equip themselves with cultural, scientific and educational institutions in response to the expectations of enlightened elites. Provincial academies thus became a driving force in towns without universities.

In 1758 the Academy of Rouen acquired from the municipality the use of a large piece of land for establishing a botanic garden in return for a token

5 Michel Adanson, *Familles des plantes* (Paris: Vincent imprimeur, 1763), vol. 1, p. cxlvii.

payment (a bouquet of flowers a year!). In Dijon, where the small medical college had virtually no resources, the initiative came from a sponsor, Le Gouz de Gerland, an eminent representative of the nobility. He arranged the acquisition of an enclosure of some 5,000 square metres adjoining the public promenade in the Porte Bourbon quarter and had a botanic garden established there in 1770; an office of natural history was associated with it, and then a glasshouse in 1773 and an arboretum in 1778. It was linked to the Academy of Dijon in 1774 which managed it up until 1793; the local authority agreed to contribute to its endowment to enable public courses in botany and chemistry to be offered there. Elsewhere there were doctor/naturalists such as Dominique Villars (1745–1814) in Grenoble and Emmanuel Gilibert (1741–1814) in Lyon who set about persuading the town corporations and intendants to finance botanic gardens. These practitioners had, at some time or another in their training or careers, attended courses in the King's Garden in Paris and were keen to reproduce an institutional model to whose utility they could bear witness. During the first three quarters of the eighteenth century in Grenoble, instruction in military surgery medicine was delivered by the Fathers of Charity in a section of the general hospital. Dominique Villars, who had done his studies there, was asked to give a course in botany, and he deplored the insufficiency of the herb garden located within the establishment's walls. The local socio-cultural context proved amenable to the development of a more ambitious project. During the 1770s and 1780s the town acquired an academy, a weekly journal, a theatre, a permanent orchestra and a public library linked with a natural history office, all financed by public subscription and with the blessing of the public authorities. In 1782 the Intendant of Dauphiné granted Dominique Villars's request relating to the foundation of a new botanic garden with a teaching professorship. This was about creating a centre for naturalist studies, initially benefiting students enrolled in the new public school of surgery, opened in 1770 and complemented by midwifery and anatomical courses in 1774–1775. Villars got wind of the financial embarrassments of his friend Gilibert in Lyon: he had founded the Brotteaux garden in 1773 with his own money at the request of the Intendant Jacques de Flesselles, who subsequently quarrelled with the Abbot Terray, controller-general of finance, and was in no position to repay the loans Gilibet had agreed to. So the Grenoble naturalist had to maintain tight control of the garden's accounts to ensure its survival.

The fine mountains surrounding Grenoble act as a source for the botanic garden sited in the town. The rare plants they provide do not just fill the garden, but also

> provide a subject instrumental in exchanges with distant territories. This is why the maintenance of the garden, believed to be expensive, costs only 300 pounds a year, apart from the appointment of employees and their rent. All these costs amalgamated amount to no more than 1,200 pounds a year.[6]

The last two decades of the *Ancien Régime* abounded in initiatives by the more dynamic sectors of the medical world, supported by the ambitious Royal Society of Medicine founded in 1778, and by enlightened intendants. Their concerns coincided with those of the royal administration which wished to improve the nation's healthcare framework and the quality of treatment. The introduction of new training schemes was intended to alleviate both the inefficacy of most of the old medical universities, accused of offering only routine and exclusively theoretical instruction, and the proliferation of private, paying courses, that were common in many towns and attracted confused students concerned to get a qualification.

The reshaping of the educational system in the revolutionary period interrupted the functioning of academic botanic gardens for a while. Some were displaced because of new issues in the management of space. From the 1800s onwards, the institutional framework for medical training was set up and it lasted for more than a century.[7] As well as the faculties of medicine located in large cities (such as Paris, Montpellier, Strasbourg, Marseille, Toulouse, Bordeaux, Lyon…), a network of secondary schools of medicine operated in average-sized towns, and there were also military hospitals. These organisations had to have botanic gardens, even if they were quite modest, in accordance with the decree of 2 December 1794, which laid down regulations for medical teaching. Botany was tackled immediately, in the first year, in order to prepare students for the study of pharmacy in the following year. These arrangements were not really challenged by future developments. The widespread mass production of chemical medicines by the pharmaceutical industry from the middle of the nineteenth century did not dispense with the need for students in the health professions to complete an apprenticeship in the therapeutic properties of plants. The large number of regularly republished treatises in medical botany is in fact an indication of the vitality of this specialisation.

Special accommodation was made for medical botany within botanic

6 Dominique Villars, 'Mémoire concernant l'École de Chirurgie, le Jardin de Botanique et les Pépinières établis à Grenoble, présenté à Messieurs du Département de l'Isère', n.p., n.d. [Grenoble, 1789].

7 Olivier Faure, *Histoire sociale de la médecine (XVIIIe–XXe siècles)* (Paris: Anthropos-Economica, 1994).

gardens, where one supposes there were also pedagogical arrangements to enable 'useful' plants to be identified without fear of error. It was feared that the profusion of vegetal species from so many different sources constituting the subject of the study of botany in general could well generate dangerous confusion in the minds of students. It was better for them to concentrate on the few dozens of medicinal plants of which doctors and apothecaries made effective use. At Montpellier in 1852 a reserve was created of 'pharmacopeial, alimentary, industrial and poisonous plants', comprising 420 species.

> They are organised in a natural way and set out in large square clumps; labels in four different colours correspond to the four divisions we have indicated. The aims of this reserve are to enable students of medicine, agriculturalists and persons in industry to take in at a glance all the species they need to know about; to supply examples for study purposes; to supply the requirements of courses and examinations, as well as the requests made by hospitals for fresh plants. The vegetal species it comprises can also be found in the botanic school; but there, lost among very many other species that have no use and are of scientific interest only, they command less attention and students are often discouraged by the amount of time they have to spend just for the sake of those they really wish to study.[8]

Most botanic gardens would undergo similar reorganisation of their planting-beds. At the end of the 1860s, those in Paris would have a bed for medicinal and useful plants, another for edible and marketable plants, and a whole area given over to the botanic school, with colour codes according to different types of plants.[9]

Tropical delights

One must, of course, realise that this rationalisation arose from the influx of plants from all corners of the earth, along with the large number of visitors. In the eighteenth century, walking in the botanic garden was in fact one of the urban leisure-time activities available to the majority of townspeople. As we saw in Chapter 1, such gardens introduced into urban life glimpses of exotic landscapes, to which the public was initiated thanks to the very popular narratives of great expeditions. Numerous tropical plants, of which the palms, baobabs and pineapples were perhaps typical, became part of the visual patrimony of one and all. The collections in botanic gardens made concrete the imaginings about remote parts and tended to legitimise colonial domination.

8 Charles-Frédéric Martins, *Le Jardin des plantes de Montpellier. Essai historique et descriptif* (Paris: Victor Masson, 1854), p. 85.

9 William Robinson, *The Parks, Promenades and Gardens of Paris* (London: Murray, 1869), pp. 72–73.

The accounts of visitors like the London doctor Lister show that at the end of the eighteenth century the King's Garden, despite its out of the way location, was already a walking-place appreciated by the public, undeterred by the medical function of the place:

> The king's botanic garden … is very extensive and well-stocked with plants, and indeed with decent people, and anyone who wants to walk there. Its appearance is very varied: there are groves, pools, lawns, hillocks, besides a great levelled plantation devoted to the cultivation of all sorts of plants … The glasshouses are well supplied with delicate foreign plants, and the terraces are full of other kinds of herbs.[10]

The fame of the King's Garden in the eighteenth century derived quite as much from its collection of plants from the whole world as from the excellent instruction delivered there.[11] It was in fact an essential part of the mechanism of a complex 'colonial machine'.[12] The network, with headquarters at Versailles, comprised scientific institutions, civil and military medical institutions, academies, commercial companies and religious orders. The king and his ministry for the Navy and the Colonies sought to optimise efforts to exploit a rapidly expanding first French empire, in a context of heightened colonial rivalry between the European powers. The aim was more ambitious than the simple amassing of exotic products brought to mainland France. It was a matter of accumulating for society potentially 'useful' knowledge in the scientific fields that reflected the preoccupations of the times: measuring and mapping the planet, making an inventory of its resources and understanding how the natural world worked. Numerous progressive applications were to be imagined deriving from the richness of the vegetable kingdom, and that is what botany dealt with.

Beginning in the last decade of the seventeenth century, there was a voluntarist policy for creating botanic gardens in the arsenals of the west and the east (Brest, Rochefort, Toulon, Marseille) under the responsibility of the Intendants. They had a therapeutic mission, in that they were often linked with a military hospital. However, above all, these Navy gardens constituted vital staging points for vegetal material in transit by sea from one point to another on the various continents. A real circuit was established around the world to assist the transport and acclimatisation of plants from overseas. In

10 *Voyage de Lister à Paris en M DC XCVIII* (Paris: Typographie Lahure, 1873), p. 167.

11 Emma Spary, *Utopia's Garden: French Natural History from Old Regime to Revolution* (Chicago: University of Chicago Press, 2000).

12 James E. McClellan III and François Regourd, *The Colonial Machine. French Science and Overseas Expansion in the Old Regime* (Turnhout: Brepols Publishers International, 2012).

the sixteenth and seventeenth centuries these were brought back in an ad hoc manner by ships' captains and crews, but at the end of the seventeenth century they received explicit instructions from experts who had been called on by the government. In the eighteenth century, botanists and naturalists regularly joined crews embarked on major exploration voyages. With specialists aboard, the specimens doubtless had a better chance of arriving at the destination port unharmed. There were problems about making these transfers successfully: transporting seeds was not particularly difficult, but living plants posed very different logistical problems, even simply that of watering in the enclosed space of the ship, where fresh water was strictly limited. The unpredictability of dates of departure and arrival, resulting from weather conditions, for instance, did not help at all and could unduly prolong the unfavourable state in which plants found themselves, often deprived of light in the bottom of a ship's hold and entrusted to the care of a crew whose chief skill was not gardening. Collaboration between the King's Garden and the merchant marine was reinforced from the 1720s on: captains were given lists of plants found in the French colonies and in Africa with which they should concern themselves.[13] In 1752 Henri Duhamel du Monceau published, with Roland Michel de la Galissonnière, the first true manual on the subject under the title of *Avis pour le transport par mer des arbres, des plantes vivaces, des semences et diverses autres curiosités d'Histoire naturelle* (*Advice on the Sea Transport of Trees, Living Plants, Seeds, and Sundry Other Curiosities of Natural History.*) Even so, difficulties and poor practices continued, and for this reason a school for young naturalists going travelling was established in 1819 in the Museum of Natural History, the institution that had succeeded the King's Garden in 1793: after a year the pupils were sent abroad, armed with precise instructions from their professors.[14]

In the course of the eighteenth century, the foundations of staging-gardens, or 'storage gardens'[15] were established; they were subordinate to the King's Garden, which oversaw the flows of material, and twinned by sea with botanic gardens established in colonial towns. On different sides of the

13 Lorelai Kury, 'Les instructions de voyage dans les expéditions scientifiques françaises. 1750–1830', *Revue d'histoire des sciences* **51** (1998): 65–91.

14 Dominique Juhé-Beaulaton, 'Du jardin royal des plantes médicinales de Paris aux jardins coloniaux: développement de l'agronomie tropicale française', in Jean Louis Fischer (dir.), *Le jardin entre science et représentation* (Paris: CTHS, 1999), online at https://halshs.archives-ouvertes.fr/halshs-00089363, p. 8.

15 Yves-Marie Allain, *D'où viennent nos plantes?* (Paris: Calmann-Lévy, 2004), p. 102.

oceans, the storage gardens enabled plants to be kept and to be given the care needed to strengthen them. In France, most plants came from already existing botanic gardens which were developed and retained their original functions. This was the case, for example, with the garden at Lorient, founded in 1724 by the Compagnie des Indes, which dominated the town: originally a large apothecarial garden, it was enriched with all the plants disembarked by the Compagnie's ships, and then sent on to Paris. In 1777 fifteen trees of thirteen different species were received in Paris after having made the journey via Lorient, including a pomegranate tree, a lemon tree, orange trees from China and one orange tree from Quito. In 1719 a decree set out to make the apothecaries' garden in Nantes such a staging-post:

> Article V. we mean that the said garden should assume the quality of a royal botanic garden and be subordinate to our King's Garden ... and should be an entrepot and a workshop for the maintenance and cultivation of plants from foreign countries. To this end, the Director ... shall be at pains to take reception of the boxes of plants, grains and roots addressed to the garden, for the account of the said garden, and to inform our Intendant of our garden of the new and rare plants that he receives from foreign countries and that he will cultivate in our said garden at Nantes.[16]

The exchanges of course went in both directions, France sending into its colonial territories plants to be cultivated - such as coffee plants to Martinique. For example, in 1815, the new botanist/gardener appointed to the Île Bourbon (La Réunion today) had to convey with him from France 71 crates from the Paris botanic garden containing about 1,000 tree and shrub plants, three crates of seeds, etc. Forced by the international situation to stay ashore at Le Havre, he had the plants cultivated in that town's garden; a year later he set off by road to Rochefort from which port his ship was to sail, and the plants were again installed in the garden of the port, and it was not until February 1817 that they eventually set sail![17] Thus, if it could at times take two years just to leave the land, one can understand the vital role of gardens in these ports. They left a lasting mark on the urban landscape, not so much by the amount of land they took up as by the special arrangements they required. For example, the botanic garden linked to the Rochefort arsenal since 1697 is a good example of this. The training of students in the navy school of surgery, founded in 1722,

16 Decree of Intendant Pierre Chirac, 1719, in Dominique Juhé-Beaulaton, 'Du jardin royal des plantes médicinales de Paris aux jardins coloniaux: développement de l'agronomie tropicale française', in Jean Louis Fischer (dir.), *Le jardin entre science et représentation* (Paris: CTHS, 1999), online at https://halshs.archives-ouvertes.fr/halshs-00089363, pp. 6–7.

17 Allain, *D'où viennent nos plantes?* p. 102.

became its main function. In the 1730s it was struggling to accommodate the accumulation of diverse plants disembarked from ships. A storage garden was accordingly attached to it in 1741, with a surface area of 6,000 square metres. This comprised two glasshouses, one tropical and one temperate, into which plants could easily be taken thanks to tracks sloping from the quay where they were disembarked. In the first half of the nineteenth century, botany enthusiasts in the little town of Rochefort took great pride in the establishment, then in its heyday, as is evident in this description from 1837:

> In its present state the school of botany comprises almost 4,000 plants. It has rare and costly plants. The fig from the Indies proudly lifts its head beside the date-palm with its massive trunk. The Egyptian papyrus grows as it does on the banks of the Nile, and it is wreathed in garlands of passion flowers from central America. Almost 1,500 exotic plants blend their unfamiliar forms with our climate. Such richness ranks Rochefort's botanic garden fourth in France.[18]

At this time botanic gardens were enhanced with new arrangements of pools, enabling them to cultivate aquatic plants.

The opening up of botanic gardens to the world made them oases of biodiversity in urban spaces. However, they should not be considered as separate islets but rather as the nodes of an ever-denser global network. Correspondence and exchanges of seeds and specimens, which had lain at the heart of the practices of the Republic of Sciences since the sixteenth century, reinforced the links between the botanic gardens of Europe, America, the West Indies and the Indian Ocean. The most famous of these regularly published catalogues of their collections, as much to impress their partners as to help them in their choices. In the eighteenth century the King's Garden was regularly sought out not only by botanists from abroad, but also by all the founders of botanic gardens in France, looking to get access to its considerable resources. Having become administrative director of the Museum in 1793, André Thouin reinforced this centralisation still further as it enabled him to direct from Paris projects for acclimatising 'useful' plants in Mediterranean gardens and in Corsica.

The restructuring of institutions effected after the fall of the monarchy was accompanied by a systematic cataloguing of patrimonial treasures, as much artistic and architectural as scientific. The collections of gardens and cabinets of natural history belonging to the clergy or the aristocracy were

18 René Primevère Lesson, 'Réponse au Dr Bobe-Moreau' (1837) in Michel Sardet, *Le Jardin botanique de la marine du port de Rochefort (1741–1896)*, DEA dissertation, under the direction of Jean-Pierre Bardet, Université Paris-Sorbonne, 1993.

transferred to the Museum, and these appropriations extended to the lands of sister republics.[19] The secondary botanic gardens played a huge part in the cataloguing work, enabling them to publish their inventories as early as the 1800s. Allowing for the size and the issues involved in the principles of classification to be adopted, it was not before the 1820s that the Museum published an *Index Seminum* of its Garden of Plants, updated each year, to this day, and distributed to French and foreign scientific institutions. At the end of the nineteenth century, it was completed by a *Catalogue de graines et de plantes vivantes* (*Catalogue of Seeds and Living Plants*) in French. These works helped greatly with exchanges between botanic gardens, who used them to convey their discoveries. The standardisation of names through the widespread adoption of Linnean classification in the first third of the nineteenth century further eased vegetal circulation between urban botanic gardens. From October 1893 to October 1894, the Jardin des Plantes in Paris sent out to its colleagues more than 24,000 packets of seeds, and more than 7,000 living plants, and in Paris alone distributed almost 30,000 samples for use in classes.[20] Private individuals could also benefit from this dense and fruitful network. However, since the 1850s, a somewhat wary discourse has emerged in respect of alien vegetal species,[21] and this has tended to hinder exchanges a little. In the nineteenth century some of these species were suspected of endangering the system of agricultural production; nowadays there are regulations which codify the battle against species deemed invasive and accused of disturbing the ecological balance. Although they are not solely responsible, the role of botanic gardens in these processes of diffusion raises questions nonetheless. They have contributed to making the cultivation of new species in metropolitan areas commonplace.

From the middle of the nineteenth century, there has been a fashion for acclimatisation, of both animal and vegetal species. It is not that before this period there was no awareness of the adaptation of new species to the French climate: we have demonstrated sufficiently, especially in respect of ornamental plants, the extraordinary influx of exotics that have modified the appearance of French gardens, particularly since 1750. However, this acclimatisation was as much due to the action of private individuals as to

19 Pierre-Yves Lacour, 'Les Amours de Mars et Flore aux cabinets. Les confiscations naturalistes en Europe septentrionale. 1794–1795', *Annales historiques de la Révolution française* (2009, 4): 71–92.

20 Allain, *D'où viennent nos plantes ?* p. 114.

21 Allain, *Une histoire des jardins botaniques*, pp. 106–108.

botanic gardens. People often refer to the famous case of *Magnolia grandiflora*, first brought into France from Louisiana in 1711: against royal rules, it was brought in clandestinely by a private individual who planted it in an orangery where, for twenty years, it just about kept going, until it was planted outside in a corner of the garden, and flourished at last. Even so, it was a few years before several examples of this species could be produced, by marcotting (air-layering) so that it could be distributed.[22] Such acclimatisation efforts, which were frequent and widespread, sometimes took place in urban gardens, notably in storage gardens, but most often they needed a lot of space and were undertaken on very large private estates or by horticultural associations. From the eighteenth century until the first half of the nineteenth century there emerged a regular itinerary with various stages for exotic plants brought into France, as the Abbé Delille explains in his 1802 poem *L'Homme des champs* (*The Countryman*):

> From the burning tropics with dusty rocks
> Malta first welcomed these venturesome plant;
> From Hyères the less scorched fields in their turn
> Offer asylum to wandering plants.
> Lyon awaits them and its kindly climate
> Offers sweet haven to its adoptive plants.
> Lastly in Paris the acclimatised tree
> Lends our gardens its borrowed shade.[23]

However, advancements in techniques for transporting plants and faster moving times in the nineteenth century soon made these staged journeys obsolete. Above all, by the mid-nineteenth century, and especially under the Second Empire, the acclimatisation of both animals and plants became a public cause supported by public authorities. In France this taste lasted for some fifty years – and in the colonies into the inter-war period, as many colonial gardens tried to acclimatise various species in order to obtain profitable cultivars, all coordinated by the colonial garden founded at Nogent in 1899.[24] The Acclimatisation Society, founded in 1854, equipped itself with a Garden of Acclimatisation in 1860 situated in the Bois de Boulogne. It is one of the few gardens in France specifically devoted to this practice. However, they are

22 Allain, *D'où viennent nos plantes?* pp. 117, 186.

23 Abbé Delille, *L'Homme des Champs* (1802), in *Œuvres complètes* (Paris: Furne, 1833), vol. VII, p. 217.

24 Christophe Bonneuil, *Des savants pour l'empire. La structuration des recherches scientifiques coloniales au temps de la "mise en valeur des colonies françaises", 1917–1945* (Paris: éditions de l'ORSTOM, 1991).

also found elsewhere, in Bordeaux for example, again set up in the middle of the century. In 1853 the city council decided to transfer the Jardin des Plantes to the site of the old public garden created by the Intendant Tourny. The aim was to establish a school of botany which would not be exclusively pedagogic in function:

> We shall also make many attempts at acclimatising useful or valuable plants ... In New Zealand] there also grow a host of useful plants, enormous trees bringing wealth to the shipyards of the English navy. It is in this direction that we shall constantly turn our gaze ... so that there will one day come to us from this rich and distant country sacks of seeds and precious plants, all of which there is hope of acclimatising in Gironde.[25]

While the acclimatisation of rare plants was achieved effectively, the first aim of the mainly Parisian initiative, of adapting 'useful' animals and plants for French agriculture, and even industry, was on the whole a failure, and from the end of the nineteenth century the Paris garden was increasingly neglected. Aside from this disappointment, at least until the middle of the nineteenth century, botanic gardens became centres for development and instruction in the vegetal sciences because they collected plants from all over the world.

When city dwellers become botanists...

The discourse on method

In Chapter 6 we saw botanists embarking on the conquest of urban space to discover the diversity of the vegetal kingdom within it, in gardens and lawns or between paving-stones. Botany became an independent scholarly discipline in the seventeenth century: it gradually freed itself from the centuries-old tutelage of medicine in order to devise its own concepts and methods. Up until the middle of the nineteenth century, the work of botanic scholars was to name, identify and classify the tens of thousands of unknown species which arrived from all over the globe. It was thought that it would be possible to explain nature by making a systematic inventory of all vegetal production, including plants that were not of immediate use to man.[26] It was necessary to

25 Michel-Charles Durieu de Maisonneuve, *Le Nouveau Jardin des Plantes, discours prononcé dans la séance publique d'hiver de la Société linnéenne de Bordeaux le 4 novembre 1853* (Bordeaux: imprimerie Justin Dupuy, 1853), pp. 8–9.

26 Émilie-Anne Pépy, 'Décrire, nommer, ordonner : enjeux et pratiques de l'inventaire botanique au XVIIIe siècle', in Florian Charvolin, Isabelle Arpin et al., *Histoire et actualité des inventaires naturalists*, special issue of *Études rurales* (June 2015).

agree on one taxonomic methodology: that advanced by the Swede Charles Linnaeus (1707–1778), based on the reproductive organs of plants, was much admired, but was not unanimously favoured in France.[27] There were many different proposals: some fifty more or less workable systems were worked out in the course of the eighteenth century. The method devised by Joseph Pitton de Tournefort (1656–1708) in the King's Garden retained fervent adherents up until the end of the century, on an equal footing with that of Linnaeus. On the eve of the Revolution a new method, called 'natural', was worked out by uncle and nephew Bernard and Antoine-Laurent Jussieu.

These sometimes virulent debates overflowed the comfortable world of academe and even spread out over the very terrain of urban botanic gardens. Buffon (1707–1788), who was for forty years the omnipotent authority as Intendant of the King's Garden, would not hear a word in favour of the Swedish scholar and his disciples, and made it known. The decision over how plants should be organised was crucial for the director of a botanic garden because it meant choosing sides. Dominique Villars explained these uncertainties in the catalogue of the Strasbourg botanic garden which he published in 1807. He explained that he favoured the Jussieu method:

> Besides having the advantage of relieving the memory and so making investigation easier by way of plants' affinities and correspondences of character, the natural method also brings the advantage of pointing out striking similarities to the eye by way of the whole look of plants and their habit, which a deeper and more considered examination will almost always confirm ... The curious, the enthusiast, the philosopher and the scholar who does not necessarily want to take his study of botany further, will find in the natural method a straightforward basis for finding his way through the realm of Flora, without being too distracted by other issues.[28]

In the second half of the nineteenth century, this issue, whose stakes had been considerable, became virtually obsolete in the face of botanists' new preoccupations such as the concepts of evolution and ecology. However, the principles of the Jussieu method, though much amended in the nineteenth and twentieth centuries, still constitute the structure on which the organisation of botanic gardens is based.

With the diminishing interest in classification during the nineteenth century, and even more after the First World War, botanic research was conducted less in gardens and more in laboratories, in herbaria or in the field:

27 Pascal Duris, *Linné et la France (1780–1850)* (Geneva: Droz, 1993).

28 Dominique Villars, *Catalogue méthodique des plantes du jardin de l'école de médecine de Strasbourg* (Strasbourg: Levrault, 1807), pp. xiv–xvi.

the founding of the INRA (Institut National de la Recherche Agronomique/ National Institution for Research in Agronomy) in 1946 bears witness to that. Botanic gardens thus saw their role dwindling, in practical research at least, but to the benefit of their function of plant distribution and of regeneration when possible – at least to ensure, as with the garden at Brest that had been destroyed by bombing, that they did not lapse into dormancy. A revival has, however, been observable over the last thirty years: interest in biodiversity, especially among the public, has involved the renovation of some gardens, giving priority to recreating 'natural' habitats rather than exhibiting species isolated from their true context. The botanic garden in Bordeaux offers a striking example of this: created in 1629 as an apothecaries' garden, it was moved several times in the ensuing centuries, and was finally located in the Jardin Public in 1858, but excited little interest from the inter-war period onwards. It was not until 1996 that programmes of urban renewal planned for its removal to the right bank of the Garonne, and not until 2002 that it reopened on its new site. Its ten hectares are still enclosed by a fairly dense urban fabric, but they offer more possibilities than the restricted site in the Jardin Public, which is more recreational. On the new site, eleven natural zones have been recreated whose dynamics and biodiversity may be studied.[29]

Similarly, since the 1980s, the growing interest in urban nature and its role in the wellbeing of citizens has brought naturalist knowledge out of botanic gardens and academic cliques. Public participation is now encouraged in the development of knowledge of nature in towns. An example of this is the foundation in 2005 of the Departmental Observatory of Urban Biodiversity in Seine-Saint-Denis, whose explicit aim is to disseminate and share knowledge about urban biodiversity. To this end, those who wish to participate in the observation of urban nature are invited to forward information they have so that it may then be processed by professionals. In the same way, but this time on the national scale, the Museum of Natural History in Paris created a programme of participative science under the title of Vigie-Nature. Started in 1989 for the observation of birds, it subsequently extended to other animals and to urban nature. In 2011 it launched a project of observation called 'Wild Things in my Street' in the Paris region, which attracted 550 volunteers, who described 119 vegetal species on 330 pavements in the Île-de-France; the project became national in 2012 with the participation of Nantes, Lille, Marseille, Vannes, Toulouse, Strasbourg

29 For this entire paragraph, see Allain, *Une histoire des jardins botaniques*, pp. 104–107.

and Montpellier, for example. On the basis of a methodology communicated to volunteers, from throughout the country it garnered citizens' observations on common biodiversity, an everyday biodiversity which a few scientists on their own could never see.[30] The programme also made the popularisation of scientific knowledge possible, to the benefit of all. This can work in a playful, spontaneous way: in 2014 a botany enthusiast in Nantes undertook to name the wild species he came across in the streets by stencilling their names on the pavements, an initiative that residents liked and that got the town hall's support.[31] Finally, many publications contribute to spreading knowledge of urban plants among children and adults.[32]

These developments explain why a Charter, drawn up in the middle of the 1990s by the organisation Jardins Botaniques de France et des Pays Francophones (Botanic gardens of France and of French-speaking countries), allots three principal tasks to these places: the conservation of vegetal material (which also enables botanic gardens to exchange resources and knowledge, and so to act as nodes in an international scientific network); the development of scientific activities; the education of the public (children; adult enthusiasts, whose training is essential in the context of a citizen-based approach to scientific work; students of biology and medicine; etc.).[33]

Green classes

Since the eighteenth century, changes in the nature of research have been accompanied by modifications in the teaching offered by botanic gardens to non-specialist members of the public. In fact, botany and its applications were not just of interest to a handful of scholars whose taxonomic research was found to be abstruse by a good number of their contemporaries. Even Rousseau, an enlightened enthusiast of botany, did not withhold his criticism, deeming that they wrote 'only for people like themselves' and that the

30 http://vigienature.mnhn.fr/

31 http://www.terraeco.net/A-Nantes-une-mysterieuse-graffeuse,55660.htm

32 See, for example, Guillaume Eyssartier, *Guide de la nature en ville* (Paris: Belin, 2015); Marie-Claire Rassemusse and Éva Châtelain, *Découvre les fleurs sauvages des villes* (Morlanne: Les P'tits Bérets, 2015); Brunhilde Bross-Burkhardt, *Mauvaises herbes, je vous aime!* (Paris: Delachaux et Niestlé, 2016); Gilles Carcassès, *La Fleurette et le camionneur. À la découverte de la nature en ville* (Paris: Ul-mer, 2016).

33 Bernard Millet, 'Les jardins botaniques : leurs nouvelles missions et leur place dans la cité', *Actes du colloque "Le Jardin et la Nature dans la cité"* (Saline Royale d'Arc-et-Senans, 7–8 June 2001) (Besançon: Institut Claude-Nicolas Ledoux, 2002), p. 80.

Linnaean system 'is a system for masters, we need one for pupils'.[34] By 'pupils' Rousseau did not mean only the captive public of medical students; in fact he recommended the stimulating study of botany, and more broadly a generous observation of nature, to all well-bred young people as being good for their souls. The philosopher described himself as 'convinced that at all times of life the study of nature abates the taste for frivolous amusements, prevents the tumults of the passions, and provides the mind with nourishment that is salutary by filling it with an object most worthy of its contemplations'.[35]

In her first treatise on education, where she presents an imaginary noble family, the Countess of Genlis, the governess of the children of the house of Orleans, contributes to the diffusion of Rousseauesque principles:

> Out walking, our children just take exercise by running and jumping; in one year we will accustom them, as Rousseau recommends, to measure any space by eye, or tell how many trees there are in an avenue, or pots of flowers on a terrace, etc. And it is also there they will learn what a foot, a measuring rod, an acre is, and they will acquire some notion of agriculture.[36]

The eighteenth century also saw the sanctification of the educational walk, that enabled a properly brought up pupil to instruct him or herself directly from the great book of nature. For educators, concrete experiences were an extension of lesson time and allowed them to introduce or to illustrate wider concepts presented in class. The pedagogic garden was a manufactory for clever children. Learning was only to be done during the period of children's legal minority, under the authority of supervising adults to whom they owed obedience, as educational treatises and other manuals never failed to remind them. 'A Collection of Instructive walks', the *Voyage au jardin des plantes* (*A Journey in a Botanic Garden*) is typical of this kind of writing for the young, in the service of pedagogy and morality. The young reader is introduced to the naturalist riches of the Museum of Natural History in Paris; he can identify with the chief character, Gustave, who discovers galleries, amphitheatres, the animal house and the botanic garden in the company of a narrator who acts as a teacher.

34 Quoted by Alexandra Cook, 'Le pluralisme taxonomique de Jean-Jacques Rousseau', in Claire Jacquier and Timothée Léchot (dir.), *Rousseau botaniste: Je vais devenir plante moi-même* (Pontarlier: éditions du Belvédère, 2012), pp. 37–56.

35 Jean-Jacques Rousseau, *Lettres élémentaires sur la botanique,* trans. Thomas Martyn (London: J. White, 1802).

36 Stéphanie-Félicité du Crest de Genlis, *Adèle et Théodore, ou Lettres sur l'éducation* (Paris: Lambert et Baudouin, 1782), vol. 1, pp. 77–78.

Such facilities were not of interest solely to children and adolescents. The useful properties and the aesthetic aspects of plants were objects of study appreciated by a broad public. A fashionable leisure activity for some, for others, botany was a real professional interest. One thinks immediately of collectors, nurserymen and other agronomists working tirelessly to improve species, but also of artists, textile workers reproducing flower motifs, wallpaper designers, and so on. For those who wished to devote themselves to regular scientific activity, learned institutions proposed a varied offer (workshops with the academies, public courses, demonstrations of experiments) to which was added the possibility of following private instruction, if money allowed. Botanic gardens were no exception to the rule.

In 1773, the doctor and botanist Jean-François Durande (1732–1794) presented the course of instruction which he was going to deliver at the newly inaugurated botanic garden in Dijon:

> Every day at six o'clock in the evening I shall dictate some part of Tournefort's method in order to enable everyone to benefit from this course, even without books, & I shall then present demonstrations. This garden, gentlemen, will present plants to you in a methodical way; but as it is not less important to see them scattered about as it has pleased Nature to spread them over the surface of the globe, every Thursday we shall go out seeking plants while walking round this Town's neighbourhoods.[37]

The address to 'Gentlemen' was purely conventional, as this discourse was delivered at an inaugural session of the Academy where several society ladies were present. Botany is one of the few sciences which social convention deemed to be appropriate for the fair sex: and was it not in any case associated with domestic economy, with keeping a garden properly and with the arts of pleasing taught to young ladies of good birth? Women attended botanic courses without any hindrance, as did young girls, even if there was an attempt to disguise from them the meaning of some Linnaean metaphors.

Thus it was a very mixed public that, as long as they treated where they were respectfully and behaved suitably, could attend free daily demonstrations or join plant hunts organised around the town. In Dijon, as elsewhere, courses took place in summer when flowers made it possible to investigate plants' anatomical details. The public was informed of the timetable of sessions and of dates for plant hunts by way of the press or of notices on the garden's gates. It was deemed that those attending could follow the course without ever having opened a botany book, as the lecturer would explain the fundamentals

37 *Séance publique tenue le 20 juin 1773 dans le sallon du Jardin des plantes par l'Académie des Sciences, Arts & Belles Lettres de Dijon* (Dijon: Causse, 1773), p. 26.

of the method he had chosen to present; Durande had even devised a specific teaching aid which he called a 'Botany Card', in fact a poster displayed in the salon of the Academy summarising classification by Tournefort's method.

After the Revolution scholars sought to convince successive governments to support the generous instruction offered by French botanic gardens. Thus, in 1793, the King's Garden in Paris was the subject of a complete reorganisation with the inauguration of twelve professorial chairs, whose number increased in the nineteenth century. Bernardin de Saint-Pierre revealed the encyclopaedic ambitions of the institution in his *Mémoire sur la nécessité de joindre une Ménagerie au Jardin des Plantes de Paris* (*Memorandum on the Need to Add an Animal House to the Botanic Garden in Paris*) (1797), which begins with this plea:

> The study of nature is the basis of all human knowledge. The National Office of Natural History and its botanic garden in Paris are destined to contain all its principal subjects for the instruction of the public. Few people know the full value of this establishment because they pay no more attention to it than to the nature within which they live. They could get some idea of this by considering how many bodies come there to learn from its luminaries. Mineralogists, botanists, zoologists; then those professing the arts that derive from the three first kingdoms of nature, lapidaries, chemists, apothecaries, distillers, surgeons, anatomists, doctors; and lastly those exercising the arts of taste, designers, painters and sculptors come every day to seek new knowledge.[38]

Artists got good value there, whether they wanted to represent the landscape of the garden or to portray plants. Besides, drawing the gates and entrances to gardens constituted part of the academic exercises demanded of architectural students. For those who wished to specialise in botanic illustration in the strict sense, the National Museum of Natural History offered courses in which artistic teaching was not separated from scientific teaching. Before the advent of photography, it was necessary to reproduce accurately the specimens that one discovered or described. Knowledge was obtained above all by observation, drawing and printing. This is why Antoine-Laurent de Jussieu, Daubenton, Thouin and Brongniart in 1790 propounded a regulation for the botanic garden in Paris, envisaging the creation of a course in the iconography of natural objects in a kind of school they believed to be unprecedented.[39] This shows a wish to institutionalise

38 Bernardin de Saint-Pierre, *Mémoire sur la nécessité de joindre une Ménagerie au Jardin des Plantes de Paris* (1797), in *Œuvres complètes* (Paris: Méquignon-Marvis, 1818), vol. XII, pp. 633–634.

39 Michel Thireau, 'Alliance de l'art et de la science au travers des peintures sur vélin du Muséum National d'Histoire Naturelle de Paris', *Journal of Traditional Agriculture and Applied Botany* **37** (1) (1995): 45–57.

botanic illustration, which had played a major role in the epistemological construction of the discipline, but which before the Revolution had been mastered by only a very restricted number of artists, who had more or less gone through the Academy or been trained on the job.[40]

The Decree of 10 June 1793 constituting the Museum thus filled a gap in instituting 'a course in natural iconography, or the art of drawing and painting all the productions of nature'.[41] The Museum library, enriched by all the collections confiscated in the nationalisation process of clergy property and from seizures targeting nobles reputed to be émigrés, facilitated this course of instruction. To this end 'the collection of plants and animals painted from nature in the Museum of Natural History and deposited at various times in the national library, will be transferred to the Museum library'.[42] In this collection, vellums – botanic and later zoological paintings on the skin of still-born calves – played a prestigious and important part. These works of art, made for the pleasure of the king and of Gaston d'Orleans, became real working tools – until the middle of the nineteenth century when photography came as competition – illustrating the history of the Museum and transmitting knowledge to other institutions by way of loans, etc. And still today, when they have been digitised, they are disseminated widely, especially among the general public.[43] Up until the years 1850–1860 the botanic garden in Paris was a place favoured by artists for studying the natural world, flora of course, but also fauna in the menagerie. And the Museum fostered this activity, giving entry cards to artists in all genres, often allowing access outside public opening hours. Gustave Moreau, for instance, made the most of these possibilities: he followed courses in palaeontology and chemistry, studied vellums, drew aquatic plants and animals, and so on. And there one might also meet decorators who came for inspiration for floral motifs for cloth, sculptors seeking to capture the posture or movement of animals, illustrators of naturalist works, as well as simple amateurs. Courses organised by the Museum took place in the library: they began on 15 May and finished in the summer, after thirty classes on the fundamentals of naturalistic representation.[44]

40 Madeleine Pinault-Sorensen, *Le Livre de botanique aux XVIIIe et XVIIIe siècles* (Paris: Imprimerie Nationale, 2008).

41 Decree of 10 June 1793 relating to the organisation of the National Plant Garden and the Natural History Cabinet, under the name of National Museum of Natural History, Title II, Article 1.

42 Ibid., Title III, Article 4.

43 Thireau, 'Alliance de l'art et de la science etc.'.

44 Luc Vézin, 'La Ménagerie du Jardin des Plantes et l'art animalier', in Nadine Beauthéac (dir.), *Les Carnets de l'exotisme*, Special issue *Les Jardins du retour* 13 (1st semester 1994): 58–59.

This type of instruction was, however, marginal in relation to the more traditional courses in horticulture and arboriculture given in botanic gardens in response to public demand and to complete the training of professionals. In the nineteenth century the botanic garden at Nantes, for example, comprised a school of fruit trees, a forestry school, a landscape school and a school of botany.[45] It was the same with the botanic garden in Montpellier, which was distinguished by having a school of vines.[46] These institutions delivered more or less specialised courses. At Nantes, the garden, run by the municipality from 1819, was entrusted in 1822 to Antoine Noisette, a Parisian landscape gardener, who was expected to establish a school of botany with 600 plants and a fruit-tree school with 670 of these – which in fact he only partly managed to do. In 1825 the town required him to give a free course in botany: he transformed it into a course on pruning fruit trees, which in 1827 took place on Wednesday and Saturday from 10 a.m. to noon for a month between February and March.[47] It was in the same spirit that the garden was opened to the public from 1829 and that a chair in botany was created in 1835; its first incumbent was none other than the future director Jean-Marie Écorchard, who started teaching in 1836. His courses took place on Tuesday, Thursday and Saturday at 6 p.m. and were open to women. Up till his death in 1882, Écorchard dispensed his knowledge prolifically, as did his successors, notably Paul Marmy, who delivered a course in arboriculture for fruit and ornament. In a letter to the mayor giving an account of his activities, he claimed that attendance at his courses had risen from about ten in 1893 to some 130 in 1896. If one believes him, all the local bourgeoisie of Nantes were there: the commander in chief of the 11th army corps, the president of the Civil Tribunal, a councillor from the prefecture, heads of institutions, large landowners, many gardeners for private employers, horticulturalists, and so on. It was a fact that the botanic garden in the nineteenth century answered the requirements as much of strollers enjoying the reasonably well-ordered exotic setting, as those of lovers of scientific leisure whose more alert gaze went straight to the labels and little notices dispersed among the plants and trees to identify them.

This opening up of instruction in botany to the public ran in parallel with

45 Service des Espaces verts et de l'Environnement de Nantes, *Jardin des Plantes de Nantes* (Nantes: n.d.), p. 58.

46 Charles-Frédéric Martins, *Le Jardin des plantes de Montpellier. Essai historique et descriptif* (Paris: Victor Masson, 1854), p. 85.

47 Service des Espaces verts et de l'Environnement de Nantes, *Jardin des Plantes de Nantes*, pp. 17–18.

Figure 50.

The pedagogical display of plants at the Jardin des Plantes in Nantes, based on a postcard.
Source: Authors' collection.

Figure 51.

School garden in Lens, botany lesson in the inter-war period.
Courtesy of the archives of the Fédération nationale des jardins familiaux et collectifs.

it being institutionalised in schools. At the end of the eighteenth century the success of instruction in general or specialised botany went along with the development of several scientific fields dedicated to the vegetal, from agronomy to the natural sciences (botany, zoology, geology, mineralogy). These disciplines made their appearance in educational curriculums at the secondary and higher levels from 1795, before being gradually adopted in primary schools in the course of the nineteenth century: think of the famous 'educational gardens' set up by the minister for public instruction Jules Simon to entrench agricultural careers for country children. One finds traces of this teaching of natural history in *Le Tour de la France par deux enfants* (*Two Children's Journey Around France)*, an 1877 novel that became a school textbook and was extraordinarily popular under the Third Republic, with six million copies being sold before World War I. In the course of his two orphaned heroes' travels, the author distils much information on natural history, and when they visit the botanic garden in Paris she tells them that the great glass houses are there for studying the vegetation of other countries and that the institution gives courses on pruning trees, seedlings, planting and so forth.[48] In order to become a teacher, it was accordingly necessary to show evidence of a real aptitude for the natural sciences and a sound knowledge of the vegetable kingdom.[49] Besides, teacher training colleges in towns made small botanic gardens available to future teachers where they could prepare for their future responsibilities: courses in practical and theoretical botany, teaching agriculture and gardening. Generations of pupils who had benefited from a systematic initiation into the sciences of nature, from the simple object lesson to an apprenticeship in Linnaean nomenclature, reinforced the ranks of the many botanic, agricultural and horticultural societies that invigorated local life in the nineteenth and twentieth centuries. Furthermore, lines of communication were created between learned institutions and schools. In Nantes, free courses open to all, which had been abandoned in 1930, were relaunched in 1999, and have been supplemented since 2009 with activities in educational workshops, both theoretical and practical, aimed at pupils.[50] They have made it possible, as

48 G. Bruno, *Le Tour de la France par deux enfants* (Paris: Belin, 1904 [1877]), pp. 293–294.

49 Nicole Hulin, 'L'enseignement des sciences naturelles au XIXe siècle dans ses liens à d'autres disciplines', *Revue d'histoire des sciences* **55** (1) (2002): 101–120.

50 For this elaboration on the teachings of the Jardin des Plantes in Nantes, see Élodie Bonnet, Jardin des Plantes, Master 2 dissertation 'Valorization of the Economic and Cultural Heritage', 2012, pp. 7–12.

we have seen, to create a network of amateur botanists who can go around the town and inform the botanic garden of the existence of new or invasive wild species, for example.

Science as spectacle

From the end of the seventeenth century, practical experimentation became indispensable in the process of building scientific knowledge. There were many procedures that took place in the open air in front of curious onlookers. The presence of witnesses was vital to give evidence of the success or failure of an experiment; and this explains the slide towards the staging of science in the eighteenth century. For this purpose, natural spaces in towns became a favoured theatre.

Parks and public or private gardens were suitable for enthusiasts of astronomy or meteorology to make observations as they offered a clear view of the sky. In the eighteenth century, ownership of specialised instruments became commonplace, at least among the enlightened elite: people used them without any constraint save that of transporting them and with very little fuss, as is apparent in the testimony of the Duke of Croÿ in 1754: 'Being in the Tuileries which I admired as an artist and philosopher, as I wandered dreamily alone I came upon Monsieur Lemonnier. We had interests in common. I sat on the grass with him and forgot my own concerns ... We moved on to talk about telescopes ... As it was a fine night I suggested that we go and get his ready so that we could observe Saturn.'[51] By contrast, experiments in physics or chemistry, much prized by members of high society, and adding to their prestige, as seen in Carmontelle's portraits, required more elaborate preparations. On 15 April 1785 the mineralogist Faujas de Saint Fond conducted an experiment aiming to investigate the transformation of coal into tar, at the request of the minister Calonne who hoped to find industrial applications for it. The cream of Paris's royal authorities gathered in the King's Garden in a special enclosure. A furnace was built there linked to a series of apparatus for treating the smoke from the combustion and extracting from it tar, petroleum and volatile alkalis.[52] The great private gardens did

51 *Journal inédit du duc de Croÿ (1718–1784), publié par le vicomte de Grouchy et Paul Cottin d'après le manuscrit autographe conservé à la bibliothèque de l'Institut, avec introduction, notes et index* (Paris: Flammarion, 1906–1921, 4 vols), vol. 1, p. 288 [*Circa* août 1754].

52 Barthélémy Faujas de Saint-Fond, *Essai sur le goudron du charbon de terre* (Paris: Imprimerie Royale, 1790), p. 38–39.

not stand aside from science, particularly the Garden of the Chartreux in Paris which willingly authorised access to scholars recommended by the Academy.[53] In 1746 one Abbot Nollet, then at the height of his career (he was at the time tutor to the royal children), repeated a memorable experiment he had already tried on the Swiss Guards at Versailles: he administered an electric shock to a human chain of monks whom the audience saw leaping all at the same time. About this time, another scholar literally transformed the garden into an experimental terrain in order to evaluate the speed of transmission of electricity:

> Monsieur le Monnier employed to make the electric circuit, a wire nineteen hundred *toises* long, laid down in the enclosure … & another wire of almost two thousand *toises*, that is to say about a league. One part of the metal wire went across a meadow where the grass was wet with dew; another was carried on an elm palisade & twisted round several trees; lastly a long section trailed across newly dug earth: despite all these apparent obstacles the transmission of the electrical fluid took place.[54]

Lemonnier conducted similar experiments in the Tuileries and in the King's Garden, immersing the wire in pools and fountains, without changing the final result.

Even more than electricity demonstrations, ballooning was the epitome of science as a spectacle coming down to street level, or rather into parks and gardens large enough to contain the floods of curious spectators.[55]

A real madness for air-balloons overwhelmed Paris in the last quarter of the eighteenth century, which saw the competition between the teams of Étienne Montgolfier and Jacques Charles. The issue between the montgolfière and the charlière was which would first send a man in a balloon up, free, in the air. While Montgolfier was the first, with two men taking off in a balloon from the Muette garden on 21 May 1783, his competitor organised the most spectacular demonstrations: on 1 December 1783 a huge crowd – some said half of Paris – was present when a charlière, financed by public subscription, took off from the Tuileries garden; it set down its occupants two hours later in the fields in Nesles.[56] Whether one belonged to the grand world of society or

53 Émilie-Anne Pépy, 'Les Chartreux et les élites du savoir dans le royaume de France, aux XVIIe et XVIIIe siècles', in *Les Chartreux et les élites, XIIe–XVIIIe siècle: colloque international du CERCOR, 30–31 Août 2012*, *Analecta Cartusiana* 298 (Saint-Étienne: CERCOR, 2013), pp. 285–300.

54 Pierre Bertholon, *De l'électricité des météores* (Lyon: Bernuset, 1787), vol. 1, pp. 345–346.

55 Marie Thébaud-Sorger, *L'aérostation au temps des Lumières* (Rennes: Presses Universitaires de Rennes, 2009).

56 Bruno Belhoste, *Paris savant. Parcours et rencontres au temps des Lumières* (Paris: Armand Colin, 2011), pp. 143–145.

Figure 52.

Engraving representing an experiment conducted by Lemonnier on electricity in the garden of the Carthusian monks in Paris in 1746.
Source: Wikimedia commons.

to the humble people of the town it was unthinkable to miss out on a balloon take-off. On 2 March 1784 Mrs Cradock, the well-born Englishwoman on holiday in Paris, was present at Blanchard's ballooning experiment on the Champ de Mars, after having given her servant a day off so that she could also attend.[57] The boundary between scientific experiment and simple cheerful spectacle became ever more imprecise. As Mrs Cradock's journal for 11 July 1784 relates, it was necessary henceforward to pay for one's place.

> A day of adventures. They were going to launch an extraordinarily large balloon from the Luxembourg Gardens. Price of a ticket: 3 pounds. At half past ten we left in a largeish party, half French half English. A dense crowd had invaded the gardens; thus, we had the greatest difficulty in getting through the barrier to take the seats we had reserved. We waited for four hours and at the end of that time someone came to announce to us that the balloon would not be leaving.

57 *Journal de Mme Cradock, Voyage en France (1783–1786)*, trans. from the original and unpublished ms by O. Delphin-Baleyguier (Paris: Perrin, 1896), Tuesday, 2 Mar. 1784, p.10.

Figure 53.

Expérience Aërostatique, engraving, Paris, Basset, 1784.
Courtesy of BNF / Gallica: https://gallica.bnf.fr

While the English people and their friends may have managed to get over their disappointment by stripping the cafés and restaurants to organise an improvised picnic, others proved less phlegmatic: the price of a ticket and the hire of a well-placed chair represented the equivalent of a day's pay for a labourer. Frustration and anger explain some disturbances that took place on the fringe of the event, to the detriment of the vegetal surroundings where the machine remained anchored to the earth. 'In the evening I learned that the public had not taken things as well as we did. They forced the gates, broke the chairs and benches, and pulled the balloon to pieces; the guard even had to be called out for fear that they would attack the palace.'[58] In the highly competitive world of pleasure-gardens, the commercial interest of the innovation was swiftly noticed: balloons became a regular part of the entertainments on offer, more and more elaborately staged to fascinate visitors and to attract more people. Thus, at Tivoli in 1798 there took place

> The experiment of a balloon filled with inflammable gas which rose majestically into the air, with a Venus lying voluptuously in the basket; at a certain height she arose and, swaying from side to side, seemed to reveal her terror. When the balloon was about to enter the clouds, the basket detached itself and the Venus landed softly by parachute in the Champs Élysées.[59]

The provinces were also smitten with the passion for ballooning, to the extent that even middling-sized towns converted their green spaces into theatres for experiments that were as much spectacular as pedagogical. *Les Affiches de Poitiers* was proud to announce that on 16 December 1783 'the priests of the Oratory of our College launched from the public promenade an Air-Balloon thirty-two feet in circumference' which succeeded in staying aloft for about five minutes before subsiding onto the roof of a house.[60]

While the eighteenth century was the time for pioneers and the first amazing experiments with air-balloons, the general public's taste for this kind of spectacle did not abate during the nineteenth century, or before the inter-war period. Every festive or charitable occasion was an opportunity for towns to advertise their technical modernity, even though they had to use large sports grounds for this kind of demonstration. The national holiday of 14 July 1902 at Nantes featured a balloon race starting from the Champ de Mars;

58 Ibid., pp. 62–63.

59 Gilles-Antoine Langlois, *Folies, Tivolis et attractions : les premiers parcs de loisirs parisiens* (Paris: Délégation artistique à la ville de Paris, 1991), p. 99.

60 Michel-Vincent Chevrier (dir.), *Annonces, affiches, nouvelles et avis divers de la Province du Poitou*, Thursday, 1 Jan. 1784, p. 3.

according to the local press, the demonstration was so successful that workers were delayed in inflating the balloons as they were so hampered by floods of enthusiastic spectators. Another innovation tested out in urban green spaces was the steam engine, which aroused great interest as we have seen. From the middle of the nineteenth century, the Champs-Élysées was traversed by a steam-powered ancestor of our little trains that still delight tourists.

And what about the earliest automobiles that paraded along Parisian promenades, competing with and then eclipsing horse-drawn vehicles, formerly admired but these days obsolete?

Over and above conveying knowledge of vegetation, green spaces provided a stage setting for science and innovation in various, even extravagant, forms. In 1801 a somewhat crazy proposal was set before Napoleon Bonaparte: on 100,000 square metres of the Luxembourg Garden bordered by terraces and the palace façade there would be reproduced in its precise form each department of France. Little hillocks for mountains, marble channels for rivers, a small lake for the ocean in the west and columns or pyramids at the site of the chief town bearing the name of the department and its distance from Paris would round off the arrangement.[61] This of course was designed to educate the people of France about its geography and history, but that was not sufficiently pertinent to persuade the First Consul to have this sumptuous work realised.

If science, however spectacular it might have been, contaminated public gardens, then by the same token botanic gardens at times became somewhat commonplace: far from their initial scientific and pedagogic functions, they found themselves doing a bit of everything, the victims of their own success. In the nineteenth century, when a town acquired a botanic garden or undertook to extend an existing garden it was no longer because an intendant or a municipality shared the views of some botanists or doctors, as was the case before the Revolution. The demand then came from a large number of citizens, especially prominent ones, very active in associations dedicating themselves to the study of nature. And among their number some amateur philanthropists will be remembered for bequeathing their private gardens to the town of their birth in order to encourage a taste for the natural sciences in their contemporaries. Tarbes still today regards the botanist Placide Massey (1777–1853) as a benefactor. From a humble background, he was

61 Marie-Blanche d'Arneville, *La France des jardins et des espaces verts de 1789 à 1870*, Ph.D. diss., Paris-Sorbonne in 1986 under the direction of Jean Tulard, p. 173.

noticed by Cuvier and by the Bonaparte family and later became one of the chief administrators of the gardens at Versailles between 1818 and 1849. From 1829 he constructed a domain in his native town that sought to reflect his exceptional social trajectory. A botanic garden, a winter garden under glass, an arboretum and nurseries allowed the study of both the vegetal and agronomy in elegantly romantic surroundings. Massey was not able in his lifetime to achieve the construction of a museum of natural history linked with an observatory tower, a task which after 1853 reverted to the Société Académique de Tarbes (Tarbes Academic Society), recently founded with that end in view. While these scientific ambitions endured, they gradually became secondary to the pure recreational pleasure of the promenade and/ or meditation. The Jardin Massey rapidly became an essential stopping place for tourists on their way to the Pyrenean summits:

> The little town of Tarbes has a jewel which many great cities could envy, the Jardin Massey. It is not a simple square ... and the title botanic garden which it has been given is no exaggeration: it is fourteen hectares in area. [It] comprises an admirable collection of natural riches which, through their intelligent arrangement, are equally alluring to the young man and the old, the businessman and the poet, the philosopher and the scientist. It is a delightful and peaceful interlude, where a man can be alone and think, dream, reflect, observe, weep or pray as his spirit moves him.[62]

* * *

In his 'Poème du Jardin des Plantes' ('Botanic Garden Poem') Victor Hugo says of this place, 'It is a complete shortcut to a vast universe'.[63] The whole world, especially vegetal but sometimes animal too, has been invited into botanic gardens since they were first created. They are places where science, medical and botanic, was created and they have had to supply plants first to doctors and then to their counterparts in studying plants, cultivating them, adapting them to the climate of France, classifying them, analysing them and finally disseminating them. This programme of work made them, in Yves-Marie Allain's fine phrase, the 'garden of the universal',[64] a symbol of the European domination of the world. This ambition is obsolete today, for the confined space of urban gardens collides with the immense vegetal

62 J.-A. Lescamela, *Guide du touriste et du baigneur à Cauterets, à Saint-Sauveur et à Barèges* (Tarbes: J.-M. Dufour, 1865), pp. 24–27.

63 Victor Hugo, 'Le Poème du Jardin des Plantes', *L'Art d'être grand-père* (1877).

64 Allain, *Une histoire des jardins botaniques*, p. 108.

wealth of our planet. It also runs counter to our growing concern about avoiding intrusion by invasive species – some studies claim that more than half of these have spread out from botanic gardens.[65] While they remain sites of conservation and of work on fundamental biological mechanisms, in the towns where they exist, botanic gardens now play a vital recreational and pedagogical role.

65 Ibid.

CONCLUSION

The inhabitants of Woodstown in the United States should have been suspicious: in building their town by cutting down 3,000 trees to use for building and furniture, they were heading for disaster. The following spring, with a tremendous surge of life and sap, the forest resumed its rights; branches and leaves regrew on now misshapen furniture, roofs collapsed, roots and creepers invaded houses and streets, and boats' masts resumed their vegetal life. In a few days the town was obliterated, taken back by a vengeful, implacable and proud nature.

In Alphonse Daudet's fantastic 1873 tale, the inhabitants' mistake is to go against nature, to injure it with their hatchets and their axes. The forest takes umbrage at this 'insolent town' full of 'robbers'.[1] Here is a vision of American nature, wild and undaunted, that has to be conquered: however, is the attitude of Europe, or France in particular, so very different?

It was certainly necessary at the beginning to clear away threatening forest in order to set up towns. But, since the seventeenth century, a more peaceful relationship between towns and their hinterland has been established. Nature was welcomed within the town boundaries and domesticated in private gardens, noble or ecclesiastical. She was seen in the streets and the streams and rivers; and she was there in the fallow places, wilder and shaggier than elsewhere; and soon she extended her empire, in the gentle guise of esplanades, promenades and the ever-increasing number of public gardens evolving down the centuries. The thieving, insubordinate town? As nineteenth century technicist pride increasingly dreamed of complete mastery over the vegetal, Daudet's fable destroys the illusion of omnipotence. The Baudelairean dream that we described in the introduction is becoming realised: not a completely mineral town, it is true, but one with nature so perfectly controlled – in parks and public spaces – that it seems to be just artifice. The decades which followed World War II came closest to this, with the use of herbicides and the dumping of fertiliser on soulless green spaces, in towns that spread themselves like parasites over their surroundings.

The counter-movement launched in the 1970s, which we have described in its various aspects, is decisive in representing the return to favour of another nature, more abundant, freer, more shared; but also, since then, bursting with

1 Alphonse Daudet, 'Woodstown', *Le Bien public*, 27 May 1873.

new urban practices, and revealing a particular vision, that of the garden-town.

Today, the garden is less and less thought of as enclosed within a limited space: it flows over its walls and spreads over the whole town, erasing the distinctions between public and private space, and between ornamental and wild plants. An ecological concern, an aspiration towards naturalness in gardens and green spaces, insists on their relationship throughout towns and even beyond: the town is seen as one stage in the continuity that is looked for between regional countryside and the microcosm of the private garden. Plants adapted to local ecosystems, ecological corridors, green or blue networks, projects for intercommunal parks, regional improvement plans – all these things come together, at least in theory, in the extending of the gardened-town. Paradoxically, this quest for the green is mediated by an intersecting technicity, reconciling the artificiality of urban space with vegetal profusion on roofs, walls and terraces and in all the little gaps between concrete and brick.

This greening of the town is laden, sometimes exploitatively, with all kinds of virtues. Should we be surprised by this? As we have sought to show in this study, urban nature is loaded with meanings, sometimes changing as time goes on, but at the intersection of urban practices and interpretations. Health is almost always central, and nature is the antidote to the town, not its opposite; but from being a breathing space or a place of rest, it has today become the cure for all ills – pollution, stress, climatic warming, and so on. These days it is ecological, it reinstalls the citizen in an ecosystem in order to sustain its diversity and its soothing, curative capacities. In terms of ideology, it implies social order and reflects dominant values, it facilitates the learning of sound behaviour, it educates and teaches morals. Today what we expect from nature is solidarity, social responsibility and inclusion. But when politics battens on to the vegetal it can become transgressive, the object or the site of conflict, offering the hope of an escape or a rejection. Aesthetics play their part, when power or rank express themselves through the vegetal, when it makes socialisation possible or by contrast favours segregation. Botanic science is never static; it extends the range of the possible and then innovates in the town and for the town. In its productive guise, then, lost for a while but today partly found again, urban nature becomes a source of physical activity, of healthy and balanced nutrition, even of an alternative economic system. These are among the innumerable aspects of the vegetal in towns, and this explains the hopes that are vested in it.

The conference 'Villes jardinées et initiatives citoyennes' (Gardened towns and citizens' initiatives) held in October 2012 in Strasbourg concluded with a 'Déclaration des droits universels à la ville jardinée' (Declaration of universal right to a gardened-town), which has become the route to a real revolution in our lifestyles:

> In all humility, we, citizens of the World, declare that, from humus to humans, gardened cities are henceforth a vital dimension of our future …
> Gardened cities contribute to the change in economic model by:
> – introducing new moneyless exchange systems (material or immaterial exchanges, cashless exchanges)
> – promoting citizen involvement in the design and management of their environment (balconies, terraces, sidewalks, green spaces, parks …)
> – encouraging self-production with the goal of increasing food security and food self-sufficiency
> – promoting local employment by producing and consuming locally
> – allowing easier access to plots of earth and gardens by the management of public lands.

In the style of this declaration, the ecological urban utopia often robes itself in controversy: the greening of towns is not thought of as a merely decorative issue, as we have understood, but as a fundamental, almost ontological, issue for western societies. It is a fairer world, where sharing dominates with nature cultivated communally, where private property is, if not abolished, much reduced. This, to give an example, is the spirit of the Jardins d'Utopie (Utopia Gardens) at Grenoble: this 8,000 square metre kitchen garden was created in 2006 on a hitherto unused piece of university land, without the endorsement of the administrative authorities, in order 'to suggest concrete answers to our questioning of the organisation of society and of the food production system in particular'. There are multiple objectives: to promote self-management, autonomy, better nutrition, avoiding commercial networks, repairing a social fabric damaged by a toxic economic system, and so on.[2] This is truly an alternative society that needs to be experimented with, like the more thoughtful version of *guerilla gardening* which we described in Chapter 3. A more fraternal society too, if one so regards the movement of support for Eritrean and Sudanese migrants set up in June 2015 in the Jardins d'Éole in Paris, where a relay of people take turns in conveying food, care, and clothing to these illegals, and even in protecting them from drug traffickers.

Alongside these controversial utopias, but rarely in contact with them, a technical movement, both pragmatic and visionary, has emerged, which puts architecture at the very centre of future urban greening. It is based on many commissions or demonstrations, like *Jardins, jardin* which, since 2004, has

2 http://jardins-utopie.over-blog.com/

Figure 54.

Jardins d'Utopie, 2017, Grenoble-Alpes University Campus.
Courtesy of Clarisse Coulomb.

brought together in the Tuileries all those with an interest in urban nature, such as businesses, landscapers, the media, students, amateurs. There one finds temporary landscape installations, and very many exhibitors and nurserymen specialising in urban gardens, activities for children, and so on. Above all, since 2010, prizes, such as that for the innovative object, and the Green City prize, awarded to designers and landscapers, have aimed at inventing the garden city of tomorrow, proposing objects and concrete actions for managing and extending urban nature. In the 2015 event the specified theme was 'the happy city'. In 2011, in an exhibition on the town of the future, the Cité de l'architecture et du patrimoine (City of Architecture and Heritage) saw it as a 'fertile city' where there would be buildings in 'vegetal concrete' with façades of 'algal photobioreactors' – already the subjects of patents.[3] It seems that the

3 *La Ville fertile. Vers une nature urbaine*, Exhibition at the Cité de l'architecture et du patrimoine, Special Issue *Paysage. Actualités* (Mar. 2011): 10.

imagination of architects, landscapers and town-planners is boundless when it comes to uniting the town and nature: squares and private gardens which are aerial (up on high), garden bridges linking one to another, vertical squares (with several levels), mobile and temporary gardens, etc.[4] A Flower Tower has seen the light of day in the seventeenth arrondissement in Paris, and a vegetal tower sixty metres high has been proposed for the Île de Nantes: the Édouard François consultancy which is behind these projects, sees glimpses of a new town-planning, combining urban biodiversity with high-rise building.[5] The boldest are not content with just building, however spectacularly, but are already imagining the green town as it will be in a century's time. This is what is occupying the architect Luc Schuiten in relation to such towns as Lyon, Strasbourg and Nantes which he envisages in 2100 as being, to use his own term, 'archiborescent': in his wonderful drawings the town takes nature as its model and even uses natural materials and structures as it evolves.[6]

Luc Schuiten is not alone in this undertaking: all over the world people are imagining, experimenting and creating. In 2015 the architect Vincent Callebaut advanced a futuristic vision of Paris entitled 'Paris Smart City 2050': to address climatic warming and population growth he and his team imagined a profoundly vegetalised city, featuring positive energy green towers, some depolluting, others as dwellings or vertical farms.[7] This is of course a futurist vision, but it is based on techniques that are already in place: it is a practical, concrete initiative to 'transform the town of tomorrow into a mature tropical forest'[8] or 'an urban natural system'. Here again, as is the case with Luc Schuiten, the recourse to nature is not thought of as purely cosmetic, but as a profound transformation of the town, which has to turn from unyielding grey to porous green. Completely reinvented, it is based on a circular economy where everything that is made and consumed is recycled; where the buildings are not inert, but create energy; and where zoning by function no longer exists, as agricultural spaces, offices

4 Jean-Baptiste Vaquin (ed.), *Atlas de la Nature à Paris* (Paris: Atelier Parisien d'Urbanisme, 2006), pp. 280–283.

5 http://www.edouardfrancois.com/fr/projets/hauteur/details/article/145/tour-vegetale-de-nantes/#.VXsJeaaZQ-8

6 http://www.vegetalcity.net/

7 http://vincent.callebaut.org/page1-img-parissmartcity2050.html

8 Vincent Callebaut, in an interview in 'Des bâtiments "mangeurs" de brouillard pour lutter contre la pollution', *Atlantico*, 5 Apr. 2015. http://www.atlantico.fr/rdv/atlantico-green/batiments-mangeurs-brouillard-pour-lutter-contre-pollution-vincent-callebaut-2075471.html

and dwellings all coexist within vast towers that Vincent Callebaut calls 'vertical villages'.[9]

Dreams with no future? Maybe, but at least they bear witness to new hopes – a bit wild at times – lodged in the redeeming virtues of urban nature. Just a passing fashion? Not so, if one thinks of all the qualitative and quantitative progress made over the last thirty years in vegetalising towns, and of the extraordinary inventiveness expressed everywhere in some measure. Renewed attention to *place* and its physical or climatic constraints should not lead to overlooking the *moment* in which it is inscribed. Nature in towns has a history which this work has set out to trace: to ignore it in apparently historically rootless projects will get one nowhere; if the future is to be vegetal, it will only succeed if it builds on the strata of known and acknowledged history. Then perhaps the dream of Julien Gracq, a peaceful version of Daudet's nightmare, will come about:

> Wherever I go today, if there is a chance, if I've got an hour to lose in an unfamiliar town, an agreeable diversion takes me along streets towards calm green enclaves surrounded in our time by the circulation of traffic and stared at from above by the high rise blocks of flats and towers which show through the leaves of cedars and catalpas around them.
>
> I see in these green Noah's arks just so many modest treasure chests, beaten everywhere, misguided, squeezed by the tide of urbanisation, but whose explosive vegetal power will one day bring new life to abandoned cities.[10]

9 'Quelle ville pour demain?' *Planète Terre*, France Culture, 16 June 2015.

10 Julien Gracq, *La Forme d'une ville* (Paris: José Corti, 1985), p. 39.

ACKNOWLEDGEMENTS

Writing this book would not have been possible without the help of many people we met during its elaboration, and whom we would like to thank warmly here. The kind welcome we received in Nantes from Jacques Soignon, Director of the Green Spaces and Environment Service and Romaric Perrocheau, Director of the Jardin des Plantes, and the interviews they gave us, were particularly useful, as was the information kindly provided by Christophe Ferlin, Director of the Annecy Green Spaces Services. The staff of the Dubreuil municipal library also opened their doors and resources to us with great care and competence. Caroline Gutleben, director of Plante & Cité, gave us access to the association's very rich documentary portal. In our search for illustrations, we were able to benefit from the precious help of the National Federation of allotment and community gardens, which opened its archives to us; of Vincent Le Gall, in charge of the archives of Plessis-Robinson; of the association of the friends of Albert Robida; of Luc Schuiten, who kindly gave us the reproduction rights of one of his plates; as well as of Clarisse Coulomb and Julie Damaggio, who kindly accepted that their photographs illustrate the pages of this book in both English and French editions. Our sincere gratitude extends to Patrick Beaune of Champvallon Editions, and to Sarah Johnson of White Horse Press, for the trust they have placed in our book and their hard work in bringing it to a successful conclusion. We would also like to thank the universities Savoie Mont Blanc and Bordeaux-Montaigne, as well as the Centre de Recherches Historiques (EHESS) and the Centre d'Études des Mondes Modernes et Contemporains (Bordeaux-Montaigne University) for their financial help in the translation of this book. Finally, we would like warmly to thank Moya Jones for her involvement in the project, and for all the care she took in the English translation.

BIBLIOGRAPHY

Abad, Reynald, *Le Grand Marché. L'approvisionnement alimentaire de Paris sous l'Ancien Régime* (Paris: Fayard, 2002).

Adamkiewicz, Éric, 'Nouvelles pratiques et sports autonomes dans la ville. Creation of new types of relationships with the urban. L'exemple lyonnais', in Christian Vivier and Jean-François Loudcher, *Le Sport dans la ville* (Paris: l'Harmattan, 1998), pp. 303–313.

Aggéri, Gaëlle, 'Le sauvage dans les villes: du wild garden à la gestion différenciée', *Le Jardin et la Nature dans la Cité* (Besançon: Institut Claude-Nicolas Ledoux, 2002).

Aggeri, Gaëlle, *Inventer les villes-natures de demain* (Dijon: Educagri, 2010).

Agulhon, Maurice (dir.), *Histoire de la France urbaine. La ville de l'âge industriel* (Paris: Seuil, 1998).

Alary, Éric, Bénédicte Vergez-Chaignon and Gilles Gauvin, *Les Français au quotidien, 1939–1949* (Paris: Perrin, 2006).

Allain, Yves-Marie, *D'où viennent nos plantes?* (Paris: Calmann-Lévy, 2004).

Allain, Yves-Marie, *Une histoire des jardins botaniques, entre science et art paysager* (Versailles: Quae, 2012).

Alphandéry, Pierre and Olivier Nougarède, 'Le silvarium de la Grande Bibliothèque', *Courrier de l'environnement de l'INRA* **24** (1995): 59–66.

Ambrosoli, Mauro, 'Marcher la nuit sans lanterne, c'est cueillir thistle pour luzerne…', *Études rurales* 151–152 (1999): 77-102.

André, Florence and Stéphanie de Courtois (dir.), *Édouard André, un paysagiste botaniste sur les chemins du monde* (n.p.: Éditions de l'imprimerie, 2002).

Andrieu, Bernard and Olivier Sirost, 'Introduction l'écologie corporelle', *Sociétés* 125 (2014/3): 5–10.

Anonymous, 'Enjeux de l'espace public (1970–2010)', in Hervé Brunon and Monique Mosser (dir.), *L'Art du jardin. Du début du XXe siècle à nos jours* (Paris: CNDP, 2011).

Anonymous, 'L'émergence internationale du paysagisme (1940–1970)', in Hervé Brunon and Monique Mosser (dir.), *L'Art du jardin. Du début du XXe siècle à nos jours* (Paris: CNDP, 2011).

Ansart, Cédric and Emmanuel Boutefeu, 'Sous le pavé, les fleurs', *Métropolitiques*, special issue *Nature(s) en ville* (February 2013) http://www.metropolitiques.eu/Nature-s-en-ville.html

Arnould, Paul et al. 'Nature in the city: The improbable biodiversity', *Geography, Economics, Society* **13** (1) (2011).

Aubry, Christine and Jeanne Pourias, 'L'agriculture urbaine fait déjà partie du "métabolisme urbain"', *Déméter* (2013) http://www.clubdemeter.com/ledemeter.php ?demeter=2013

Audouy, Michel and Michel Péna, *Petite histoire du jardin et du paysage en ville* (Paris: Alternatives, 2011).

Audouy, Michel, Jean-Pierre Le Dantec, Yves Nussaume and Chiara Santini (eds), *Le grand*

Pari(s) d'Alphand: création et transmission d'un paysage urbain (Paris: Éditions de La Villette, 2018).

Bailly, Antoine and Lise Bourdeau-Lepage, 'Concilier désir de nature et préservation de l'environnement : vers une urbanisation durable en France', *Géographie, économie, société* **13** (1) (2011): 27–43.

Baratay, Éric and Élisabeth Hardouin-Fugier, *Zoos. Histoire des jardins zoologiques en Occident (XVIe–XXe siècle)* (Paris: La Découverte, 1998).

Baridon, Michel, *Les Jardins* (Paris: Laffont, 1998).

Barles, Sabine 'Les villes transformées par la santé, XVIIIe–XXe siècles', *Les Tribunes de la santé* **33** (4) (2011): 31–37.

Barles, Sabine et al., 'Grain, meat and vegetables to feed Paris: Where did and do they come from? Localising Paris food supply areas from the eighteenth to the twenty-first century', *Regional Environmental Change* **12** (2) (2012).

Barles, Sabine and Nathalie Blanc (dir.), *Ecologies urbaines: sur le terrain* (Paris: Economica, 2016).

Baumier, Béatrice, *Tours entre Lumières et Révolution, pouvoir municipal et métamorphoses d'une ville (1764–1792)* (Rennes: PUR, 2007).

Beauthéac, Nadine (dir.), *Les Carnets de l'exotisme,* Special issue, *Les jardins du retour* 13 (1st semester 1994).

Beck, Robert, 'La promenade du peuple des villes (fin XVIIIe–XIXe siècles). L'exemple du peuple de Paris', in Philippe Guignet (dir.), *Le Peuple des villes dans l'Europe du Nord-Ouest* (Lille: Centre de Recherches sur l'Histoire de l'Europe du Nord-Ouest, 2002), vol. I, pp. 247–266.

Béguin, Katia and Olivier Dautresme (dir.), *La ville et l'esprit de société*, proceedings of the study day 27 May 2002 (Tours: Presses universitaires François Rabelais, 2004).

Belhoste, Bruno, *Paris savant. Parcours et rencontres au temps des Lumières* (Paris: Armand Colin, 2011).

Belmas, Élisabeth, *Jouer autrefois: essai sur le jeu dans la France moderne XVIe–XVIIIe siècle* (Seyssel: Champ Vallon, 2006).

Bernard de Raymond, Antoine, *En toute saison: le marché des fruits et légumes en France* (Rennes: PUR, 2013).

Béroujon, Anne, *Peuple et pauvres des villes dans la France moderne* (Paris: Armand Colin, 2014).

Berque, Augustin, 'Des toits, des étoiles', *Les Annales de la Recherche Urbaine*, 'Natures en villes', 74 (March 1997).

Berque, Augustin, Philippe Bonnin and Cynthia Ghorra-Gobin (dir.), *La Ville insoutenable* (Paris: Belin, 2006).

Berque, Augustin, *Histoire de l'habitat idéal* (Paris: Le Félin, 2016).

Béthemont, Jacques and Guy Mercier, *La Ville en quête de nature* (Québec: Septentrion, 1998).

Bizet, Michel and Alain Meyrier, 'Annecy côté jardin', *Revue Annesci* 31 (1990).

Blanc, Nathalie et al., 'Governance of urban nature', *Articulo - Journal of Urban Research* (2017), http://articulo.revues.org/3212

Blanchon-Caillot, Bernadette, 'Pratiques et compétences paysagistes dans les grands ensembles d'habitation, 1945–1975', *Strates* 13 (2007), http://strates.revues.org.janus.biu.sorbonne.fr/5723

Bonnet Élodie, Jardin des Plantes, Dossier documentaire de l'exposition 'Le public du jardin des Plantes, d'hier à aujourd'hui', Nantes, Master's dissertation 'Valorisation du Patrimoine Economique et Culturel' (2012).

Bonneuil, Christophe, *Des savants pour l'empire. La structuration des recherches scientifiques coloniales au temps de la 'mise en valeur des colonies françaises', 1917–1945* (Paris: éditions de l'ORSTOM, 1991).

Bordes, Maurice (dir.), *Histoire d'Auch et du pays d'Auch* (Roanne: Horvath, 1980).

Borne, Dominique, *Histoire de la société française depuis 1945* (Paris: Armand Colin, 1992).

Bourdeau-Lepage, Lise and Roland Vidal (dir.), *Nature en ville: attentes citadines et actions publiques (Nature in the city : expectations and public actions)* (Paris: Archibooks, 2014).

Bourdeau-Lepage, Lise and Roland Vidal, 'Nature urbaine en débat: à quelle demande sociale répond la nature en ville?' *Déméter* (2013): 195–210.

Bourgery, Corinne, 'Castres, le renouvellement des arbres urbains', *Metropolis (urbanism, regional planning, environment)*, Special Issue, *L'urbanisme végétal* 96–97 (1992).

Bourguet, Marie-Noëlle and Pierre-Yves Lacour, 'Les mondes naturalistes: Europe (1530–1802)', in Pestre Dominique (ed.), *Histoire des sciences et des savoirs*, vol. 1, *De la Renaissance aux Lumières*, (Paris : Seuil, 2015) pp. 255–281.

Boursier-Mougenot, Ernest J.-P. and Michel Racine, *Les Jardins de la Côte d'Azur* (Aix-en-Provence: Édisud-Arpej, 1987).

Boutefeu, Emmanuel, 'La nature en ville: des enjeux paysagers et sociétaux', *Géoconfluences*, 28 April 2007, http://geoconfluences.ens-lyon.fr/doc/transv/paysage/PaysageViv.htm

Boutefeu, Emmanuel, *Composer avec la nature en ville* (Paris: CERTU, 2001).

Bowie, Karen, *La Modernité avant Haussmann. Formes de l'espace urbain à Paris 1801–1853* (n.p., Éditions Recherches, 2001).

Bradel, Vincent, 'Du jardin à la ville: Lunéville-Nancy', in Daniel Rabreau and Sandra Pascalis (eds), *La Nature citadine au siècle des Lumières* (Bordeaux: Arts & Arts, 2005).

Brand, Caroline and Serge Bonnefoy, 'L'alimentation des sociétés urbaines: une cure de jouvence pour l'agriculture des territoires urbains?' *VertigO* **11** (2) (2011).

Brault, Yoann, 'Fortifications, esplanades et champs de Mars. Nature citadine et principes de contiguïté entre civils et militaires', in Daniel Rabreau and Sandra Pascalis, *La Nature citadine au siècle des Lumières* (Bordeaux: Arts & Arts, 2005), pp. 203–213.

Brunon, Hervé and Monique Mosser (dir.), *L'Art du jardin. Du début du XXe siècle à nos jours* (Paris: CNDP, 2011).

Brutel, Chantal and David Levy, 'Le nouveau zonage en aires urbaines de 2010', *Insee Première*, 1374 (October 2011), http://www.insee.fr/fr/ffc/ipweb/ip1374/ip1374.pdf

Buridant, Jérôme, 'Flottage des bois et gestion forestière: l'exemple du Bassin parisien du XVIe au XIXe siècle', *Eau et forêt, Revue forestière française* 4 (July–August 2006): 389–398.

Burstin, Haim, *Le Faubourg Saint-Marcel à l'époque révolutionnaire. Structure économique et composition sociale* (Paris: Société des études robespierristes, 2012).

References

Cabedoce, Béatrice and Philippe Pierson, *Cent ans d'histoire des jardins ouvriers* (Grâne: Créaphis, 1996).

Calenge, Christian, 'De la nature de la ville', *Les Annales de la Recherche Urbaine*, 'Natures en villes', 74, (March 1997).

Callais, Chantal and Thierry Jeanmonod, *Bordeaux, World Heritage* (La Crèche: Geste éditions, 2012).

Cénat, Jean-Philippe, 'Chamlay (1650–1719), le stratège oublié de Louis XIV', *Revue historique des armées* 263 (2011): 53–62.

CEREMA, *Implication citoyenne et nature en ville* (Bron: Éditions du Cerema, 2016).

Chabaud, B., 'Les jardins de la Côte d'Azur', in A. Robertson-Proschowsky, G. Roster and B. Chabaud, *La Résistance au froid des palmiers* (Marly le roi: Champflour, 1998).

Chansigaud, Valérie, *Histoire des Fleurs* (Paris: Delachaux and Niestlé, 2014).

Choay, Françoise, 'Pensées sur la ville, arts de la ville', in Maurice Agul-hon (dir.), *Histoire de la France urbaine. La ville de l'âge industriel* (Paris: Seuil, 1998), pp. 251–265.

Choay, Françoise, *L'Urbanisme, utopies et réalités* (Paris: Seuil, 1965).

Chomarat-Ruiz, Catherine (dir.), *Nature urbaine en projets* (Paris: Archibooks, 2014).

Chomarat-Ruiz, Catherine (dir.), *Nature Citadine series* (n.p., Editopics, 2015):

- Donadieu, Pierre (dir.), *Agriurbanization: Dreams or Reality?*
- Chomarat-Ruiz, Catherine (dir.), *The Utopia of a Sustainable City.*
- Santini, Chiara (dir.), *Forms and Patterns of Urban Nature (19th and 20th Centuries).*
- Chomarat-Ruiz, Catherine (ed.), *Urban Art Eclipses. Vers une éthique de la nature citadine.*
- Chomarat-Ruiz, Catherine (dir.), *Nature/City: A New Alliance.*

Choquette, Leslie, 'Homosexuals in the City', *Journal of Homosexuality* **41** (3–4) (2002): 149–167.

Cirès, Jean-Louis, *La construction des jardins publics à Paris sous le Second Empire*, Master's dissertation, under the direction of Alain Corbin, University of Tours, 1985.

Clément, Gilles, *Le Jardin en mouvement* (Paris: Pandora, 1991).

Clément, Gilles, Yves Laissus, Pascal Heurtel et al., *Le Jardin des Plantes* (Paris: MNHN, 2006).

Clergeau, Philippe (dir.), *Ville et Biodiversité* (Rennes: PUR, 2011).

Clergeau, Philippe and Nathalie Blanc (dir.), *Trames vertes urbaines* (Paris: Éditions du Moniteur, 2013).

Conan, Michel and Juliette Favaron, 'Comment les villages devinrent des paysages', *Annales de la recherche urbaine*, 'Natures en villes', 74 (March 1997).

Conan, Michel, 'Les hortillons', in Michel Racine (dir.), *Créateurs de jardins et de paysage*, volume II (Arles: Actes Sud, 2002), pp. 64–69.

Conan, Michel, *Dictionnaire historique de l'art des jardins* (Paris: Hazan, 1997).

Contoz, Pierre, 'Besançon. L'histoire et les arbres', *Métropolis, Dossier L'urbanisme végétal* 96–97.

Cook, Alexandra, 'Le pluralisme taxonomique de Jean-Jacques Rousseau', in Claire Jacquier and Timothée Léchot (dir.), *Rousseau botaniste: Je vais devenir plante moi-même* (Pontarlier: éditions du Belvédère, 2012), pp. 37–56.

Corajoud, Michel, 'Territorialité du paysage', *Temps Libre* 9 (Spring 1984).

Corbin, Alain et al., *Les Usages politiques des fêtes aux XIXe–XXe siècles* (Paris: Publications de la Sorbonne, 1994).

Corbin, Alain, 'Les balbutiements d'un temps pour soi', in Alain Corbin (ed.), *L'Avènement des loisirs, 1850–1960* (Paris: Flammarion, 1995), p. 448–469.

Coulomb, Clarisse, *Les Pères de la patrie. La société parlementaire en Dauphiné au temps des Lumières* (Grenoble: PUG, 2006).

Couplan, François, *Plantes urbaines* (Paris: Sang de la Terre, 2010).

Cronier, Emmanuelle, 'The Street', in Jay Winter (ed.), *Capital Cities at War. Paris, London, Berlin, a Cultural History* (Cambridge: CUP, 2007).

Cronon, William, *Nature's Metropolis. Chicago and the Great West* (New York: Norton, 1991).

Croze, Philippe, 'Étude de potentialité des sites sur la ville de Montpellier', in Proceedings of the colloquium *Vers la gestion différenciée des espaces verts* (Strasbourg: CNFPT, AIVF, October 1994), pp. 73-81.

D'Anthenaise, Claude, 'Jardins de papier', in Catherine de Bourgoing (dir.), *Jardins romantiques français* (Paris: Les musées de la ville de Paris, 2011).

D'Arneville, Marie-Blanche, *La France des jardins et des espaces verts de 1789 à 1870*, Ph.D. thesis defended at the Université Paris-Sorbonne in 1986 under the supervision of Jean Tulard.

D'Orgeix, Émilie, 'Zones Non aedificandi. La politique du vide dans les places forteresses (1550–1789)', dissertation by HDR, University of Bordeaux Montaigne, 2016.

De Bourgoing, Catherine (dir.), *Jardins romantiques français* (Paris: Les musées de la ville de Paris, 2011).

Debié, Frank, *Jardins de Capitales* (Paris: CNRS editions, 1992).

Démeter, *Dossier Nature et Agriculture pour la Ville* (2013) http://www.clubdemeter.com/ledemeter.php ?demeter=2013

Denis, Laurent, *Du jardin partagé au jardin de trottoir, Nature de quartier et éco-citoyenneté à Lyon*, Master 2 dissertation, National Museum of Natural History, 2010.

Descola, Philippe, *Par-delà nature et culture* (Paris: Gallimard, 2005).

Despommier, Dickson, *The Vertical Farm* (New York: St Martin's Press, 2010).

Deverre, Christian and Jean-Baptiste Traversac, 'Manger local, une utopie concrète', *Métropolitiques*, 26 October 2011, http ://www.metropolitiques.eu/Manger-local-une-utopie-concrete.html

Dubost, Françoise, *Vert Patrimoine* (Paris: MSH, 1994).

Duby, Georges, *Histoire de la France urbaine*, volume IV, *La Ville de l'âge industriel*, dir. Maurice Agulhon (Paris: Seuil, 1998).

Duréault, Jérôme, *Architecture contemporaine et nature en ville*, AgroCampus Ouest final dissertation, 2013, https://dumas.ccsd.cnrs.fr/dumas-00906453/document

Duris, Pascal, *Linné et la France (1780–1850)* (Geneva: Droz, 1993).

Ébert-Cau, Isabelle, 'Aimé Bonpland, Les Carnets de l'exotisme', special issue *Les Jardins du retour* 13 (1st semester 1994), dir. Nadine Beauthéac.

Elliott, Paul A., *British Urban Trees. A Social and Cultural History, c. 1800–1914* (Winwick, Cambridgeshire: The White Horse Press, 2016).

Emanuel, M.B., 'Hay fever, a post industrial revolution epidemic: a history of its growth during the nineteenth century', *Clinical Allergy* **18** (1988): 295–304.

Emelianoff, Cyria, 'Pour un partage de la fabrique urbaine', *Revue urbanisme*, special issue, 'La ville durable en question(s)', 363 (November–December 2008).

Estavoyer, Lyonel, *Besançon au siècle des Lumières* (Besançon: Cêtre, 1978).

Farge, Arlette and Laurent Turcot, *Flagrant délis à la promenade des Champs-Élysées, les dossiers Ferdinand de Federici, 1777–1791* (Paris: Gallimard, 2008).

Farge, Arlette, *Essai pour une histoire des voix au XVIIIe siècle* (Paris: Bayard, 2009).

Faure, Olivier, *Histoire sociale de la médecine (XVIIIe–XXe siècles)* (Paris: Anthro-pos-Economica, 1994).

Fillinger, Gilbert, *Art, villes et paysage. Hortillonnages Amiens* (Amiens: Éditions trois cailloux, 2014).

Fournier, Patrick, 'La ville au milieu des marais aux XVIIe et XVIIIe siècles', *Histoire urbaine* **18** (1) (2007): 23–40.

Frioux, Stéphane, 'Des espaces libres aux espaces verts, 1908–1952', communication, ENS-LSH, 4 March 2008.

Gérard Bory et al. 'L'arbre et les opérations de taille', in Louis-Marie Rivière (dir.), *La Plante dans la ville* (Paris: INRA, 1997).

Germain, Michel, *La Vie quotidienne à Annecy pendant la guerre, 1939–1945* (Montmélian: La Fontaine de Siloé, 2005).

Goerg, Odile and Xavier Huetz de Lemps, *La Ville coloniale XVe–XXe siècles* (Paris: Seuil, 2012).

Grésillon, Étienne, *Une géographie de l'au-delà? Les jardins de religieux catholiques, des interfaces entre profane et sacré*, doctoral thesis in geography, Paris IV, 2009.

Guignet, Philippe (dir.), *Le Peuple des villes dans l'Europe du Nord-Ouest* (Lille: Centre de Recherches sur l'Histoire de l'Europe du Nord-Ouest, 2002).

Guillot, Pascal, *La Nature en révolution – de la liberté de la chasse aux arbres de la liberté*, Master's dissertation, Lille, Délégation Régionale à l'Architecture et à l'Environnement, 1989.

Guineau, Claude, 'Saint-Quentin-en-Yvelines. Le comportement des arbres en ville nouvelle', *Metropolis (urbanisme, planification régionale, environnement)*, Special Issue 'L'urbanisme végétal', 96–97.

Hallé, Francis and Pierre Lieutaghi, *Aux origines des plantes* (Paris: Fayard, 2008).

Hardy-Hémery, Odette, 'Les cités-jardins de la Compagnie du chemin de fer du Nord: un habitat ouvrier aux marges de la ville', *Revue du Nord* 374 (2008/1): 131–151.

Hedelin Claude et al., 'L'architecture végétale dans la conduite des arbres urbains', in Louis-Marie Rivière (ed.), *La Plante dans la ville* (Paris: IN-RA, 1997).

Hiegel, Charles, 'Les arbres de la Liberté dans le département de la Moselle', *Les Cahiers lorrains* 4 (December 1999).

Hopkins, Richard S., 'Sauvons le Luxembourg: Urban greenspace as private domain and public battleground, 1865–1867', *Journal of Urban History* **37** (1) (2011): 43–58.

Hopkins, Richard S., *Planning the Greenspaces of Nineteenth-century Paris* (Baton Rouge: Louisiana State University Press, 2015).

Hulin, Nicole, 'L'enseignement des sciences naturelles au XIXe siècle dans ses liens à d'autres disciplines', *Revue d'histoire des sciences* **55** (1) (2002): 101–120.

Ile de France, Service Patrimoines et Inventaires, *Montreuil, patrimoine horticole* (Lyon: Lieux dits éditions, 1999 and 2016).

Ives, Colta, *Public Parks, Private Gardens. Paris to Provence* (New Haven/London: Yale University Press/the MET, 2018).

Jarassé, Dominique, *Grammaire des jardins parisiens* (Paris: Parigramme, 2007).

Jovet, Paul and Bernadette Lizet, *Les Herbes folles du Jardin des Plantes* (Paris: Muséum National d'Histoire Naturelle, 1990).

Jovet, Paul, 'Végétation des lignes aériennes du chemin de fer métropolitain de Paris I', *Bulletin de la Société Botanique de France* 92 (1945): 92–97.

Jovet, Paul, 'Végétation des lignes aériennes du chemin de fer métropolitain de Paris II', *Bulletin de la Société Botanique de France* 92 (1945): 105–109.

Juhé-Beaulaton, Dominique, 'Du jardin royal des plantes médicinales de Paris aux jardins coloniaux : développement de l'agronomie tropicale française', in Jean Louis Fischer (dir.), *Le Jardin entre science et représentation* (Paris: CTHS, 1999), p. 8, https://halshs.archives-ouvertes.fr/halshs-00089363

Kaplan, Steven, *Les Ventres de Paris: pouvoir et approvisionnement dans la France d'Ancien Régime* (Paris: Fayard, 1988).

Kebir, Leïla and Bernard Barraqué, 'Éditorial', *Espaces et sociétés* 158 (2014/3): 9–12.

Kern, Catherine, 'Du jardin d'Hildegarde de Bingen aux jardins thérapeutiques contemporains en Alsace', paper given at the first symposium of the Association Jardins et Santé, 'Jardins à but thé-rapeutique en milieu hospitalier et médico-social', 23 May 2008, http://www.jardins-sante.org/2008/80-symposium-jets/symposium2008/253-s2008-deroulement

Kury, Lorelai, 'Les instructions de voyage dans les expéditions scientifiques françaises. 1750–1830', *Revue d'histoire des sciences* **51** (1998): 65–91.

La ville durable et ses territoires de nature (Colloquium proceedings) (Dardilly: Société des éditions horticoles de France, 2008).

Lacour, Pierre-Yves, 'Les Amours de Mars et Flore aux cabinets. Les confiscations naturalistes en Europe septentrionale. 1794–1795', *Annales historiques de la Révolution française* 4 (2009): 71–92.

Laille, Pauline, Damien Provendier, François Colson and Julien Salanié, *Les Bienfaits du végétal en ville: étude des travaux scientifiques et méthode d'analyse* (Angers: Plante & Cité, 2014).

Lambin, Éric, *L'Ecologie du bonheur* (Paris: Éditions Le Pommier, 2009).

Langlois, Gilles-Antoine, *Folies, Tivolis et attractions: les premiers parcs de loisirs parisiens* (Paris: Délégation artistique à la ville de Paris, 1991).

Larbey, Vincent, *Jardins et jardiniers. Les pieds dans la terre, la tête dans les nuages. Une Anthropologie du potager*, Sociology thesis under the direction of Pr Martine Xiberras, Université Paul Valéry - Montpellier III, 2013.

Larné, Aurélien, *Jean-Nicolas Pache, Maire de Paris. Mouvement populaire et question sociale en l'an II*, thesis in progress under the direction of Marc Bélissa, CHISCO, Université Paris-Ouest Nanterre La Défense.

Lasserre, Madeleine, *Villes et Cimetières en France de l'Ancien Régime à nos jours* (Paris: L'Harmattan, 1997).

Lauras, Clarisse, *Firminy-Vert, de l'utopie municipale à l'icône patrimoniale* (Rennes: Presses Universitaires de Rennes, 2014).

Laurent, Catherine (dir.), *Histoire(s) de jardins, usages et paysages à Rennes* (Rennes: PUR, 2009).

Lavedan, Pierre, Jeanne Hugueney and Philippe Henrat, *L'Urbanisme à l'époque moderne, XVIe–XVIIIe siècles* (Geneva: Droz, 1982).

Le Dantec, Denise and Jean-Pierre, *Le Roman des jardins de France* (Paris: Bartil-lat, 1998).

Le Dantec, Jean-Pierre, *Jardins et Paysages* (Paris: Larousse, 1996).

Le Jardin et la nature dans la cité (Conference Proceedings) (Arc-et-Senans: Institut Claude-Nicolas Ledoux, 2002).

Le Roy Ladurie, Emmanuel and Bernard Quillet, 'Un urbanisme frôleur', in Georges Duby (ed.), *Histoire de la France urbaine*, 5 vols, vol. 3 (Paris: Seuil, 1983).

Lebeau, René, review of Michel Philipponneau, *La vie rurale de la banlieue parisienne* (1956), in *Revue de Géographie de Lyon* **34** (1) (1959): 75–79.

Leclerc, Bénédicte (dir.), *Jean-Claude Nicolas Forestier. Du jardin au paysage urbain* (Paris: Picard, 1994).

Lefebvre, Sylvain, Romain Roult and Jean-Pierre Augustin *Les Nouvelles Territorialités du sport dans la ville* (Québec: Presses de l'Université du Québec, 2013).

Lejeune, Daniel, Édouard André (Paris: Société Nationale d'Horticulture de France, 2013).

Lesot, Sonia and Henri Gaud, *Les Jardins en troc de Bitche* (Moisenay: Éditions Gaud, 2009).

Limido, Luisa, *L'Art des jardins sous le Second Empire* (Seyssel: Champ Vallon, 2002).

Lizet, Bernadette, 'Introduction', in Marie Mianowski, Sylvie Nail and Pierre Carboni (eds), *La Nature citadine. En France et au Royaume-Uni. Concevoir, Vivre, Représenter* (Rennes: PUR, 2015).

Lizet, Bernadette, 'Théâtres végétaux dans la ville: jalons pour une ethnobotanique urbaine', in Francis Hallé and Pierre Lieutaghi, *Aux origines des plantes* (Paris: Fayard, 2008), vol. 2.

Lizet, Bernadette, Anne-Elizabeth Wolf and John Celecia, *Sauvages dans la ville. De l'inventaire naturaliste à l'écologie urbaine* (Paris: MNHN, 1999).

Lunel, Alexandre, *La Maison médicale du roi, XVIe–XVIIIe siècles. Le pouvoir royal et les professions de santé* (Seyssel: Champvallon, 2009).

McClellan III, James E. and François Regourd, *The Colonial Machine. French Science and Overseas Expansion in the Old Regime* (Turnhout: Brepols Publishers International, 2012).

Machon, Nathalie, *Sauvages de ma rue* (Paris: MNHN, 2012).

Marraud, Mathieu, *La Noblesse de Paris au XVIIIe siècle* (Paris: Seuil, 2000).

Marrey, Bernard and Jean-Pierre Monnet, *La grande histoire des serres et des jardins d'hiver, France 1780–1900* (Paris: Graphite, 1984).

Massard-Guilbaud, Geneviève, 'Pour une histoire environnementale de l'urbain', *Histoire urbaine* **18** (1) (2007): 5–21.

Mayeur, Jean-Marie, *Un prêtre démocrate: l'abbé Lemire* (Paris: Castermann, 1969).

Mehdi, Lotfi, Christiane Weber, Francesca Di Pietro and Wissal Selmi, 'Évolution de la place du végétal dans la ville, de l'espace vert a la trame verte', *VertigO* **12** (2) (September 2012).

Méliani, Inès, Isabelle Roussel and Saïda Kermadi, 'Politiques et pratiques de la santé environnementale à l'exemple de la commune de Meyzieu', *Pollution Atmosphérique* 206 (2010).

Menozzi, Marie-Jo (dir.), *Les Jardins dans la ville, entre nature et culture* (Rennes: PUR, 2014).

Métropolis, Dossier *L'urbanisme végétal*, 96–97.

Mianowski, Marie, Sylvie Nail and Pierre Carboni (eds), *La Nature citadine. En France et au Royaume-Uni. Concevoir, Vivre, Représenter* (Rennes: PUR, 2015).

Millet, Bernard, 'Les jardins botaniques: leur nouvelles missions et leur place dans la cité', Proceedings of the conference 'Le Jardin et la Nature dans la cité' (Saline Royale d'Arc-et-Senans, 7–8 June 2001) (Besançon: Institut Claude-Nicolas Ledoux, 2002).

Molinier, Jean-Christophe, *Jardins de ville privés, 1890–1930* (n.p.: Ramsay de Cortanze, 1991).

Mollie, Caroline, *Des arbres dans la ville, l'urbanisme végétal* (Arles: Actes Sud, 2009).

Monjaret, Anne, 'Les vertus du jardin à l'hôpital', in Marie-Jo Menozzi (dir.), *Les Jardins dans la ville, entre nature et culture* (Rennes: PUR, 2014).

Montenach, Anne, *Espaces et pratiques du commerce alimentaire à Lyon au XVIIe siècle, l'économie du quotidien* (Grenoble: PUG, 2009).

Morovich, Barbara, 'Hautepierre: de l'espace conçu à l'espace vécu', in *L'Urbanisme à Strasbourg au XXe siècle* (Strasbourg: Ville de Strasbourg, 2010), www.strasboug.eu

Mosser, Monique, '"Cette amiable manifestation de l'esprit humain": Édouard André et l'histoire des jardins', in Florence André and Stéphanie de Courtois (eds), Édouard André, un paysagiste botaniste sur les chemins du monde (n.p., Éditions de l'imprimerie, 2002).

Mosser, Monique, *Histoire des jardins: de la Renaissance à nos jours* (Paris: Flammarion, 2002).

Musée d'histoire de Besançon, *La Ville en ses jardins* (Besançon: Catalogue of the exhibition at the Palais Granvelle, 8 August–24 September 1984).

Nahmias, Paula and Emmanuelle Hellier, 'La gouvernance urbaine en question: le cas des lieux de nature cultivée', *VertigO* **12** (2) (September 2012), http://vertigo.revues.org/13109

Nourry, Louis-Michel, *Les Jardins publics en province* (Rennes: PUR, 1997).

Observatoire Départemental de la Biodiversité Urbaine de Seine-Saint-Denis, Natureparif, Plante & Cité, Muséum National d'Histoire Naturelle, *Réaliser des toitures végétalisées favorables à la biodiversité* (October 2011), http://www.natureparif.fr/attachments/Documentation/livres/Toitures-vegetalisees.pdf

Nougaret, Marie-Paule, *La Cité des plantes. En ville au temps des pollutions* (Arles: Actes Sud, 2010).

Oillic, Pascal, Jean-Louis Yengué and Alain Génin, 'Le jardin individuel au cœur des enjeux fonciers et écologiques dans une métropole régionale: le cas de Tours en France', *VertigO* **12** (2) (September 2012), http ://vertigo.revues.org/13023

Ozouf, Mona, *La Fête révolutionnaire* (Paris: Gallimard, 1989).

Paris, Magali, *Le Végétal donneur d'ambiance. Jardiner les abords de l'habitat en ville*, Ph.D. thesis, École nationale supérieure d'architecture, Grenoble, 2011.

Pastorello, Thierry, 'Sodom in Paris: Protohistory of masculine homosexuality, late eighteenth-mid-nineteenth centuries', Ph.D. thesis, 2009, Paris-Diderot University (Paris VII).

Pelt, Jean-Marie (ed.), *Un jardin de chartreux. Les conseils de jardinage d'un chartreux de Vauvert: histoire, patrimoine, savoir-faire* (Grenoble: Glénat, 2004).

Perrot, Jean-Claude, 'Rapports sociaux et villes au XVIIIe siècle', in Marcel Roncayolo and Thierry Pacquot (eds), *Villes et civilisation urbaine, XVIIIe–XXe siècles* (Paris: Larousse, 1992).

Paysage. Actualité, Special issue *La Ville fertile. Vers une nature urbaine*, Exhibition at the Cité de l'architecture et du patrimoine, March 2011.

Pépy, Émilie-Anne, 'Les Chartreux et les élites du savoir dans le royaume de France, aux XVIIe et XVIIIe siècles', in *Les Chartreux et les élites, XIIe–XVIIIe siècle*, international conference of the CERCOR, 30–31 August 2012, *Analecta Cartusiana* 298 (Saint-Étienne: CERCOR, 2013), pp. 285–300.

Pépy, Émilie-Anne, 'Descrire, nommer, ordonner: enjeux et pratiques de l'inventaire botanique au XVIIIe siècle', in Florian Charvolin, Isabelle Arpin et al. *Histoire et actualité des inventaires naturalistes*, special issue of Études rurales (June 2015).

Percheron, Bénédicte, *Les Sciences naturelles à Rouen au XIXe siècle*, doctoral thesis in history, University of Rouen, 2014.

Peter, Jean-Michel and Gérard Fouquet, 'Du jeu de paume au tennis, les discours des médecins au XVIIIe et XIXe siècles', in Grégory Quin and Anaïs Bohuon, *L'Exercice corporel du XVIIIe siècle à nos jours* (Paris: Glyphe, 2013), pp. 61–80.

Picon, Antoine, 'Nature et ingénierie: le parc des Buttes-Chaumont', *Romantisme* 150 (2010/4).

Pigeaud, Jacquie and Jean-Paul Barbe, *Histoires de jardins, lieux et imaginaires* (Paris: PUF, 2015).

Pinault-Sorensen, Madeleine, *Le Livre de botanique au XVIIe et XVIIIe siècle* (Paris: Imprimerie Nationale, 2008).

Pinol, Jean-Luc (dir.), *Histoire de l'Europe urbaine*, vol. I: *De l'antiquité au XVIIIe siècle, genèse des villes européennes*; vol. II: *De l'ancien Régime à nos jours. Expansion et limites d'un modèle* (Paris: Seuil, 2003).

Pinol, Jean-Luc, *Le Monde des villes au XIXe siècle* (Paris: Hachette, 1991).

Plumauzille, Clyde, 'Le "marché aux putains": économies sexuelles et dynamiques spatiales du Palais-Royal dans le Paris révolutionnaire', *Genre, sexualité & société* 10 (Fall 2013), http ://gss.revues.org/2943 ; DOI : 10.4000/gss.2943

Pluvinage, Manuel and Florence Weber, *Les Jardins populaires: pratiques culturales, usages de l'espace, enjeux culturels*, research report for the mission of the ethnological heritage of the Ministry of Culture, 1992.

Portet, François, *L'Ouvrier, la terre, la petite propriété. Jardin ouvrier et logement social 1850–1950* (Le Creusot: CRACAP Écomusée de la communauté, 1978).

Pryce-Jones, David, *Paris in the Third Reich* (London: Collins, 1981).

Quelle biodiversité dans la ville ? Cahier Spécial de La Recherche, 422 (September 2008).

Quellier, Florent, 'Le bourgeois arboriste (XVIIe–XVIIIe siècles)', *Histoire urbaine* **6** (2) (2002): 23–41.

Quellier, Florent, 'Le jardin fruitier-potager, lieu d'élection de la sécurité alimentaire à l'époque moderne', *Revue d'histoire moderne et contemporaine* **51** (3)(2004): 66–78.

Quellier, Florent, *La Table des Français, une histoire culturelle, (XVe–début XIXe siècles)* (Rennes: Presses Universitaires de Rennes, 2007).

Quin, Grégory and Anaïs Bohuon, *L'Exercice corporel du XVIIIe siècle à nos jours* (Paris: Glyphe, 2013).

Rabreau, Daniel and Sandra Pascalis (eds), *La Nature citadine au siècle des Lumières* (Bordeaux: Arts & Arts, 2005).

Racine, Michel (ed.), *Créateurs de jardins et de paysages en France du XIXe au XXIe siècle* (Arles: Actes Sud, 2002).

Rastetter, Vincent, 'La flore adventice de Mulhouse et de ses environs', *Bulletin de la société industrielle de Mulhouse*, 784 (1982): 55–67.

Réseau National de Surveillance Aérobiologique, *Végétation en ville*, http://www.vegetation-en-ville.org/PDF/Guide-Vegetation.pdf

Revenin, Régis, 'L'émergence d'un monde homosexuel moderne dans le Parie de la Belle Époque', *Revue d'Histoire Moderne et Contemporaine*, **53–54** (4) (2006).

Revue urbanisme, dossier: *la Ville durable en question(s)*, 363 (November–December 2008).

Reygrobellet, Bernard, *La Nature dans la ville, biodiversité et urbanisme*, Rapport du Conseil économique et social (2007).

Reynolds, Richard, *La Guérilla Jardinière* (n.p., Yves Michel, 2010).

Rioux, Jean-Antoine, *Le Jardin des plantes de Montpellier* (Graulhet: Odysée, 1994).

Rivière, Louis-Marie (ed.), *La Plante dans la ville* (Paris: INRA, 1997).

Rizzotto, Milena, 'Le amene mostruosita: coltura, selezione e manipulazione delle piante ornemantali nel XVIIe seculo', in Allen J. Grieco et al. (eds), *Le Monde végétal, (XIIe–XVIIe siècles), savoirs et usages sociaux* (Presses Universitaires de Vincennes, 1993), pp. 141–155.

Robertson-Proschowsky, A., G. Roster and B. Chabaud, *La Résistance au froid des palmiers* (Marly le roi: Champflour, 1998).

Roncayolo, Marcel and Thierry Pacquot (eds), *Villes et civilisation urbaine, XVIIIe–XXe siècles* (Paris: Larousse, 1992).

Roussel, Claude-Youenn and Arièle Gallozzi, *Jardins botaniques de la Marine en France* (n.p.: Coop Breizh, 2004).

Roussel, Christiane, 'Besançon au XVIIIe siècle', *Histoire urbaine* **8** (2) (2003).

Sansot, Pierre, *Jardins publics* (Paris: Payot, 2003).

Santini, Chiara, 'Promenades plantées et espaces verts: un regard historique sur la ville de Paris', *Déméter* (2013): 216–218, http://www.clubdemeter.com/ledemeter.php ?demeter=2013

Sardet, Michel, *Le jardin botanique de la marine du port de Rochefort (1741–1896)*, DEA dissertation (Master 2), under the supervision of Jean-Pierre Bardet, Université Paris-Sorbonne, 1993.

Scheromm, Pascal et al., 'Cultiver en ville... cultiver la ville ? L'agriculture urbaine à Montpellier', *Espaces et Sociétés* 158 (2014/3): 49–56.

Schorske, Carl, *De Vienne et d'ailleurs* (Paris: Fayard, 2000).

Sciences Humaines, Special issue: *Villes durables : quelles villes pour demain* 40 (2015).

Sibalis, Michael, 'Les espaces des homosexuels dans le Paris d'avant Haussmann', in Karen Bowie, *La Modernité avant Haussmann. Formes de l'espace urbain à Paris 1801–1853* (n.p:, Éditions Recherches, 2001).

Sibalis, Michael, 'The Palais-Royal and the homosexual subculture of nineteenth-century Paris', *Journal of Homosexuality* **41** (3–4) (2002): 117–129.

Spary, Emma, *Utopia's Garden: French Natural History from Old Regime to Revolution* (Chicago: University of Chicago Press, 2000).

Strub, Christelle, *Assainir et embellir Strasbourg au XIXe siècle: étude sur la municipalité de Georges Frédéric Schützenberger (1837–1848)* (Strasbourg: Société académique du Bas-Rhin, 1998).

Terrin, Jean-Jacques, *Jardins en ville, villes en jardin* (Marseille: Parenthèses, 2013).

Tesseyre-Sallmann, Line, 'Urbanisme et société: l'exemple de Nîmes aux XVIIe et XVIIIe siècles', *Annales. Economies, Societies, Civilizations* 5 (1980): 965–986.

Tétard, Matthieu, *Le Sauvage dans la ville*, Master's thesis, IEP de Toulouse, 2012.

Tétard, Philippe (dir.), *Histoire du sport en France, du Second Empire au régime de Vichy* (Paris: Vuibert, 2007).

Theys, Jacques, 'L'approche territoriale du "développement durable", condition d'une prise en compte de sa dimension sociale', *Développement durable et territoires*, Dossier 1/2002, http://developpementdurable.revues.org/1475

Thébaud-Sorger, Marie, *L'Aérostation au temps des Lumières* (Rennes: Presses Universitaires de Rennes, 2009).

Thireau, Michel, 'Alliance de l'art et de la science au travers des peintures sur vélin du Muséum National d'Histoire Naturelle de Paris', *Journal d'agriculture traditionnelle et de botanique appliquée* **37** (1) (1995): 45–57.

Toriumi, Motoki, *Promenades de Paris, de la Renaissance à l'époque haussmannienne. Esthétique de la nature dans l'urbanisme parisien*, Ph.D. dissertation, EHESS, 2001, under the supervision of Augustin Berque.

Torre, André, 'Introduction générale', *Natures urbaines: l'agriculture au cœur des métropoles?*, *Demeter* (2013).

Traversac, Jean-Baptiste, 'Inventaire statistique: état des lieux de l'agriculture dans et à proximité des villes', *Demeter* (2013).

Turcot, Laurent, 'Forming a public promenade: the Champs-Élysées in the eighteenth century', in Daniel Rabreau and Sandra Pascalis (eds), *La Nature citadine au siècle des Lumières* (Bordeaux: Arts & Arts, 2005).

Turcot, Laurent, 'L'émergence d'un espace plurifonctionnel: les boulevards parisiens au XVIIIe siècle', *Histoire urbaine* **12** (1) (2005): 89–115.

Turcot, Laurent, *Le Promeneur à Paris au XVIIIe siècle* (Paris: Gallimard, 2007).

Urbanisme, Special issue, *La Ville durable en question(s)*, 363 (November–December 2008).

Urbia. Les Cahiers du développement urbain durable Special issue, *Urbanisme végétal et agriurbanisme* 8 (June 2009).

Van Damme, Stéphane, *Métropoles de papiers* (Paris: Les Belles Lettres, 2012).

Van Waerbeke, Jacques, 'Le motif végétal dans les regards portés par les artistes sur les périphéries parisiennes', in Augustin Berque, Philippe Bonnin and Cynthia Ghorra-Gobin (eds), *La Ville insoutenable* (Paris: Belin, 2006).

Vaquin, Jean-Baptiste (dir.), *Atlas de la Nature à Paris* (Paris: Atelier Parisien d'Urbanisme, 2006).

Vernes, Michel, 'Les jardins contre la ville', *Temps libre* 9 (Spring 1984).

Veyret, Yvette, 'Ville et "nature" dans le monde occidental', in Élisabeth Dorier-Apprill, *Ville et environnement* (Paris: Sedes, 2006).

Veyret, Yvette and Renaud Le Goix, *Atlas des Villes durables* (Paris: Autrement, 2011).

Vézin, Luc, 'La Ménagerie du Jardin des Plantes et l'art animalier', in Nadine Beauthéac (ed.), *Les Carnets de l'exotisme*, Special issue *Les jardins du retour* 13 (1st semester 1994): 58–59.

Vidal, Roland and André Fleury, 'L'autosuffisance agricole des villes, une vain utopie?', *La Vie des idées*, 4 June 2010, http ://www.laviedesidees.fr/L-autosuffisance-agricole-des.html

Vigouroux, André, 'Les dépérissements d'arbre en ville', in Louis-Marie Rivière (ed.), *La Plante dans la ville* (Paris: INRA, 1997), pp. 249–265.

Vincent, Johan, 'Origine des rapports complexes à la nature dans les stations balnéaires françaises', *VertigO* **13** (3) (December 2013), http ://vertigo.revues.org/14401

Vivier, Christian and Jean-François Loudcher, *Le Sport dans la ville* (Paris: l'Harmattan, 1998).

Walter, François, *Hiver. Histoire d'une saison* (Paris: Payot, 2014).

Werquin, Ann-Caroll and Alain Demangeon, *Jardins en ville, nouvelles tendances, nouvelles pratiques* (n.p.: Dominique Carré, 2006).

Winter, Jay (ed.), *Capital Cities at War. Paris, London, Berlin, a Cultural History* (Cambridge: CUP, 2007).

Younès, Chris (ed.), *Ville contre-nature. Philosophie et architecture* (Paris: La Découverte, 1999).

Zask, Joëlle, *La Démocratie aux champs: du jardin d'Éden aux jardins partagés* (Paris: La Découverte, 2016).

Websites

Scientific websites

CNRS: animation vidéo: http://www.cnrs.fr/cw/dossiers/dosbiodiv/ ?pid=decouv_chapC_p6

Programme Interdisciplinaire de Recherche Ville et Environnement: http ://www.pirve.fr

Observatoire de la biodiversité des jardins: http ://obj.mnhn.fr

Museum National d'Histoire Naturelle, particulièrement: http ://www.mnhn.fr/fr/participez/contribuez-sciences-participatives

Institutional websites

Ministère français de l'environnement:

- http://www.developpement-durable.gouv.fr/Plan-nature-en-ville.html
- http://www.nature-en-ville.com/content/plan-nature-en-ville
- http ://www.afbiodiversite.fr

Nature France: http ://www.naturefrance.fr

Agenda 21: http://www.agenda21france.org/agenda-21-de-territoire/index.html

Plate-forme d'observation des projets et stratégies urbaines: http://www.popsu.archi.fr/popsu-europe/accueil

Réseau National de Surveillance Aérobiologique: http ://www.pollens.fr

Association and professional websites

Jardins et Santé: http://www.jardins-sante.org

Plante et Cité: http ://www.plante-et-cite.fr

Ecophyto Pro: https ://www.ecophyto-pro.fr

Union Nationale des Entreprises du Paysage, annual surveys available at http://www.lesen-treprisesdupaysage.fr/decouvrir-l-unep/publications

Guerilla gardening en France: http://guerilla-gardening-france.fr/wordpress/

Laissons Pousser: http://www.laissonspousser.com

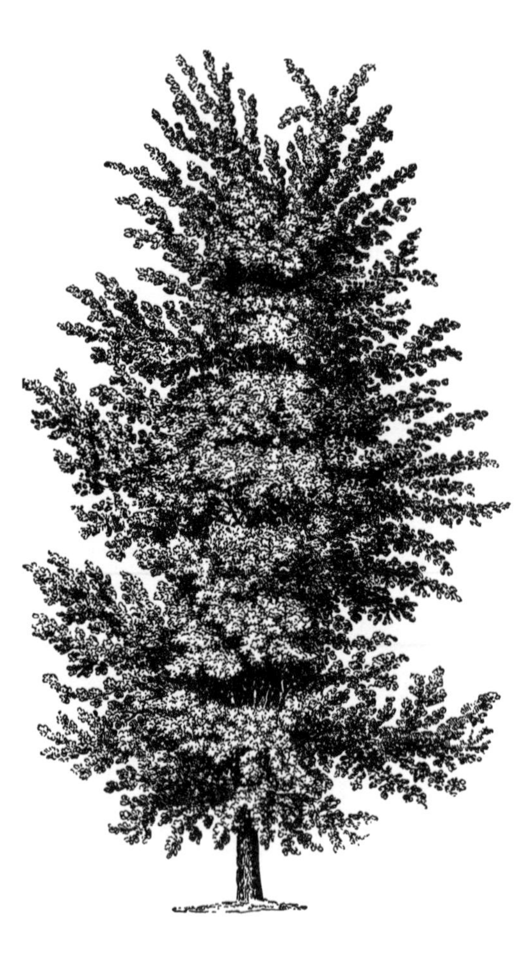

INDEX

Index

Index

Lightning Source UK Ltd.
Milton Keynes UK
UKHW020857050720
366023UK00001B/23

9 781912 186136